THE MEN BEHIND BOYS' FICTION

W. O. G. Lofts and D. J. Adley

*This is the book that every collector of British juvenile
literature—and every enthusiast—has long been awaiting.
It contains the names of well over two thousand authors
and editors, together with biographical details of many of
them, including the pen-names they used and the papers to
which they contributed. One can tell at a glance what one's
favourite author wrote, and where.*

*It contains many new facts, never before revealed, all
checked either through official records or by personal contact
with the author or editor concerned.*

*This book is the result of fifteen years' painstaking
research by two of the foremost experts in the field, and
whether your interest is in Henty, Rider Haggard, Frank
Richards of Billy Bunter fame, or the creator of the Tiger
Tim stories, you will find in this book all the information
you desire.*

Also by
W. O. G. Lofts and D. J. Adley

THE BRITISH BIBLIOGRAPHY OF EDGAR WALLACE

THE SAINT AND LESLIE CHARTERIS

THE EDGAR WALLACE ANTHOLOGY

published by Howard Baker

W. O. G. Lofts and D. J. Adley

THE MEN BEHIND BOYS' FICTION

HOWARD BAKER, LONDON

W. O. G. Lofts and D. J. Adley
THE MEN BEHIND BOYS' FICTION

First publication, 1970

A HOWARD BAKER BOOK

SBN 09 3047703

Howard Baker books are published by
Howard Baker Publishers Limited
47 Museum Street, London, W.C.1

Printed in Great Britain by The Anchor Press Ltd,
and bound by William Brendon & Son Ltd,
both of Tiptree, Essex

Contents

Introduction by Leslie Charteris

I have a great nostalgic affection for British juvenile literature, because I was brought up on it.

The *Boys' Own Paper* and the much less glossy *Chums* (which I preferred) were an important part of my youthful reading. Since most of that pre-teen youth was spent in Singapore during World War I, the delivery of periodicals was erratic and often completely missing, but the arrival of the bound *Chums* Annual always seemed to succeed in landing under the Christmas tree. And this was not only worth waiting for but in a way even better, for then I could read the serials straight through, like books, instead of waiting out a week's suspense between instalments.

And what fine lusty fare it was! In those simple bygone days, before the child psychologists were invented, there was meat in those tales for a boy to get his teeth into – instead of getting them into his playmates. The pirates were unregenerate cut-throats, the international spies and criminals were prodigal with murder and torture; even the denizens of other planets were bloodthirsty monsters. There was no sparing of violence and gore. Before Our Side inevitably triumphed, the scuppers ran with blood, the sinister cellars rang with screams, the bug-eyed Martians devoured any available humans except our heroes. Hardly any of those stories would have survived today's namby-pamby criteria of what the young should be allowed to read. But they were a good introduction to the classics which we would move on to in adolescence, from Henty to Sabatini, from Rider Haggard to Sax Rohmer.

What frightful effects this diet had on me I had perhaps better leave others to estimate. As a writer, it did not seriously inspire me to step into that field. I took a leap ahead, of sorts, after an exploratory book or two, into what might be called the adolescent-of-all-ages pasture of the *Thriller*. Which still had much the same uninhibited principles.

I

I would love to see some advanced evangelist, uncorrupted by airy-fairy theory, start out from the bald fact that my generation, raised on this kind of reading, produced an infinitely smaller percentage of juvenile delinquents and layabouts than the brood which is currently supposed to be raised on today's approved wishy-washy pabulum. And I hope this truly monumental collective biography may add to his ammunition.

About the Compilers

W. O. G. Lofts

Full name William Oliver Guillemont Lofts, born at St Marylebone, London, 1923. Attended Barrow Hill Road Elementary School behind the Lord's Cricket Ground, St John's Wood. Worked for a famous carburettor firm from 1940 until 1968, in engineering. It was during war service in the jungle-fighting in Burma that he first became interested in juvenile fiction, after finding a Sexton Blake Library in a disused Japanese bamboo hut.

On his return to England, his curiosity was aroused as to who had created Sexton Blake, and in time he became greatly interested in all aspects of juvenile fiction. Over the years he has written more than a thousand articles in this connection, and has acquired a considerable reputation for solving 'mysteries' pertaining to Old Boys Literature. He has also done research for Fleetway Publications, and on behalf of Leslie Charteris. Probably his greatest discovery was finding a long-lost story written by Sir Winston Churchill, which was reprinted in Argosy.

He has several times appeared on television and radio, and is known as the 'Sir Bernard Spilsbury' of Old Boys Books. A bachelor, he still lives in St Marylebone, now known as the City of Westminster, and has probably the largest collection of 1st editions of boys' and comic papers in the world. Chairman of the London Old Boys Book Club, 1966.

D. J. Adley

Full name Derek John Adley, born at Shepherd's Bush, London, 1927. Educated at Secondary Modern Schools in London and Stanmore, Middlesex. Served in the gunnery sections of the Royal Navy and Fleet Air Arm. After training

3

in all aspects of photography he took up accountancy and has been employed for a number of years as a Financial Accountant by a large American Company in London.

He has a strong and avid interest in all aspects of popular fiction, both British and American, and has written a number of articles on the subject. Apart from possessing a large library of his own, he has built up a vast statistical reference library of his own writings dealing with authors, artists and catalogues of hundreds of periodicals and publications published during the last hundred years.

He has corresponded with many authors, and has a vast filing system to assimilate all these facts concerned with fiction which has inspired the imagination of the reading public through the last two centuries.

He is married, with two young daughters, and lives in Middlesex.

Foreword

Perhaps it is because I live so close to Baker Street, the home of those immortal detectives, Sherlock Holmes and Sexton Blake, that I possess such a keen detective 'instinct'. Nothing gives me greater pleasure than the solving of mysteries – and these have been considerable throughout the years, in connection with boys' authors. Writers and their pen-names have always fascinated me, and I find no greater satisfaction than in tracing a long-lost author, to discuss with him his writings, career, and perhaps from what source he inherited his writing skill – above all, to discover any pen-names he may have used. I believe it was Charles Hamilton, perhaps the greatest and best-loved school-story writer of all time, who mentioned in his autobiography that out of the hundreds of thousands of readers only one or two ever guessed that, apart from being 'Frank Richards', he was also 'Martin Clifford', 'Owen Conquest', and 'Ralph Redway'.

The results of this work could be said to have covered over fifteen years of extensive research, during which time I personally met several hundred authors and editors, ranging from the obscure to the world-famous such as Leslie Charteris. Many of them, including Leslie Charteris, could be classed as personal friends – and what good, co-operative people they have all been! To give a full list of them would require almost a Who's Who on its own, but needless to say I have met editors from almost every type of boys' paper – C. M. Down of the MAGNET and GEM, H. W. Twyman of the UNION JACK, W. Howard Baker of the SEXTON BLAKE LIBRARY, 'Jackie' Hunt of DETECTIVE WEEKLY, Jack Cox of the BOYS OWN PAPER, Philip Davis of FILM FUN, and E. L. (Mac) McKeag of THE SCHOOLFRIEND, not counting sub-editors galore.

Practically every living author not met personally has been contacted by correspondence, and all details carefully perused and

5

checked wherever possible for accuracy against official records. Even where authors have passed on – and unfortunately they are many – we have done the next best thing and contacted their nearest relatives. Amongst these are Mrs Gwyn Evans, the late Mrs E. S. Brooks, Mrs G. H. Teed, Mrs Robert Murray Graydon, Mrs Richard Goyne, and the niece of Charles Hamilton, Mrs Una Hamilton Wright, to mention only a few.

It is inevitable that some authors whom I met have since departed this life, but I shall always remember with affection the large, good-natured John Hunter, whom I met at the Wine Lodge, in Worthing, many times; George E. Rochester, who had fallen on lean times and was living in a back bed-sitting room at the rear of Victoria Station, and who let me type details about him on his own machine, which was literally on its last legs. Also Major Donnelly Aitken, who although severely handicapped with only one arm, must have taken hours to type out details about himself for me, as well as other authors, in the early days of the Amalgamated Press.

The first acknowledgement I must make is to my very good friend and hobby enthusiast, Brian Doyle, who brought out an abridged Authors' and Artists' Who's Who in duplicated form in 1963, and whose success convinced me that a more complete and printed version would be well received by a much wider public. Brian, honest fellow that he is, readily admitted in his foreword that the majority of the information was collated from articles in the collecting magazines to which I am a prolific contributor – and as I wrote these articles I cannot be accused of plagiarism!

I must also convey my deep gratitude to Mr Leonard Matthews, Director of juvenile publications at Fleetway House, for having given me permission to peruse official records and glean from them priceless information which has enabled me to solve hundreds of minor 'mysteries'. In this respect I must also mention Mr Leslie Lawrence, Chief Literary Cashier, whose co-operation and friendliness will always be appreciated. Thanks are due also to Mr W. Howard Baker, the editor of the SEXTON BLAKE LIBRARY, who not only introduced me to nearly all the modern Sexton Blake writers, but put me in touch with many other old Amalgamated Press staff as well.

Finally, in acknowledgement, I would like to express my admiration to all those of the 'old brigade' of enthusiasts in the collecting world, who created an interest in authors and their pen-names long before I became involved: the late Herbert Leckenby, editor of the

6

COLLECTORS DIGEST, Bill Gander, late editor of THE STORY PAPER COLLECTOR, Walter Webb, Harry Dowler, Len Allen, Len Packman, and Eric Fayne, present editor of the COLLECTORS DIGEST, for permission to include extracts from my articles published in his magazine. Nor must I forget Frank Vernon-Lay, whose enthusiasm over the years has many times stimulated my own interest when it showed signs of flagging.

Perhaps this biography is unique in that it is titled THE MEN BEHIND BOYS' FICTION, and does not include artists. A survey conducted amongst enthusiasts brought to light the fact that only a few were really interested in artists, and then only in famous ones. But as there seemed to be considerable interest shown in editors, it was decided to break with tradition and include them where known, though it should be added that the majority of editors were also authors in their own right.

Whilst this biography does not claim to list every single boys' author who ever wrote, it does claim to list every single Amalgamated Press writer, plus many hundreds of principal writers for other papers and publishers. The sharp reader may note that in some cases the Amalgamated Press author is still not identified – i.e., as to whether the name used was his own or a pen-name. The reason for this is simply that either the story was submitted by agents who now have no record of the transaction, or the story was editorially rewritten from an old one and a new name inserted.

Revealed also for the first time are many of those obscure D. C. Thomson authors. Who does not remember THE WIZARD, SKIPPER, ROVER, ADVENTURE, and THE HOTSPUR, whose stories of Red Circle are still recalled? It cannot be too strongly emphasised that many of the serials and series of stories were written by a syndicate of writers and editorially suggested – consequently the editors of this group can lay claim to their great success.

It has been a truly mammoth research job, compiling this data with Derek Adley, and I can only trust and hope that readers will get the same enjoyment from reading it.

W. O. G. Lofts
London, February, 1970

A Tribute to the D. C. Thomson Papers and Red Circle School

While this biography predominantly features the AMALGA-MATED PRESS and FLEETWAY PUBLICATIONS, it is only right and proper to say that they were far from being the only publishers of boys' papers. Indeed, the Scottish firm of D. C. Thomson & Co. Ltd., could be said to have been their biggest rival for the last fifty years. All the big publishing houses which concern themselves with juvenile publications can lay claim to having created their own particular set of characters or series, and certainly Thomson's are no exception. A tremendous number of long-running series are nostalgically sought after today, and it is astonishing to think that many of the original boys' papers which cost twopence, are worth as much as thirty times that amount today. It is even more fantastic to see an advertiser offering as much as £2 each for issues of The Rover, dated 1936!

As far as is known, D. C. Thomson entered the juvenile field in 1919, with the Dixon Hawke Library, this being a rival, of sorts, of the Sexton Blake Library. The ADVENTURE, the first weekly boys' paper, came in 1921, followed by THE ROVER, and then THE WIZARD in 1922. 1923 saw THE VANGUARD and THE SKIPPER in 1930. The RED ARROW ran for exactly one year, starting from 1932, and the last, THE HOTSPUR, classed as a school-story paper, came in 1933. All of these, with the exception of THE VANGUARD and THE RED ARROW, had very long runs, and the remaining five became known as 'The Big Five'.

Each paper had their own seemingly popular and outstanding character, who appeared in a long series, had a short rest, then appeared again in another new series. Probably THE WIZARD's most famous was the Wolf of Kabul – a British Secret Service Agent who operated in the North West Frontier of India. His real name was actually Bill Sampson, but unfortunately his blue eyes used to betray him when he was disguised as a native. Still, armed with twin knives and accompanied by his native servant, Chung, he took on all comers. Chung was himself a colourful character who, after surveying the battered heads of his enemies, would remark – his eyes filled with sadness – that his 'Clicky-ba' merely turned in his hand! 'Clicky-ba' being a cricket-bat bound with copper and brass, with some ominous reddish-brown stains on it.

Dixon Hawke appeared in the ADVENTURE with his assistant Tommy Burke in weekly adventures, as well as appearing in the Dixon Hawke Library, and is in fact still going strong today in the Scottish DAILY POST. The Black Sapper was another long and popular series which ran in THE ROVER. These stories were about a man dressed in a black, tight-fitting costume who caused a great upheaval in more ways than one – he travelled through the earth in a 'burrowing' machine, shaped like a submarine, which sometimes cut right through the Underground, in London!

'The Truth about Wilson' was another tremendously long popular series in THE WIZARD. This was about an incredible athlete who broke all the world records, and was dressed in a black Victorian bathing costume. He was reputed to be nearly 120 years old, and he attained this great age by a series of special breathing exercises and by eating wild roots, which he collected from the Yorkshire Moors. I do know, for a fact, that these stories inspired more than one young athlete to later become International runners.

THE HOTSPUR really had some wonderful characters. The Big Stiff – real name Semptiminus Green – was about a schoolmaster who had an uncanny knack of taming wild boys and interesting them in education. Later on, in another series, as in real life, he was promoted to a School Inspector. I often suspected that my old schoolteacher was a HOTSPUR fan, as often in the middle of a rather boring lesson, and when the class was fidgety, he would suddenly let us out of the class-room into the playground to have a game of football. On our return we did seem to give more attention to the boring subject which had been interrupted.

One could really write a book on the colourful and never-to-be-forgotten characters in the Thomson papers: Lion-Hearted Logan the Mountie in THE WIZARD; Mustard Smith the teacher of circus children in THE SKIPPER; Cast-Iron Bill, a wonderful goalie in THE ROVER, and many more too numerous to mention. But in view of their almost non-stop run from 1933 to 1958 and their immense popularity, I would say that the greatest series ever to appear in The Big Five was the Red Circle School stories in THE HOTSPUR.

Red Circle was a completely new and modern school situated at Lington. One went from Liverpool Street, London, in order to get to it, so one assumes that it lay somewhere on the East Coast. The buildings were made of red sandstone and its houses were built in a circle around the quadrangle, hence its name. Boys came to it from all over the world; from all parts of the British Empire and from America.

For this reason the junior boys were divided into three sections, according to their place of birth. The captain of the Home House was Tubby Ryan; this house faced the main school buildings and all its inhabitants were British boys. The building to the east was the Trans-Atlantic House, its captain being Cyrus Judd, and it was nicknamed the 'Yank House'. All its boys were American or Canadian. The building to the west held pupils coming from all parts of the British Empire; its captain was Kit Delaney and it was called 'The Conk House'.

Like nearly all schools, the rivalry between the Houses was very fierce, and it formed the basis of many plots for the stories. What was certainly original and true to life about this school was the fact that the boys did eventually grow up and move to higher forms; then in time they left.

Extensive research into the whole history of the school, when every single character, location, synopsis of stories, etc., has been catalogued, makes a tremendous dossier which should one day be made into a Red Circle Prospectus; and this proves that the whole series were very intelligently planned. There were actually four stages of moving upwards in the school's history:

Stage 1	1933–35	1– 106
2	1935–37	107– 209
3	1937–41	210– 500
4	1941–58	501–1155

New Hotspur, picture strips of Red Circle, 1959 onwards.

Strangely enough, the most famous and best-remembered character at Red Circle was Mr Alfred Smugg, the extremely unpopular master of the Home House, who was a brilliant piece of character-

11

isation, so much so that at times one felt a sneaking sympathy for him. He was followed by Dixie Dale, the most popular master of Conk House, who was eventually promoted to Headmaster. Richard Doyle – better known as Dead-wide Dick because of his lazy habits – is also well remembered, due to the fact that he featured largely in the series and eventually became School Captain. He actually left the school in No 500 to join the Royal Navy.

Of course there have been many generations of Red Circle School readers, and those in 1941, say, would find that Cripple Dick Archer was the School Captain, and that another wonderful character – Weepy Willie Smugg, Alfred's younger brother (arrived No 232) was at the school, eventually retiring by 514 (1945).

Whilst probably many of the stories were humorous, there were also stories of real drama. No 175 (1936) saw an epidemic of small-pox at the school, when 'Jumbo' James, captain of the Senior House football, and who had a host of young and Old Boy brothers at the school, died. Many of the stories at the beginning were complete in themselves, but later on there were series featuring holidays abroad, world tours, athletics series and almost every conceivable adventure one could think of; even a spider invasion of Red Circle!

It would be foolish to say that the stories were written in such prose as by Frank Richards of Greyfriars fame, but they were certainly in the style that a boy found easy to read, and which made few demands on him. One could say further that they were penned in an interesting style and read more willingly by the modern boy, and were more to the taste of the average boy in the thirties. If the editors of D. C. Thomson, behind the scenes, had not decided to make their career in journalism they might have become psychologists, as they seemed to know exactly what boys wanted to read and prepared their papers accordingly.

When I was a boy I don't think I worried at all because no authors' names appeared on the stories, and I don't honestly think any other reader cared, either. Certainly circulation did not suffer because of this policy, and after all that was the main thing that mattered. Now an adult researcher, I must confess that I find this rather vexing, however, although the explanation of this omission is quite simple. Nearly all the stories, characters and series were editorially suggested to the author, and he was commissioned to write them. The writer not only had to have many long discussions with the editors on how to pen these stories, but even when the story was finished it was subject to much editorial subbing and rewriting. Very few authors could lay claim to any particular character or to the whole writing of a popular series, for more often than not several authors wrote various series (as in the case of Wilson); and with the editorial rewriting it is probably the reason why the style of all the stories appeared the same.

Indeed, on the question of which was the easiest firm to write for – D. C. Thomson or Amalgamated Press – many authors have told me (in writing for both firms) that the former was the most difficult and their stories had to be right up to the highest standard every time.

Dealing with the important question as to who created Red Circle School, the answer is simply that it was created editorially. The badge which shows the school houses in a circle with the flagpole in the middle, was designed long before any stories were written. The first stories commissioned were by A. R. Linden of Portsmouth (now deceased) but were used from No 3 onwards with the introduction of Dead-wide Dick. The first actual stories were written by the late R. G. Thomas, who also wrote a considerable number in the first seven or eight years.

Later writers were the late B. H. Bulman, J. H. Stein, C. V. Frost, the late G. L. Dalton, R. A. Carpenter and possibly a few from Frank Howe. But in many cases the editor could lay as much claim to have his name attached to the story as could the author.

A survey conducted a few years before the last war in a very large elementary school showed the astonishing fact that out of roughly a thousand boys, about 75% were reading the Thomson papers, with the MAGNET and GEM well down the scale and the B.O.P., SCOUT and CHILDREN'S NEWSPAPER in bottom places. There is no question at all that in the 1930's the Thomson papers were giving the Amalgamated Press editors a great deal of worry, as the Amalgamated Press circulation was dropping rapidly. Several have confessed to me that they were told by their Department chiefs to 'modernise' their papers, and this they were loth to do, mainly because of the old traditions and seemingly high standard of literature held at Fleetway House. The main trouble was that they were still producing papers appealing to boys of the twenties and did not move with the times. Whilst an educated man may shudder at boys being named 'Spiv Ringer' and 'Wild Cat McCoy' – two popular characters at Red Circle – and ask his own writers to refrain from

13

using such names (perhaps for snobbish reasons), the fact remains that boys at school did have such nicknames.

Another modern approach was the use of long, colourful titles – 'Caned Six Times in his First Day at School' and 'Never Hang a Big Shot by his Braces' were more acceptable to the boy with a vivid imagination than, say, 'Fool's Luck'.

The Thomson editors had a far friendlier and happy-go-lucky approach to boys, and treated them as equals and personal friends. The editor of THE HOTSPUR had an editorial chat entitled 'Sez Me!' which showed a young, friendly man in shirt-sleeves grinning from his office chair, making you feel at home instantly. No editor here with a grim face, wearing a stiff wing collar and pin-striped suit, telling boys not to smoke, to 'always play the game' and to be sure to have a cold bath every morning!

Many of the Amalgamated Press papers in the middle and late thirties realised that the Thomson modern approach was best, and such papers as TRIUMPH, STARTLER and WILD WEST WEEKLY were not only up-to-date, but the author's names were dropped. Proof that this policy was best is shown by the fact that Thomson papers went on for years longer than the more established papers at Fleetway House.

Whilst, unfortunately, there is some unfair criticism today of the contents of the Thomson papers throughout the years, it is only fair to say they should be judged entirely on the market at which they were aimed, and not from an adult viewpoint. All the stories were clean and entertaining and gripped the young reader, and they had a high moral standard. They sold in millions, and the D. C. Thomson editors deserve the highest possible praise for contributing – by thus entertaining the young – to a part of our social history.

I, for one, was very happy to be one of their readers when I was a boy.

The Charles Hamilton Schools

As stated in the biography, Charles Hamilton was not only the best-loved of all school-story writers, but easily the most prolific. Whilst he is best remembered for his Greyfriars, St Jim's, and Rookwood stories, and to the female generation for his creation of Bessie Bunter of Cliff House School, he did create a great many other schools.

Many indeed, it could be said, may have become almost as famous as the already mentioned, if he had only taken the trouble to develop them. Whilst this list is claimed to be the very first published in chronological order, and the most lengthy ever compiled by personal research of the writer, it certainly is not claimed to be complete. Schools of his creation are still being discovered, and it is certain that when every boys' paper has been traced and perused, the grand total will far exceed the hundred and seven mark now known.

This is only a list of schools where they featured first as the main theme in the story. Cliff House and Highcliffe, for example, featured in many MAGNET stories before they appeared in a separate publication as an individual school. Readers will note with interest that another Greyfriars, Rookwood and Cliff House School appeared long before the more famous schools of the same name – although in the case of the latter, this was a boys' school situated in Devonshire and not a girls' establishment. Many characters had very familiar names, such as Wharton, Quelch, Glyn, Wingate, Trimble, Railton and Clavering. Some names of schools were also duplicated but had, of course, different sets of characters and settings.

Whilst Charles Hamilton is known to have written his first story in 1895, there are really curious gaps until his first school story was traced in 1902. This can be explained perhaps by the fact that in the early days he wrote romance, adventure, football, cricket and other non-school stories. Research is still going on into his early field of writing.

School	Date	Paper	No.
Redclyffe	3. 5.1902	Best Budget	8
Cliff House	27. 6.1903	Marvel	503
St Winifred's (1)	18. 2.1905	Marvel	56
St Cynthia's	25. 3.1905	Union Jack	76
Castlemoor School	6. 5.1905	Funny Cuts	774
Clavering (1)	29. 7.1905	Pluck	38
Fernley	21.10.1905	Union Jack	106
Westmoor	27. 1.1906	Boys Friend	242
Chilcote	10. 4.1906	Boys Friend	252
Clivedale College	16. 6.1906	Boys Realm	211
Northmoor	25. 8.1906	Pluck	94
Rookwood (1)	8. 9.1906	Pluck	96
St Edith's	8. 9.1906	Boys Friend	274
St Hilda's (1)	22. 9.1906	Boys Realm	229
Melthorpe	13.10.1906	Pluck	101
Carbrooke	3.11.1906	Boys Realm	231
Lyndale	10.11.1906	Pluck	105
St Jim's	17.11.1906	Pluck	106
St Oliver's	24.11.1906	Funny Cuts	855
Headland School	8.12.1906	Marvel	150
Chumley School	29.12.1906	Smiles	35
St Kit's	26. 1.1907	Pluck	116
Carnforth	2. 2.1907	Boys Realm	244
St Egbert's	9. 2.1907	Boys Realm	245
Grayle College	12. 2.1907	Smiles	42
St Hilda's (2)	26. 2.1907	Smiles	44
Clivedale (2)	5. 3.1907	Smiles	45
St Freda's (1)	12. 3.1907	Smiles	46
Dormer College (Oxford)	16. 3.1907	Boys Realm	250
St Winifred's	19. 3.1907	Funny Cuts	872
Greyfriars School (1)	19. 3.1907	Smiles	47
St Kit's (2)	26. 3.1907	Smiles	48
Clavering (2)	30. 3.1907	Gem	3
Swarthmoor College	23. 4.1907	Smiles	52
Northcote	4. 5.1907 (approx.)	Vanguard	1
Northorpe	14. 5.1907	Smiles	55
Norchester Board School	11. 6.1907 (approx.)	Vanguard	7

School	Date	Paper	No.
Friardale School	18. 6.1907	Smiles	60
Larkshall College	30. 7.1907	Vanguard	13
Netherby	10. 8.1907	Marvel	185
Cliveden	26.10.1907	Boys Herald	223
St Seriol's College	12.11.1907	Smiles	81
St Ronan's (1)	16.11.1907	Boys Realm	285
St Kate's (1)	17.12.1907	Vanguard	33
Blackdale School	Jan. 1908	B.F.L.	36
Beachwood Academy	18. 1.1908	Marvel	208
St Friar's	8. 2.1908	Boys Realm	297
Greyfriars (2)	15. 2.1908	Magnet	1
St Ronan's (2)	18. 2.1908	Funny Cuts	920
Birchemwell House	17. 3.1908	Smiles	99
Winwood College	13. 5.1908	Boys Realm	312
St John's	June 1908 (approx.)	Diamond Lib.	36
Cranmere	July 1908 (approx.)	Diamond Lib.	39
St Cecilia's	29. 9.1908	Funny Cuts	952
St Winifred's (3)	Dec. 1908	B.F.L.	67
St Freda's	16. 1.1909	Boys Realm	346
Mornington	19. 6.1909	Boys Realm	368
St Dorothy's	3. 7.1909	Boys Realm	370
Professor Crammer's School for Young Gentlemen	10. 8.1909	Funny Cuts	39
Chigville School	14. 9.1909	Vanguard	124
Pelham	18. 9.1909	Boys Realm Football Lib.	1
Ravensbourne College	12.10.1909	Picture Fun	35
Clarence College	2.11.1909	Picture Fun	38
Dugdale College	16.11.1909	Picture Fun	40
Rylcombe Grammar School	19. 2.1910	Empire Library	1
St Cuthbert's	15. 3.1910	Picture Fun	57
St Michael's	29. 3.1910	Picture Fun	59
St Tim's	12. 4.1910	Picture Fun	61
St Denny's	19. 4.1910	Picture Fun	62
St Steve's	24. 4.1910	Picture Fun	63
St Mick's	19. 7.1910	Picture Fun	75
St Andrews	18.10.1910	Picture Fun	88

School	Date	Paper	No.
St Freda's (3)	29.10.1910	Empire Lib. (2nd)	1
Clyffe	10.12.1910	Boys Realm Football and Sports Library	65
St Wode's	14. 1.1911	Empire Library	12
St Mary's	14. 2.1911	Picture Fun	105
Headland College	4. 4.1911	Picture Fun	112
St Luke's	2. 5.1911	Picture Fun	116
St Dennis's	13. 6.1911	Picture Fun	122
Clifton College	20. 6.1911	Funny Cuts	136
Banleigh	11. 7.1911	Funny Cuts	139
Courtfield Council School	10. 1.1914	Chuckles	1
St Mildred's	28.11.1914	Picture Fun	303
Highcliffe	Jan. 1915	B.F.L.	288
Rookwood	20. 2.1915	Boys Friend Weekly	715
Cedar Creek	18. 8.1917	Boys Friend Weekly	845
Cliff House (2)	17. 5.1919	School Friend	1
Benbow	1.11.1919	Greyfriars-Herald (2nd)	1
St Kit's (3)	17.12.1921	School & Sport	1
Grimslade	27. 8.1932	Ranger	81
Packsaddle	19. 1.1935	Gem	1405
High Combe	16. 3.1935	Modern Boy	371
Oakshot	12.12.1936	Modern Boy	462
Bendover	13. 2.1937	Pilot	72
Carcroft	Dec. 1944	Pie Magazine	
Sparshott	16. 7.1946 (approx.)	Sparshott Series	
Headland House	16. 7.1946 (approx.)	Headland House Series	
Topham	13. 5.1947	Mascot Series	
Lynwood	cir. 1944/9	Published at Manchester.	
Tipdale	cir. 1944/9	No record in	
High Lynn	cir. 1944/9	British Museum.	
Barcroft	Sept. 1949	Tom Merry's Own	1
Felgate	Sept. 1949	Raymond Glendenning Book of Sport No. 1	
St Kate's	Reported to have been published circ. 1950. No record of it found.		

St Ethelbert's, Ferndale, are other schools recorded but details missing.

The Sexton Blake Roll of Honour

When Harry Blyth wrote the first story of Sexton Blake in No 6 of THE HALFPENNY MARVEL, in 1893, neither he nor the great Alfred Harmsworth (later Lord Northcliffe) could possibly have imagined that, some seventy-six years later, he would still be going strong; and that, not only in several publications, but through the medium of television and radio, millions of people (especially the younger ones) were reading about, hearing about and seeing the great Baker Street detective.

Some years ago I met the son (now deceased) of Harry Blyth, also named Harry, at his home in Broadstairs, Kent. A very friendly man, he told me how the first story featuring Sexton Blake came to be written. Although firmly convinced that his father had coined the name, this fact was disputed by a former editor of the old Harmsworth boys' papers, who asserted that the detective was originally called 'Frank Blake', but that the Christian name was rejected on the grounds that it was not colourful enough.

The name of 'Sexton' was suggested, and as it was a name which conjured up the sombre and somewhat mysterious atmosphere of graveyards and gloomy crypts, it was finally chosen in order to give the character an element of eeriness. But irrespective of whose was the final decision, the fact remains that since 1893 Sexton Blake has been the copyright of, firstly, The Harmsworth Brothers; later, the Amalgamated Press, and now the present-day Fleetway Publications.

Harry Blyth, sad to relate, died in 1898 of typhoid fever, aged only 46, so he did not live long enough to see how famous his creation was to become. Since that first story, nearly two hundred different authors have penned over four thousand stories – a grand total of roughly two hundred million words. The stories have also been translated into at least twenty different languages. His chroniclers have been from all walks of life, including the following formidable list:

19

Clergymen, Doctors, Soldiers, Sailors, Airmen, Sheep Farmers, Gold Prospectors, Engineers, Actors, Bank Clerks, Artists, a Golf Caddy, a Boxer, an Orange Picker in South Africa, a Lumberjack, a Ship's Doctor, an Explorer, an Irish Peer, a Tramp, a Woman Playwright, a Laundryman, a Fly-Driver, a British Secret Service Agent, a Clerk in a Glass-blowing Factory, and a man who was 'down and out' on the Embankment and wrote his stories on scraps of paper. Also included is a woman who writes Westerns and is an expert on Nelson Lee, various Newspaper Men, and three writers who shall be nameless but who penned their stories whilst being themselves 'penned' in Dartmoor, Wormwood Scrubs and Durham Jail!

It has been no easy task to compile a complete list of Sexton Blake authors in strict rotation from the beginning, as so many difficulties were encountered. Many authors never saw their names in print at all, as for years it was a strict policy that all stories should be anonymous. When names eventually did appear, some authors, as well as using their own names, adopted nom-de-plumes. In these cases the author is recorded first when he wrote a story, then if at a later date he adopted a pen-name, this is given as well. The number at the side will indicate whether it is the same author.

Another headache lay in the 'stock' names of 'Arnold Davis', 'John Andrews', 'Desmond Reid' and 'Richard Williams'. They were used editorially when the original author's story had to be re-written or revised for certain reasons. In these cases, it has been re-corded when the stock names first appeared, followed by the name of the author concerned. The original author, obviously, must take credit for writing the story.

In my investigations over the years, I have found several authors who claim to have written Blake stories, although no official records can be found of their names. A few claim to have 'ghosted' for more established writers, but as the latter were obviously paid for the stories, the claimants cannot be included in these lists.

In the years from approximately 1908 to 1912, there were how-ever many short stories of Sexton Blake published in the adult magazines, ANSWERS and PENNY PICTORIAL. Although it has been established that the majority were written by established Blake authors, there is always the possibility that a few odd ones were penned by other writers. Unfortunately it is not now possible to trace them.

Two well-known names which are missing from The Roll of Honour are those world-famous writers, Edgar Wallace and Leslie Charteris. Neither of them ever wrote a Blake story, which fact has been confirmed by official records. The belief that they did arose simply because both at one time were writing for the Amalgamated Press and in THE THRILLER. This paper was controlled by P. M. Haydon and edited by Len Pratt, who both also ran THE SEXTON BLAKE LIBRARY. Leslie Charteris told me that the reason he never wrote a story about Blake was because he wanted to build up his own brain-child, The Saint.

Edgar Wallace's son, Brian, did however write a short play featuring Sexton Blake in THE DETECTIVE WEEKLY. To be perfectly accurate, half-an-author could be included in the list, as J. D. S. Hunt, editor of THE DETECTIVE WEEKLY, once had to write the latter half of a story when the original author became indisposed after writing the opening chapters. But as the original author's name was on the cover of The Sexton Blake Library when it appeared, he is credited by records as having written it, and Mr Hunt's name is not included. Probably there were many other such cases which have not yet been brought to light.

From Harry Blyth in 1893 to the present day here is presented

THE SEXTON BLAKE ROLL OF HONOUR

No. of Author	Writer	Paper	Date
1.	Hal Meredith	Marvel	13.12.1893
1.	Harry Blyth	Marvel	17. 1.1894
2.	Patrick Morris	Chips	24.12.1894
3.	Sexton Blake	Union Jack	16. 2.1895
4.	W. Shaw Rae	Union Jack	1. 6.1895
5.	Arnold Grahame	Union Jack	7. 9.1895
6.	Melton Whyte	Union Jack	28. 9.1895
7.	Herbert Maxwell	Union Jack	16.11.1895
8.	Stanhope Sprigg	Union Jack	27. 2.1897
9.	Julian Rochefort	Union Jack	23. 9.1899
10.	Campbell Brown	Union Jack	7.10.1899
11.	Paul Herring	Union Jack	29. 9.1900

No. of Author	Writer	Paper	Date
10.	G. W. Brown	Union Jack	24.11.1900
9.	Christopher Stevens	Union Jack	16. 2.1901
12.	Norman Goddard	Union Jack	25. 5.1901
13.	Percival Cooke	Union Jack	23.11.1901
14.	J. H. Thompson	Union Jack	21.12.1901
15.	Alec G. Pearson	Union Jack	8. 3.1902
—	Arnold Davis (stock name)	Union Jack	1.10.1904
16.	T. G. Dowling Maitland	Union Jack	26.11.1904
17.	W. Murray Graydon	Union Jack	17.12.1904
18.	W. B. Home-Gall	Union Jack	28. 1.1905
19.	E. J. Gannon	Union Jack	18. 2.1905
20.	E. A. Treeton	Union Jack	29. 4.1905
12.	Mark Darran	Union Jack	24. 6.1905
21.	Edgar Pickering	Union Jack	2. 9.1905
22.	F. H. Evans	Union Jack	25.11.1905
23.	T. C. Bridges	Union Jack	20. 1.1906
7.	W. Lomax	Union Jack	27. 1.1906
24.	E. W. Alais	Union Jack	17. 2.1906
25.	Cecily Hamilton	Union Jack	7. 4.1906
26.	E. H. Burrage	Union Jack	5. 5.1906
27.	Cecil Hayter	Union Jack	19. 5.1906
28.	C. E. Pearce	Union Jack	18. 8.1906
29.	A. C. Murray	Union Jack	1. 6.1907
30.	Arthur Joseph Steffens	Union Jack	8. 6.1907
31.	L. J. Beeston	Union Jack	4. 1.1908
32.	E. Sempill	Union Jack	11. 1.1908
33.	G. Carr	Union Jack	4. 7.1908
34.	W. J. Bayfield	Union Jack	22. 8.1908
35.	D. H. Parry	Union Jack	12. 9.1908
36.	Andrew Murray	Answers	12. 6.1909
37.	Maxwell Scott	Boys Herald	17.11.1909
38.	E. J. Murray	Answers	16. 4.1910
39.	J. G. Jones	Union Jack	18. 6.1910
40.	Douglas Walshe	Union Jack	4. 3.1911

No. of Author	Writer	Paper	Date
41.	Colin T. Baine	Union Jack	5. 8.1911
42.	Ernest Brindle	Union Jack	16.12.1911
43.	W. A. Williamson	Union Jack	6. 1.1912
44.	Edwy Searles Brooks	Union Jack	13. 1.1912
45.	G. H. Teed	Union Jack	30.11.1912
37.	J. Staniforth	Union Jack	6. 9.1913
46.	H. E. Inman	Union Jack	25.10.1913
47.	J. W. Bobin	Union Jack	17. 1.1914
48.	Lewis Carlton	Boys Journal	1914–15
49.	Jack Lewis	Union Jack	28. 8.1915
50.	Robert Murray Graydon	Union Jack	16. 9.1916
51.	George Norman Phillips	Union Jack	25.10.1919
52.	R. H. Poole	Union Jack	15.11.1919
53.	Oliver Merland	S.B.L.	Dec. 1919
54.	W. W. Sayer	Union Jack	24. 1.1920
55.	L. H. Brooks	S.B.L.	Mar. 1920
56.	T. C. Wignall	S.B.L.	Mar. 1920
57.	H. G. Hill	Union Jack	26. 6.1920
58.	R. C. Armour	Union Jack	28. 8.1920
59.	S. G. Shaw	Union Jack	25. 9.1920
60.	F. A. Symonds	Union Jack	5. 2.1921
61.	Alfred Edgar	Union Jack	2. 7.1921
58.	Hartley Tremayne	Champion	11. 3.1922
62.	Arkus Sapt	Union Jack	16. 9.1922
63.	H. H. C. Gibbons	Union Jack	3. 3.1923
64.	Richard Goyne	Union Jack	4. 8.1923
65.	W. H. Jago	Union Jack	29.12.1923
66.	Warwick Reynolds	S.B.L.	Jan. 1924
67.	Walter Shute	Union Jack	29. 3.1924
68.	Gwyn Evans	Union Jack	19. 4.1924
69.	H. W. Twyman	Union Jack	3. 5.1924
70.	J. W. Wheway	Union Jack	21. 6.1924
71.	H. Crichton Miln	S.B.L.	Sept. 1924
72.	D. Thomas	Union Jack	4.10.1924
73.	Anthony Baron	Union Jack	27.12.1924

No. of Author	Writer	Paper	Date
74.	John Nix Pentelow	Union Jack	3. 1.1925
75.	Noel Wood Smith	Union Jack	25. 4.1925
76.	F. W. Young	Union Jack	26. 9.1925
77.	Arthur Paterson	Union Jack	17. 7.1926
78.	Ladbroke Black	Union Jack	8. 1.1927
79.	Tom Stenner	Union Jack	26. 3.1927
80.	Houghton Townley	S.B.L.	30. 4.1927
81.	C. M. Hincks	Union Jack	30. 7.1927
82.	R. L. Hadfield	Union Jack	13. 8.1927
83.	Gerald Verner	S.B.L.	Aug. 1927
84.	Lester Bidston	S.B.L.	Aug. 1927
85.	Stacey Blake	Union Jack	10. 9.1927
86.	E. W. McLean	Union Jack	19.11.1927
87.	Rex Hardinge	Union Jack	14. 1.1928
88.	R. F. Foster	S.B.L.	May 1929
89.	W. Tremellin	Union Jack	7. 9.1929
90.	W. E. S. Hope	S.B.L.	Oct. 1929
63.	Gilbert Chester	Union Jack	23.11.1929
51.	Victor Fremlin	Union Jack	30.11.1929
58.	Reid Whitley	Union Jack	28.12.1929
51.	Anthony Skene	Union Jack	1. 2.1930
91.	Edward C. Davis	S.B.L.	Mar. 1930
83.	Donald Stuart	Union Jack	22. 3.1930
92.	L. C. Douthwaite	S.B.L.	June 1930
34.	Allan Blair	S.B.L.	June 1930
93.	R. C. Elliott	S.B.L.	June 1930
50.	Robert Murray	Union Jack	5. 7.1930
58.	Coutts Brisbane	S.B.L.	July 1930
38.	Sidney Drew	S.B.L.	July 1930
52.	Michael Poole	S.B.L.	7. 8.1930
94.	Lewis Essex	S.B.L.	4. 9.1930
95.	Francis Warwick	Union Jack	6. 9.1930
96.	David Macluire	Union Jack	11.10.1930
67.	Walter Edwards	S.B.L.	April 1931
47.	John Ascott	S.B.L.	7. 5.1931

No. of Author	Writer	Paper	Date
75.	Norman Taylor	Union Jack	16. 5.1931
49.	Stephen Hood	S.B.L.	4. 6.1931
30.	A. S. Hardy	S.B.L.	Sept. 1931
47.	Mark Osborne	S.B.L.	Sept. 1931
49.	Lewis Jackson	Union Jack	19. 9.1931
78.	Paul Urquhart	S.B.L.	1.10.1931
59.	Stanley Gordon	Union Jack	21.11.1931
97.	W. J. Elliott	Union Jack	19.12.1931
98.	W. P. Vickery	S.B.L.	4. 2.1932
95.	Warwick Jardine	S.B.L.	Mar. 1932
99.	Stawford Webber	Union Jack	30. 7.1932
100.	J. G. Brandon	S.B.L.	5. 1.1933
101.	Arthur J. Palk	Union Jack	7. 1.1933
—	John Andrews (stock name)	Boys Friend Library	1. 6.1933
102.	Frank Lelland	D.W.	14.10.1933
54.	Pierre Quirroule	S.B.L.	4. 1.1934
103.	Gerald Bowman	D.W.	27. 1.1934
104.	George E. Rochester	D.W.	3. 2.1934
105.	Roland Howard	D.W.	31. 3.1934
45.	Louis Britanny	D.W.	5. 5.1934
106.	Bruce Chaverton	D.W.	2. 6.1934
107.	George D. Woodman	D.W.	25. 8.1934
81.	Charles Malcolm	Sports Budget	1935
108.	Anthony Ford	D.W.	27. 4.1935
109.	Francis Brent	D.W.	11. 5.1935
57.	Hylton Gregory	S.B.L.	July 1935
109.	John Hunter	S.B.L.	Aug. 1935
110.	Maurice B. Dix	S.B.L.	5. 3.1936
111.	Martin Frazer	S.B.L.	2. 4.1936
34.	Allan Maxwell	S.B.L.	3.12.1936
112.	John Creasey	S.B.L.	4. 2.1937
113.	Cyril Vernon Frost	S.B.L.	6. 5.1937
114.	Barry Perowne	S.B.L.	3. 6.1937
115.	John L. Garbutt	Pilot	21. 8.1937

No. of Author	Writer	Paper	Date
116.	Anthony Parsons	S.B.L.	7.10.1937
117.	George Dilnot	S.B.L.	4.11.1937
73.	John Baron	D.W.	26. 3.1938
44.	Berkeley Gray	S.B.L.	6.10.1938
118.	Hedley Scott	S.B.L.	3.11.1938
115.	John Brearley	B.F.L.	5. 1.1939
119.	Ernest Dudley	D.W.	25. 3.1939
45.	George Hamilton	D.W.	10. 6.1939
120.	Brian Edgar Wallace	D.W.	9. 9.1939
121.	Donald Bobin	D.W.	23. 9.1939
122.	Edward Holmes	D.W.	20. 1.1940
123.	Stanley Hooper	D.W.	27. 4.1940
124.	Clifford Gates	S.B.L.	Jan. 1941
125.	D. L. Ames	S.B.L.	Aug. 1942
126.	John Purley	S.B.L.	Mar. 1943
127.	John Sylvester	S.B.L.	May 1943
128.	Joseph Stamper	S.B.L.	July 1943
129.	Walter Tyrer	S.B.L.	Aug. 1943
109.	Peter Meriton	S.B.L.	Oct. 1943
130.	John Drummond	S.B.L.	May 1944
64.	Richard Standish	S.B.L.	Dec. 1944
131.	Derek Long	S.B.L.	Dec. 1946
132.	Hilary King	S.B.L.	Jan. 1951
133.	Stephen Blakesley	S.B.L.	Dec. 1951
134.	Quentin Ford	Knockout Fun Book for 1953	Sept. 1952
135.	Hugh Clevely	S.B.L.	6.11.1952
136.	W. J. Passingham	S.B.L.	7. 5.1953
137.	George Rees	S.B.L.	3.12.1953
138.	W. Howard Baker	S.B.L.	3.11.1955
138.	Peter Saxon	S.B.L.	2. 2.1956
139.	Arthur Maclean	S.B.L.	July 1956
140.	Arthur Kent	S.B.L.	Aug. 1956
141.	James Stagg	S.B.L.	Oct. 1956
142.	Jack Trevor Story	S.B.L.	4.12.1956

No. of Author	Writer	Paper	Date
143.	Jacques Pendower	S.B.L.	
—	Desmond Reid (stock name)	S.B.L.	Mar. 1957 Mar. 1957
144.	Gordon Sowman	S.B.L.	Mar. 1957
145.	Brian McArdle	S.B.L.	Apr. 1957
146.	Lee Roberts	S.B.L.	4. 6.1957
147.	Jonathan Burke	S.B.L.	2. 7.1957
148.	A. L. Martin	S.B.L.	2. 7.1957
138.	William Arthur	S.B.L.	Aug. 1957
149.	Frank Lambe	S.B.L.	Sept. 1957
150.	Martin Thomas	S.B.L.	Oct. 1957
151.	Edwin Harrison	S.B.L.	May 1958
152.	D. Herbert Hyde	S.B.L.	Feb. 1959
153.	Rex Dolphin	S.B.L.	Mar. 1959
154.	Noel Browne	S.B.L.	Aug. 1959
155.	E. C. Tubb	S.B.L.	Oct. 1959
138.	W. A. Ballinger	S.B.L.	Jan. 1960
156.	Eddie Player	S.B.L.	Feb. 1960
157.	Philip Chambers	S.B.L.	Apr. 1960
158.	Ross Story	S.B.L.	May 1960
139.	Arthur Kirby	S.B.L.	June 1960
—	Richard Williams (stock name)	S.B.L.	July 1960
159.	F. Dubrez Fawcett	S.B.L.	Oct. 1960
141.	Gilbert Johns	S.B.L.	Jan. 1961
160.	Colin Robertson	S.B.L.	May 1961
161.	Wilfred McNeilly	S.B.L.	June 1961
162.	Stephen Francis	S.B.L.	Aug. 1961
163.	Anthony Glyn	S.B.L.	Oct. 1961
164.	A. Cahil	S.B.L.	Nov. 1961
165.	A. Garstin	S.B.L.	Dec. 1961
166.	V. J. Hanson	S.B.L.	Jan. 1962
—	George Sydney (stock name used once only)	S.B.L.	Feb. 1962

No. of Author	Writer	Paper	Date
167.	S. J. Bounds	S.B.L.	Feb. 1962
168.	Anthony Douse	S.B.L.	Mar. 1962
169.	Michael Moorcock	S.B.L.	June 1962
170.	T. C. P. Webb	S.B.L.	Dec. 1962
130.	J. N. Chance	S.B.L.	Jan. 1963
171.	S. O. Franes	S.B.L.	Feb. 1963
172.	M. Marquis	S.B.L.	May 1963
173.	B. Hopkins	S.B.L.	May 1963
174.	Ross Richards	S.B.L.	Mar. 1966
175.	Stephen Christie	S.B.L.	1968
174.	Matt Mead	S.B.L.	1968
176.	Tony Power	Sexton Blake Annual/1969	Sept. 1968

SPECIAL NOTE:
Since these lists were compiled, it has been established that Maxwell Scott wrote a Sexton Blake serial in the comic, Jester, in 1901. Consequently the numbers before No 38 need revising, as unfortunately the exact date cannot be confirmed.

NEW DATA

In compiling a biography of this nature, one of the most frustrating factors is that with fresh data coming in all the time one can never be satisfied that it is as complete as one would wish. It would be easy to insert additional information in a yearly publication, but in this case it is, of course, not possible.

Certainly one important change since this work was written is that 'Fleetway Publications' is now known as 'The I.P.C.' (Magazine Division) and was legally so since the 1st September 1968. Consequently, editorial positions mentioned in this biography may now be altered, although it is of course a record of those held at the time. Another big change is that Mr Leonard Matthews left the firm in December, 1968, to start his own publishing business in Fleet Street. He was succeeded in a sense by Mr John Saunders, a most capable man, who was editor of LOOK AND LEARN.

THE MEN BEHIND BOYS' FICTION

Notes

The following abbreviations will be found in this collective biography:

A.P.	..	Amalgamated Press
B.O.P.	..	Boys Own Paper
S.O.L.	..	Schoolboys Own Library
B.F.W.	..	Boys Friend Weekly
B.F.L.	..	Boys Friend Library
S.B.L.	..	Sexton Blake Library
U.J.	..	Union Jack
Lib.	..	Library
(anon)	..	Story written anonymously
(1st)	..	Denotes that it was written in the 1st series (or where the case may be) of that particular paper.
(r.n.)	..	Real name of Author

1. It should be emphasised that this work is mainly intended to cover the writers of stories which appeared in boys' papers. This is, roughly, up to 1950, as after that date most boys' papers mainly consisted of picture stories. Some writers of boys' books are, however, included where it is felt that they should be inserted for general interest.

2. All the names have been personally checked by the compilers, either through official records or by personal contact with the editors or writers concerned. Much information has also been gained by personal correspondence, and in the case of 'classical' authors long since dead, information has been taken from reliable reference books.

3. No theories have been included, and whilst it could be strongly suspected that an author may have written under another name by the style of writing, this is not taken as proof. Official records show that in many cases the style of writing is not a true guide, and any assumptions made along these lines could well be false.

4. Many of the names listed not marked (*r.n.*) may possibly be the real name of the author. This has only been inserted when the real name has been proved to be authentic.

5. All the authors of D. C. Thomson papers have been anonymous, excepting the yearly Annuals. In all probability many hundreds of other names could be added if they were known. A 'W. G. Bagnall', 'Campbell', 'Loader', 'Cornes' and 'Cummings' are known to have written stories, but as nothing is known about them, or what papers they wrote for, they are not included.

6. Most of the serials in comic papers did not have the author's name, and they are only included where they have been located by research. It would take almost another full-length work to include them all, and this is really another field of research.

THE MEN BEHIND BOYS' FICTION

Abbott, Lawrence   *(r.n. Christopher George Holman Lawrence)*
Union Jack (1st).   True Blue (2nd).
Abdullah, Sheikh Ahmed   *(r.n. Ali Ikbal Shah)*
Chums.   Lloyds Detective Series.
Adams, Edward C.
Boys Journal.   Lloyds Boys Adventure Series.   B.O.P.
Chums.
Adams, Frederick K.   *(r.n.)*
Sub-editor on GEM (1921) and on staff of other boys' papers
at Amalgamated Press Ltd.
Boys Cinema.   Rocket.   Champion.   Scout.
Adams, Gerald Drayson
Thriller.
Adams, Harry
Pluck (2nd).
Adams, H. C.
B.O.P.
Adams, John   *(r.n. J. A. McLaren)*
Boys Realm (2nd).
Adams, Major J. Verney
Boys Journal.
Adams, Lawrence
Boys Favourite.
Adams, M. P.
B.O.P.
Adamson, Cecil
Scout.
Adare, Allen
Racing Novels (1st Aldine).
Addiscombe, John
Flag Library.
Addison, Captain
Vanguard Library.   Diamond Library (1st).

Addison, G. Douglas
Chums.
Agent '55'   *(r.n. Percy Longhurst)*
Gem (2nd).
Agnew, Stephen Hamilton   *(r.n.)*
Prolific writer of boys' stories around the turn of the century
and after. Took up writing the Aldine Dick Turpin Library
where the original author, Charlton Lea, left off. Lea's stories
were full-blooded enough, but Agnew's were even more so.
He had a notably picturesque, colourful, descriptive style and
his stories were mainly of the weird, fantastic and hair-raising
variety. Penned many other stories for Aldine Libraries, and
was killed on the Western Front in 1915.
Pen-names: Arthur Stephens. Kenneth Stephens. Colin
Summers. Roy Allyne.
Fun and Fiction. Boys Comic Library. The Comic Library.
Dick Turpin Library. Diamond Library (1st). Black Bess Lib.
Vanguard Lib. Newnes Adventure Lib. Nugget Lib. (1st and
2nd). Comic Life. Lot-O'-Fun. Chums. Lion Lib.
Aimard, Gustave
Captain Library.
Ainsworth, William Harrison   *(r.n.)*
Born 1805. Died 1882. Educated at Manchester Grammar
School. First novel, Rookwood, 1834. Editor of Bentleys
Miscellany, 1840–2. Ainsworth Magazine, 1842–53, and
then acquired New Monthly Magazine. Wrote 39 novels in-
cluding Jack Sheppard, 1839. Tower of London, 1840. Old St
Paul's, 1841. Guy Fawkes, 1841. The Miser's Daughter, 1842.
Windsor Castle, 1843. Lancaster Witches, 1848. The South Sea
Bubble, 1868.
Union Jack (1st). Pluck (1st).
Aitken, A. Donnelly   *(r.n.)*
Born London 1892. Died 1962. Educated at Emmanual School,
Cambridge. Worked on staff of A.P. 1909 until being called up
for war service. Editor Modern Man 1910. Editor of Fun and
Fiction, 1911–14. Also wrote many stories for it including 'The
Woman with the Black Heart' series, and some in the series
about 'Adam Daunt, Detective' and 'The Sign of the Twisted
Tooth'. He also started the series of music-hall interviews called
'Footlight Favourites'. After serving with distinction in the

Great War, reaching the rank of Major and suffering the loss of an arm, he returned to Fleet Street and edited CHUMS 1918–20. He joined Newnes in 1927, and was assistant editor of TITBITS until his death.

Pen-names: A. Donnelly. A. Donnelly Shannon.

Fun and Fiction (anon). Dreadnought (anon). Butterfly (anon). Favourite Comic (anon). Merry and Bright (anon). Chums.

Aitken, B. W.

Young England.

Akbar

Chums.

Alais, Ernest W. *(r.n.)*

Born Reading, 30.12.1864. Died at Streatham, 7.1.22. Was brother-in-law to James Harwood Panting. Born with only one lung, yet was a continuous heavy smoker of the strongest tobacco, his favourite being the old Irish Twist. When he was writing there was a ceaseless volume of smoke from his pipe. A marvellous raconteur, and told all his yarns without a facial movement. He could literally smell a fog coming, when he would retire to his bed until it had cleared. He was sixth of a family of seven, and his tact in any emergency was unsurpassed, his mental ability making up for his delicate physical condition. He made his début into the literary world by a contribution to the Golden Penny. In addition to his literary work he was a brilliant caricaturist and was also a fine black-and-white and water-colour artist. He also did some steel engraving. He probably acquired this skill from his father, W. J. Alais, who was a well-known steel engraver, engraving many of Landseer's works and other works of historical and military nature.

According to his family, with whom D. J. Adley was in lengthy correspondence, the name is pronounced to rhyme with 'Calais'. Created Kit and Cora.

Pen-names: Lawrence Miller. Cedric Wolfe.

Popular (1st) (anon). Boys Herald (anon). B.F.L. (1st) (anon). S.B.L. (1st) (anon). N.L.L. (Old Series) (anon). U.J. (2nd) (anon). B.F.W. (2nd) (anon).

Aldcroft, Arthur *(r.n.)*

Sub-editor on the Companion Papers – Magnet, Gem, Penny Popular, Empire Library, almost from the beginning to end, and worked mainly on reprint stories. Wrote at least one short

Greyfriars story in Boys Herald (the continuation of the Greyfriars Herald) and other bits and pieces. After leaving A.P. he went to work in a Government Department in London.

Alfriston, Louis
B.F.L. (2nd). Gem (2nd).

Allan, F. Carney *(r.n.)*
Pen-names: Duncan Neish. Eric MacDonald.
Pioneer Football Weekly. B.F.L. (2nd). Boys Wonder Lib. Bullseye (anon). Sport & Adventure (anon). Boys Realm of Sport & Adventure. Boys Realm (2nd). Chums. Magnet. Startler (anon). Chums Annual. Holiday Annual.
Lived in Putney for many years. Now in semi-retirement in Scotland.

Allan, John
Marvel (2nd). B.F.L. (2nd). Modern Boy.

Allen, Chris
Detective Tales (2nd). Boys Pocket Lib. Lloyds Boys Adventure Series. Comic Life. Lot-O'-Fun. Boys Weekly.

Allen, George J.
Union Jack (1st). Pluck (1st). B.F.W. (1st).

Allen, Lewis
Chums.

Allen, Mark
B.F.W. (2nd).

Allen, Oswald
Boys World.

Allingham, Claude and Claud
Marvel (1st). Boys Cinema.

Allingham, Herbert John *(r.n.)*
Born 1867. Died Jan. 1935. Son of William Allingham, who was owner and one-time editor of a weekly called 'The Christian Globe'. He was educated at Ardingly and Cambridge University; was intended for the Church but changed his mind and went into journalism. He became editor of the London Journal and retired in 1905 or 1906 to write boys' school stories and others for the Amalgamated Press, John Leng and Thomsons. He was also a successful serialist and wrote many tales. Two of the better-known at the time were 'The Duffer' and 'Human Nature', which ran weekly for over five years. Was the top-price writer for A.P. in 1911 at £2 2s. od. per thousand words

(later 2½ guineas). He married his cousin, Emily J. Hughes, and had three children, of whom Margery Allingham was the eldest. He was an old friend of Richard Starr, and they collaborated once or twice. His uncle was John W. Allingham (Ralph Rollington); a man considered to be somewhat wild by the rest of the family. (Much of this data came from Margery Allingham during her lifetime, and she also sent a copy of 'The History of Old Boys Books', written by her great-uncle, to Derek Adley.) Fun & Fiction (anon). B.F.L. (2nd). Gem (2nd). Young Britain (1st). Bullseye (anon). Dreadnought. Boys Own Lib. (1st). True Blue (2nd). Butterfly (anon). Favourite Comic (anon). Merry & Bright (anon) and Thomson publications.

Allingham, John W. *(r.n.)*
Editor and publisher of papers such as 'Boys World' and 'Our Boys Paper' which ran in the 1870's and 1880's. In writing the popular 'Ralph Rollington's Schooldays' and its varied sequels for his own papers, Allingham created the name by which he eventually became generally known, in much the same way as Charles Hamilton became more widely known as Frank Richards. He penned most of his later stories under the 'Ralph Rollington' pen-name, and also wrote a 'History of Old Boys Books' which mainly told of the rivalry between such 19th century publishers as Brett, Emmett, etc. He was the uncle of Herbert Allingham – who was, of course, the father of Margery, the famous detective and story writer.

Allingham, Margery Louise *(r.n.)*
Born London, 1904. Died 1967. Educated at Perse High School, Cambridge. Daughter of H. J. Allingham. Married P. Youngman Carter, 1927. She began writing at the age of 7, and her first novel was published when she was 16. Created and wrote best-seller novels about Albert Campion.
Broadsheet Novels. Thriller. Thriller Lib. U.J. (2nd).

Allyne, Roy *(r.n. Stephen H. Agnew)*
Chums.

Ames, Delano *(r.n.)*
Married first to romantic novelist Maysie Greig, then to Kit Woodward. Wrote one S.B.L. in 1942, and has since written many successful detective novels in book form, one of the most popular being 'Corpse Diplomatique'.
Thriller. S.B.L. (3rd).

Anderson, Frank *(r.n.)*
   Editor of Young Folks Tales (A.P. – after Henderson's) and
   Playtime. Wrote in A.P. comics as 'Uncle Dan'.
Anderson, G. J. B. *(r.n.)*
   Pen-names: Captain Dangerfield. Viscount Y. Melton Whyte.
   Howard Fielding. Max Lynn.
Anderson, Captain Linsay
   Marvel (1st). Boys Home Journal.
Anderson, Warwick
   Hotspur Book for Boys. Skipper Book for Boys.
Andom, R. *(r.n. Alfred W. Barratt)*
   Captain Library. Nugget Library. Nuggets.
Andrews, Jack
   Chips.
Andrews, John (stock name)
   A stock name used by A.P. editors for reprinted stories. This
   was used mainly when an author's name had been frequently
   employed and it was thought that a new 'author's' name would
   be more suitable. It was also used in cases where out-dated
   stories had to be modified and brought up-to-date, when the
   author had died many years previously. The best-known case in
   point was when Cecil Hayter's original 1909 stories of Sexton
   Blake at school and at Oxford were reprinted in the B.F.L. in
   the 1930's, and also where Maxwell Scott's famous 'Silver
   Dwarf' was reprinted. All these stories had the 'John Andrews'
   pen-name.
   Thriller. Pilot (anon). B.F.L. (2nd).
Andrews, Mervyn
   Chums.
Angas, John
   Football & Sports Favourite.
Anson, Piers *(r.n. Draycot Montagu Dell)*
   B.F.L. (2nd). Boys Wonder Library. Chums.
Anstey, F. *(r.n. Thomas Anstey Guthrie)*
Anthondyke, Captain Harry
   Marvel (1st). B.F.W. (1st). Boys Herald. Boys Realm (1st).
Appelbee, A. S.
   B.O.P.
Appleton, Cecil
   Boys Realm (1st).

Applin, Arthur G. T. *(r.n.)*
Born 1883 at Chelston Manor, Devon. Died 1948–9. Educated at Newton Abbot and privately. Author and producer. Married Edyth Olive, the actress. Edited Court Circular 1910 and Novel Magazine, 1914. Joined R.N.V.R. 1915. Pilot and Observer R.N.A.S. 1916. Captain 1917. Intelligence Dept., R.A.F. 1918-19. Dramatic and Film critic, St James's Gazette. Daily Sketch. Lloyds Weekly News.
Union Jack (1st). All Sports.

Archibald, C. M.
B.O.P.

Armitage, Alfred *(r.n. William Murray Graydon)*
Armitage, Vincent *(r.n. John W. Wheway)*
Champion. Boys Realm (2nd). Rocket. Sport & Adventure. B.F.L. (2nd). Pluck (3rd).

Armour, R. Coutts *(r.n.)*
An Australian who was fond of writing historical tales, especially about Robin Hood, for he wrote all the A.P. Robin Hood Library. A writer with a great sense of humour, which he incorporated into many of his stories, he also wrote of Gunga Dass in the Sexton Blake field.
Pen-names: Hartley Tremayne. Coutts Brisbane. Reid Whitley.
Robin Hood Lib. (A.P.) (anon). S.B.L. (1st) (anon). S.B.L. (2nd). U.J. (2nd) (anon). Popular Book of Boys Stories.

Armstrong, Anthony *(r.n. Captain Anthony Armstrong Willis)*
Thriller.

Armstrong, Jack *(r.n. F. A. Felton)*
B. F. W. (2nd).

Armytage
Boys Herald. B.F.L. (1st and 2nd). Popular (2nd). N.L.L. (old). British Boys.

Arnold, Blake
Chums.

Arnold, Clement *(r.n. Arnold Clement Panting)*
Boys Herald. Boys Realm (1st). B.F.W. (2nd).

Arnold, Eben
Young Britain(1st).

Arnold, Edgar
Young Britain (1st).

Arnold, Edwin Lester *(r.n.)*
Captain.

Arnold, Frank *(r.n. F. W. Young)*
Football & Sports Lib. Thriller. Boys Favourite. Sports Budget (2nd).

Arnold, J. E.
Boys World.

Arnold, Captain Malcolm *(r.n. Andrew Nicholas Murray)*
Boys Realm Football & Sports Library. B.F.L. (1st and 2nd). Champion. Boys Realm (1st and 2nd). Gem (2nd). Young Britain (1st). Sports for Boys. Rocket. Pluck (3rd). Boys Herald. Sports Fun. Football & Sports Favourite.

Arnold, Rex
Nugget Library.

Arter, Wallace E. *(r.n.)*
Member of the Institute of Journalists and the Guild of Agricultural Journalists, and Councillor on Local Government for over 20 years. Has made many broadcasts, including some for Woman's Hour and has also written for Children's Hour. Together with his wife wrote a great deal for children's Annuals of Blackies, Nelson's, Birns, Wills & Heyworth, Warnes, Dean and also for Chatterbox. During First World War served with R.E. Signals. Quite possibly may be the author listed below, Elmer K. Arter, but he had an agent and cannot remember the stories in question.
Pen-name: Wallace Kay.
Lengs Fairy Tales.

Arter, Elmer K.
Boys Realm (2nd). B.F.W. (2nd). Gem (2nd).

Arthur, Bruce
Chums.

Arthur, Arthurs, Harry *(r.n. A. H. Base)*
Union Jack (1st). Pluck (1st). Wonder.

Arthur, William *(r.n. William Howard Baker)*
S.B.L. (3rd).

Ascott, John *(r.n. John William Bobin)*
Rocket. B.F.L. (2nd). S.B.L. (2nd). Triumph. Champion. Nelson Lee Lib. (3rd New Series). Champion Lib. Thriller.

Ash, Derek *(r.n. F. T. Bolton)*
Pluck (3rd). Champion Annual.
Ash, Fenton *(r.n. F. A. Atkins)*
B. F. W. (2nd). B. F. L. (1st). Boys Herald. Nelson Lee Lib.
(old). Union Jack (2nd). Chuckles. Boys Leader.
Ash, Mark
Boxing novels (1st) (Aldine). War Stories (Aldine).
Ashley, Fred
Marvel (2nd).
Ashworth, Chadwick
Champion.
Atkey, Philip *(r.n.)*
Was on the staff of Newnes producing such popular magazines
as Happy and Sunny at the age of 18. Wrote a great deal of
stories for Newnes Dick Turpin Library at £20 per 31,000
words. Author of the world-famous 'Raffles' stories after the
creator, E. W. Hornung. He wrote at least 50 or 60 of these at
lengths varying between 7,000 and 140,000 words. In 1931,
Monty Haydon, a director of the A.P., made the original
arrangements for him to continue the character of Raffles. An
editor on the staff of Sexton Blake material in the middle 30's –
'Jackie' Hunt – thought of the idea of pitting Raffles against
Sexton Blake, and these adventures appeared in the S.B.L. His
uncle was Bertram Atkey, the novelist.
Pen-name: Barry Perowne.
Atkins, Frank A. *(r.n.)*
An extremely mysterious author, of whom very little is known;
extensive research has proved fruitless. Biographical details
which are known show that he was brought up in South Wales,
on the shores of the Bristol Channel. Later he studied to be an
engineer, but subsequently took up writing and specialised in
science fiction and fantasy. Wrote several stories and serials for
various papers in the early 1900's.
Easily his most famous story was 'The Radium Seeker' in Boys
Realm, and when this tale was produced in book form by
Pitmans in 1906, it was enthusiastically received, especially by
the Daily Telegraph, who stated: 'It suggests Jules Verne, Rider
Haggard and Fenimore Cooper in their boldest and most
entrancing moods.' He received £40 only for the copyright of
another story, 'A Trip to Mars', published by Chambers in

41

1909. He was film critic on a London Sunday paper around this period, when he wrote many stories adapted from the films. Records do show a F. A. Atkins Junior, so there may have been a father and son who were both writers.
Pen-names: Fenton Ash. Frank Aubrey.
Union Jack (2nd) (anon). Captain Library.
Atkins, F. J.
Boys Realm (1st).
Atkinson, Reginald *(r.n. Lewis Carlton)*
B.F.W. (2nd).
Atkinson, W. A.
Young England. Chatterbox.
Aubrey, Frank *(r.n. Frank A. Atkins)*
B.F.L. (1st).
Audley, Captain
Pluck (2nd).
Austin, F. Britten
Chums.
Austin, Mortimer *(r.n. John Gabriel Rowe)*
Union Jack (1st).
Austin, Stanley E.
Whilst a prolific and splendid author in his own right, he became somewhat more famous as being a leading substitute writer for the Magnet and Gem, chiefly the latter. Starting with 'The Fag's Honour' for the Gem in 1919, he continued until the early 1930's, writing a considerable number of stories of Greyfriars, St Jim's, and Rookwood. Unlike many other substitute writers he was trusted to write long series, Holiday Caravan, Motor Cruiser, Norfolk Broads amongst them. His last long series for the Gem was known as the 'Who Shall be Captain?' series, which consisted of eight stories with a cricketing background. His first story (not a substitute) was in 1910 in the Boys Herald. He died in the 1950's.
Pen-names: (as sub-writer) Owen Conquest. Martin Clifford. Frank Richards.
Boys Herald. Boys Realm (1st and 2nd). B.F.W. (2nd). Chums. Nelson Lee Library (3rd New Series). Lloyds Sports Library. Lloyds School Yarns. British Boy.
Avery, Harold *(r.n.)*
Born at Headless Cross, Worcestershire, 1867. The son of a

local J.P., William Avery. Educated at New College, Eastbourne. Served in the Army, 1914–18. Wrote his first story for boys in 1884. It was a very popular serial for the B.O.P. in 1896 which really put him on the map, this being entitled 'The Triple Alliance', an excellent school story. This was later published in book form and ran into several editions, proving very popular as a school and Sunday School prize.

He subsequently wrote numerous school stories, some of them suitable for younger readers. His serials appeared in Captain as well as B.O.P. His many bound books include 'The Dormitory Flat', 'Mobsley's Mohicans', 'Play the Game', 'The Cockhouse Cup', 'Heads or Tales' and 'Off the Wicket'. He was also a prolific short-story writer, contributing to many juvenile papers and Annuals. Also wrote a few adult novels, including 'A Week at the Sea', 'Every Dog has his Day', and 'Thumbs Up'. But it was really as a school-story writer that he excelled.

Most of his life was spent at Evesham, Worcestershire, where he died in 1943.

Captain. B.O.P. Chums. Young England.

Aynesworth, Cecil   *(r.n. E. Burton Childs)*

Champion.

Back, William   *(r.n.)*

Editor of the Union Jack in the early 1900's, and one to whom all Sexton Blake enthusiasts should be grateful. For it was W. H. Back who recalled Blake to the pages of the Union Jack after he had been discarded for nearly two years. Back's brilliant hunch in October 1904 paid rich dividends and Blake was featured in every issue from No 107 onwards. Wrote an article in B.F.W. (1st) and was Editorial Director of Amalgamated Press until his sudden death abroad in the early 1920's.

Bacot, J. T. W.

Union Jack (1880).

Baden-Powell, Lord Robert   *(r.n.)*

Born 1857 and was famous for his defence of Mafeking during the Boer War. It is as founder of the Scout Movement and of the paper 'Scout' that most boys know him, however. He founded the Boy Scouts in 1908 after writing his book 'Scouting for Boys' the same year. (This appeared in six fortnightly parts.)

These booklets were extremely successful and letters came pouring in to the publishers from interested readers who wanted to know more about scouting.

'B.P.', as the Chief Scout, felt that a paper should be launched which catered for the Boy Scout Movement; so, after considerable talks with advisers and consultations with the publishers (C. Arthur Pearson Ltd), The Scout was born, and the first issue appeared on the 18th April, 1908. The first article was 'How I Started Scouting' by Lord Baden-Powell himself, and he continued to contribute articles almost to the time of his death in 1941. Marvel (1st). Scout. Boys Journal (under B.P. – Be Prepared).

Bagshotte, Annerley
Scout.

Bailey, Robert Ernest *(r.n.)*
B.O.P.

Baine, Colin T. *(r.n.)*
Wrote stories for many papers and magazines, mainly with a sailing-boat theme in the 1910 period, this including a Sexton Blake story for the Union Jack No 408 in 1911, entitled 'Sexton Blake – Yachtsman'.
Union Jack (2nd) (anon). Boys Herald. Boys Journal. Marvel (2nd). Boys Realm (2nd). Diamond Library (1st).

Baines, R. Read
Boys Home Journal.

Baird, G.
Chatterbox.

Baker, A.
B.O.P.

Baker, Augustus *(r.n.)*
Was Deputy Editor-in-Chief to Reeves Shaw, who was in charge of Newnes juvenile publications. These included The Captain, Merry Moments, Tubby Haig, Nick Carter, Buffalo Bill, Treasure Trove, Joe Pickford and Redskin Libraries, which appeared around the early 1920's. Also did a lot of writing, and under the pseudonym of 'Anthony Baron' (although the story was anonymous he had to mask his own name when writing for a rival firm) wrote one story for the Union Jack in 1924, which was later reprinted in the Detective Weekly in 1938 under the name of 'John Baron'.

He left the juvenile field in the late 20's and died only a few years ago.

Baker, H. S.
True Blue (2nd).

Baker, Johnny
Thomson's Red Lion Library.

Baker, Olaf
B.O.P.

Baker, Sir Samuel
Chums.

Baker, Tom
Triumph.

Baker, William Arthur Howard   *(r.n.)*
Born in Cork, Eire, 1925. As a boy he was a regular reader of the Magnet and still has some of his original copies today. He edited the school magazine The Centaur, and during the last war he served in the Armed Forces. After his demobilisation he travelled a great deal in Australia, Asia, North Africa, Central America and on the Continent as a freelance writer. He also contributed many articles and short stories to popular magazines and newspapers. Later, he settled in London as correspondent for a group of European papers and afterwards became Editor of Panther Books. When L. H. Pratt retired as Editor of the S.B.L. Howard Baker was invited to take over, with a brief to give a new and modern look to the Sexton Blake saga. This he did, and from the moment he took over as editor in 1956, many changes were made and many new authors of the modern school were recruited. Whilst many of the old brigade of readers did not like the transition from Baker Street to Berkeley Square, and the introduction of female assistants into the Blake/Tinker ménage, most agreed that his changes were for the better.
His own first contribution for the S.B.L. was No 347 – 'Without Warning' – and many others followed. During his first year, in 1956, he turned out 6 S.B.L.s under his own name and another 5 were produced as 'Peter Saxon'. Probably his best-remembered S.B.L. was the one in which he introduced Paula Dane (who afterwards became Blake's personal secretary); this was No 359, 'The Frightened Lady'.
His story 'The Sea Tigers' was considered to be one of the best-written stories of all time, and another of his S.B.L.s was made

into a film (1958) featuring Geoffrey Toone as Blake. The film was called 'Murder at Site Three' and was adapted from the story entitled 'Crime is My Business'.

When the Amalgamated Press was taken over by a larger company and, under a new policy, decided to publish only those periodicals of best-selling potential (a role to which the S.B.L. did not aspire) he left Fleetway House and entered into negotiations with Mayflower/Dell Books of London/New York, with a view to continuing the Sexton Blake saga under a new imprint. Against all predictions, negotiations were successful, with the result that Bill Howard Baker became Editor and Director of the New Sexton Blake Library, produced in paperback format on a monthly basis. In 1968, he set about the formation of his own publishing company, Howard Baker Publishers Ltd, which is rapidly growing into a large concern. This new company continues to produce Sexton Blake novels, now in hard-cover format, in addition to its many other lines.

Former pen-names: Peter Saxon, Richard Williams, W. A. Ballinger, William Arthur, etc. (no longer exclusive pseudonyms).

S.B.L. (3rd and 5th).

Baldwin, Basil *(r.n. Balfour Ritchie)*
Sport and Adventure. B.F.L. (2nd). Boys Realm (2nd). Champion Annual. Playtime.

Balfour, David S.
Chums Annual.

Balantyne, Robert Michael *(r.n.)*
Born Edinburgh, 1825. As a youth spent some years in the service of the Hudson's Bay Company in Canada and later worked for Constables, the publishers. In 1856 he wrote his first book, 'The Young Fur Traders', which was an immediate success. His later and more famous books for boys include: 'Coral Island', 'Martin Rattler', 'The World of Ice' and 'The Gorilla Hunters'. Altogether during the period from 1848–94 he wrote more than 100 books, of which 72 were adventure stories. He also contributed numerous magazine articles as well as several serials to the B.O.P., including 'The Prairie Chief' and 'Twice Bought'. Also a serial to Samson Low's Union Jack around 1880. Also an accomplished artist, he occasionally illustrated his own stories. More often, however, he gave an illustrator a rough

sketch of how he wanted a scene to appear, and he went to a great deal of trouble to make sure that he gave his stories an authentic background. For example, he spent six years in the wilds of North America and Canada before writing 'The Young Fur Traders', visited Algiers for 'The Pirate City', spent two weeks on the North Sea with deep-sea fishermen for 'The Young Trawler' and sat up every night with London firemen, going out to fires with them, for 'Fighting the Flames'. He also lived for several weeks in a lighthouse for 'The Lighthouse'. He died in Rome in 1894.

A full list of Ballantyne's first editions appear in 'Book Collecting & Library Monthly', No 1, May 1968, and the full story of his life can be read in 'Ballantyne the Brave' (Rupert Hart-Davis, 1967). B.O.P. Union Jack (1880).

Ballantine, Jack

Hotspur Book for Boys. Skipper Book for Boys.

Ballard, Eric Alan

A modern prolific writer for magazines and newspapers, who lives in Spain.

Pen-name: Edwin Harrison.

S.B.L. (3rd).

Ballinger, William A. *(r.n. in relation to S.B.L. William Arthur Howard Baker)*

S.B.L. (3rd and 5th).

Bancks (M.A.), Rev. G. W.

Boys Journal.

Bander, James Wynne

Bulldog Breed Library.

Banfield, F. *(r.n.)*

Pluck (1st). Marvel (1st) (anon).

Banks, Marsh

Chums Annual.

Bardsley, Colonel John

Pluck (1st). Marvel (1st). Union Jack (1st).

Bardwell, Denver *(r.n. James Denson Sayers)*

Western Library.

Barker, C. Hedley

Lloyds Detective Series.

Barnard, Alfred J. *(r.n.)*

Born 1878, in Plaistow. Editor of 'The Era', 1911–18.

Special articles Editor in 'The Daily Mirror' 1918–20. Proprietor and editor of 'The Encore' 1928–30. Was with Amalgamated Press until 1911, when he wrote many serials and stories around this period. He also wrote a substitute story for the Gem. He was the father of R. J. Barnard and R. I. Barnard.

Pen-names: Leonard Hart. Martin Clifford (in Gem).
Empire Library (1st). Pluck (2nd). Marvel (2nd). B.F.L. (1st).

Barnard, Captain C. D.
Modern Boy.

Barnard, Richard Innes *(r.n.)*
Son of Alfred Barnard. Wrote many short pieces for Boys Realm group in the 20's. Was believed killed in the Black & Tan fighting in Ireland.
Pen-name: Frank Richards in Magnet.
Boys Realm (2nd). Sport & Adventure.

Barnard, Robert J. *(r.n.)*
Son of Alfred Barnard. Like his brother, he contributed short bits and pieces, but there is some confusion, as both signed themselves 'R. Barnard'.
Boys Realm (2nd).

Barnard, Wilfred
Boys Realm (2nd).

Barnes, G. G.
Boys Torch Adventure Library.

Barnes, Herbert
B.O.P.

Barnes, John *(r.n. Peter O'Donnell)*
Champion.

Barnett, John *(r.n. J. R. Stagg)*
Boys Journal. Cheer, Boys, Cheer.

Barnum, P. T.
Bad Boys Paper. Boys of the Isles.

Baron, Anthony *(r.n. Augustus Baker)*
Union Jack (2nd) (anon).
Special note: The above name was used when he was writing for a rival firm.

Baron, John *(r.n. Augustus Baker)*
Detective Weekly.

Barr, Nat *(r.n. Norman Goddard)*
Gem (1st).

Barradale-Smith, William *(r.n.)*

Famous for his many fine school stories under the name of Richard Bird. He was a schoolmaster by profession, so he knew what he was writing about. He began penning short stories for The Captain in 1911, then in 1915 he contributed his first full-length serial, 'The Dipcote Skippers' (later published in book form as 'The Rival Captains'). This was followed by four more 'Captain' serials: 'Bats versus Boats', 'The Ripswayd Ring', 'Hooligan Hall' (later published as 'The Deputy Captain') and 'The Liveliest Term at Templeton'. He wrote numerous short stories for all the better-class boys papers and many hard-cover stories as well. He also contributed many adult stories to 'The Strand' and other magazines.

Pen-name: Richard Bird.

Captain.

Barrett, Alfred Walter *(r.n.)*

Born London, 1st May 1869. Author of several broadly humorous novels, mainly concerning the adventures of 'Troddles' and his friends. His style was reminiscent of Jerome K. Jerome's. His serial 'The Waltham Wobblers' (the Misadventures of a Boys Cycling Club) ran in 'Comic Life' and was later reprinted in 'Nuggets' under the title of 'Our Sikle Club'. He also wrote many serials for 'Nuggets' and 'Boys World'. His bound books included 'We Three and Troddles' and 'Martha and I'. As well as 'Nuggets' he also edited Henderson's 'Garland' and 'Scraps' (1900 to 1910). It was whilst he was editor of 'Nuggets' that he gave the popular school-story writer, R. A. H. Goodyear, his first big chance by publishing his stories in that paper.

Pen-name: R. Andom.

B.F.W. (2nd). Boys World. Comic Life. Nuggets. Nugget Lib. (1st) (anon).

Barrett, Joseph

Diamond Library (1st).

Barrie, S.

A rather mysterious writer who wrote some substitute Greyfriars stories for the Magnet in the early 1920's. Titles were 'Bunter's Baby', 'A Bid for the Captaincy', 'A False Hero', 'Loder's Luck' and 'The Council of Action'. It is suspected that the name of this writer hid the identity of a top editor who shortly afterwards left the Amalgamated Press.

Pen-name: Frank Richards in Magnet.

Barron, A. Elton   *(r.n. E. H. Burrage)*
Bullseye (Aldine). True Blue (1st).

Barrow-North, H.   *(r.n.)*
Born in Leavengreave, Lancs. Wrote all types of stories for many magazines in the 1900 period. Was probably best in humorous school stories, several of which appeared in Chums. His best-known was probably 'Jerry Dodds, Millionaire' which told of the adventures of a South African boy at an English Public School (1900). This was later reprinted in book form with great success. Other serials included 'The Chronicles of St Simon's', 'Boys of Dormitory Three', 'Tom Durncombe's Peril' and 'Gomburg's Revenge'.
Chums.

Barry, Arthur
Young Britain (1st).

Barry, Gerald R.   *(r.n.)*
Born Belfast, 1887.
Thriller.

Barry, Wolfe
Pluck (1st).

Bartlett, Charles C.   *(r.n.)*
Boys Realm, Football and Sports Lib. Boys Realm (1st). B.F.W. (2nd). Boys Journal. Cheer, Boys, Cheer. Dreadnought.

Bartlett, J. Allen
B.O.P.

Barton (Christian name unknown)   *(r.n.)*
Butterfly. Favourite Comic. Merry & Bright (all anon).

Bartram, Lieut. G. B.
Boys Home Journal.

Base, A. H.   *(r.n.)*
Pen-names: Harry Arthur, Harry Arthurs.

Basset, Arthur, Ward
Boys Weekly.

Batchelor, Richard A. C.   *(r.n.)*
Pen-names: Arthur Mayne. Collett Henton.
Chums.

Bateman, Frederick   *(r.n.)*
Chums.

Bateman, H.
Scout.
Bates, Lieutenant
B.F.W. (2nd).
Batten, Harry Mortimer   *(r.n.)*
Born Singapore 1888 and educated at Oakham. Served with the
Canadian Police Force for some years then, after war service,
was awarded the Croix de Guerre. Famous for his writings on
wild animals, birds, etc., and on natural history. Author of
many memorable and moving animal stories. Contributed to
many adult and high-class magazines such as 'Blackwoods',
'Illustrated London News', 'Chambers', 'Field', etc., and of
course to many boys' papers. Wrote a Western serial in Chums
1918 entitled 'Ishmael of the Prairies', and a Red Indian serial
'Birdett the Trailer' for the Captain in 1913. Published many
books, including 'Tales of the Wild, 'Tracks and Tracking',
'Wild Animal Romances', 'Starlight' etc., also broadcast
numerous talks in the days of 2LO in the 20's. Lived for many
years at Connel, Argyll.
Chums. Scout. Captain. British Boy. B.O.P.
Batten, Peter W.   *(r.n.)*
Born Tranmere, Cheshire 1893. Educated at Baldock College,
Herts. Had six sons and three daughters. Served in France and
Gallipoli 1914–19. Awarded the Military Cross. News Editor
Sunday Dispatch 1926. Chief Sub-Editor Sunday Express 1929.
Football Stories. Football Novels. Boxing Novels (1st and 2nd).
Bauman, M. J.
Boys Torch Adventure Lib.
Bax, Arthur H.   *(r.n.)*
Editor of Comic Home Journal, 1904.
Baxter, George Owen   *(r.n. Frederick Faust)*
Western Library. Lloyds Boys Adventure Series.
Baxter, Horlyor
Young England.
Bayfield, William John   *(r.n.)*
Born at St Edmunds, Suffolk, on the 5th January 1871. He was
the son of a sergeant in the West Suffolk Militia. He started
writing at the turn of the century, and wrote his first serial in
the new series of the Boys Friend in 1901; it was originally en-
titled 'Through Thick and Thin' but this was changed to 'The

Boys of Repley College' after the first three instalments to avoid confusion with another story of a similar title. He wrote many further serials for Boys Friend, including 'Pluck Will Tell', 'Only a Highland Laddie', 'Storm Island' and 'A Lad o' Liverpool'. The rags-to-riches theme was a favourite one with Bayfield.

When the Boys Realm started in 1902 he was given pride of place in the front page with his new serial 'The Muff of Melthorpe College' and when a new series of the Union Jack began in 1903 so did his serial 'The Chums of Ashbourne School'. He also wrote a story in collaboration with Hamilton Edwards for the Boys Herald. His first Sexton Blake yarn was in the Union Jack around 1912, and he subsequently wrote many more, both for this paper and the S.B.L. Under one of his pen-names, 'Allan Maxwell', he was the author of S.B.L. 555 (2nd series), which he re-wrote from the original by W. M. Graydon. He also wrote for adult papers, including 'Penny Pictorial' in which a serial of his 'Slaves of the Pen' ran.

Bayfield spent the last years of his life in an Old Folks Home, but content, and in happy surroundings. He died at the Eventide Home, Staines, on the 3rd June 1958, at the ripe age of 87.

Pen-names: James Egerton Wing. Allan Maxwell. Allan Blair. Gordon Carr (at times). One S.B.L. (2nd) as Mark Osborne and another as Warwick Jardine.

Nelson Lee (old) (anon). Popular (1st) (anon). B.F.L. (1st) (anon). Detective Weekly (anon-rewrite). S.B.L. (1st and 2nd) (anon). Union Jack (2nd) (anon).

Bayly, Captain George
B.O.P.

Bayne, Charles S. *(r.n.)*
Born 26th Nov., 1876, Editor of Little Folks 1908–15. Girls Realm 1908, and on all Cassells book publications for young people. Originated British Boys Annual 1910. British Girls Annual 1910. Cassells Annual 1909. He also wrote Robin Hood & His Merry Men (new version).

Bayne, Peter *(r.n. Ernest Brindle)*
B.F.L. (1st). Gem (2nd). Magnet. Boys Herald.

Beal, George *(r.n.)*
Former newspaper reporter who switched to editing Children's Annuals. Worked at Odhams, and is at present at Fleetway House. Has a very large collection of children's Annuals and

boys and girls papers, and is probably one of the greatest authorities on this branch of literature. Was the last editor of the Fleetway House Magazine, and is very interested in all aspects of juvenile literature. Has also written children's stories.

Bean, E. A.
Boys Torch Adventure Lib.

Beaumont, Brenchley *(r.n. Walter Viles)*
Boys World.

Beaver, Barrington
Union Jack (1880).

Bebb, Fisher
Boys Journal.

Beck, Ashley
Lot-O'-Fun.

Beck, Christopher *(r.n. Thomas Charles Bridges)*
Captain. Newnes Adventure Lib. Britons Own Lib. Cheer, Boys, Cheer. Fun & Fiction. Boys Herald. Scout. British Boy.

Becke, Louis
Captain. B.O.P.

Beckenham, John
Boys Friend Weekly (2nd).

Beckerley, L. C.
Chums.

Bedford, Lee
Boys Cinema. Chums. Boys Friend Weekly (2nd).

Beeding, Frances *(r.n/s. John Palmer and H. A. St G. Saunders)*
Union Jack (2nd).

Beeston, L. J. *(r.n.)*
A story by Beeston appeared in the first volume of Chums, in 1892, and he continued to write for that paper for many years, sometimes using the name of 'Richard Camden'. His serials for Chums include 'The Shadow of St Basils', 'The Secret of St Udolph's' and 'The Spy of Sedgemere School'. As can be expected from such titles, he specialised in school mystery stories for this paper. He also wrote prolifically for nearly all the adult magazines. Someone once pointed out that Beeston had a vigorous enough style, but had an audacious habit of using the same plot time and time again, without giving it a new twist. He wrote several Sexton Blake yarns for the Union Jack in the 1908-9 period, and died at an extremely advanced age.

Pen-names: Lucian Davies. Richard Camden.
Popular (1st) (anon). Boys Herald. B.F.W. (2nd). B.F.L. (1st).
Boys Realm (1st). Nelson Lee (old). Union Jack (2nd) (anon).
Chums.

Beeton, Samuel Orchart   *(r.n.)*
Publisher husband of Mrs Beeton of cookery fame. As well as
publishing his wife's original books, he also launched an early
boys' paper called 'Boys Own Magazine' 1855. It only ran
until 1874, and Beeton died three years later. It was in 1887
in 'Beeton's Christmas Annual' (then published by Ward Lock
Ltd) that Sir Arthur Conan Doyle's 'Sherlock Holmes' made
his début. This was 'Study in Scarlet' – for which Conan Doyle
received a lump sum of £25, and not a penny more.

Beith, John Hay   *(r.n.)*
Born 1876, and educated at Fettes and Cambridge. Several of
his books deal with public-school life. Notably 'The Housemaster' (1936) which was produced as a successful London play
as well as being a best-seller in novel form. 'Pip' was another
book set in part at Grandwich School, and he also wrote a book
of essays called 'The Lighter Side of School Life'.
He served with great distinction in World War I, gaining the
M.C. and C.B.E. He wrote some fine war books also. During
the Second World War he was Director of Public Relations at
the War Office, and found time to write successful light novels
and plays. A member of the Royal Company of Archers, he was
one of the finest bow shots in Britain. He died in 1952.
Pen-name: Ian Hay.

Belbin, Harry   *(r.n. Harold J. Garrish)*
Pluck (2nd).

Belfield, Harry Wedgwood   *(r.n.)*
Wrote all the Colwyn Dane stories in the Champion from 1939
to the end, with the exception of one short period. Also wrote a
large number of Falcon Swift tales for the Boys Magazine and
Derek Lawson tales for the Wonder.
Pen-names: Harry Belfield. Cecil Wroxham. Rupert Drake.
Mark Grimshaw. E. Wedgwood Belfield (in error).
Chums. Pluck (3rd). Champion. Boys Realm (2nd). Champion
Lib. Young Britain (1st). B.F.L. (1st and 2nd). Tiger. Wonder
(anon). Boys Magazine (anon). Champion Annual.

Bell, George *(r.n.)*
Scout.

Bell, John Keble *(r.n.)*
Younger brother of well-known school-story writer, 'Captain' editor, novelist and playwright R. S. Warren Bell. Wrote many articles and one or two stories for 'Captain' and for other boys' papers. Later worked as reporter for the Press Association, as dramatic critic for 'The Daily Mail' and as editor of 'The Sketch'. As 'Keble Howard' he wrote more than 30 novels, 20 humorous books (including the popular 'Chicot' series) and over 20 plays, some of which were produced in the West End. His novels were so popular that several were printed in Braille. Author of a controversial novel called 'Lord London', which was a thinly-disguised portrait of Lord Northcliffe. Published his Autobiography 'My Motley Life' in 1927. He died on 23rd March, 1928.
Pen-names: Keble Howard. John Methuen.

Bell, Robert Stanley Warren *(r.n.)*
Born in 1871 and died 26th Sept., 1921. Was the eldest son of the Rev. G. E. Bell, Vicar of Henley-in-Arden, Warwickshire. Was originally intended for a career in the legal profession but eventually gave up reading for the Bar. Educated at St John's College, Leatherhead, he later became master at a private school, writing his first novel for adults in his spare time. This was 'The Cub in Love' and was published in 1897. The year before he began his long association with boys' papers by writing a serial 'The Boys of Daneleigh College' for the first number of George Newnes' short-lived 'British Boys'. He wrote this under the pen-name of 'Hawkesley Brett'. Later, under his own name, he contributed another serial to the paper, 'The Boy in Black'. In 1899, at the age of only 28, he joined George Newnes Ltd, as the founder and first editor of the 'Captain'. For over ten years he was the original 'Old Fag' and also contributed 10 serials and numerous short stories over the years.
His school stories were usually about Greyhouse, but he wrote about Claverdon too. One of his Greyhouse stories 'Sir Billy' was reprinted later in the Gem as a serial. One or two of his Greyhouse stories appeared in Chums also. Published many books, both for boys and adults. One of the best was 'Smith's Week', which deserved the highest praise, as it described sympa-

thetically the trials of a junior schoolmaster's first term, and was probably based in parts on his own experiences.

Other popular books included 'J. O. Jones', 'The Duffer', 'Jim Mortimer' and 'Tales of Greyhouse'. In 1907, he launched another Newnes magazine, a weekly this time, called 'Boys Life', editing the first eight issues. It failed to ring the bell, however, and lasted for a little over six months. Bell resigned from the 'Captain' in 1910, at the end of the 23rd volume, to write primarily for the theatre. The following year saw the successful production of his comedy, 'A Companion for George', at London's Kingsway Theatre.

Towards the end of World War I he was drafted into the Royal Flying Corps and served with G. R. Samways. After service he settled down at Westcliff-on-Sea and resumed his novel and short-story writing. His last story, written shortly before his death, was 'A Good Egg' which appeared in 'Captain'.

His brother was John Keble Bell, who also wrote boys' and adults' stories as 'Keble Howard'.

Gem (2nd). Boys Realm (1st). Boys Journal. Sports for Boys. Cheer, Boys, Cheer. Captain. Boys Life.

Bellamy, R. L.
Scout.

Bellasis, Brian
Comic Life (in collaboration with Toye Vise).

Bellingham, Cathel
Racing Novels (1st).

Belmont, Claude
Boys Realm (1st).

Bennett, Charles Moon *(r.n.)*
Born at Canterbury, 1899, and educated at Simon Langton's School. Was a schoolmaster by profession and, in 1933, became Headmaster of Eastfield Road School, Enfield, Middx. If he was as exciting a teacher as he was an adventure writer, his boys must have had a marvellous time. He made his début in boys' writing in the early 1920's by winning a nation-wide competition (organised by Nesbet & Co., Publishers) for the best boys' adventure story. His prize novel, which the panel of judges voted unanimously into first place, was a thrilling pirate story called 'Pedro of the Black Death'. It was serialised in Chums in 1926, being graphically illustrated by Paul Hardy.

Bennett's later books were all of the same type and included 'Tim Kane's Treasure', 'A Buccaneer's Log', 'Mutiny Island' and 'Red Pete the Ruthless'.

Three of the titles were subsequently issued by Nesbets in Omnibus form called 'The Pirate Omnibus'. Bennett also wrote a play chiefly for school called 'Hereward the Wake'. He lived in Enfield, Middx., for many years.
Chums.

Bennett, C. N.   *(r.n.)*
Pen-name: Norman Collier.
Chums.

Bennett, Hilda R.
Chatterbox.

Bennett, John
Boys Favourite.

Bennett, Rolfe   *(r.n.)*
Born London, 1882.
Captain.

Benson, Edward Frederic   *(r.n.)*
Born in Wellington College (where his father was headmaster, later to become Archbishop of Canterbury) in 1867, he was educated at Marlborough and Cambridge. Worked as an archaeologist in Athens between 1892–95. His first novel was 'Dodo' in 1893, followed by many light novels and other tales. In 1915 came 'David Blaize', set in Helmsworth School. An entertaining school story, it today suffers from touches of sentimentality, but it was one of his most popular books. He also wrote two other books about the same character, 'David Blaize and the Blue Door', and 'David at King's', the latter telling of his adventures at Cambridge. Was the younger brother of A. C. Benson, the writer, essayist and scholar, who was a housemaster at Eton and later became master of Magdalene College, Cambridge. E. F. Benson was Mayor of Rye from 1934–37, and died in 1940.

Benson, Richard (Captain)
Captain. Bulldog Breed Lib.

Benton, Clive
Boys World (Storey). School Cap.

Beresford, John   *(r.n. George Ernest Rochester)*
S.O.L. B.F.L. (2nd). Modern Boy.

Beresford, Leslie *(r.n.)*

Wrote stories for many papers, mostly for Champion, when F. Addington Symonds was editor. Probably his best-known serial for the latter was 'War of Revenge', which told of the Germans starting World War II in 1962. As this story was written in the 1920's it was a remarkable prophecy. He also wrote serials for Young Britain, including a science-fiction adventure called 'The Purple Planet'. He was also once a reader on the staff of Stephen Aske, the literary agents (Mr and Mrs Knight).

British Boy. Champion. Gem (2nd). Chums. Young Britain (1st). B.F.L. (2nd).

Berkeley, Anthony *(r.n. Anthony Berkeley Cox)*

Detective Weekly.

Berry, Len *(r.n.)*

Was on the staff of Amalgamated Press Ltd., and became editor of Detective Weekly around 1934. He left afterwards and went to the U.S.A., where he was on the staff of the United Nations.

'Bertie'

Marvel (2nd) No 83.

Besier, George

Diamond Library (1st).

Bevan, Tom *(r.n.)*

Born in Risca in 1868, and educated at Sir Thomas Rich's School in Gloucester and St Paul's College, Cheltenham. Was originally a schoolmaster and then later became Education editor to Sampson Low and Marston (Publishers), holding this position from 1917–31. Wrote many stirring and historical stories for boys, including, for the B.O.P., 'The Goldsmith of Chepe' (1907), 'The Beymouth Scouts' (1911) and 'The Hair of Wyselwood' (1913). Had many boys' books published including 'The Chancellor's Spy', 'The Grey Fox of Holland', 'The Heroic Impostor', etc. Also the 'Tom Bevan Omnibus'.

He also wrote a series of handbooks on English history for students. Contributed to numerous boys' and juvenile Annuals, also adult magazines. Lived at Ringwood, Hampshire, for many years.

B.O.P.

Bewley, Christopher

Chums.

Bey, Commander R. R. Hubbard
Scout.
Beynon, John
Modern Wonder.
Bidston, Lester   *(r.n.)*
Born in 1884, was a Liverpool schoolmaster whose first work appeared for 'Champion' and 'Pluck'. Specialised in off-beat fantasy stories. His titles include 'The Radio Planet', 'Wireless Wizard', 'The Crimson Claw', and, in the declining days of the Boys Friend, 'The Space Destroyer' and 'Scund the Eternal'. Under the name of Paul Hotspur he wrote 'Northwood Ho!', 'Isles of Gold' and 'Treasure of the North'. He also wrote an S.B.L. in 1927.
Pen-name: Paul Hotspur.
Champion. B.F.W. (2nd). Gem (2nd). Rocket. B.F.L. (1st and 2nd). Boys Wonder Library.
Biggers, Earl Derr   *(r.n.)*
Born Warren, Ohio, 26th August, 1884. Died 5th April, 1933. Famous as creator of the Chinese detective, Charlie Chan. Detective Weekly.
Billings, Buck
Western Library.
Bindloss, Harold Edward   *(r.n.)*
Born Liverpool 1866. Died 30th December, 1945.
Captain. Chatterbox.
Bingham, Major Arthur   *(r.n. W. Rowe)*
Union Jack (1st).
Birch, J.
Scout.
Birch, J. Weedon
Diamond Lib. (1st). B.O.L. (1st). Boys Comic Lib. Comic Lib.
Birchwood, Reginald
Chums.
Bird, Lewis   *(r.n. Cecil Hayter)*
Gem (1st).
Bird, Richard   *(r.n. William Barradale-Smith)*
Chums. B.O.P. Captain.
Birnage, Derek A. W.   *(r.n.)*
Joined the staff of R. T. Eves in 1930, and was on the Amalgamated Press Champion/Tiger group of papers. Now editor of

Sunday Companion, a post which was also held by his father.
Pen-names: Dick Birnage, Frank Winsor, Frank Windsor.

Birnage, Dick   *(r.n. Derek A. W. Birnage)*
Triumph.

Bishop, Julian Truitt
Captain.

Bishop. Percy Cook   *(r.n.)*
Editor of Union Jack and Pluck in a period in the 1890's.
Wrote one or two early Sexton Blake tales for the former, when
he introduced a character named Lorrimore Wallace.
Pen-name: Percival Cooke.

Black, Ian
Scout.

Black, Ladbroke Lionel Day   *(r.n.)*
Born in Burley-in-Wharfedale, Yorks, 21st July, 1877. Educated
at Foyle College, Ireland, and Queens' College, Cambridge,
where he received a B.A. degree. Became assistant editor of 'The
Phoenix' in 1897, assistant editor of 'The Morning Herald' in
1900, assistant editor of the 'Echo' 1900–1. Editor of 'Today'
1904–5, and special writer on the 'Weekly Dispatch' 1905–11.
Wrote his first Sexton Blake story for the S.B.L. in 1927 and
subsequently wrote many more, including some for the 'Union
Jack' and 'Detective Weekly', many of them under the pseudonym of 'Paul Urquhart'. (This name incidentally was used by
another writer named Thomas Cox Meech, a non-Blake writer,
though one time they both wrote in collaboration.)
Black's creations for the Sexton Blake field were 'The Spider'
and 'Mr Preed', a solicitor with a sword-stick. The latter especially became very popular with readers. He also wrote for many
adult papers (sometimes using the name of 'Lionel Day') but
his main work was for the national newspapers.
He wrote several books, including 'The Love Letters of King
Henry VIII', 'The Gorgon's Head', 'Old Mother Hubbard',
'Some Queer People' and 'The Poison War'. He was an expert
on history and biography and his favourite recreations were
boxing and rugby. He lived at Wendover, Bucks, for many
years and was Chairman of the Mid-Bucks Liberal Party in
1922–24. He died on July 27th, 1940.
Pen-names: Lionel Day. Paul Urquhart.
Pilot (anon). Union Jack (2nd). Popular (1st) (anon). Nelson

Lee Lib. (2nd N.S.). Thriller. Detective Weekly. S.B.L. (2nd).
Football Favourite (anon).
Blackledge, William James *(r.n.)*
Born 1886.
Detective Weekly.
Blackmore, Fred
Sports Budget (1st). Football and Sports Favourite.
Blackwood, William *(r.n.)*
Was Director of Amalgamated Press. Editor of Answers. Died
some years ago.
Blaikley, Ernest
Scout.
Blaiklock, E. M.
Chums Annual.
Blain, W. *(r.n.)*
Editor of Thomson Papers (juvenile section) since 1924. Was
the first editor of Hotspur and the artist who designed the
spreading eagle on the cover, this data coming from a Canadian
magazine. According to writers who had contributed to D. C.
Thomson, Mr W. Blain is a very versatile man, with tremendous
energy and ideas, and it is small wonder that his papers were
so successful.
Blair, Allan *(r.n. William J. Bayfield)*
A writer by the name of 'Gordon Carr' used this pen-name for
a time: ex-Boys Friend Weekly (2nd) No. 324.
Empire Lib. (2nd). Boys Friend Weekly (2nd). B.F.L. (1st).
Pluck (2nd). S.B.L. (2nd). Boys Journal. Boys Realm (1st).
Boys Realm Football and Sports Lib. Cheer, Boys, Cheer.
Champion. Dreadnought. Union Jack (2nd). Boys Herald.
Boys Home Journal.
Blair, Anthony *(r.n. Rowland Walker)*
Boys Realm (2nd).
Blair, Edward
Chums.
Blair, Erskine
Rob Roy Lib.
Blake, Bernard
Champion.
Blake, C. J.
Chatterbox.

61

Blake, Paul *(r.n. Harry Major Paull)*
B.O.P. Lloyds School Yarns.

Blake, Royston *(r.n. Edmund Burton Childs)*
Boys Friend Weekly (2nd).

Blake, Robert
Pals (Hultons).

Blake, Sexton
Stories about Sexton Blake appeared under this name in two issues of the very early ½d Union Jack, but the real identity behind the name is untraceable.

Blake, Stacey *(r.n.)*
Born Bradford, 1878. Started out as a black-and-white artist and was also a very keen bicycle rider on journeys abroad, including Gibraltar, Finland, Antwerp, Athens, Norway, Sweden, Denmark and Lapland. He used to write up his adventures for magazines and weekly papers. Has worked for Newnes, Pearsons, Cassell's and Thomsons. His first book was 'The Blue Highway' and some of his best stories were about 'Moreton Stowe', Special Correspondent, which appeared in 'Big Budget' at the beginning of the century.

When the A.P. 'Champion' started 20 years later, its editor – F. Addington Symonds – engaged him to revive the characters. Other popular creations by this author included 'Captain Kettle Jnr.' (in Big Budget) and Captain Christmas (in Penny Pictorial). Two of his most popular serials were 'Black Diamond' (Boys Leader) and Wilbur Wright, Apprentice (Boys Friend). He wrote several Sexton Blake stories, which appeared in 'Union Jack', 'Detective Weekly', and the S.B.L. In some of them he introduced his character, Captain Christmas.

He died in Nottingham on the 5th May 1964, aged 91.

Captain (in coll. with W. E. Hodgson). Big Budget Lib. Football & Sports Favourite. Champion. Modern Boy. Union Jack (2nd). Boys Herald. Boys Friend Weekly (2nd). Thriller. Football & Sports Lib. Detective Weekly. B.F.L. (1st and 2nd). S.B.L. (2nd). Scout. Thomson Papers. Boys Leader. Big Budget.

Blake, Captain Wilton (sometimes D.S.O. following) *(r.n. D. H. Parry)*
Pluck (2nd). Boys Herald. Boys Friend Weekly (2nd). Boys Journal. Cheer, Boys, Cheer. B.F.L. (2nd). Magnet.

Blakesley, Stephen *(r.n. F. Bond)*
S.B.L. (3rd).
Blayne, Roger
Modern Boy.
Blaze, Don
Thriller.
Blinders, Belinda *(r.n. Desmond Coke)*
Bloomer, Jack *(r.n. J. G. B. Lynch)*
Boys Friend Weekly (2nd).
Bloomer, Steve and Ambrose Earl *(r.n. J. G. Jones)*
Dreadnought. B.F.L. (1st).
Bloundelle-Burton, John Edward *(r.n.)*
Born 1850.
Chums. Young England.
Bluett, A. T. Q.
Comic Life.
Blyth, Harry *(r.n.)*
    Born in 1852. Now known throughout the world of juvenile
fiction as the man who first wrote about Sexton Blake. Worked
mainly as a free-lance journalist, and for some years ran his own
paper in Glasgow. This was 'Chiel' (sub-titled 'Scottish Punch')
and was originally produced in partnership with Robert Arthur
(who built the Kennington Theatre, London, S.E.) but in later
years the latter dropped out of the enterprise. It ran for almost
8 years. Blyth also had an interest in the Theatre Royal,
Glasgow, for which he wrote a very successful pantomime. He
was a busy writer, having three different serials running in
English and Scottish papers at one time. He also wrote a series
of articles for 'The Sunday People', called 'Third Class Crimes',
which was very successful. These caught the eye of Alfred
Harmsworth (later to become Lord Northcliffe and founder of
the Amalgamated Press), and he commissioned Blyth to write
a series of detective stories for his new boys' paper, 'Marvel'.
According to Blyth's son (now deceased), his father coined the
name of Sexton Blake, but this has been disputed by an old
editor of Harmsworth Ltd., who claimed that it was editorially
suggested. But whoever originated the name, Harry Blyth wrote
the first story of Sexton Blake, which appeared in No 6 of the ½d
'Marvel', December 1893. The story was entitled 'The Missing
Millionaire' and the sequel, 'A Christmas Crime', was printed

the following week. The author's name was given as 'Hal Meredith', one of Blyth's pen-names. He was living at Peckham Rye, London. He also wrote for many of the other early Harmsworth papers, including the Union Jack and Pluck. One of his favourite writing characteristics was to always begin his stories with the spoken word. For his first Sexton Blake story he received the sum of £9 9s. 0d., and this included the full copyright of the character as well.

He died of typhoid fever in February 1898, and never lived to see how famous Sexton Blake was to become in later years.

Pen-names: Hal Meredith. Policeman Paul.

Popular (1st) (anon). Union Jack (1st). Pluck (1st). Chums. Marvel (1st).

Blyth, Spencer R.
B.O.P.

Bobin, Donald E. M. *(r.n.)*

Son of the well-known Sexton Blake author John W. Bobin (Mark Osborne) and a writer himself just before the Second World War. Worked at Amalgamated Press for some years and was the last editor of Detective Weekly circa 1939. It was Donald Bobin who rewrote and brought up to date all the early Sexton Blake stories which were reprinted. Also wrote an original Blake story himself for D.W. entitled 'The Banknote Bandits' (No 344). He also worked on the girls' papers 'Girls Crystal' and 'Schoolgirls Own Library' and wrote stories under the name of 'Shirley Halliday'. He worked also for a time as secretary to another Blake writer, John G. Brandon, who used to dictate all his stories to Bobin, usually whilst lying on a bed. Now has his own large bookshops at Southend-on-Sea, Essex, and runs the Technical section.

Pen-name: Warren J. Lawson.

Detective Weekly (anon).

Bobin, John William *(r.n.)*

Wrote his first story, 'The Case of the Anonymous Letters', for the Union Jack in 1912. At this time he was a laundry-man with a horse and cart at Southend, and his tale was written on scraps of paper. But it was as 'Mark Osborne' that he was to make his biggest contribution to the Blake Saga, as he took over the popular character of George Marston Plummer from Norman Goddard (who was killed on war service in 1916), who turn had taken over from the creator, Michael Storm. Bobin did, however, create his own characters, amongst them Aubrey Dexter, who appeared, and was very popular, in the Sexton Blake stories. Apart from his detective tales he was prolific in other fields, especially in girls' fiction. Two of his pen-names were 'Adelie Ascott' and 'Gertrude Nelson'. He was also very fond of sport and wrote a number of stories featuring horse and dog-racing. Bobin died at an early age at Southend on the 9th April 1935.

Pen-names: Steve Nelson. Matthew Ironside. Jack W. Bobin. Mark Osborne. John Ascott. Victor Nelson.

Boys Journal. Pluck (2nd). B.F.W. (2nd). S.B.L. (1st and 2nd) (anon). Union Jack (2nd) (anon). Nelson Lee Lib. (old) (anon). Startler (anon).

Boff, Charles *(r.n.)*
On the staff of Amalgamated Press, and was in various editorial positions, including at one time Modern Boy.

Boque, J. Russell *(r.n.)*
Author of a Sexton Blake play called 'Sexton Blake on the East Coast' which was produced in 1916 at several London suburban and provincial theatres. Blake was played in this production by James Duncan and Tinker by Lee Gilbert. Pedro appeared as 'Himself'.

Bolee, Harold
Captain.

Bolin, Mayne
B.O.P.

Bolingbroke, William *(r.n. William Bolinbroke Home-Gall)*
Champion Annual.

Bolton, Charles
Scout.

Bolton, F. H. *(r.n.)*
Wrote three exciting and graphic science-fiction adventure serials for B.O.P. between 1908–15. 'In the Heart of the Silent Sea', 'Under the Edge of the Earth' and 'Into the Soundless Depths'. All were later reprinted in book form. Bolton also contributed stories of other kinds to B.O.P., and one school serial 'Noblesse Oblige'.
B.O.P.

Bolton, F. T. *(r.n.)*
A prominent writer down Fleet Street, and an agent, who
'ghosted' articles and stories reputed to have come from stars
in the world of sport. He was at one period Chairman of the
Press Club, and contributed boys' stories.
Pen-names: Wally Hammond. Derek Ash.
B.F.L. (2nd).

Bond, F. *(r.n.)*
Wrote three Sexton Blake stories for the S.B.L. (3rd series).
Pen-name: Stephen Blakesley.

Bond, Richard
Chums.

Bond, Stephen
Boys Realm (1st). Boys Friend Weekly (2nd).

Bonser, A. E.
B.O.P.

Booth, Christopher B.
Thriller. Detective Weekly.

Booth, D. E. (Miss) *(r.n.)*
Scout.

Booth, Ned
Scout. B.O.P.

Booth, Patrick
B.O.P.

Boothby, Guy
Lot-o'-Fun.

Borg, Jack
Western Library.

Borlase, Skip *(r.n. J. G. Bradley)*
British Boys.

Boswell, James
B.O.P.

Bott, H. L.
Was personal assistant to Harold J. Garrish, editor-in-chief of
the Comics at Amalgamated Press. Bott wrote in a book some
of his interesting experiences whilst on the staff, and especially
an authentic account of the creation of Tiger Tim.

Bouchard, William *(r.n. W. G. Wright)*
Boys Friend Weekly (2nd).

Bouchier, W. W.
All Sports.
Bounds, S. J. *(r.n.)*
Wrote Sexton Blake stories published under the editorial names
of George Sidney and Desmond Reid.
S.B.L. (3rd).
Bourne, George
Thomson's Red Lion Library.
Bourne, Lawrence *(r.n.)*
Popular boys' adventure story author of the 1920's and 1930's.
Wrote a series about a tough red-headed adventurer on the
high seas named 'Coppernob Buckland', including a special
omnibus edition containing three of his Coppernob books.
Other titles include 'The Channel Pirate', 'Treasure of the
Hebrides', 'The Adventures of John Carfax', 'The Radium
Casket', and 'Well Tackled'. He also contributed to several
magazines, including B.O.P.
B.O.P.
Bow, Ross
Racing Novels (1st).
Bowman, Alice Bertha *(r.n.)*
Born Birkenhead, educated privately. Married George Bow-
man and was the mother of Frederick Bowman. She was both
authoress and poetess. Wrote also for at least one comic paper.
Comic Cuts.
Bowman, Frederick H. U. *(r.n.)*
Born Liverpool, 1894. Educated Liverpool Inst., editor, author,
songwriter, dramatist, dramatic critic. Worked on Liverpool
Weekly Mercury, 1916. Founder of Independent Political
League, Liverpool. Editor and sole proprietor 'Trade Show
Critic' and 'Critic Annual'. First story for A.P. was 'For Life
and Law'. His work included two serials for 'Fun & Fiction',
'The Firefighters' and 'Behind the Scenes'. Mainly his work
was confined to the comic papers.
Bullseye (anon). Fun and Fiction (anon). Chips (anon).
Favourite Comic (anon).
Bowman, Gerald *(r.n.)*
Was on the staff of Amalgamated Press, and also a most prolific
writer of all kinds of stories. Some of them appeared in the
popular Bullseye. Later he wrote some detective tales of Sexton

Blake in the S.B.L. and Detective Weekly. During the Second World War he served as an officer in the RAF, rising to the rank of Group Captain. His experiences stood him in good stead, as afterwards, in 1955, he wrote a best-selling book about parachutists called 'Jump for It'. Another novel entitled 'Pattern in Poison Ivy' received excellent reviews. For a long period he was Features editor on the Evening News.

Died on the 30th Dec. 1967 at his home in Queen Annes' Grove, Turnham Green.

Pen-names: Captain Robert Hawke (used at times by Hedley O'Mant). Gerald Magnus. J. M. Bowman (probably in error). Warder Lynk.

Startler (anon). Pioneer. Sports Budget (2nd). Football & Sports Lib. S.B.L. (2nd). Boys Cinema. Boys Friend Weekly (2nd). Bullseye (anon). Ranger (2nd). Thriller Lib. Thriller. Detective Weekly.

Bownes, William E.
Chums.

Boxall, Ernest
Chatterbox.

Boyd, Don
Champion.

Boyes, Howard C.
Boys Journal.

Boyle, Frederick
B.O.P. (In collaboration with Ashmore Russan.)

Boyle, Robert
B.O.P.

Boyten, H. E.   *(r.n.)*
On the staff of Amalgamated Press for many years, mainly working on girls' papers. Did, however, write boys' yarns. Was the creator of Jill Crusoe in June and Schoolfriend. Was mainly scriptwriting for the latter in the 1950's. Now retired after more than forty years in Fleet Street.
Chums.

Brace, Dudley
Young Britain (1st).

Bradby, Godfrey Fox   *(r.n.)*
Born in 1863, the son of Dr E. H. Bradby, D.D. One-time assistant Master of Harrow and Headmaster of Haileybury.

Educated at Rugby, and then at Balliol College, Oxford, where he gained a Blue at rugger, as well as achieving scholastic distinction. Going to Rugby as a master in 1888, he became a Housemaster in 1908, a post which he held until he retired in 1920. Whilst at Rugby, Bradby wrote a novel, from the adult viewpoint, about public-school life called 'The Lanchester Tradition' (1914). It was reprinted in 1954 and has been broadcast as a radio play on more than one occasion. It is a fine story of a new Headmaster and the troubles he encounters, chiefly amongst his own staff, and is generally regarded as one of the best adult school novels ever written.

Bradford, Rev. Edwin Emmanuel *(r.n.)*
Born Torquay, 1860.
Young England. Captain. B.O.P.

Bradford, Captain L. *(r.n. Captain L. B. Carson)*
Boys Herald.

Bradish, J. S.
B.O.P.

Bradley, Albert W. *(r.n.)*
Pen-name: Charles Wentworth (in Marvel 363 only).
Diamond Lib. (1st and 2nd). Boys Own Lib. (2nd). True Blue (2nd). Marvel (1st) (anon). Vanguard (Trapps Holmes). Aldine Robin Hood (1st and 2nd). Aldine Buffalo Bill (1st and 2nd). Boys Leader.

Bradley, J. J. G. *(r.n.)*
Pen-names: Captain Leslie. Skip Borlase.
Big Budget. Boys Standard (2nd). Boys Leisure Hour.

Bradshaw, Percy V. *(r.n.)*
Illustrated many stories in B.O.P. in the 1890's and early 1900's. In 1905 decided to write as well as illustrate a serial; and the result was a humorous school story called 'The Fourth Form Ferret'. Several more serials followed, and he illustrated them all: 'The Cockler's Club', 'Pages from the Prefect's Diary', 'After School Hours', etc. Sold his first drawings to B.O.P. and Chums when a 15-year-old boy in a London advertising agency.
Later he decided to concentrate on drawing and had work accepted by most leading magazines: Windsor, Tatler, Sketch. Home Chat and Sunday Companion. He was also on the Art staff of the Daily Mail for a time. Later he founded his well-

known Press Art School through which passed many artists afterwards to find considerable fame. In 1943 he wrote an entertaining autobiography, entitled 'Drawn from Memory'.
B.O.P.

Brain, H. D.
B.O.P.

Braithwaite, Coulton   *(r.n. G. W. Brown)*
Union Jack (1st).

Brampton, Peter
Thriller.

Brand, Charles E.
Aldine Robin Hood (1st and 2nd). True Blue (2nd).

Brand, Dudley   *(r.n. H. Hild)*
Union Jack (1st and 2nd). Pluck (1st). Marvel (2nd).

Brand, Max   *(r.n. Frederick Faust)*
Thriller. Western Library.

Brandon, John Gordon   *(r.n.)*
Born in Australia in 1879 and was one of the most prolific S.B.L. authors in the 1930's. His most popular creation to the Sexton Blake saga was Ronald Sturges Vereker Purvale, better known as R.S.V.P., whom he introduced in all his Blake stories but one. His first S.B.L. appeared in 1933 and the last in 1941. Other characters of his in the S.B.L. included 'Flash' George Wibley, the reformed crook and manservant to R.S.V.P., and Big Bill Withers, the taximan. Besides being a successful writer he was a heavyweight boxer. His hobby was pigeon-keeping, and he even wrote an S.B.L. around the subject – 'The Pigeon Loft Crime'.
Many of his Blake stories, with the character changed, appeared in book form published by Wright and Brown.
The author lived for many years at Southend-on-Sea, and died at Newbury, Berks., in 1941. He was also a successful playwright.
Thriller. Detective Weekly. S.B.L. (2nd). Union Jack (2nd). Dixon Hawke Lib. Greyfriars Holiday Annual.

Brandt, Richard
Aldine Robin Hood Library.

Brash, M. M.
Chums.

Brayley, Captain Leonard
Pluck (1st).
Breakspear, Norman
Union Jack (1880).
Brearley, John   *(r.n. John Garbutt)*
B.F.L. (2nd). Modern Boy. Magnet. Nelson Lee Lib. (2nd New series). Ranger (1st and 2nd). Popular Book of Boys Stories. Greyfriars Holiday Annual.
Breck, Alan
Boys Wonder Library. Chums. British Boy.
Bredon, John   *(r.n. W. T. Taylor)*
B.F.L. (2nd). Modern Boy. Magnet.
Brent, Charlton   *(r.n. Emmett)*
Brent, Ernest   *(r.n. Emmett)*
Our Boys Paper. Boys World. Young Briton. Half-Holiday. Garfield Boys Journal. True Blue (1st). Boys Own Journal. Boys.
Brent, Francis   *(r.n. Alfred John Hunter)*
Detective Weekly.
Brereton, Lt. Col. F. S.   *(r.n.)*
Prolific best-selling boys' author of the early years of the century. His many typical titles include: 'The Great Airship', 'On the Field of Waterloo', 'With the Allies to the Rhine', 'With Allenby in Palestine', 'With Rifle and Bayonet', 'Indian and Scout', 'The Great Aeroplane' and 'Scouts of the Baghdad Patrols' – the latter being a serial in Chums in 1921.
Chums.
Breton, Guy
Union Jack (1st).
Breton, Captain Pierre
Marvel (1st).
Brett, Edwin James   *(r.n.)*
Born in Canterbury, Kent, 1828, the son of an Army officer. Little is known about his early career, but it has been established that he was a political associate of writer and editor G. W. M. Reynolds in 1848. He began his journalistic career as an artist, but the few illustrations he did for Harrison's 'The Blue Dwarf show a mediocre style. Later Brett became partner to a minor publisher, Ebeneezer Landells, until the latter's death in 1860. Then he joined forces with W. L. Emmett and

Joseph Hardiman, but Brett and Hardiman soon left Emmett, with some bad feeling on both sides.

Emmett in particular was later to become Brett's prime rival in the boys' publishing field. Brett joined the Newsagents Publishing Company, where his early efforts were penny-number reprints of the Boys Miscellany serials, 'Mazeppa' and 'Sixteen-String Jack', but he soon progressed to original works which became leaders in the field. They included such titles as 'The Boy Detective', 'The Boy Pirate', 'The Wild Boys of London', and 'The Wild Boys of Paris'. They caught on remarkably well, so much so that Brett decided to start publication of a weekly paper for boys, and the 'Boys Companion' appeared in 1865. It was short-lived and in 1865 Brett tried again with 'Boys of England'. This could truthfully be described as long-lived, as it ran right up to 1899. It was in this paper that the infamous and highly popular Jack Harkaway made his bow. Brett soon became one of the leading publishers of boys' papers in the country and issued no fewer than 21 papers during his lifetime. (The succeeding Edwin J. Brett Ltd added 6 more.) They included 'Young Men of Great Britain', 'Boys Comic Journal', 'Halfpenny Surprise' and 'Our Boys Journal'. Brett's colourful life and his accounts of rivalry would in themselves fill a book, and he died in 1895, wealthy, successful and somewhat arrogant by nature, having made publishing history.

Brett, Hawksley *(r.n. R. S. Warren Bell)*
Chips. British Boys.

Bridges, Thomas Charles *(r.n.)*
Born in France 1868, the son of a clergyman and was educated at Marlborough College. In 1886 he went to Florida to work on an orange plantation, but after much hard work and many adventures he returned to England in 1894, almost penniless, and decided to try his hand at writing. His first two articles on fishing in Florida appeared in 'The Field', then, after contributing free-lance items to many magazines, including Answers – where he joined the latter as a sub-editor – he resigned after about four years to concentrate on free-lance writing.

In 1902 he wrote his first boys' story. Gilbert Floyd, who was the editor of Boys Realm, suggested that he write a serial for the paper, and the result was 'Paddy Leary's Schooldays' – the adventures of an Australian boy at an English public school. It was so popular that he wrote two further long sequels and several short stories about the characters.

He also wrote the first story in the new series of the Union Jack, 'With Pick and Lamp'. Apart from being a prolific contributor to many boys' papers, he also wrote books for boys, mainly adventure stories.

In the early 1900's, Bridges and his wife (whom he married in 1899) went to live at Dartmoor, only two miles from the prison. This, no doubt, is why he was fond of writing tales featuring prison life. He wrote Sexton Blake stories for the Union Jack and as late as 1939 he was still contributing to B.O.P., Scout, and Children's Newspaper, where he was affectionately known as T.C.B. In 1928 he published his autobiography 'From Florida to Fleet Street'. His recreations were fishing, golf and gardening, and he was a good friend of Sidney Gowing. He died in Torquay, where he lived during his declining years, in June 1944.

Pen-names: Christopher Beck. Tom Bridges.
Champion. Modern Boy. Boys Friend Weekly (2nd). Boys Herald. Boys Realm (1st). Magnet. Thriller Lib. B.F.L. (1st and 2nd). Pluck (2nd and 3rd). Union Jack (2nd). S.B.L. (2nd). Boys Realm Football and Sports Lib. (anon). Chums. Scout. Lloyds School Yarns. Newnes Adventure Library. British Boy.

Bridges, Victor *(r.n.)*
Pen-name: Vernon James.
Boys Realm (1st).

Bright, C. A.
Hotspur Book for Boys. Skipper Book for Boys.

Bright, James *(r.n. John Gabriel Rowe)*
Marvel (1st).

Brightly, Ben
Pluck (1st) *(see Ned Neolan)*.

Brightwell, Leonard Robert *(r.n.)*
Little Folks. B.O.P. Toby. Captain.

Brindle, Ernest *(r.n.)*
Born Burton-on-the-Water, Glos. Educated at King Edward's School, Witley, Surrey. During the Boer War he was quite a

73

famous war correspondent for the Daily Mail. Later he turned to boys' writings and wrote at least one Sexton Blake story, 'The Rajah's Vow' for the Union Jack (No 427) in 1911.
Pen-name: Peter Bayne.
Sport & Adventure. Marvel (2nd). Boys Herald. Boys Realm (1st and 2nd). Union Jack (2nd) (anon).

Brisbane, Coutts   *(r.n. R. Coutts Armour)*
B.F.L. (2nd). S.B.L. (2nd). Nelson Lee Lib. (1st new series). Thriller. Detective Weekly. Ranger (1st).

Briscoe, Ernest Edward   *(r.n.)*
Born in 1882, and was really an artist, although he did write a story in 1920. Many of his drawings, which were of an exceptionally high quality, appeared in the Nelson Lee Library (old series), where he did a series on British Public Schools.
Boys Realm (2nd).

Bristowe-Noble, J. C.
Chums.

Brittany, Louis   *(r.n. George Heber Teed)*
Detective Weekly.

Britten, Frank Curzon
B.O.P.

Britton, Herbert   *(r.n. Reginald T. Eves)*
B.F.L. (1st). Boys Friend Weekly (2nd). Boys Realm (2nd).

Broadbent, Abel
Union Jack (1880)

Broadbent, David
Scout.

Brockington, Rev. Alfred Allen   *(r.n.)*
Born Birmingham, 1872. Educated at King Edward VI, Birmingham. London University and Bishop's University, Canada. Wrote several books of a religious nature.
B.O.P.

Brocklehurst, Tyrer   *(r.n.)*
Union Jack (1st).

Brood, Norman
Union Jack (1st).

Brook, Eric   *(r.n. of famous footballer)*
Wrote one single story, probably was ghosted for him. *Read F. T. Bolton.*
Football Weekly.

Brooke, Arthur   *(r.n. Arthur C. Marshall)*
Champion. Scout. Champion Annual.
Brooks, Colin
Knockout.
Brooks, Edwy Searles   *(r.n.)*
Born at Hackney, London, 11th November 1889. Was the son
of George Brooks, a Congregational minister, and well-known
political writer for 'The Times' and leading magazines. The
Rev. Brooks had three other sons and one daughter. At an early
age Edwy moved to Norfolk, and later attended Banham
Grammar School. As a boy he was tremendously interested in
The Magnet and Gem, and he wrote his first story when a
schoolboy. This was the forerunner of thousands to come from
his pen.
Easily his most famous stories were those in which he featured
the school of St Frank's in the Nelson Lee Library, and he wrote
every story except one, covering a span of over sixteen years.
In the Sexton Blake field, one of his most famous characters was
Waldo the Wonderman, and in one of the Nelson Lee Library
series he featured Waldo's son.
Because of his knowledge of Greyfriars and St Jim's, he also
wrote quite a few substitute stories for The Magnet and The
Gem. Shortly before the last war he turned to writing novels
and these were published under the pen-names of 'Berkeley
Gray' and 'Victor Gunn', the former featuring the famous
Norman Conquest stories.
Edwy died very suddenly in December 1965, and his wife
Frances in 1968. A large collection of original manuscripts,
letters, papers and other documents was left on loan to the
London Old Boys Book Club, and in the custody of Robert
Blyth, the Nelson Lee Librarian. They can be seen, provided
an appointment is made beforehand with Mr Blyth.
Pen-names: Norman Greaves. C. Heddingham Gosfield.
E. Sinclair Halstead. Berkeley Gray. Victor Gunn. Robert W.
Comrade. S. B. Halstead. Martin Clifford (in Gem). Frank
Richards (in Magnet and Popular). Reginald Browne. Edward
Thornton.
Monster Lib. Detective Lib. Detective Weekly. B.F.L. (1st and
2nd). Boys Friend Weekly (2nd). Boys Realm of Sport and
Adventure. Sports Budget (2nd). Boys Realm (1st and 2nd).

Nelson Lee Library (all series). Thriller. Schoolboys Own Library. Popular (2nd) (anon). Nugget Library. S.B.L. (1st) (anon) (2nd and 3rd). Gem (2nd). Nugget Weekly. Union Jack (2nd). Holiday Annual. Dixon Hawke Lib. (anon). Pilot (anon). Modern Boy. Boys Magazine, and Thomson boys papers. Pluck (2nd) (anon). Pluck (3rd). Ranger (anon).

Brooks, Leonard Harold *(r.n.)*

Brother of Edwy Searles Brooks, and a very minor author. It was suspected by many editors, and confirmed later by Mrs Frances Brooks, that many of his stories were written almost entirely by Edwy. Leonard died in tragic circumstances, being found dead by gas-poisoning at Blackburn, Lancs, in 1950.

Pen-name: Howard Steele (in Champion).

S.B.L. (1st and 2nd) (anon). Union Jack (2nd) (anon).

Broome, Lady Mary Ann *(r.n.)*

Died 6th March 1911.

B.O.P.

Broughton, A. J.

Chums.

Brown, Campbell *(r.n. G. W. Brown)*

Union Jack (1st).

Brown, Charles Perry *(r.n.)*

Founder of the famous Aldine Publishing Company in the late 1880's and continued for a period of some forty years to publish a fair number of boys' publications. Also some of a more adult nature, but still widely read by boys.

Brown, Duncan *(r.n. T. Nelson)*

Ranger (2nd) Pioneer.

Brown, Captain Eric

Union Jack (1st).

Brown, G. W.

Believed to have been a doctor, as articles from a Dr G. W. Brown appeared in Harmsworth early publications.

Pen-names: Alexis Graham. Campbell Brown. G. W. Campbell. Coulton Braithwaite.

Union Jack (1st) (anon). Popular (1st) (anon). Pluck (1st) (anon).

Brown, Howard

Boys Torch Adventure Lib.

Browne, Leslie
Boys Realm (1st).
Browne, Noel *(r.n.)*
One of the writers of Sexton Blake under the 'Desmond Reid' pen-name.
S.B.L. (3rd).
Browne, Reginald *(r.n. E. S. Brooks)*
Schoolboys Pocket Library (G. Swan Ltd).
Browne, William
B.O.P.
Bruce, David
Scout.
Bruce, W. A.
Scout.
Bryant, Bruce *(r.n. W. G. Wright)*
Pluck (3rd). Boys Realm (2nd).
Bryce, William Alexander *(r.n.)*
Born Glasgow, 1886. Educated at Mason's College and Birmingham University. Physician and surgeon, and chief recreation is the study of pirate literature.
B.O.P. (in collaboration with H. de Vere Stacpoole).
Buchan, Charles *(r.n. of famous footballer)*
Probable ghosted story. *See F. T. Bolton.*
Chums.
Buchan, John *(r.n.)*
Born Perth, 1875, and later became Lord Tweedsmuir. Educated at Glasgow University and Oxford and won high academic distinctions. He practised as a lawyer, went to South Africa as assistant secretary to Lord Milner, the High Commissioner, returned to his law practice, then in 1906 entered publishing as a partner in the firm of his friend, Thomas Nelson. He was elected to Parliament in 1911, served in World War I, and returned to the House of Commons in 1927, as M.P. for the Scottish Universities. In 1935 he became Lord Tweedsmuir and Governor-General of Canada. In 1937 he became Chancellor of Edinburgh University. He actually started writing stories of adventure in 1914, featuring Richard Hannay, when he was confined to bed after an accident. His creation, Hannay, figured in such best sellers as 'The 39 Steps', 'Green Mantle', 'The Three Hostages' and 'Mr Standfast'. His one serial in

77

Captain was 'The Black General' in 1910, which was later published in book form as the now famous 'Prester John'. Lord Tweedsmuir died in 1940.
Captain.

Buchanan, Carl
Thriller.

Buck, Frank
Modern Boy.

Buckley, F.
Captain.

Buckley, Richard
Jester and Wonder.

Buffalo Bill
This name was used as the 'author' in several magazines, including Chums and the Aldine Buffalo Bill Libraries (all series). It is obvious that several writers hid behind this name, all now unfortunately lost in the mists of time.

Buley, Bernard *(r.n.)*
Editor of Boys Magazine (Hulton).
Pen-names: Bat Masters. Roy McRae.
Champion Lib. B.F.L. (2nd). Boys Realm (2nd). Chums. Champion.

Buley, E. C. *(r.n.)*
Born Ballarat, Australia, July 1869. Educated at Granville College, Ballarat and Melbourne University. Chief sub-editor of 'Reynolds'. (See 'He Laughed in Fleet Street' by Bernard Falk.) This writer is probably of some close relationship with Bernard Buley, as both wrote racing stories of a similar nature. Racing Novels (1st). Football Novels.

Bull, Albert E. *(r.n.)*
Educated privately and at Mannamead School (now Plymouth College). Editor on the staff of Pearson's, Amalgamated Press, Hutchinson and Hendersons. Author of the famous 'Mabel' in Young Folks Tales.
Pen-name: Victor Cromwell.
Young Folks Tales (anon).

Bullen, Ravenor *(r.n.)*
Educated at University College School, London, and lived for many years at Bampton, Oxfordshire. Wrote several mystery and adventure serials for B.O.P., the first in 1910, called 'The

Mystery of Cabin No 7'. Had several novels published. Later he went to Canada to look after mining interests and subsequently became associated with the production of crude petroleum in the oil fields of Ontario.
B.O.P.

Bullivant, Cecil Henry *(r.n.)*
Born 1882. Author, editor, traveller and lecturer. On the staff of 'Men and Women' (Cassell) 1903. Joined Harmsworth 1904, editor of Boys Herald, 1904–7. On staff of Answers, 1908. Editor of Ladies Home Paper 1909–10. Founder and editor of Tit-Bit Novels, managing editor of Captain, 1911–12. Expert on English language and literature. Editor of 'Boys Best Story Paper' and 'Scholars Own'.
Pen-names: Henry Turville. Maurice Everard. Carlton Grey. Colonel North.
Pluck (2nd).

Bulman, B. H. *(r.n.)*
One of the authors of the famous Red Circle school stories in The Hotspur, but obviously wrote a large number of other stories as well. Now known to be deceased.

Bungay, E. Newton *(r.n.)*
Prolific writer of stories and serials for many papers, especially for the comic papers. He wrote the long-running school serial 'Tom Topping', which began in the first issue of 'Young 'Britain'.
Pen-names: John Lance. H. B. Richmond.
Wonder Lib. Dreadnought (anon). Young Britain (1st). Fun & Fiction (anon). Chums. Butterfly (anon). Favourite Comic (anon). Merry & Bright (anon).

Buntline, Ned *(r.n. E. Z. C. Judson)*
Wild West Library (anon).

Burke, Jack
Golden Penny Comic.

Burke, Jonathan *(r.n.)*
Made his début in the Sexton Blake field in 1957. Also is a very well-known writer in the realms of science-fiction and has had several novels published. Was also one of the 'Desmond Reid' writers.
S.B.L. (3rd).

Burke, Thomas *(r.n.)*
Born 1867, and after working in Fleet Street on the Tribune, and contributing articles and short stories to many papers and magazines, found fame as a depictor of London life and locales with his book of stories set in London's Chinatown called 'Limehouse Nights'. Later he wrote more books about the city, including 'City of Encounters', also a very popular novel entitled 'Twinkletoes'. Was editor of Boys Realm for a very short time in 1920.
Pen-name: Oakmead Rhodes.

Burns, Jock
Chums. Chums Annual.

Burrage, Alfred McLelland *(r.n.)*
Born Hillingdon, Middlesex, 1st July 1889, and was the son of A. S. Burrage. He began to write and sell stories whilst still at school and at 17 was a busy professional writer contributing stories, articles and poems to nearly 150 publications, including Strand, Pearsons and Tatler. Probably his most famous story was about a schoolboy who masqueraded as a schoolgirl in a girls' public school. This was entitled 'Poor Dear Esme' and ran as a serial in the Modern Boy (Nos 102–15) in 1930, having been previously published in book form by George Newnes around 1925. Prior to this it had first appeared in a Newnes popular magazine.
Under the pen-name of 'Frank Lelland' he wrote his first Sexton Blake story for the Detective Weekly in 1933, 'The Singing Clue', and followed it a little later with another, 'Murder at Full Moon'. In 1908 he wrote several stories about a character called 'Tufty' in Henderson's short-lived Triumph Library. They proved so popular that they were reprinted a few years later. He was the nephew of E. Harcourt Burrage, and died around 1956/7.
Pen-names: Stewart Young. Frank Lelland. Jack Lancaster. Cooee.
Diamond Lib. (1st). Comic Life. Triumph Lib. Modern Boy. Marvel (2nd). Gem (2nd) (anon). Boys Friend Weekly (2nd). Vanguard (Trapps Holmes).

Burrage, Alfred Sherrington *(r.n.)*
One-time editor of Emmet's 'Young Englishman' in the 1870's, and also wrote stories for several other papers. Author

of several Robin Hood Libraries, including the first number. It is said that he started writing professionally when he was only 15. (His son, A. M. Burrage, followed in his father's footsteps, for he also began at a very early age.) Was the brother of Edwin Harcourt Burrage.

Pen-names: Alf Sherrington. Cyril Hathway. Philander Jackson. Aldine Robin Hood (1st, 2nd and 3rd). True Blue (2nd).

Burrage, Athol Harcourt *(r.n.)*

Born Earlswood, 1899. Educated at Reigate Grammar School. Nephew of A. S. Burrage and son of E. H. Burrage.

Chums. Scout.

Burrage, Edwin Harcourt *(r.n.)*

Born in 1839, in Norfolk, and became one of the greatest and most prolific of the Victorian boys' writers. Originally came to London with artistic rather than literary ambitions, but found little scope and less money. Discouraged and almost destitute, he was on the point of returning home when he met Charles Stevens, one of the Emmett publishing brothers' leading authors, who urged him to try his hand at writing. Burrage doubtfully did so – and had his first effort accepted. From that moment he never looked back.

His long career started with a poem entitled 'John Brown, Ye Modern Knight' in Emmett's 'Young Gentlemen of Britain' in 1869. His first serial was 'Harry Power the Wanderer' in the same paper that year, and thereafter many serials flowed from his pen. In time the Emmett's made him editor of 'Young Gentlemen of Britain' but after being away ill for a long time he found on his return that he had been replaced.

He parted from Emmett's and joined Henry Fox, who had just started the 'Boys Standard'. It was appropriate that Burrage should begin this association with his most famous story, 'Handsome Harry of the Fighting Belvedere', which introduced to the rapt readers of that generation the immortal 'Ching Ching'. Later this character had his own paper called 'Ching Ching's Own', and written of course from cover to cover by Burrage. Some of his other well-known serials were 'Broad Arrow Jack', 'Jack the Rover', 'Dick Strongbow' and 'Tom Tarter at School' (serialised in the Nelson Lee Library, old series); also the famous 'Island School' and 'Lambs of Littlecote' for Aldine around 1895. Burrage finished his writing career in control of the competition section at Amalgamated Press, and was also a highly-respected councillor at Redhill, Surrey. He died on the 6th March 1916. He was the uncle of A. M. Burrage, ʟather of A. H. Burrage, and brother of A. S. Burrage. **Pen-names:** Walter Darrell. A. Elton Barron. Bart Morland. Boys Realm (1st). Popular (1st) (anon). Boys Herald. Nelson Lee Lib. (old). Union Jack (1st and 2nd). B.F.L. (1st). Pluck (1st). Marvel (1st). Boys Friend Weekly (2nd). B.O.P. Life & Adventure Lib. First Rate Lib. Bullseye (Aldine). Diamond Lib. (1st). Boys Own Lib. (1st). Cheerful (1st). True Blue (2nd). Boys Standard. Young Briton.

Burroughs, Edgar Rice *(r.n.)*

Born in Chicago, U.S.A. 1st September 1875, and educated at Harvard School, Chicago, Phillips Academy, Andover, Mass., and Michigan Military Academy. Enlisted in the U.S. 7th Cavalry at 16 and saw service in the West against the Apache Indians, including Chief Geronimo. He was discharged from the Army when it was discovered that he was under age. In the next 15 years he was successively cattle drover, gold dredger, storekeeper and railway detective. At the age of 35, Burroughs looked upon himself as a failure in life, but when reading through some magazine adventure yarns, he decided that he could do better than many of the writers in question.

His first book 'Tarzan of the Apes' appeared in the U.S.A. in 1912 and was the first of some 20 Tarzan novels. Burroughs had never visited Africa, but the books were so popular that they sold over 25,000,000 copies throughout the world. More than 20 films were made about Tarzan and his adventures still sell today in paperback form.

Apart from his Tarzan books, Burroughs wrote many Martian novels and numerous Western, detective, historical, adventure and science-fiction books. In his first ten years as an author he had become a millionaire and built his own ranch called Tarzana in California. He was capable of writing a full-length novel in a weekend, and did so once for a bet. During the Second World War he was a special correspondent in the Pacific campaigns. His recreations were flying, motoring and riding. He died a very wealthy man, in 1950.

Pluck (3rd). Boys Cinema.

Burrows, Harold
Captain.
Burton, Alan
Chums.
Burton, Edmund *(r.n. Edmund Burton Childs)*
Popular (2nd). Champion. Boys Friend Weekly (2nd). Gem
(2nd). Magnet. Sport & Adventure. Chums. Young Britain
(1st and 2nd). B.F.L. (1st). Boys Realm (1st and 2nd). Grey-
friars Holiday Annual. British Boy. Scorcher Novels.
Butler, Professor
Marvel (1st) in coll. with Franklyn Wright.
Buzzacroft, John
B.O.P.
Byrd, Franklyn
Boys Favourite.
Cahill *(r.n.)*
One of the writers of Sexton Blake stories under the Desmond
Reid pen-name.
S.B.L. (3rd).
Calkins, Franklin Wells
Captain.
Callam, Tex
Ranger (2nd).
Calvert, William Robinson *(r.n.)*
Born St Bees, 1882. Wrote for many adult papers. Editor of
Newnes Publications 1911. News editor Sunday Times 1915.
Daily Telegraph 1920.
Pen-names: Roy Croft. Austin Dale.
Chums (anon).
Camden, Richard *(r.n. L. J. Beeston)*
Chums.
Cameron, Brian
B.F.L. (2nd).
Cameron, Captain
Marvel (1st).
Cameron, Clifford *(r.n. John L. Garbutt)*
Modern Boys Annual. Popular Book of Boys Stories. B.F.L.
(2nd). Modern Boy. Greyfriars Holiday Annual.
Cameron, V. Lovett (Commander)
B.O.P.

Campbell, Big Bill *(r.n. of famous radio star)*
Probable 'ghosted' stories.
Wild West Weekly. Radio Fun.

Campbell, Donald
Gramol Thrillers.

Campbell, Sir Gilbert
B.O.P.

Campbell, G. Wells *(r.n. G. W. Brown)*
Union Jack (1st). Pluck (1st). Marvel (1st).

Campbell, Harry *(r.n. Bernard Smith)*
Triumph. Champion.

Campbell, Kenneth
Diamond Library (1st).

Campbell, Sir Malcolm *(r.n. of famous racing driver)*
Probable 'ghosted' story.
Modern Boy.

Campbell, Sydney G. *(r.n.)*
Pen-name: Chester Lawrence.
Chums.

Campling, F. Knowles *(r.n.)*
Editor of Chums, 1915–18. Editor of Little Folks and Little Folks Annual. Worked on several more of Cassells publications until the early 20's, when he left to do free-lance writing. Was also editor of 'Toby' until succeeded by Gwyn Evans. One of his favourite themes in writing articles was how to avoid accidents, and several of these appeared in boys' papers; ironically, he was killed at Lancing, Sussex, in 1940, when he stepped in front of a bus.
Pen-name: Eric Wood.
Chums.

Campson, Kaye
Modern Boys Annual. B.F.L. (2nd). Modern Boy. Greyfriars Holiday Annual.

Canning, V. *(r.n.)*
Startler (anon).

Cannon, J. R. *(r.n. Norman Goddard)*
Empire Lib. (1st). B.F.L. (1st). Pluck (2nd).

Cansford, John
Boys Life.

Cantle, G. H. *(r.n.)*

Editor of many famous comics in the 1904 period. These include Chips, Comic Cuts and Puck.

Capper, Cecil

Boys Leader.

'Captain, The'

Nelson Lee Library (3rd New Series).

Cardinal, John C.

Captain.

Cardon, Guy

Champion Annual.

Carew, Burleigh *(r.n. Fred Gordon Cook)*

Chums. Chums Annual. Schoolboys Pocket Lib. (Swan).

Carew, Conway

Boys Life.

Carew, Jack

Boxing Novels (1st).

Carew, Sidney

Boys Herald.

Carew, Singleton

Scout. New Adventure Lib. Boys World (Cassells). Boys Leader.

Carins, Dixon

Boys World (Storey).

Carlton, Lewis *(r.n. G. E. L. Carlton)*

Born in Devon around 1886. Son of a local Insurance manager. Joined the staff of Amalgamated Press around 1910 and held several editorial posts, including that of editor of Union Jack for a time, also last editor of Boys Journal. Wrote several stories of Sexton Blake. Left Fleetway House to go on the stage, where it was said that because of his youthful looks he actually played the part of Tinker. Resumed writing as a free-lance in the 20's and 30's, including more Blake tales and girls' fiction.

Lewis Carlton was last heard of in Fleet Street around 1950, since which date he has completely disappeared. Despite exhaustive research, including newspaper publicity in the Romford Times, no trace of him has come to light, nor is there any record of his death. During the 30's he formed a syndicate writing pool, which consisted of himself, John G. Brandon, J. W. Bobin and Donald Bobin.

He was married, with two sons and a daughter, and his total and inexplicable disappearance is a mystery that even the great Sexton Blake himself would find difficult to solve.

Pen-names: Martin Clifford (Gem). Reginald Atkinson. S.B.L. (2nd). Union Jack (2nd). Boys Realm (1st). Boys Journal. B.F.L. (1st). Pluck (2nd). Dreadnought.

Carmichael, Roy
B.O.P.

Carpenter, R. A. *(r.n.)*
One of the syndicate of writers who penned the famous Red Circle School stories in The Hotspur. He wrote, in particular, a large number of the later ones.
Hotspur (anon).

Carpentier, Georges *(r.n. world-famous French boxer)*
Stories probably 'ghosted'.
Chums. All Sports.

Carr, Adams *(r.n. Douglas Walshe)*
Boys Friend Weekly (2nd).

Carr, Andrew
B.O.P.

Carr, Frank
Boxing Novels (1st).

Carr, George
Boys Herald.

Carr, Gordon *(r.n.)*
Reported to have been on the Amalgamated Press staff in the 1900–10 period. The name was used also by W. J. Bayfield (Boys Realm (1st) No 510).
Pen-names: Edgar West. Charles Westcombe.
Boys Herald. Boys Realm (1st). Boys Friend Weekly (2nd). Union Jack (2nd) (anon). Popular (1st) (anon). B.F.L. (1st).

Carr, Captain Howard
Diamond Lib. (1st and 2nd).

Carr, Kent *(r.n. Gertrude Kent Oliver)*
A woman school-story writer, and considered by many of the 'classic' experts to be the best of that period.
B.O.P. Boys of our Empire.

Carr, Melton
Marvel (1st and 2nd). Worlds Comic.

Carr, Wallace *(r.n.)*
Born Paddington, 1890. Educated at Westbourne School, Paddington.
B.O.P.

Carr-Clements, J.
Chums.

Carrington, Hepworth
Coloured Comic.

Carrington, J. K.
Chums.

Carruthers, Captain Pat
Boys Friend Weekly (2nd).

Carson, Kit (Jnr.)
Boys Friend Weekly (1st and 2nd).

Carson, Captain L. B. *(r.n.)*
Pen-name: Captain L. Bradford.
Chums.

Carson, Matt
Red Lion Library.

Carstairs, Rod *(r.n. G. L. Dalton)*
Ranger (2nd). B.F.L. (2nd).

Carter, Alec
Modern Boy.

Carter, A. B. *(r.n.)*
Writer who was probably on the Amalgamated Press staff. Wrote some of the famous 'House of Thrills' stories in Bullseye.
Bullseye (anon).

Carter, Herbert S.
Scout.

Carter, Val
Rocket.

Cartwright, A. *(r.n. Harold W. Twyman)*
B.F.L. (2nd).

Carvalho, Clare N. *(r.n.)*
Wrote several novels.
Chums. B.O.P.

Cassidy, Martin
Pluck (3rd).

Cassilis, Ina Leon
Aldine Mystery Novels.

Casson, R. T.
Comic Cuts. Worlds Comic.
Castleton, A. G.
Boys Torch Adventure Lib.
Catchpole, William Leslie *(r.n.)*
Born Northampton, around 1900. As a boy was an avid reader
of The Magnet and Gem. In 1915 he entered the Greyfriars
Story Competition and won a prize. (This was a copy of Longfellow's poems.) His original entry was never published,
although a later story was, entitled 'Linley's Legacy', No 596.
Disappointed at the rejection of his stories he switched to film
story writing and did this for about 8 years. A chance meeting
with C. M. Down, The Magnet and Gem editor, brought him
back to the fold, and with G. R. Samways giving up writing
the Greyfriars Herald supplement and St Sam's Pieces, he took
his place. He probably wrote all the small contributions from
1926 until the end in 1940.
Apart from his school paper contributions, he also wrote for
Ranger, and some Sexton Blake tales. Always interested in
insurance, he later took this up full-time and became a prominent administrator in one of England's leading Insurance
Companies. Since then he has written articles dealing with
insurance and finance, and he retired a few years ago. He still
retains many of his old papers containing his own contributions,
including many of the famous Holiday Annuals.
Pen-names: Martin Clifford (Gem). Owen Conquest (Gem).
Frank Richards (Magnet). Roland Howard. Rowland Hunter.
John Hawkins.
Catcombe, George *(r.n.)*
Better known as an artist of many Amalgamated Press Papers.
Only one contribution as a writer found.
Union Jack (1st).
Cathel, E. E.
B.O.P.
Catherall, Arthur *(r.n.)*
In 30 years as a writer had about 1,000 short stories and about
50 books published. Contributed also to Scouting papers and
D. C. Thomson's. His own estimate of his work is as follows:
  3,000,000 words in book form
  5,000,000 words in short stories

1,000,000 words in serials
250,000 words in articles for boys on Scouting.
He also wrote a book in Braille, and a play in collaboration with David Read, which went the rounds of the Rep. Companies.

Pen-name: Peter Hallard.

Sports Budget (2nd). Comet. Chums Annual. Scout. Startler (anon). Pioneer. Boys Favourite. Football Weekly. Adventure (anon). Rover (anon).

Catling, G.
Chums.

Catling, Thomas G. *(r.n.)*
Chums.

Cauldwell, H. T. (Jimmy) *(r.n.)*
Was the very last editor of the Nelson Lee Library. Left Amalgamated Press to go on Mickey Mouse Weekly and later with his own original idea started Odhams Modern Wonder in 1937. Also an illustrator and a man with an inventive mind. In post-war years he started up a boys' paper entitled 'Boys Venture', price 2s. monthly, but this only ran for two issues.

Cavin, Wilfred
Chums.

Chaffee, Allen (Miss) *(r.n.)*
Has written several novels.
Scout.

Chalfont, Peter
Chums.

Chambers, Derek *(r.n. Derek Hyde Chambers)*
Very closely connected with current Editor of TV's 'William Tell' series.

Pen-name: D. Herbert Hyde.

Chambers, Philip *(r.n.)*
Born 1936 and educated at Stonyhurst College. Later trained at the School of Military Intelligence. Engaged on official Security work for a time, which earned him three citations. Has also written several TV and film scripts, as well as many short stories. Made his début in the S.B.L. in 1960, writing several Blake novels. One of the writers who revised stories for the Richard Williams pen-name.
S.B.L. (3rd).

Chambers, Rex
Scout.
Chambers, Sydney
Marvel (1st).
Champ, Tom
Racing Novels (1st).
Chance, John Newton *(r.n.)*
Born at Streatham Hill, London, in 1911 and educated at Streatham Hill College and privately. Writing was in the family as his grandfather was the famous theatre critic 'Referee', whilst his father controlled those world-renowned comics, Comic Cuts, Chips, etc. He wrote for his father the Dane Detective stories in the latter, and also Sexton Blake stories – which are regarded by many as the best of the period. His first was No 71, 'The Essex Road Crime' (S.B.L. 3rd series) under the nom-de-plume of John Drummond.

Has also published numerous books under his own name for Gollanz, Cassell, MacDonald and Hale. Several books also for Oxford University Press under the name of 'David C. Newton'. During the last war he served in the RAF and was eventually invalided out in 1944. Since then has poured out hundreds of stories for newspapers, especially The Evening News (London). He had one book made into a film, which did the children's Saturday rounds for a long time, whilst another well-written Science Fiction book 'The Night of the Big Heat' was made into a film. Has written under many other pen-names in the Science Fiction field. Lived for a time in the Isle of Wight, but now lives in Sussex.

Pen-name: John Drummond. Also one of the 'Desmond Reid' writers in the S.B.L. (3rd).
Chips (anon).

Chance, Richard Newton *(r.n.)*
Father of John Newton Chance and the son of the famous theatre critic. For many years he was the controlling editor of Chips, Comic Cuts, Joker, Puck, Golden Comic and many others. Retired from the Amalgamated Press about the early 1950's and died in 1957.
Firefly (anon).

Chancellor, John
Football and Sports Lib. B.F.L. (2nd). Boys Magazine.

Chandos, Herbert *(r.n. T. G. Dowling Maitland)*
At times the name was printed incorrectly as 'Chandros'.
Marvel (2nd). Union Jack (2nd). Pluck (2nd).
Channel, A. R.
Scout.
Chapman, Arthur Edward
Chums. Scout. Young Britain (1st). British Boy.
Chapman, G. H. Murray *(r.n.) (Flight-Lieut.)*
Chatterbox.
'Charlie'
Young Britain (2nd).
Charlton *(r.n. H. Charlton Emmett)*
Boys Standard. Champion Journal. New Boys Paper. Boys
Own Journal.
Charteris, F. C.
Scout.
Charteris, Leslie *(r.n.)*
Born 12th May 1907 in Singapore, the son of a leading surgeon.
Was christened Leslie Charles Bowyer Yin, but changed this
name legally by deed-poll in 1926 to Leslie Charteris.
Came to England and was educated at Rossall and Cambridge
Universities. After leaving Cambridge, he had a great variety
of jobs, including one of blowing up balloons in a fairground.
His first story, however, was published when he was only 16;
a story set in the Pacific, concerning a pearl.
In 1927 he wrote his first novel entitled 'X, Esquire', followed
by 'The White Rider'. His third book, which appeared in
September 1928, introduced The Saint in 'Meet the Tiger'.
When The Thriller started in 1929 the adventures of The Saint
were to be found quite often in its pages. They soon caught the
imagination of the general public in the years that followed, and
in the bound books later published.
Going to Hollywood, he wrote screen plays, and the first Saint
film was made in 1938, with Louis Hayward in the leading role.
Radio plays featuring The Saint followed, and soon his books
were being sold by the million in countries throughout the
world. The Saint on TV, with Roger Moore in the leading
role, has proved to be one of the most successful series ever
produced in this medium, and in markets abroad it is one of
Britain's best exports in this field.

Lofts wrote the whole history of The Saint some years ago, published for Fleetway Publications, and later reprinted in The Saint Mystery Magazine, and has also undertaken many commissions of research for Leslie Charteris throughout the years. Leslie Charteris now shares his time between England and France.
Thriller. Detective Weekly. B.F.L. (2nd) (anon).

Charteris, Leslie K. (L.L.B.)
This writer is no relation to the famous Leslie Charteris, creator of The Saint. In fact, Mr Charteris was so amused by finding another writer with the same name in his boyhood favourite paper, that he made a reproduction of part of the story in The Saint Mystery Magazine.
Chums.

Chase, Powell
B.O.P. (also did illustrations).

Chasefield, H. Carlton
Young Britain (1st).

Chaseton   *(r.n. H. Charlton Emmett)*

Chatham, Frank   *(r.n. George E. Rochester)*
Boys Wonder Lib. Chums. Chums Annual.

Chaverton, Bruce   *(r.n. Fred Gordon Cook)*
Detective Weekly.

Chaytor, Rev. Henry John   *(r.n.)*
Born Worcester 1871. Wrote several books.
B.O.P.

Cheetham, Tom   *(r.n. of Q.P.R. centre-forward)*
Probable 'ghosted' story.
Football Weekly.

Cheshire, Clive
Rocket.

Cherub, The   *(r.n. John Gerard)*
Modern Boy.

Chester, Captain George
Marvel (1st).

Chester, Gilbert   *(r.n. H. H. Clifford Gibbons)*
Pluck (3rd). Ranger (2nd). Sport & Adventure. Young Britain (1st). Union Jack (2nd). Boys Realm (2nd). Gem (2nd). Thriller. Rocket. Detective Weekly. B.F.L. (1st and 2nd).

Hotspur Book for Boys. Skipper Book for Boys. S.B.L. (2nd and 3rd). Modern Boy. Greyfriars Holiday Annual.

Chesterton, Rupert *(r.n.)*
This writer was discovered when quite young by Arthur C. Marshall, editor of Boys Leader. Chesterton wrote many serials for this paper, mainly in the early 1900's, including 'The Chronicles of Crosfield College'.
Scout. Boys Leader. Big Budget. Newnes Adventure Lib.

Cheyney, Peter *(r.n. Reginald Southouse Cheyney)*
Thriller. Detective Weekly.

Cheyney, Reginald Southouse *(r.n.)*
Born in London of Irish descent, his first story was published when he was only 14. He was once news editor of The Sunday Graphic, and in sport a crack pistol shot, and holder of an International Fencing licence. He was the originator of Tinker's Notebook in the Union Jack and contributed to this for about 18 months. Is also reputed to have once written a Sexton Blake story for the same paper and had it rejected by the editor, H. W. Twyman – who, in recent years, has denied ever seeing one from his pen! In his early years, Cheyney adopted a stage career, acting in many plays up and down the country, also appearing in several silent films. In the 1914 war he joined the Royal Warwickshire Regiment and was severely wounded in the second Battle of the Somme. Later he became crime reporter and special investigator to a London Magazine Group. Also a keen student of Criminology he wrote several non-fiction books. Later when he became famous, radio plays also issued from his pen. Subsequently he wrote over 30 novels featuring such well-known characters as Lemmy Caution and Slim Callaghan. He died in 1951 at St John's Wood, London.
Pen-name: Peter Cheyney.
Union Jack (2nd) (anon).

Child, R. W.
Captain.

Childs, Edmund Burton *(r.n.)*
Born at Drumcondra, Dublin, in 1887. Went to Merchant Taylor School, Dublin, and afterwards was employed in the insurance business for 9 or 10 years. His first story was published in Boys Friend Weekly in 1912, but later he became a professional competition man. In some stories he collaborated with

his friend, Captain Reginald Glossop. Still writes juvenile fiction, and is a familiar figure in Fleet Street.

Pen-names: Cecil Aynsworth. Edmund Burton. Royston Blake.

Christie, Agatha Clarissa *(r.n.)*

Born at Torquay. Educated privately. She wrote her first story during the 1914–18 war – 'The Mysterious Affair at Styles' – which was published after the Armistice. She created the famous Belgian detective, Hercule Poirot, and many other characters, and all her books are best-sellers. Many of her novels have been filmed and one of her plays – 'The Mousetrap' – is in its 17th year (a world-beating run) in the West End. She has travelled widely and is called, with justification, 'The Queen of Thriller Writers'.

Thriller. Detective Weekly.

Christie, Stephen *(r.n. D. S. C. Kuruppu)*

S.B.L. (5th).

Chute, B. J.

B.O.P.

Cinnamond, Lieut. H. P.

Chums.

Clare, Ronald

Triumph.

Clare, Vincent (Captain)

Union Jack (1st).

Clark, Alfred *(r.n.)*

Captain.

Clark, Geoffrey H.

Thriller.

Clark, H. R. D.

Chums.

Clark, Mrs Henry

Young England.

Clark, W. Fordyce *(r.n.)*

Born 1865, he also wrote for many adult magazines. A Scotsman, who lived in Edinburgh.

B.O.P. Young England.

Clarke, C. E.

Scout.

Clarke, E. Lidner
Chums. Scout.
Clarke, G. R. Lidner
Chums.
Clarke, Captain Maurice   *(r.n. S. Clarke Hook)*
Pluck (1st).
Clarke, Percy A. *(r.n.)*
On the staff of Amalgamated Press for many years until he
retired a few years ago, as well as being a prolific writer. Held
an editorial post on The Boys Friend Library when, apart from
writing a number of stories (including two about Ferrers Locke
and another about Nelson Lee), he worked on the revision of
the original stories, cutting down to Library size.
Was well-known in the Sexton Blake field as 'Martin Frazer'
and also had a long-running series in Knockout for over 5 years,
entitled 'The Boys of St Clements'. Also had several thrillers
published under this name by Wright & Brown, as well as many
Westerns under the name of 'Dane Lander'. He also wrote
romantic novels under the nom-de-plume of 'Jane Lytton'.
Was for a time editor of Jack & Jill and Knockout. Probably
older readers may recall the Jim, Buck and Rastus stories in The
Ranger in the 1930's, which were his work, being actually re-
writes of original Jack, Sam and Pete stories.
Pen-names: St John Watson. Steve Rogers. Vernon Neilson.
Martin Frazer. Charles Wentworth.
Football & Sports Lib. Detective Weekly. B.F.L. (2nd).
Modern Boy. Boys Realm (2nd). Boys Favourite. Boys Realm
of Sport & Adventure. Sports Budget (2nd). Nelson Lee
Library (1st and 2nd New Series). Ranger (1st). Football &
Sports Favourite. Gem (2nd). Startler (anon). Knockout
(anon). Greyfriars Holiday Annual.
Clarke, S. Dacre *(r.n.)*
Publisher of several, often unsuccessful, boys' papers in the 1880's
and 1890's. These include probably the rarest boys' papers of
all: Bad Boy's Paper, Bonnie Boys of Britain, Boys Champion
Paper and Boys Graphic. In another, 'Young Briton's Journal',
Clarke wrote a serial called 'Guy Rayner's Schooldays' and
followed it with other serials about the same character. In time
Clarke himself became widely known as 'Guy Rayner'. He
tried to compete with such formidable rivals in the boys' pub-

lishing world as Emmett, Brett, and Fox, but without any marked success.

Pen-name: Guy Rayner.

Clarke, Silvey *(r.n.)*

An editress who was in charge of some coloured comics at Amalgamated Press, including 'My Favourite'. Later she joined Odhams and became the first editor of the Mickey Mouse Weekly in 1936.

Clarke, Vincent

Golden Penny Comic.

Cleaver, Hylton Reginald *(r.n.)*

Born London, 1891, and educated at St Paul's School. It was during his war service in 1914 that he first started writing seriously, mainly to take his mind off things. As a boy his favourite paper was the Captain, and it was here that his first story was accepted when he was 22. This tale was entitled 'The Red Rag'. He rapidly became one of the leading school-story writers in the country. Most of his tales were about Harley or Greyminster, and some were based loosely on his own schooldays. He took a keen interest in sport, especially boxing, boating and riding, and in later years became a sports writer on these subjects for the London Evening Standard, a position he was to hold for over 20 years.

His first novel was 'Roscoe Makes Good' (1921) which originally appeared in the Captain as 'Who Cares?'. He published many other books, mostly school stories, and also several adult novels. He wrote several plays, and also an Autobiography in the 1950's called 'Sporting Rhapsody'.

He died at St John's Hospital, Battersea, London, on 9th September, 1961, aged 70.

Pen-name: Reginald Crunden.

Captain. B.O.P. Modern Boy. Chums. Chums Annual. Film Fun (reprints).

Cleghorn, Lieutenant C. A.

Boys Life.

Cleig, Charles

Captain.

Clements, Harry

Champion Annual.

Clementson, W. A. B.
B.O.P. Boys Own Novels.

Cleveland, Frank   *(r.n. Frank H. Shaw)*
Chums.

Clevely, Hugh   *(r.n.)*
Born in Bristol, and brought up in a country vicarage, where
he was educated by his uncle, who was the vicar. A keen flyer,
he obtained his pilot's licence before the last war, and also
joined the RAF Reserve. Served on active service all through
the war and finished as a Wing Commander.

Despite his 'quiet' upbringing, Clevely has written thrillers for
almost all his working life, and wrote more than 25 stories for
The Thriller, including 'Lynch Law', the long complete yarn
that comprised No 2 in 1929. Is also remembered for his
popular 'Gang-Smasher' stories for later issues of that paper.
Author of many hard-cover mystery novels, when he wrote
adult thrillers under the 'Tod Claymore' pen-name. Believed to
have died a few years ago in the mid-1960's.

Thriller. Thriller Lib. Detective Weekly. S.B.L. (3rd). B.F.L.
(2nd) (anon).

Cliffe, Gunton
Scout.

Clifford, Lionel B.
Chums.

Clifford, Lloyd
B.O.P.

Clifford, Martin   *(r.n. Charles Hamilton)*
This nom-de-plume was also used by the following other writers,
when Hamilton's stories were unavailable, in the St Jim's
stories: *S. E. Austin. A. Barnard. E. Searles Brooks. L. Carlton.
W. L. Catchpole. F. G. Cook. C. M. Down. R. T. Eves. P. Griffith.
H. Harper. J. Herman. H. A. Hinton. H. C. Hook. H. Hutt. R. S.
Kirkham. C. D. Lowe. K. E. Newman. H. O'Mant. K. Orme.
J. N. Pentelow. L. E. Ransome. C. Russell. G. R. Samways. N. Wood-
Smith. F. Warwick.*

Special Note: R. S. Kirkham also wrote a story under this
name, featuring Cedar Creek.

Popular (1st and 2nd). B.F.L. (1st). Pluck (2nd). Gem (1st and
2nd). Marvel (2nd). Triumph. Boys Friend Weekly (2nd).

Schoolboys Own Lib. Empire Lib. (2nd). Greyfriars Holiday Annual. Goldhawk Books.

Clifford, Read
Thriller.

Clifton, Henry   *(r.n. Charles Hamilton)*
Chuckles.

Clifton, Richard
Football and Sports Library.

Clinton, Garth
Chums. Chums Annual.

Clinton, Harry   *(r.n.)*
True Blue (1st and 2nd). Union Jack (1st) (anon). Pluck (1st) (anon).

Clive, Clifford   *(r.n. Charles Hamilton)*
A few stories towards the end of School and Sport by E. R. Home-Gall.
School and Sport.

Clive, Keith (Captain)
Boys Magazine.

Close, H. P.
Boys Torch Adventure Library.

Cobb, G. Belton   *(r.n.)*
Chatterbox.

Cobb, Thomas   *(r.n.)*
Born 1854, and lived at Brighton for many years. Wrote a number of novels.
B.O.P.

Cobham, Sir Alan   *(r.n.)*
The first stories featuring King of the Islands in Modern Boy were credited to 'Sir Alan Cobham & Charles Hamilton', the former name no doubt giving the stories a 'boost'. But the fact of the matter was that Charles Hamilton wrote all the stories himself.

Cochrane, Alfred   *(r.n.)*
Born Mauritius 1865, educated at Repton, Hertford College and Oxford.
Captain.

Cockton, Henry   *(r.n.)*
Born in London, 1807. Is remembered almost entirely for his long book 'Valentine Vox, the Ventriloquist', published in

1840, which was the forerunner of every other story of ventriloquism ever published. A great many have appeared in the realms of comic and boys' literature since then – 'Val Fox' in Puck, and stories about Billy Bunter in the Magnet. There were many other successors and imitators of 'Vox', including the publisher, Lloyd – 'Valentine Vox' by Timothy Portwine and 'Silas the Conjuror' in Beeton's Boys Own Magazine in 1855. Cockton died fairly early in life in 1852.

Union Jack (1st). Pluck (1st).

Cody, Stone   *(r.n. G. A. Lansborough)*
Western Library.

Cogger, Percy
Scout.

Coke, Desmond   *(r.n.)*
Born in London on 5th July 1879, the son of a Major Talbot Coke. Educated at Shrewsbury, where he became school captain, and also edited the Salopian, thus beginning his literary career while still a schoolboy. A photograph of him as Shrewsbury's captain appeared in The Captain's first volume in 1899. Later, at Oxford University, he edited The Isis. While still at Oxford he wrote an amusing burlesque of the famous Victorian children's book 'Sandford and Merton', calling it 'Sandford of Merton' and it was published in 1903 under the name Belinda Blinders. In 1906 came the classic of his life at Shrewsbury College, 'The Bending of the Twig', which he dedicated to his Housemaster, the Rev. Churchill.

Around this time he was a schoolmaster himself at Claymore and remained there for six years. Wrote many other adult and boy's novels. Served as Captain and Adjutant with the Royal North Lancs Regiment between 1914–17 and saw active service in France. Was mentioned in despatches and finally invalided out. His main hobby was browsing around antique shops and art galleries, and he possessed a fine and valuable art collection at his home in London.

His name, curiously enough, is pronounced the same as 'Cook'.
Captain.

Colbeck, Alfred   *(r.n.)*
A Yorkshireman by birth, the Rev. Colbeck was educated at Batley and at Ranmoor College, Sheffield. His ministry was spent in Lancashire, Yorkshire, Shropshire and Staffordshire.

His first story appeared in the B.O.P. in 1895, and he subsequently wrote several stories and serials for that paper. His tales were usually about the adventures of young Englishmen in foreign parts. His backgrounds were authentic, as he had travelled widely, especially in Egypt, Palestine, Greece, Turkey and Russia.
B.O.P.

Colchester, Captain
Marvel (1st).

Cole, Alan
Young England.

Cole, Jackson
Western Library.

Coles, Detective Inspector *(r.n. E. Sempill)*
Marvel (2nd). B.F.L. (1st).

Colinski, A. J. *(r.n.)*
Pen-names: Captain Angus Scott. Captain Angus McPherson.

Collier, John C. *(r.n.)*
Union Jack (1st). B.F.L. (1st). Marvel (1st).

Collier, Norman *(r.n. C. N. Bennett)*
Pluck (2nd). Marvel (2nd). Boys Herald. True Blue (2nd). Comic Life.

Collingwood, Harry *(r.n. W. J. C. Lancaster)*
Chums. Union Jack (1880). Garfield Boys Journal.

Collins, Colin *(r.n. Oliver Merland)*
Nelson Lee Lib. (1st New Series). Pluck (3rd). Dreadnought. Wonder. Lloyds Detective Series. Lloyds School Yarns.
Special Note: Houghton Townley used this name in one instance.

Collins, E.
B.O.P.

Collins, Wilkie *(r.n. William Wilkie Collins)*
World-famous as one of the earliest detective and mystery writers. Born 8th January 1824, in Tavistock Square, London. His younger brother, Charles, also a writer, married Charles Dickens's sister. Amongst his best-known novels are 'The Woman in White' and 'The Moonstone'.
He died on 23rd September 1889.
B.O.P.

Colo, Edwin
Scout.
Comfort, John
B.O.P. Chatterbox.
Compton, Herbert Eastwick *(r.n.)*
Chums.
Comrade, Robert W. *(r.n. Edwy Searles Brooks)*
Dreadnought. Gem (2nd). Nelson Lee Lib. (old and 2nd New Series). Boys Friend Weekly (2nd). B.F.L. (1st and 2nd).
Conner, Henry *(r.n. H. Gilbert)*
Boys Herald.
Conquest, Owen *(r.n. Charles Hamilton)*
This name was also used by the following other writers when stories by Hamilton were not available:
S. E. Austin. W. L. Catchpole. C. M. Down. R. T. Eves. K. E. Newman. H. O'Mant. W. E. Pike. G. R. Samways. N. Wood-Smith.
Popular (1st and 2nd). Boys Friend Weekly (2nd). Gem (2nd). Magnet. Schoolboys Own Lib. Greyfriars Herald (2nd). B.F.L. (1st). Greyfriars Holiday Annual. Knockout.
Conway, Gordon *(r.n. Charles Hamilton)*
Vanguard Lib.   (Trapps Holmes). Funny Cuts. Smiles.
Conway, Richard
Sports Budget (2nd).
Conyers, Captain and Reginald Wray *(r.n. W. B. Home-Gall)*
Marvel (1st).
Cooee *(r.n. A. M. Burrage)*
Gem (2nd).
Cook, Fred Gordon *(r.n.)*
Born in 1900 and educated at Marylebone Grammar School, London. On leaving school he worked as a junior clerk in a Chartered Accountant's office, but he left soon afterwards and worked as a junior sub-editor on Chums. He wrote his first story in this paper about 1918, when F. Knowles Camplin was editor. Being an avid reader of the Magnet and Gem in his boyhood days, he knew all their history and began to contribute small items for the Greyfriars Herald and Magnet, run then by J. Nix Pentelow. In 1919 his first substitute Magnet story was published (No 591), 'Weggie of the Remove', followed by about 30 more, and probably twice as many for the Gem. Also he contributed many stories to Chums, including several series of

humorous school stories under the name of Burleigh Carew. He also re-wrote many of the American originals for Newnes 'Nick Carter', 'Buffalo Bill' and 'Treasure Trove' Libraries, as well as contributions to 'Tubby Haigh' and the comic, 'Merry Moments'.

In 1921 he wrote one or two St Frank's stories for the Nelson Lee Library, but they were never used, as Edwy Searles Brooks's own stories were always on schedule. Between 1927–33 he contributed a very popular series for The Boys Magazine featuring The Boys of St Giddy's as well as a number of humorous tales illustrated by Jack Greenall, later to become famous as the creator of Useless Eustace, the famous Daily Mirror cartoon feature, which is still running today.

He also wrote a series 'Madcaps of Merrydew' for the little-known boys' paper called Toby.

Later Fred Cook gave up boys' fiction writing and worked as a wireless engineer for a famous firm near White City, London. Now retired, Fred Cook lives not far from Newbury, Berks.

Pen-names: Fred Smeaton. Bruce Chaverton. Vincent Owen. Burleigh Carew. Peler Foy. Frank Richards (Magnet). Martin Clifford (Gem). Popular (2nd).

Rover (anon). Adventure (anon). Chums. Greyfriars Herald (2nd) (anon).

Cooke, W. Bourne   *(r.n.)*

Author of several exciting adventure stories for boys, probably the best-known being 'The Black Box' which ran as a serial in The Captain in 1913. With 'Wreck Cove' in the same paper in 1915–16. Chums also saw his serials 'Grey Wizard' and 'The Curse of Ameris' in 1920 and 1923 respectively. 'Wreck Cove' in particular was an extremely dramatic yarn with plenty of atmosphere, dealing with adventurers searching for treasure in the 18th century in Cornwall. Most of these serials were later published in book form.

Cooke also wrote several adult novels, including 'The Horned Owl' and 'Madame Domino'.

Chums. Captain.

Cooks, Percival   *(r.n. Percy C. Bishop)*

Boys Comic Lib. Union Jack (1st). Boys Friend Weekly (1st and 2nd). Pluck (1st).

Cooper, Alfred Benjamin *(r.n.)*

Born Preston, and wrote many adult novels as well as contributing to such adult magazines as Strand, Answers, Pearsons, etc.

Scout. B.O.P.

Cooper, Charles Henry St John *(r.n.)*

Born in London, 3rd November, 1869, and educated both in England and France. Was the grandson of Henry Russell, the composer of several songs, including 'Cheer, Boys, Cheer'. He was also the nephew of William Clark Russell, the famous sea-novelist, who also wrote for boys, and a half-brother of Gladys Cooper, the well-known actress.

Originally intending to become an artist, he had his own studio at the age of only 15, where he turned out many sketches and paintings, including several of Richmond, Surrey. But he turned to writing and at 17 he became sub-editor of the short-lived boys' paper, 'Pleasure'. He wrote practically the whole of the paper himself, including 'Answers to Correspondents'. In 1890 he wrote a biography of his grandfather, which was published by McQueens. In 1896 he wrote his first serial for the ½d Boys Friend and called 'A Middy of Nelson's Day'. It marked the start of a long, prolific and highly successful career as a boys' writer, during which time he contributed around 400 serials, and many more short stories for the Girls Friend under the 'Mabel St John' pen-name. Probably the most famous in this field was 'Pollie Green's Schooldays'. He also contributed to many adult papers such as 'Penny Pictorial', 'Family Journal' and 'Merry'.

When the Boys Realm was revived in 1919 he wrote for it 'Henry St John's Schooldays', in which he was a junior at the school of St Basil's himself. He also had many books published, including a best-selling romance 'Sunny Ducrow' in 1919, which also achieved success in America. It sold over 40,000 copies in its first year of publication.

St John Cooper was also a keen breeder of bulldogs and wrote four text books on the subject. His other hobbies included wood-carving, antique furniture, hammering in brass and copper, and making model ships, gramophones, etc. He had three sons, one an artist who originated the Mr Cube on Tate and Lyle's product during the last war.

Henry St John Cooper died at Sunbury on Thames, 9th Sept. 1926.
Pen-names: Clifford Hoskin. Gordon Holme. Henry St John. Lieut. Paul Lefevre.
Football & Sports Library. Playtime.

Cooper, E. Fitzgerald
Diamond Library (1st).

Cooper, Freemont   *(r.n. Arthur Steffens)*
Boys Friend Weekly.

Cooper, James Fenimore   *(r.n.)*
Born at Burlington, New Jersey, U.S.A. 1789 and educated at Yale College. Entered U.S. Navy when he was 19 and served for 3 years. Later became a business man and did not write his first novel 'Precaution' until 1821; from then on he wrote over 30 novels, including the classic 'Last of the Mohicans'. Has often been called the American Walter Scott. Cooper died in 1851.
Union Jack (1st). Chums. Captain Lib. Pluck (1st). Marvel (1st).

Cooper, J. Lawrence
Skipper Book for Boys.

Corbett, Mrs George
Larks (Trapps Holmes).

Corbett-Smith, Major A.
Chums.

Corbin, J. A.
Boys Torch Adventure Library.

Corcoran, Brewer
Scout.

Cordry, Clem.
Junior Pyramid Books.

Cordwell, F. C. G.   *(r.n.)*
Editor of Fleetway Publications in the period 1910–35, editing such famous papers as Fun & Fiction, Firefly, Merry & Bright, Favourite, Film Fun, Kinema Comic, Bullseye and Startler. Wrote many of the well-known series including the Jack Johnson stories in Butterfly, Favourite and Merry & Bright. Also wrote many of the Jack Keen detective stories in Film Fun. Died before World War II.
Bullseye (anon). Surprise (anon). Favourite Comic. Butterfly. Merry & Bright (all anon).

Cork, Barry Joynson *(r.n.)*
  Pen-name: Barry Joynson.
Cornier, Vincent
  Detective Weekly.
Cornish, W. H.
  Boys Friend Weekly (2nd).
Corydon, Paul
  Chums. Chums Annual.
Cotteril, Grant
  Rocket.
Coulsdon, John *(r.n. Cyril Malcolm Hincks)*
  Boys Friend Weekly (2nd).
Courtney, Charles
  Boys Realm (1st).
Cousland, D. C.
  Boys Torch Adventure Library.
Cowan, C. England *(r.n.)*
  Union Jack (1st).
Cowan, Edward *(r.n.)*
  Pen-name: Ted Cowan.
Cowan, Francis
  Chums. Chatterbox.
Cowan, Ted *(r.n. Edward Cowan)*
  Champion. Champion Annual.
Cowdy, Alan
  Boys Torch Adventure Library.
Cox, Anthony Berkeley *(r.n.)*
  Pen-name: Anthony Berkeley.
Cox, Douglas *(r.n. H. D. Cox)*
  Boys Realm (1st).
Cox, H. D. *(r.n.)*
  Pen-name: Douglas Cox.
Cox, Jack *(r.n.)*
  Was editor of the B.O.P. from 1946 until it finished, taking over
  from Robert Harding. Born in Worsley, Lancs in 1915, and
  educated at Eccles Grammar School and Manchester Univer-
  sity. Also studied at the Institute of International Relations in
  Geneva. Was originally a schoolmaster – having an M.A.
  degree – but gave up teaching in 1937, to join the staff of the

Manchester Guardian and write mainly on educational subjects. Previously, during University vacations, he had worked as a reporter on the Daily Mail. Also a prolific writer for boys, he has written over 20 books, mostly on outdoor pursuits such as camping, etc. His stories include 'Dangerous Water' and 'Calamity Camp'. Is now editor of 'The Boys Own Companion' which takes the place of the pre-war B.O.P. Annual. Regularly writes scripts for, and appears in, Children's and Schools TV and radio programmes. Lives in Northwood, Middlesex.
B.O.P.

Cox, James Roberts *(r.n.)*
Scout. B.O.P.

Cox, Palmer *(r.n.)*
Born in Canada, 28th April 1840.
B.O.P.

Cox, Reginald H. W. *(r.n.)*
Scout.

Coxe, George Harmon *(r.n.)*
Born New York, 23rd April 1901.
Thriller.

Craig, Andrew
Dreadnought.

Craig, Eric
Champion Annual.

Crane, Berkeley *(r.n. A. C. Marshall)*
Champion.

Craven, Essex
Triumph. Champion.

Creasey, John *(r.n.)* M.B.E.
Born in Southfields, Surrey, in 1908 and the son of a motor engineer. Educated at Fulham Elementary School and Sloane Secondary School. As a boy was a keen reader of the Boys Friend and especially stories of Jimmy Silver of Rookwood. Published his first book in 1932 after collecting 700 rejection slips! Has since set up a world record for writing over 400 books, mainly thrillers, about such popular characters as The Toff, The Baron, Inspector West, Dr Palfrey, Gideon of the Yard, Department Z, and Patrick (Rock) Dawlish. His pseudonyms for adult fiction are: Michael Halliday, Kyle Hunt, Anthony Morton, Jeremy York, Gordon Ashe, Norman Deane, Peter

Manton, Richard Martin, J. J. Marric, Tex Riley, William K. Reilly and Ken Ranger. Under the last three names he wrote Westerns. He wrote his first Sexton Blake story in 1936, 'The Case of the Frightened Financier' and wrote four others shortly afterwards. He also penned many Dixon Hawke Libraries for D. C. Thomson.

Up to 1957 it was reported that his books had sold two-and-a-half times as many as the prolific Edgar Wallace, with nearly 2,000 editions in 13 different languages, including Russian. These figures must have grown considerably since then, as Creasey today is writing as prolifically as ever. Fond of travel, he frequently visits the U.S.A., where he was the very first Englishman to be elected to the Board of the Western Writers of America. He was also the Founder-Chairman of the Crime Writers Association. He owns a literary agency, and published his own 'Creasey Mystery Magazine' each month. He was also co-publisher of the 'John O' London's Magazine', now discontinued. Has in recent years taken an interest in politics, and has several times contested a parliamentary seat. Many of his books have been filmed, and several of his famous characters have been featured in popular TV series. Married, with two sons, he lives at Boddenham, Salisbury, Wilts.

Pen-name: (in Western Library) William K. Reilly.

Dixon Hawke Lib. (anon). Flag Lib. Thriller. Detective Weekly. S.B.L. (2nd and 3rd).

Creighton, Donald
    Captain.

Creswick, Maurice *(r.n.)*
    On the staff of Amalgamated Press, and held many editorial posts including All Sports (after Arthur Steffens) and the popular Boys Cinema. Was also an expert golfer and captained a Fleetway team. Retired many years ago and now lives not far from Brighton in Sussex.

Creswick, Paul *(r.n.)*
    Born 1866, and lived at Beckenham, Kent. Wrote many books especially with a historical flavour. Quite probably he was the father of Maurice Creswick, but this still has to be confirmed.
    Chums. Greyfriars Herald (2nd). Boys Cinema.

Crichton, Jack *(r.n. H. Crichton Miln)*
    B.F.L. (2nd). Boys Favourite. Sports Budget (1st). Boys Friend

Weekly (2nd). Gem (2nd). Chums. Football & Sports Lib.
B.F.L. (1st). Champion. Football & Sports Favourite.

Crichton, Steve
Football and Sports Favourite.

Crick, Vernon
Champion Annual.

Crockett, Lindsay
Chums Annual.

Croft, Roy   *(r.n. W. R. Calvert)*
Chums.

Crompton, Richmal   *(r.n. Richmal Crompton Lamburn)*

Crompton, William
B.O.P.

Cromwell, Victor   *(r.n. A. E. Bull)*
B.F.L. (1st). Gem (2nd).

Cronin, Bernard
Chums.

Crosbie, W. J.
Lot-O'-Fun.

Crosfield, H. C.
Captain.

Cross, Anthony
B.O.P.

Cross, Dennis   *(r.n. William Gibbons)*
Pluck (3rd).

Cross, John
Triumph. Champion.

Cross, May
Captain.

Cross, Pennington
Scout.

Cross, Thomson   *(r.n. Samuel Andrew Wood)*
Chums. Captain.

Crouch, D.
Chatterbox.

Crump, Irving
Scout.

Crundal, Anson
Chums.

Crunden, Reginald *(r.n. Hylton Cleaver)*
B.F.L. (2nd). Chums.
Crystal, H. Y.
Hotspur Book for Boys.
Cudlip, Mrs Pender *(r.n.)*
Pen-name: Annie Thomas.
Cule, W. E.
Wrote many school stories in the 1890's and early 1900's including serials for the paper 'Boys'. Also several serials for B.O.P., including 'Rollinson and I' and 'Stories from the School-House'. Wrote a number of hard-cover books of school stories including 'Black Fifteen' and 'Baker Secundus'.
Boys. B.O.P. Young England.
Culley, John J.
Chums.
Cullum, Ridgwell *(r.n.)*
Born 1867. Wrote a serial for 'Boys of our Empire' called 'The Secret of Wondergat' in collaboration with Charles Wingrove. Also the author of many hard-cover adult novels of adventure, mainly set in the American West.
Boys of our Empire.
Culshaw, W. J.
Boys Torch Adventure Lib.
Cumberland, A. M.
Larks (Trapps Holmes).
Cummings, Ken *(r.n. Dugald Matheson Cumming-Skinner)*
Boys Realm (2nd).
Cumming-Skinner, Dugald Matheson *(r.n.)*
Born at Findhorn, Scotland, 1902 and educated at Norton Academy, Dundee, and St Andrews and Durham Universities. Began writing for magazines and papers in 1922 and while still at University. During his first 8 years as a free-lance writer he contributed over 8,000,000 words to various publications, including adult magazines such as 'Answers' and 'Woman's Way'. Was the winner of a big juvenile literary competition run by John Leng and Co., which was associated with D. C. Thomson Ltd. and soon became their most prolific contributor. A frequent broadcaster in the twenties and thirties, he gave talks on natural history, science and history, as well as telling many of his own humorous short stories. He also wrote several radio

plays. His chief relaxations were fishing, billiards and cooking.
He lived at Dundee – the home of the world-famous D. C.
Thomson headquarters – and also had a residence in Lot,
France.

He died some years ago.

Pen-names: Douglas Dundee. Dugald Morey. Donald Dane.
Ken Cummings. Henri De Beauregard.

(the last-named not yet traced in boys' fiction.)

Adventure (anon). Hotspur (anon). Rover (anon). Wizard
(anon). Startler (anon). Dixon Hawke Lib. (anon).

Cuneo, Terrence
Champion Annual.

Cunnison, C. V. L.
Hotspur Book for Boys.

Curwood, J. Oliver
Chums.

Custer, Claude *(r.n. Norman Goddard)*
B.F.L. (1st). Dreadnought. Boys Friend Weekly (2nd).

Dacre, Captain Stanley *(r.n. Stanley Portal Hyatt)*
Boys Friend Weekly (2nd).

Dagnall, J. Deveral
Boys Life.

Dakers, Manton
Chums.

Dale, Austin *(r.n. W. R. Calvert)*
Chums.

Dale, Edwin *(r.n. Edward R. Home-Gall)*
Tiger. Champion. Champion Lib. Triumph. Lion. Champion
Annual.

Dale, Leonard
B.O.P.

Dale, Martin
Ranger (1st).

Dale, Roland
 Rowland
Young Britain (1st).

Dale, Victor
Chips.

Dale, Winston
Popular Book of Boys Stories.

Dallas, Oswald   *(r.n.)*

Educated Scotland and France. Staff Captain in South African Constabulary. Staff Officer in New Zealand. Saw service all over the world; active service in West Africa. Was once a first-class sportsman. Wrote many books for boys and some adult novels. Wrote also for English and French magazines – and was also a painter in water colours.

B.O.P. Chums. Young Britain (1st). British Boys. Aldine Mystery Novels. Chums Annual.

Dalton, Gilbert   *(r.n.)*

Journalist who turned author. Gave up newspaper work in the 1930's to write fiction for boys. Was Coventry correspondent for The Times. For some years he wrote for Amalgamated Press, Newnes and D. C. Thomson, then he decided to write entirely for the latter publishers. His output was really remarkable, and he must have written thousands of stories in all sorts of series. He claimed at one time to have written every short in the Hotspur for eight weeks running.

He was one of the writers in the series of Red Circle School stories, and he penned the 'Mr Barrell' and the 'Arrival of Spiv Ringer' series. Another series in which he was only one of the writers was the 'Wilson' sportsman series. Apart from his boys' writing he also wrote about 100 plays for the B.B.C. Children's Hour as well as half-a-dozen books.

Gilbert Dalton died a few years ago.

Pen-names: Victor Norton. Rod Carstairs.

Boys Friend Weekly (2nd). Modern Boy. Hotspur (anon). Wizard (anon). Rover (anon); probably all Thomson papers.

Daly, Carrol John   *(r.n.)*

Born in New York. Educated Yonkers High School, De La Salle, and American Academy Dramatic Art. Travelled extensively.

Detective Weekly.

Dan, 'Uncle'   *(r.n. Frank Anderson)*

Playtime.

Dane, Arnold

Chums.

Dane, Donald   *(r.n. Dugald Matheson Cumming-Skinner)*

Triumph. Champion. Champion Lib. Champion Annual. Triumph Annual.

Dane, Lawrence
Pluck (3rd).
Dane, Merton
Boys Life.
Dane, Richard
Triumph. Champion.
Dane, Rupert
Newnes Adventure Library.
Danesford, Earle   *(r.n. F. Addington Symonds)*
Chums. Rocket. Champion. Boys Wonder Lib. B.F.L. (1st).
Champion Annual. Chums Annual.
Dangerfield, Captain   *(r.n. G. J. B. Anderson)*
Union Jack (1st).
Daniel, Roland
Probably the real name of the author, but never confirmed.
Lived at Brighton in 1934. Was a very good writer of mystery
novels, especially those with a Chinese atmosphere. His books
are still being published today by Wright & Brown, and to
date he must have written at least a hundred.
His popular 'Wu Fang' stories appeared in the Thriller in the
30's.
Thriller.
Daniels, Arthur James   *(r.n.)*
Born in St John's Wood, London, in 1863. Was one of the most
prolific contributors to Chums in the 1890's and early 1900's.
Wrote 10 serials and several hundred short stories. His stories
were mostly of the 'mystery at school' type, and very popular
with readers of this period.
Chums.
Daniels, Roger
Captain.
D'Arcy, Edgar
Young Briton's Journal.
Dare, Arthur C.
Marvel (1st).
Dare, Captain   *(r.n. S. G. Shaw)*
Boys Herald.
Dare, Franklyn
Sports Budget (2nd). Football & Sports Library.

Dare, Gordon
C.I.D. Library (1st).
Dare, Harold
Champion Annual.
Dare, Roderick
Robin Hood (1st, 2nd, 3rd). True Blue (2nd).
Daring, Major
Marvel (1st).
Daring, Victor   *(r.n. E. J. Gannon)*
B.F.L. (1st).
Darling, Dick
Newnes Adventure Library.
Darran, Mark   *(r.n. Norman Goddard)*
Note: A few stories were under the bi-line of *Mark Darran* and
Claud Custer.
Boys Friend Weekly (2nd). Union Jack (1st and 2nd). B.F.L.
(1st). Pluck (1st and 2nd). Marvel (1st and 2nd). Boys Journal.
Boys Realm Football and Sports Lib. Magnet. Boys Herald.
Boys Realm (1st).
Darrell, Guy
Boys Realm (1st).
Darrell, Walter   *(r.n. E. H. Burrage)*
Union Jack (1st). Marvel (1st).
Darwin, Desmond
Target Library.
Daryl, A. J.
Boys Friend Weekly (1st).
Dashwood, Percy
Modern Boy.
Daunt, Atherley   *(r.n. F. H. Evans)*
B.F.L. (1st). Pluck (2nd). Boys Herald. Boys Realm (1st). Boys
Friend Weekly (2nd).
Davenport, Tex   *(r.n. H. Hessell Tiltman)*
Young Britain (1st). Pluck (3rd). Champion.
Davis, Arnold   *(stock name)*
Davies
This name was used to hide the identities of the following
authors: *G. W. Brown. F. H. Evans. N. Goddard. W. M. Graydon.
W. B. Home-Gall. T. G. D. Maitland. A. G. Pearson.* who
wrote mainly in the pink Union Jack. Why this was done

was known only to the editor concerned. This name will not be found credited to the individual authors mentioned in this bibliography.

Marvel (2nd). Pluck (2nd). Union Jack (2nd).

Davies, Edward C. *(r.n.)*

Wrote for many adult magazines from 1919, including Hutchinson's Mystery Magazine, Adventure Magazine, Detective Magazine and all the well-known magazines. Had a crime book published by Hodders, 'The Maker of Frocks'. Wrote one single S.B.L. in 1930 (2nd series, No 231). Was last known to be living in the Southampton area.

S.B.L. (anon). B.O.P.

Davies, John

B.O.P.

Davies, Lucian *(r.n. L. J. Beeston)*

Chums.

Davies, M. C. D.

Boys Friend Weekly.

Davies, A. W. *(r.n.)*

Writer who wrote two substitute Greyfriars stories for the Magnet, in 1927, 'The Schoolboy Broadcasters' and 'Fishy's Travel Agency', which were better than some of those penned by other substitute writers in this field. Was reported to own a greengrocery business in Reading, then moved to Bournemouth, but to date no trace of him has been found.

Pen-name: Frank Richards (Magnet).

Davis, Frederick Clyde *(r.n.)*

Thriller.

Davis, Philip *(r.n.)*

An editor at Amalgamated Press, who started on the staff of the Bullseye in the early 30's and on F. G. Cordwell's group of papers. On the latter's death he became editor of Film Fun and held this post for many years until he left to go on to Annuals. Left Amalgamated Press in 1960.

Dawlish, John

Scout.

Dawson, Arnold H.

Scout.

Dawson, A. W.

Scout.

Dawson, Colin
Lot-O'-Fun.
Dawson, C. T.
A writer for the Thomson papers in the period 1922–5, who wrote many complete serials. Last heard of living in Brighton. Wizard. Rover. Vanguard and probably other Thomson papers. All anon.
Dawson, F. Morton
Chums.
Dawson, Hugh
Thriller.
Dawson, Ray
Hotspur Book for Boys.
Dawtrey, John
B.O.P.
Day, George *(r.n.)*
Pen-name: Bruce Howard.
Big Budget.
Day, Lionel *(r.n. Ladbroke Lionel Day Black)*
Boys Realm (2nd). Magnet. Nelson Lee Lib. (1st new series). B.F.L. (2nd).
Dayle, Malcolm *(r.n. Cyril Malcolm Hincks)*
Boys Realm (1st). Boys Friend Weekly (2nd). B.F.L. (1st). Boys Leader.
Dayne, Clement
Union Jack (1st).
Deakin, Guy
Champion. Lion.
Dean, Donald *(r.n. W. E. Stanton Hope)*
Ranger (2nd). Boys Realm (2nd). Football & Sports Lib. Football & Sports Favourite. Football Weekly.
Dean, Leon W.
Scout.
Deane, Vesey *(r.n. Andrew Nicholas Murray)*
B.F.L. (1st). Boys Herald. Boys Friend Weekly (2nd).
Deane, Wallace
B.O.P.
De Beauregard, Henri *(r.n. D. M. Cumming-Skinner)*
The writer claimed to have written juvenile stories under this pen-name but they have never been traced.

Dedham, Richard *(r.n.)*
Champion. B.F.L. (2nd).

Dee, Dare *(r.n. Arthur Steffens)*
Boys Herald. Boys Realm (1st). Boys Friend Weekly (2nd).

Defoe, Daniel *(r.n.)*
Born c. 1660 and died in 1732. Writer of the immortal 'Robinson Crusoe' in 1719. Was the son of James Foe – a butcher, and changed the name to Defoe in 1703. Published over 250 works and died in his lodgings in Ropemaker's Alley, Moorfields. This is another instance (as in the case of Charles Dickens) where a classical author was used in a 'blood and thunder' paper in an attempt to give it a touch of 'class'.
Union Jack (1st).

Dell, Draycot Montagu *(r.n.)*
Born 5th March, 1888. Educated at Manchester Grammar School. Stories with historical backgrounds were his favourite subject. Editor of Chums between 1926–39, and editor of Young Britain for the first two years. Was quite a lively character in his time and extremely popular with all writers, editors and artists. Died at the beginning of the Second World War.
Pen-names: Piers Anson. Stephen Thompson.
Pioneer. Young Britain (1st). B.F.L. (2nd). Champion. Union Jack (2nd). Champion Annual. Chums Annual.

Delisle, Harcourt
Young Britain (1st).

Delmere, F.
Nugget Library. Boys Realm (2nd). Grammol Thrillers.

Demage, G.
B.O.P.

Denbigh, Maurice *(r.n. Maurice Nutbrown)*
Boys Realm (2nd).

Dene, Alan *(r.n. Trevor C. Wignall)*
Boys Realm (1st and 2nd). Boys Journal. Boys Realm Football & Sports Lib. B.F.L. (1st). Marvel (2nd).

Dene, Hampton *(r.n. S. Clarke Hook)*
Boys Friend Weekly (2nd).

Denman, George
Marvel (1st).

Dennis, Hugh
Boys Friend Weekly (2nd).
Denny, Norman G.
Chums.
Dent, C. H. *(r.n.)*
Pen-names: Cecil Fanshaw. Robert Hudleston. John Hudleston.
Dent, Denis *(r.n. Graeme Williams)*
Boys Herald. Boys Realm (1st). Boys Friend Weekly (2nd).
Denton, George
Triumph. Champion Annual.
Denton, Pete
Pluck (3rd).
Denver, Athol
Chums.
Denver, Bruce *(r.n. W. E. Stanton Hope)*
Ranger (2nd).
Denvers, Jake *(r.n. Alfred Edgar)*
Rocket. Pluck (3rd). B.F.L. (1st and 2nd).
Denville, Hugh
Pluck (1st). Marvel (1st).
Dering, Richard
Triumph.
Derwent, Captain Vernon
Union Jack (1st).
Deslys, Charles
B.O.P.
Desmond, Frank
Triumph. Champion Annual.
D'esque, Count Jean Louis
Detective Weekly.
De Vigne, H. Rosier
Aldine Mystery Novels.
Dexter, Mark
Marvel (2nd).
Dexter, Philip
Diamond Lib. (1st).
Dexter, Ralph
Marvel (2nd).

Dexter, Walter *(r.n.)*
> Born London, 1877. Wrote many books and articles on Charles Dickens and was a member of a society connected with research into his work. Took a keen interest in the history of comic papers and it was he who first discovered that the first story of Sexton Blake appeared in the ½d Marvel and not in the Union Jack. Died in the late 1950's.
> B.O.P.

Dickens, Charles *(r.n.)*
> Born 1812, died 1870. Son of a Government clerk, he wrote many books which have become classics – 'Oliver Twist', 'David Copperfield', 'Great Expectations', 'The Pickwick Papers', etc. He experienced much poverty in his early life and many experts think that his classic story of David Copperfield was based on his own early adventures.
> As in the case of Defoe, Dickens's stories were included in the Union Jack to give an impression of good and high-class reading.
> Union Jack (1st).

Dickson, James Grierson *(r.n.)*
> Wrote a series of factual articles on secret societies for the Union Jack entitled 'Our Masked Menaces' and also factual articles on espionage. Many years later wrote a series called 'The Truth about Cowboys' for the Eagle. Wrote some really high-class Sexton Blake stories after World War II, using the nom-de-plume of Hilary King.
> **Pen-name:** Hilary King.
> Thriller.

Dignam, C. B.
> Captain.

Dillon, Dixie
> Ranger (2nd).

Dilnot, George *(r.n.)*
> Born in Hayling Island, Hampshire, in 1883. Was on several newspaper staffs, including the Daily Mail. Was a crime reporter and wrote many books on the subject, including 'The History of Scotland Yard'. Author also of the famous edition of The Romance of the Amalgamated Press, which was published in 1925, and which was based on an earlier edition of 1910. Wrote several Sexton Blake stories, and many thriller stories

for magazines. Had a brother named Frank, who was also a writer.

Dilnot was a leading member of the Press Club, and possibly may have once been Chairman. He died, aged 68, on the 23rd February 1951 at East Molesey, Surrey.

Thriller. S.B.L. (2nd).

Dimmock, Frederick Haydn *(r.n.)*

Born Luton, 1895. Joined the staff of The Scout at Pearsons, as an office boy in 1913. Served in World War I, and was seriously wounded, but recovered and was appointed editor of The Scout in succession to the war-time editor, Nancy M. Hayes. Apart from a brief period in 1919 he remained editor until 1954, when he retired, only to die the following year at his home in Welwyn Garden City.

As well as being an editor, Dimmock also wrote stories, serials and articles for the paper; and in the true Scouting spirit he originated the famous Soap-Box Derbies and the Bob-a-Job Week.

W. O. G. Lofts has in his possession the last copy of The Scout which Dimmock edited, personally autographed by him and his sub-editor, and presented by Bernard Smith, a former sub-editor.

Scout.

Dingle, Aylward Edward *(r.n.)*

Born Oxford 1876. Educated Central School, Oxford (Elem.).

Pen-name: Sinbad.

Dix, Maurice Buxton *(r.n.)*

Born London, 1889. Wrote at least 5 Sexton Blake stories, the first in 1936. Created the airman-crook, Punch Bennett. Wrote at least 20 novels and also contributed prolifically for newspapers and magazines. Died in Canada, 1957.

Thriller. S.B.L. (2nd and 3rd).

Dixon, Tom

Champion.

Dixon, Cross

Football Novels (2nd). Boxing Novels (1st).

Dixon, Don *(r.n. J. H. Stein)*

Ranger (2nd).

Dixon, James

Modern Boy.

Dixon, Robert W. *(r.n. Cecil H. Bullivant)*
Cecil Bullivant listed this as being one of his names in boys' fiction, but it has yet to be traced.

Dobson, W. H.
Scout.

Doherty, P. J.
Boys Torch Adventure Library.

Dolphin, Rex *(r.n.)*
Writer of Sexton Blake stories of the modern school. His first was in 1959. Has also written many short stories and articles for various publications. Is somewhat of an authority on Sexton Blake, belonging to the Sexton Blake Circle. Also wrote stories for the very first Tom Merry Annual.
Lives in Buckinghamshire.
Wrote of Sexton Blake under the pen-names of Richard Williams and Desmond Reid
S.B.L. (3rd and 5th).

Donaghue, Derek
Ranger (1st).

Donaldson, Major
Boys Realm (1st).

Donnelly, A. *(r.n. A. Donnelly Aitken)*
Boys Journal.

Donovan, Dick *(r.n. Joyce Emmerson Preston Muddock)*
Newnes Adventure Library.

Dorling, Captain Henry Taprell *(r.n.)*
Pen-name: Taffrail.

Dorning, Harold *(r.n.)*
Boys Journal. Cheer, Boys, Cheer. Scout. Chums.

Dorrian, Harry *(r.n. Charles Hamilton)*
Pluck (2nd). Gem (2nd).

Douglas, David
Boys Cinema. Diamond Lib. (1st). Popular Book of Boys Stories.

Douglas, James
Diamond Library (1st).

Douglas, Leonard
Radio Fun.

Douglas Marg.
C.I.D. Lib. (1st).

Douse, Anthony *(r.n.)*

One of the writers of Sexton Blake stories under the Desmond Reid pen-name.

S.B.L. (3rd).

Douthwaite, Louis Charles *(r.n.)*

Born in Hull, Yorkshire, 1878, and educated at Trent College. At an early age he prospected for gold in the Hudson Bay area in Canada, a background he was fond of using in his stories. Served in the 1914–18 war with a Canadian contingent in France and Belgium. After working in several newspaper departments, and as a book editor for Cassell's, he contributed his first serial for Chums in 1924. Others soon followed. He wrote his first S.B.L. in 1930 and several others. For the Thriller he wrote a great deal, as well as contributing to adult magazines. He also had a great interest in boxing and this, like gold-prospecting, was a popular feature in his writings. Collaborated on at least one story with A. Carney Allen, the latter using the name of Eric MacDonald.

Boys Realm (2nd). Chums. All Sports. Thriller. B.F.L. (2nd). Detective Weekly. S.B.L. (2nd and 3rd). Modern Boy. Chums Annual. Wild West Weekly (anon). Pioneer (anon).

Down, C. Maurice *(r.n.)*

Born at Harpenden, where his father was a J.P. Educated at a well-known public school. Joined the Amalgamated Press around 1904 and was sub-editor on the Percy Griffith group of papers which included Pluck, Gem and Empire Library, and later, the famous Magnet. At the outbreak of war he took a commission and on his return rejoined the same group. In 1921, when H. A. Hinton left, he became editor of the Magnet, Gem, Schoolboys Own, Holiday Annual and Modern Boy group until the Second World War.

Mr Down was probably the best substitute writer of them all, as he wrote stories of all Hamilton's schools, including many of Gordon Gay and Co in the Empire Library. They so closely resembled Hamilton's own work that they could, in the early days, have been mistaken for Hamilton's. He also conceived the idea of producing the Holiday Annual, probably the most popular Annual of them all, and easily the one most sought-after by Collectors today.

Charles Hamilton said in his autobiography that he based his character of Gussy on Mr Down.

On his retirement Mr Down went into a famous store near Victoria as a consultant, and later into his own family business. In his retirement he can still look back with pride as having controlled the finest boys' papers of all time.

Pen-names: Owen Conquest (Boys Friend Weekly). Martin Clifford (Gem and Popular) (1st). Frank Richards (Magnet and Popular) (2nd). Prosper Howard (Empire Library). Modern Boy (article).

Downey, Thomas
B.O.P.

Doyle, Sir Arthur Conan *(r.n.)*
Born in Edinburgh, Scotland, 1859, and educated at Stony-hurst Academy and Edinburgh University, where he studied medicine and qualified as a doctor. His first practice at Southsea was not very remunerative, so he started writing stories for magazines. One of his very early attempts was published in the B.O.P. entitled 'An Exciting Christmas Eve' – or 'My Lecture on Dynamite', when he was 24.

Other contributions followed, also many novels. His first story of Sherlock Holmes appeared in the novel 'A Study in Scarlet' and he then began to write short stories about the famous detective for The Strand Magazine. They caught the public's imagination and success for him was assured.

He was knighted in 1902 and became a world traveller, war correspondent, sportsman, lecturer and very deeply interested spiritualist. He even wrote a history on the subject of spiritualism in 1926.

Conan Doyle died in 1930, but the immortal character he created – Sherlock Holmes of Baker Street – lives on and now seems to be with us for all time.

Boys Friend Weekly (2nd). All Sports. B.O.P.

Doyle, Drac
B.O.P.

Doyle, Captain J. E.
Scout.

Doyle, Stanton
Football & Sports Lib. B.F.L. (2nd). Flag Library.

Drake, Alan
  Hotspur Book for Boys.
Drake, Dick
  Boys Cinema. Young Britain (1st).
Drake, Frank *(r.n. Charles Hamilton)*
  Funny Cuts. Picture Fun. Vanguard Lib. (Trapps Holmes).
Drake, John *(stock name)*
  A name used by Amalgamated Press, usually in rewritten or
  reprinted stories by authors who probably already had stories
  under their own name in the same publication.
  Sports Budget (1st and 2nd). Boys Favourite. Football and
  Sports Lib. Chums.
Drake, Rodney
  Chips.
Drake, Rupert *(r.n. H. Wedgwood Belfield)*
  Champion. Boys Realm (2nd). Young Britain (1st). Rocket.
  B.F.L. (2nd). Pluck (3rd).
Draper, Ben *(r.n.)*
  Pen-name: Holt Roberts.
  Ranger (2nd). B.F.L. (2nd). Startler (anon). Scout. Popular
  Book of Boys Stories. Greyfriars Holiday Annual (anon).
Draper, Hastings
  B.O.P.
Drave, Winston
  Boys Leader.
Drayson, A. W. *(r.n. Sidney Warwick)*
  Union Jack (1st).
Drayson, Col. R. A.
  Union Jack (1880).
Drew, Gordon
  Hotspur Book for Boys.
Drew, Melville
  Lot-O'-Fun.
Drew, Michael
  Junior Pyramid Books.
Drew, Reginald *(r.n. William Benjamin Home-Gall)*
  Boys Friend Weekly (2nd).
Drew, Sidney *(r.n. Edgar Joyce Murray)*
  Popular (2nd). Pluck (1st and 2nd). Detective Lib. Greyfriars
  Herald (2nd). Dreadnought. Young Britain (1st), Cheer, Boys,

Cheer. B.F.L. (1st and 2nd). Boys Herald. Boys Realm (1st).
Gem (2nd). Magnet. Nelson Lee Lib. (old). Big Budget. Boys
Leader. Wonder. Greyfriars Holiday Annual. S.B.L. (2nd).

Drew, Vaughan
Chums.

Drinkwater, Hartley
Marvel (1st).

Drummond, John   *(r.n. John Newton Chance)*
Thriller. S.B.L. (3rd).

Drury, C. W. C.
Chums. B.O.P.

Dudley, Ernest   *(r.n.)*
Born Dudley, Worcestershire, and educated privately. Famous
for his radio feature 'The Armchair Detective' in the 40's and
50's. Wrote the script for the first B.B.C. Sexton Blake series in
1939, in collaboration with Edwy Searles Brooks; also wrote an
account of Baker Street's famous sleuth in the Radio Times in
the same period. Wrote many detective novels, his character
being Dr Morelle. Has also taken a deep interest in real-life
crime, and written accounts of many cases for the National
Press.
Surprisingly, he only wrote two stories of Blake for the Detective Weekly, in which he introduced Syd Walker, the 'rag-and-
bone' man. More surprisingly, he never contributed to The
Thriller.
Detective Weekly.

Dudley, Frank
Scout. Chums.

Duffy, Michael Francis   *(r.n.)*
Born London, 1906. Educated at Wimbledon College. Worked
as a trade journalist for many years. Had the distinction of
penning the last substitute story to appear in the Magnet. This
was No 1220 – 'Speedway Coker' in 1931. All the remainder
until 1683 were written by the creator, Charles Hamilton.
Michael Duffy was a great sportsman, his main hobbies being
cross-country running and motor-boating.
Pen-name: Frank Richards (Magnet).

Duke, Derek   *(r.n. Horace Phillips)*
Boys Herald.

Dumas, Alexandre *(r.n.)*
Born 1803, died 1870. World-famous dramatist and novelist. His most famous classics were 'The Three Musketeers' and 'The Count of Monte Cristo'.
Captain Library.

Duncan, Francis
Detective Weekly.

Duncan, James *(r.n. J. E. Gunby Hadath)*
Captain.

Duncan, Leslie
Boys Torch Adventure Library.

Duncan, William Murdoch *(r.n.)*
Born in Glasgow, 1909 and educated at Walkerville, Ontario, Canada, and Glasgow University. Is an M.A. He started writing as a result of winning a £100 prize offered for an original book-length thriller in The Thriller in the 30's. This made his name and since then he has produced about 100 novels, mainly for adults, under such pen-names as John Cassell, Will Graham and L. Marshall. Also contributed to D. C. Thomson papers as yet unknown.
Thriller.

Dundee, Douglas *(r.n. Dugald Matheson Cumming-Skinner)*
Chums. Champion. Champion Lib. Triumph. Modern Boy. Champion Annual.

Dunlop, M. P.
B.O.P.

Dunn, Joseph Allan Elphinstone *(r.n.)*
Wrote his first novel in 1919, and has written hundreds of stories since that date, including Westerns, thrillers and adult fiction. It is believed that there were two authors with the same initials (J. A. Dunn) who wrote similar stories, but nothing definite has been established.
Thriller. Detective Weekly. B.F.L. (2nd). Wild West Weekly (anon).

Dunnett, R. F.
Boys Torch Adventure Library.

Dunstan, Gregory *(r.n. John Gabriel Rowe)*
Union Jack (1st). Newnes Adventure Library.

Dyce, E. Archer
Marvel (1st).

125

Eady, K. M. and R.
Wrote a school serial entitled 'Chisholm's Chums' in Boys of our Empire (Melrose) in the early 1900's. Also several books for boys and for younger children.
Young England.

Earl, Frank
Nugget Lib. (2nd). Comic Life. Boys Weekly.

Earle, Ambrose *(r.n. J. G. Jones)*
Boys Herald. Boys Realm (1st). B.F.W. (2nd). Football & Sports Favourite. B.F.L. (1st). Pluck (2nd and 3rd). Dreadnought. Boys Leader.

Earle, Michael
B.F.W. (2nd).

Ede, Detective Inspector
B.F.W. (1st).

Eden, Charles H.
British Boys.

Edgar, Alfred *(r.n.)*
Born London, 1896. Originally worked as a clerk in an engineering office at Queen Anne's Gate by St James's Park. Wrote his first Sexton Blake story for the Union Jack in 1921 (No 925, 'The Saracen's Ring'). Later he wrote many others for the U.J. as well as the S.B.L., including one under the editorial name of 'Hylton Gregory', which was also used by other authors. Was chief sub-editor (with John W. Wheway) under F. Addington Symonds on the Champion in the early 20's and also wrote stories about Panther Grayle, Detective, under another editorial name, that of 'Howard Steel' (which was used by Symonds and Arthur Brooke, amongst others). Editor of Pluck in the early 30's, he also contributed to the blue Bullseye and wrote at times three serials or stories every week. He created the famous 'House of Thrills' serial, which was later revived in Film Fun, as were the Bullseye serials.
Amongst his others were 'The Phantom of Cursitor Fields' and 'Octavius Kay'. Edgar also probably created another famous detective read by millions – Jack Keen, whose adventures ran in Film Fun and Kinema Comic. He was editor for a short while of The Nelson Lee Library in the 1928-30 period. In the early 30's he made a very successful name as a playwright; and under the name of 'Barrie Lyndon' he wrote the long-running

play 'The Amazing Dr Clitterhouse', which was produced at the Haymarket Theatre in London; and transferred after many months to the Savoy. Later this ran on Broadway, New York and was made into a Hollywood film featuring Edward G. Robinson. It is today still a firm repertory favourite and has been shown on TV. Another great success of his (also filmed) was 'The Man from Half-Moon Street'.

He later went to Hollywood to write scripts, one of which was for a screen success version of Mrs Belloc Lowdes' 'The Lodger' (based on the story of Jack the Ripper).

During his 15 years of writing for juveniles he had an exceptionally large output, but unfortunately he does not remember much of his old work, and regards it mainly as a closed book.

Pen-names: Tom Rogers. Patsy Hendren (ghosted for the famous cricketer). Barrie Lyndon. Roger Fowey. Jake Denvers. Howard Steele. Hylton Gregory (one S.B.L., 2nd story). Edgar Sayers. Steven Ryder.

Surprise (anon). Startler (anon). Union Jack (2nd) (anon). Gem (2nd). Champion. Sports Budget (1st). Football & Sports Favourite. Rocket. Bullseye (anon). Football & Sports Lib. B.F.L. (1st and 2nd). Boys Favourite. Boys Realm of Sport & Adventure. Football Weekly. Nelson Lee Lib. (1st and 2nd New Series). Young Britain (1st). Popular (2nd). Pluck (3rd). S.B.L. (1st and 2nd) (anon). Pilot (anon). Modern Boy. Boys Realm (2nd). Chums. Film Fun (anon). Champion Annual. Chums Annual. Holiday Annual.

Edgar, Lewis
Pluck (1st).

Edmonds, Frank
B.O.P.

Edmonds, Harry *(r.n.)*
Started to write as a hobby. As a boy he sailed in a windjammer. He later served in a naval ship-building works as an engineer. He rose from the ranks to become a Major in Australian artillery. Was wounded and gassed during World War I, and on recovery he worked in Naval Intelligence Division.
Chums.

Edmonds, Percy
Union Jack (1880).

Edwardes, Charles *(r.n.)*
>Boys Herald. Boys Realm (1st). B.F.W. (1st and 2nd). Scout.

Edwards, Alan
>**Alan W.**
>Marvel (2nd). Sport and Adventure.

Edwards, Johnson *(r.n. Walter Shute)*
>B.F.L. (2nd).

Edwards, Robert Hamilton *(r.n.)*
>Born 1872 and educated privately. Famous for many years as editor-in-chief of the Boys Friend, Realm and Herald group of papers. Particularly noted for his frank editorial chats to readers, in which he dispensed advice, answered queries, and attacked 'Penny Dreadfuls'. He also wrote several stories for boys, which were, however, not very good. These included 'Britain in Arms', 'The Russian Foe' and many others. He also wrote a serial in collaboration with another well-known author, W. J. Bayfield, though it was suspected that Bayfield did all the writing. It is believed that Hamilton had a serious disagreement with Lord Northcliffe, after an association of some 20 years, and the outcome was that he resigned.
>Towards the end of his life he lost most of his money as a racehorse owner, and some other business ventures in Ireland were also unsuccessful. He was at one time a managing director of Amalgamated Press, and also worked for George Newnes. He died in 1932.
>**Pen-names:** E. Gordon Grant. W. Sapte.
>Boys Friend Weekly (1st and 2nd). B.F.L. (1st). Pluck (1st). Marvel (1st and 2nd).

Edwards, R. W. K.
>B.O.P.

Edwards, Walter *(r.n. Walter Shute)*
>Greyfriars Herald (2nd). Pluck (2nd). S.B.L. (2nd). Gem (2nd). Boys Realm of Sport & Adventure. Thriller. Sports Budget (2nd). Boys Favourite. Boys Realm Football & Sports Lib. B.F.L. (1st and 2nd). Boys Journal. Football & Sports Lib. Ranger (1st). Pioneer. Chums. Boys Friend Weekly (2nd). Boys Realm (1st and 2nd). Magnet. Union Jack. Football & Sports Favourite. Holiday Annual. Popular Book of Boys Stories.

Egan, Pierce
One of the mid-19th century's most prolific and popular authors of 'Penny Dreadfuls'. Wrote for Edward Lloyd and several other publishers, and had a *penchant* for scenes of cruelty and slaughter. Amongst his many titles were 'The London Apprentice', 'Quintin Maysys the Blacksmith of Antwerp' and 'Robin Hood and Little John'. Several of his stories appeared as serials in the London Journal.

Egliston, E. H.
Nugget Library.

Eiloart, Mrs
B.O.P.

Eke, G. S.
Modern World.

Elias, Frank
Wrote several stories for the B.O.P. in the 1920's, including an historical yarn called 'The Mystery of the Mayflower' and four serials. Had many books published, including two adapted from the above-mentioned serials.
B.O.P.

Eliot, George
Lads and Lassies Library.

Eliot, Major George Fielding   *(r.n.)*
Modern Boy. Modern Boy Annual.

Elkington, W. M.
Young England. Captain.

Ellbar, George
B.O.P. Captain.

Elliott, J. Arthur
Union Jack (1st).

Elliott, Michael
Football & Sports Favourite.

Elliott, Robert Cowell   *(r.n.)*
Wrote a single S.B.L. in 1930 (No 244 – 2nd series), 'The Phantom Bat', and also a few stories in other juvenile fiction. His main speciality was romantic fiction, in which he was a prolific contributor to women's magazines.
Mr Elliott had, for a time, served in the French Foreign Legion, and put his experiences to good use in his stories. He once

shared a flat with those other two great authors of Sexton Blake
– G. H. Teed and Gwyn Evans.

S.B.L. (2nd).

Elliott, William James *(r.n.)*

Wrote at least one Sexton Blake story for the Union Jack around
Christmas 1931, when the usual contributor, Gwyn Evans, was
indisposed. Also published many books, ranging from Ameri-
can-type thrillers to historical romances. Herbert Jenkins published several of them in the 1930's and at least another 30 were
brought out by Gerald Swan Ltd in the 1940's. Mainly, Elliott
wrote for minor magazines and his work can be found in the
Gramol-type libraries.

Union Jack (2nd). Chums. Gramol Thrillers.

Ellis, Frank

Champion.

Ellison, Dick

Schoolboys Pocket Lib. (Swan).

Ellison, Ellis *(r.n. E. L. Snell)*

Union Jack (1st and 2nd). Marvel (1st).

Ellson, Ellis *(r.n. E. L. Snell)*

B.F.W. (2nd). Young Britain (1st). Pluck (1st and 2nd). Boys
Herald.

Elston, Alan Vaughan

Thriller.

Ely, George

(All details are given under the pen-name of Herbert Strang.)

Emmett Brothers

The five Emmett Brothers (William, Lawrence, George, Henry
C. and Robert) ran their own publishing house headed by the
two first-named. They issued many popular boys' papers during
the latter half of the 19th century, including such titles as
'Young Gentleman's Journal', 'Young Gentleman of Britain',
'Rover's Log', 'Sons of Britannia' and 'The Young Englishman'.
All were also prolific writers and their stories, of course, appeared in their own papers. George Emmett, who was an ex-
Cavalry officer, and who had taken part in the famous charge
at Balaclava, penned many popular yarns including 'Shot and
Shell', a series of military stories; 'The Boys of Bircham School'
and the early part of the almost classic 'Tom Wildrake's School-
days'. He also wrote for Aldine's British Boys paper. The other

four brothers wrote occasionally under their own names, but more often as W. E. Lawrence, Charlton Brent and Ernest Brent. Later George Emmett junior joined the company and took charge of several papers. The Emmetts had a running rivalry, almost amounting to feud, with fellow-publisher Edwin J. Brett, but the Emmetts' publications, although they did very well, were never so successful as Brett's.

Enderby, W. D.
Chums.

England, Allan
Young Britain (1st).

English, Don *(r.n. Miss D. E. Owen)*
Modern Boy. Gem (2nd).

Enten, Harry
The American author of the popular 'Frank Reade', famous for his 'Steam Man' series, etc., stories which were reprinted in the Aldine 'Invention, Travel and Adventure Library' in the late 1890's and early 1900's.

Epps, Francis
B.O.P.

Ericson, Ian
Chums.

Erikson, Eric
Young Britain (1st).

Errym, Malcolm J. *(r.n. J. M. Rymer)*

Esmark, Dorrien
Comic Life.

Espinasse, Bernard *(r.n.)*
Chums.

'Esses, Emma'
British Boy.

Essex, Captain *(r.n. Richard Starr)*
Boys Broadcast.

Essex, Lewis
    Louis *(r.n. Levi Isaacs)*
Champion. Young Britain (1st). Rocket. S.B.L. (2nd). Triumph. Playtime. Comic Papers (anon).

Essex, Richard *(r.n. Richard Starr)*
B.F.L. (2nd). Young Britain (1st and 2nd). Thriller. Wonder (64-issues series). Chips. Wonder.

Estel, P. G.
Captain.
Etherton, Colonel P. T.
Chums.
Evans, A. Eurule
Chums.
Evans, B. E.
B.O.P.
Evans, B. J.
Boys Realm (2nd).
Evans, Rear Admiral
   Vice Admiral *(r.n. Edward Radcliffe Garth Russell, R.N., C.B., D.S.O.)*
Chums. Modern Boy. Chums Annual.
Evans, Eubule
B.O.P.
Evans, Frank Howel *(r.n.)*
An author who was fond of writing stories of the stage, and who was probably an ex-actor.
Pen names: Howel Evans. Atherley Daunt. Crutchley Payne. Newnes Adventure Library. Champion. Union Jack (2nd) (anon). Popular (anon). Chums. Scout.
Evans, Gwyn *(r.n. Gwnfil Arthur Evans)*
Born at Portmadoc, North Wales, in 1899. Wrote his first Blake story in 1924 after being a newspaper man in Egypt. He soon became one of the most popular and best-loved writers of all time in the field of juvenile fiction. His creations included 'Splash' Page, 'Mr Mist', 'Ruff Hanson', 'Julius Jones', 'The League of Robin Hood' and 'The League of Onion Men'. It was Evans who, by his brilliant characterisations, depicted Mrs Bardell as the amusing and lovable person she is today. He had a slick, racy style of writing, and liked rather bizarre plots, but often he finished off his stories too quickly, as though he had grown tired of them. Many editors said that he was brilliant, mercurial, enthusiastic, but unstable and unreliable. He always wrote his MSS in long-hand. He wrote a few novels and one, at least, was filmed. At one time he was on the editorial staff at Amalgamated Press under F. Addington Symonds, and also edited a boys' magazine entitled 'Toby', but he was so erratic that his tenure did not last long.

His father was a Welsh clergyman, and his great-aunt was 'George' Eliot, the classic writer. He died at a very early age (he was only 39) on the 7th April 1938, at Paddington Hospital.

A book could be written about the colourful character of Gwyn Evans, but an expert on Blake lore summed up everything admirably when he remarked that 'Evans never created anyone in his stories so remarkable as himself.' He left a widow and daughter, the latter now living in the U.S.A.

Pen-names: Arthur Gwynne. Barry Western.

Pluck (3rd). S.B.L. (2nd). Champion. Boys Realm (2nd). Union Jack (2nd). Broadsheet Novels. Thriller. Detective Weekly. B.F.L. (2nd). Golden Penny Comic. Champion Annual. Sexton Blake Annual. Rocket.

Evans, Hubert
Chums.

Evelyn, A. W. *(r.n. W. Wilkes)*
Boys Herald.

Everard, Maurice *(r.n. Cecil Henry Bullivant)*
B.F.W. (2nd) B.F.L. (1st and 2nd). Popular (2nd). Modern Boy. Newnes Adventure Library. Boys Life.

Everard, Walter
Marvel (1st). Pluck (1st).

Everett, Bernard *(r.n.)*
Editor of the Scout from 1910 until about 1914. He was brother of its first editor, Percy W. Everett.
Scout.

Everett, Percy W. *(r.n.)*
Born at Ipswich, 1870. Educated there and at Trinity College, Cambridge. Was with the editorial management of C. Arthur Pearson Ltd. from 1893 until 1933. The first editor of Scout in 1908, but only held the post for a short time. Was Deputy Chief Scout to Lord Baden-Powell, and later he was knighted.
Lived at Elstree, Herts.

Everett-Green, Evelyn *(r.n.)*
Born 1856. Popular light novelist of the late 19th/early 20th century. Also wrote books for children. Amongst her adult titles were 'The Last of the Dacres', 'Dare Lorimer's Heritage', 'The Heir of Hawcombe Hall' and 'Dufferims Keep'. Also contributed many serials to magazines. She also had the distinction of writing the second serial to appear in Chums, an adventure

story called 'The Haunted House at Hoe', in Vol I, 1892. Miss Green once wrote a story entitled 'Greyfriars' but it had no relation to Frank Richards' famous school.

Chums. Lads and Lassies Lib. Young England.

Eves, Reginald T. *(r.n.)*

Started as a junior sub-editor on the Companion Papers in 1908, when he worked in the Magnet and Gem office. Wrote a few of the early substitute stories of St Jim's. During the First World War he became editor of the Boys Friend, and was considered to be an expert on all Charles Hamilton's writings. An assessment of the very large number of readers of the female sex gave him the idea of bringing out a school-story paper for girls. This was called 'The Schoolfriend', and it had Bessie Bunter in the leading role in stories of Cliff House. The first six were written by Charles Hamilton, and other writers followed. Very soon it was a great success.

Later he took over the Champion group of papers from F. Addington Symonds, which included The Triumph and Rocket. He was so conscientious where his readers were concerned that he often took their letters home with him to answer. In his early days he wrote stories, and probably his best-known were those of Redcliffe School for the Boys Friend, in which he introduced Greyfriars and St Jim's. These were under the 'Herbert Britton' pen-name. Later, stories were written about 'Jack Jackson' and 'Barker the Bounder'. Eventually, he was made a Director of the firm and retired some years ago after over 50 years' service.

Probably R. T. Eves has the distinction of being the only editor ever to reject a Hamilton manuscript. The story in question was one of a popular series of Rookwood.

R. T. Eves lives at Bexhill, Sussex.

Pen-names: Herbert Britton. Martin Clifford (Gem). Owen Conquest (B.F.W.).

Boys Realm (2nd). St Frank's stories (anon).

Ex Constable Y.

Chums Annual.

Ex Private

Aldine War Stories.

Fairbanks, Nat *(r.n. C. L. Pearce)*

B.F.L. (1st).

Fairfield, Charles
British Boy.
Fairlie, Gerard *(r.n.)*
Born London, 1889, and educated at Downside and R.M.C., Sandhurst. Was on the staff of The Times, Britannia and The Bystander, and contributed to many magazines. He wrote film scripts in Hollywood, plays in London and numerous thrillers, and was probably most famous as the 'original' of Sapper's 'Bulldog Drummond'. Was a great personal friend of Sapper, as well as writing the stage play 'Bulldog Drummond on Dartmoor', in collaboration with him. He continued to write novels about Drummond after Sapper's death.
Published his autobiography – 'Without Prejudice' – in 1952. Thriller. Union Jack (2nd).
Fairly, T. S.
Chums.
Falkner, Leonard
Detective Weekly.
Fallow, Burnett
B.O.P.
Fane, Essex *(r.n.)*
Buffalo Bill Lib. (Aldine) (1st and 2nd). True Blue (2nd). Boys Leader.
Fane, Rupert
Pluck (1st).
Fanshaw
Fanshawe, Cecil *(r.n. C. H. Dent)*
Modern Boy. Boys Friend Weekly (2nd). Champion. Champion Lib. Triumph. Boys Realm (2nd). Gem (2nd). Popular Book of Boys Stories. Champion Annual. Greyfriars Holiday Annual. Scout.
Farjeon, Joseph Jefferson *(r.n.)*
Born in London, 1883. Educated at Peterborough Lodge and privately. Author and playwright. Wrote many novels, sometimes using the names of Leonard White and Anthony Swift. Held various editorial posts with the Amalgamated Press 1909–18. Brother of Eleanor Farjeon. Died 7th June, 1955.
Farley, C. R. L.
Lot O' Fun (in collaboration with L. H. Woods).

Farmer, Henry *(r.n.)*
Educated at Harrow and Oxford University. Rowed for the latter in the Oxford versus Cambridge Boat Race. Was later an actor for a time and was the original Charley in 'Charley's Aunt'. Was literary editor of the Daily Express and as an author was on the staff of Big Budget from its beginning in 1897. He was seldom absent from its pages for some years afterwards, and he specialised in exciting, fast-moving adventure stories.
Pen-name: Franklin Wright.
Marvel (1st). Boys Friend Weekly (2nd). Boys Leader. Big Budget.

Farquhar, George G.
Boys Friend Weekly (1st). Captain. Chums. Boys Life.

Farris, Herbert
Scout.

Farrow, George Edward (Captain) *(r.n.)*
Born 1866, author of a number of books and contributed to adult magazines such as Pall Mall Magazine, etc.
Captain.

Faust, Frederick *(r.n.)*
Born 19th May 1892. One of the most prolific writers of the century, his numerous books, mainly Westerns, appeared in several countries under 19 different names, the most well-known being 'Max Brand'. Faust was an American and died from a shell fragment in his chest whilst working as a war correspondent: he was then 52. Most of his original books were published in the U.S.A. by Street & Smith. His most famous creation was Dr Kildare.
Pen-names: Martin Dexter. Peter Dawson. Lee Bolt. Walter C. Butler. George Challis. Evan Evans. Evin Evan. Frank Austin. Peter Henry Morland. Hugh Owen. Henry Uriel. 'M.B.' David Manning. Nicholas Silver. Frederick Frost. Dennis Lawton. John Frederick. Max Brand. George Owen Baxter.
Special Note: Only the last three names are included in this biography as they were used in the Juvenile fiction market.

Fawcett, Captain
Marvel (1st).

Fawcett, F. Dubrez *(r.n.)*
A free-lance writer who has written a large number of child-

ren's books and short stories, also a novel on Charles Dickens's works on stage, screen and radio. This was entitled 'Dickens the Dramatist', and appeared in 1952. Wrote one S.B.L. (3rd). S.B.L. (3rd).

Fear, Duncan
Boys Pictorial.

Fearn, C. Eaton *(r.n.)*
On the staff of Amalgamated Press boys' papers, chiefly the Champion group. Was responsible to F. Addington Symonds for the production of The Rocket. Also editor on girls' papers. Speciality was writing war stories.
Pen-names: Jim Merrick. Herbert Macrae. Peter Lang. Rocket. Pluck (3rd). Champion.

Felton, Frederick A. *(r.n.)*
Pen-name: Jack Armstrong.
Boys Realm (1st).

Fenn, Clive Robert *(r.n.)*
Born at Fifield, Essex, approximately 1870. Was the son of the famous Victorian boys' writer, George Manville Fenn, and had a brother who was an artist. Contributed to many adult magazines, and was the author of several boys' books as well as writing stories, but he never reached the same height of fame as his father. Was Competitions editor of the Amalgamated Press, and also held a post on the Magnet/Gem group of papers. His job was to answer the hundreds of readers' letters that poured in, and he often wrote 50 lengthy replies in one day.
He wrote an article in 'Tom Merry's Annual' in 1949. Lived for many years at Isleworth, Middx, and believed to have died at the age of 80.
Fun & Fiction. Boys Herald. Pluck (2nd and 3rd). Dreadnought. B.F.L. (1st). Boys Realm (1st). Boys Friend Weekly (2nd). Champion. Gem (2nd). Boys Journal. Sports for Boys. Greyfriars Holiday Annual. Diamond Library (1st). Boys Comic Library. Champion Annual. Cheer, Boys, Cheer.

Fenn, George Manville *(r.n.)*
Born 3rd January 1831 in London, the son of well-to-do parents, his early years were passed in comparative luxury. Then, because of family misfortunes, he was literally thrown on the world at the age of 13. He spent five unhappy years, and later said that he would 'never talk about them and only wanted to

forget them'. Living a life of solitude, and dependent on his own resources for amusement, he soon developed a great love of reading. This self-education led to his entering one of the training colleges for teachers run in connection with the National Society.

After periods of study and probation, he became a teacher at a school in Lincolnshire, and worked later as a private tutor. He went to London to take up writing and after a while began to have his stories accepted by such papers as 'Once a Week', 'All the Year Round' and 'Chambers Journal'. His first book, a collection of short stories, was published in 1866. His first novel appeared in three volumes, in 1867, and was called 'Hollowdell Grange'.

He wrote over 150 books in all, including many for adults. In addition he wrote parliamentary sketches for the London Evening Star, and a series of articles for the Evening Standard. For 12 years he was the Dramatic critic of the Morning Echo and was editor of 'Cassell's Magazine' and 'Once a Week'. He wrote the definitive biography of his distinguished contemporary and great friend, G. A. Henty.

Died on the 26th August 1909.

Pen-name: George Manville.

Boys Herald. B.O.P. Chums. Boys Leader. Young Folks Tales. Lads and Lassies Library.

Fenn, W. W.

B.O.P. Worlds Comic (in coll. with Edward Salmon). Grip.

Fennell, Hugh Wordsworth *(r.n.)*

Was on the staff of the Amalgamated Press in his early years, drawing cartoons for the comic papers and writing many stories which appeared in them, including several of the 'Dr Dread' stories which appeared in The Butterfly. Was an expert on Victorian and Edwardian papers and had a large and varied collection. He died at Kilburn, London, 29th July 1956.

Butterfly. Comic Cuts. Merry & Bright. Boys Magazine. Golden Comic. Monster Comic. Bullseye. Thomson Big Five Group (all stories were anon).

Fenner, Ralph

Champion.

Fennes, Clinton

Union Jack (1st).

Fenton, Roderick
Champion Annual.
Ferguson, A.
B.O.P.
Ferrar, W. J.
B.O.P.
Feveril, Hubert *(r.n. A. C. Murray)*
Chums.
Field, Marcus
Champion.
Field, Peter
Western Library.
Field, Wilford E.
Chums.
Fielding, Howard *(r.n. G. J. B. Anderson)*
Union Jack (1st).
Fielding, Vernon
Union Jack, 1880.
Finch, Bernard
B.O.P.
Finn, Jack M. *(r.n.)*
Issued many adverts in The Boys Herald from his address in
Colchester for comedians' cross-talk, etc., for sale. Writer of
short amusing pieces in many popular magazines.
Boys Herald. Boys Journal. Cheer, Boys, Cheer.
Finnemore, Hilda *(r.n.)*
Born Hampstead, 1891. Educated at Northwood College.
Childrens Newspaper. B.O.P.
Finnemore, John E. *(r.n.)*
Best known for his stories about Teddy Lester and Co., of
Slapton School, which originally ran in the Boys Realm in the
early 1900's. They later appeared in six volumes in book form.
His historical story 'The Black Gallery' was one of the three
serials which began in No 1 of The Boys Realm in 1902. Wrote a
famous scouting story 'The Wolf Patrol' which was published
in 1908. Also wrote a number of other popular books.
Boys Journal. Boys Realm Football & Sports Lib. Boys Realm
(1st). Boys Friend Weekly (2nd). Empire Lib. (2nd) (anon).
B.O.P.

Finney, Escott
Dreadnought.
Fisher, Murray
Chums.
Fisher, M. (Junior)
Boys Friend Weekly (1st).
Fisher, W. *(r.n.)*
Editor of the popular coloured comic 'Rainbow' for many years.
Fison, Roger
Scout.
Fitchett, Rev. William Henry *(r.n.)*
B.O.P.
Fitzgerald, Gerald *(r.n. Gerald B. Green)*
Union Jack (1st).
Flaxman, E. *(r.n.)*
Pen-name: Gordon Grey.
Fleet, Maxwell
Champion.
Fleming, Ronald *(r.n.)*
Pluck (3rd). Champion.
Fletcher, Andrew
Marvel (1st). Also stories by Andrew Fletcher and S. Steele.
Fletcher, Charles Seton
Chums.
Flintoff, Kit H. *(r.n.)*
Boys Journal.
Flood, Paul
Comet.
Flower, Sir Walter Newman *(r.n.)*
Born 1897. Editor of Chums 1925. Chairman of Cassells.
Flowerdew, Herbert *(r.n.)*
Broadsheet Novels.
Floyd, Gilbert *(r.n.)*
Editor of the Boys Realm in 1902 and a Departmental Manager under Hamilton Edwards. Being of independent means, in time he resigned and took to writing. He had a great passion for the sea and his favourite hobby was to embark as a passenger on a cargo ship bound for foreign parts. He would make friends with the Captain during the voyage and on his return

write up his experiences, with a good deal of imagination thrown in. Under the pen-name of 'Duncan Storm' he wrote many stories of the adventures aboard the ship Bombay Castle – a floating school-ship with a group of schoolboys on board headed by Dick Dorrington and Co.

He was also very fond of writing about shipwrecks and cast-aways-on-the-desert-island, and these were tremendously popular with readers. As 'Captain Shand' he wrote about Captain Handyman, though it has been established that T. C. Bridges also wrote about this character, probably when Floyd was away on a long sea voyage.

Known as 'The Skipper', Floyd had a sailing yacht on the Norfolk Broads. He wrote a novel in collaboration with Sidney Gowing entitled 'Sea Lavender', published around 1925. He was also a JP, and is presumed to have died in the late 20's.

Pen-names: Captain Shand. Harry Revel. Duncan Storm. John Grenfell.

Boys Realm (1st) (anon). Boys Friend Weekly (2nd) (anon).

Flynn, Hamilton
Diamond Library (1st).

Forbes, Athol *(r.n. Rev. Forbes A. Phillips)*
Captain.

Forbes, E. Howard
Union Jack (1st). Marvel (1st).

Forbes, Grant
Marvel (2nd).

Forbes, H. Campbell
Buffalo Bill Library (Aldine) (1st and 2nd).

Forbes, H. Wilson
Vanguard (Trapps Holmes). Big Budget. Boys Leader.

Ford, Anthony *(r.n.)*
Sports Budget (2nd). Football & Sports Lib. B.F.L. (2nd). Detective Weekly. Pilot (anon). Ranger (2nd). Pioneer. Boys Favourite. Magnet. Chums Annual. Football Weekly. Startler (anon).

Ford, Barry *(r.n. Joan Whitford)*
Western Library. Comet. Knockout. Sun. Knockout Fun Book.

Ford, Herbert *(r.n.)*
Popular Book of Boys Stories. Chums. All Sports. Nelson Lee

Library (2nd new series). B.F.L. (2nd). Boys Friend Weekly.
Ranger (1st) (anon).

Ford, Quentin *(r.n. Raymond Pothecary)*
Knockout Fun Book (Sexton Blake Story).

Ford, T. Murray *(r.n.)*
Born 29th May 1854 in London. Editor of 'The Joker' 1891 and
'Encore'. Editor of 'Pick-Me-Up' 1897. First novel 'Miss
Tudor' (1897). Manager of E. J. Brett's Company (1900).
Originated 'My Pocket Novels'. Was a captain in the army.
His autobiography was published in 1926 entitled 'Memoirs of
a Poor Devil'.
Boys Own Library. British Boy.
Pen-name: Thomas Le Breton.

Fordcliffe, W. G.
Pluck (3rd). Champion.

Forde, R. Asheton
Chums.

Forder, Walter
C.I.D. Library.

Fordwych, Jack *(r.n. Harold J. Garrish)*
Young Britain (1st).

Fordwych, John Edmund *(r.n. Harold J. Garrish)*
Boys Friend Weekly (2nd). Wonder Lib. Wonder (64-issue
series). Funny Wonder. Chips.

Forester, C. S.
B.O.P.

Forge, John *(r.n. Harold W. Twyman)*
Boys Realm (2nd).

Forrest, Geoffrey
B.O.P.

Forrest, George
Champion. Champion Annual.

Forrester, Edwin *(r.n.)*
Wrote a serial 'Jack Alone' which ran for a lengthy period in
the opening numbers of 'Young Britain'. Was a Civil Servant.
Young Britain (1st). Boys Friend Weekly (2nd). Wonder (64-
issue series).

Forsey, Peter Q. *(r.n. John Garbutt)*
Ranger (1st). B.F.L. (2nd).

Fortune, Neil
Chips.
Foster, Alfred Edye Manning *(r.n.)*
Captain.
Foster, Ernest *(r.n.)*
Born Herts, educated privately. Editor who took over the editorship of Chums from Max Pemberton in 1894 and held the position until 1907. Editor of 'Little Folks' 1890–4. Wrote a book entitled 'An Editor's Chair'.
Foster, Grant *(r.n. Harold J. Garrish)*
Marvel (2nd).
Foster, Rev. Reginald Frank *(r.n.)*
Born in Portsmouth 13th April 1896 and educated privately. Captain in the Indian Army (retired 1923). Ordained as a priest, and in 1940 volunteered for the army and eventually became Commanding Officer of an Infantry unit. Invalided out with the rank of Major. Contributed to a wide range of juvenile and adult publications including Strand and Daily Mirror. Wrote several hard-cover mystery novels, and many other types of books. Also many radio plays. In 1938 he wrote his autobiography entitled 'Separate Star'.
S.B.L. (2nd) (anon). Chums.
Foster, Walter *(r.n.)*
Marvel (2nd).
Fotheringham, E. M.
B.O.P.
Fowey, Roger *(r.n. Alfred Edgar)*
Nelson Lee Lib. (1st New Series). Boys Friend Weekly (2nd). B.F.L. (2nd).
Fowler, Tom H.
Chums.
Fox, Charles *(r.n.)*
One of the leading publishers of boys' papers and Penny Dreadfuls in the latter half of the 19th century. He took over many of Edward Lloyd's titles, including the famous 'Sweeney Todd' and also published many of his own papers, including the popular 'Boys Standard' which started in 1875 and ran for nearly 20 years. His other papers included 'Boys Champion', 'Boys Half-Holiday' and 'Boys Weekly Novelette'.

Fox, Franklin
B.O.P.
Fox, Freeman *(r.n. Charles Hamilton)*
Coloured Comic. Worlds Comic.
Fox, Norman A.
Western Library.
Foy, Peter *(r.n. Fred Gordon Cook)*
Boys Friend Weekly (2nd).
Frampton, H. F.
Chums.
Francis, Stephen D. *(r.n.)*
Was the creator and writer of the famous 'Hank Janson' novels, which have sold in millions. Born in South London about the end of the 1914–18 war. Later he sold the copyright of the pen-name and other authors wrote the stories. Married with two children, he now lives in Spain.
Pen-name: Richard Williams. (Also one of the writers of Sexton Blake under the Desmond Reid pen-name in S.B.L. (3rd and 5th).)
Francis, T. M.
B.O.P.
Franes, S. O. *(r.n.)*
Had a Sexton Blake story published under the Richard Williams pen-name.
S.B.L. (5th).
Fraser, Ella J.
Young England.
Fraser, W. A.
Captain.
Frazer, Martin *(r.n. Percy A. Clarke)*
S.B.L. (2nd and 3rd). Knockout. Sun.
Frazer, Commander R. H. *(r.n.)*
Cheer, Boys, Cheer.
Frazer, R. M.
Skipper Book for Boys. Hotspur Book for Boys.
Frederick, J. George *(r.n.)*
Lloyds Boys Adventure Series.
Frederick, John *(r.n. Frederick Faust)*
Lloyds Boys Adventure Series.

Freeman, Alfred S.
Boys Life.
Freeman, Miss E. *(r.n.)*
Pen-name: Jack Freeman.
Freeman, Jack *(r.n. Miss E. Freeman)*
Pluck (2nd).
Freeman, John Henry Gordon *(r.n.)*
Born Croydon, 1903. Educated St Joseph's, Streatham. On editorial staff of Daily Mirror 1918–32. Was 'Merry Andrew' on the Daily Mirror, 1929.
Lloyds School Yarns. Lloyds Boys Adventure Series.
Freeman, (Mrs) John *(r.n.)*
As Nancy M. Hayes was an author and journalist, editor of Scout during the period 1914–18.
Freeman, Lewis R.
Modern Boy.
Freeman, William *(r.n.)*
Boys Broadcast.
Fremlin, Victor *(r.n. George Norman Phillips)*
Union Jack (2nd).
French, Allen
B.O.P.
Friend, Patrick
Boys Realm (1st).
Frith, Henry
B.O.P.
Frost, Conrad
Rocket (N.O.W.).
Frost, C. Vernon *(r.n.)*
Wrote several stories for the Red Circle School series in 'Hotspur'. Also contributed largely for D. C. Thomson papers. An expert on colour photography he wrote several text books on the subject.
S.B.L. (2nd). Rocket (1956). Hotspur (anon). Pilot (anon). Wild West Weekly (anon).
Frost, Thomas
Wrote 'bloods' for George Purkess, including Sixteen String Jack, 1845.
Fry, Charles Burgess *(r.n.)*
Born in Croydon, 1872 and educated at Repton and Wadham

145

College, Oxford. Brilliant all-round athlete who was also Captain of England cricket team on several occasions. Was the first athletic editor of the 'Captain' in 1899 and his contributions were so popular that he soon left to edit his own sporting journal, 'C. B. Fry's Magazine' (1900–13). Was also associate editor in charge of sports for The Daily Chronicle, 1902–12. Wrote several books including a novel, and an autobiography, 'Life Worth Living'. Stood three times, unsuccessfully, as a Liberal Parliamentary Candidate. Was once offered the Kingship of Bulgaria by an Anglo-maniacal Bishop of the Balkans, but refused it. Was a Director of the Naval Training Ship 'Mercury' for over two generations. Wrote the foreword to E. S. Turner's 'Boys will be Boys'.

Lived for some years at Hamble, Southampton, and died on the 7th September, 1956.

Fry, Reginald C.
Chums. Scout. British Boy.

Fryars, Austin *(r.n.)*
Born 1865. Whilst this is credited in many records as being the real name of the author, a writer, T. Murray-Ford, has stated that his real name was Cleary.
Pen-name: Eddie Waters.
Boys Friend Weekly (1st).

Fulke, Commissioner *(r.n. W. J. Lomax)*
Union Jack (1st).

Fullerton, Hubert
Chums.

Furniss, L. M.
Pluck (2nd).

Furse, Barton *(r.n. George E. Rochester)*
Chums.

Gaboriall, Emile *(r.n.)*
Born at Saujon in the Charente Inferieure, 9th November 1833. Began turning out daily instalments of lurid fiction for the ½d press in 1859. Died 28th September 1873.
Tip-Top Detective Tales.

Gabriel, John *(r.n.)*
All Sports. Sport and Adventure. Boys Realm (2nd). B.F.L. (1st and 2nd).

Gabriel, John *(r.n. John Gabriel Rowe)*
Here is an example of an author who used a nom-de-plume and did not expect to find another writer whose real name was John Gabriel. Both were writing in approximately the same period, and there is still some confusion over 'who wrote what'. But an editorial in one of the boys' papers makes it quite clear they were two different people.

Gadson, W. H.
Worlds Comic.

Gale, Alan *(r.n. E. Sempill)*
B.F.L. (1st). Boys Realm (1st).

Gale, H. Winter *(r.n. T. G. Dowling Maitland)*
Pluck (1st). Marvel (2nd). Union Jack (2nd). Boys Friend Weekly (2nd). Diamond Library (1st).

Gale, John *(r.n. H. Openshaw)*
Champion. Champion Library. Triumph.

Galoway, Trevor
Comet.

Gammon, D. J. *(r.n.)*
Pen-name: Fenton Robins.

Gannon, E. J. *(r.n.)*
Pen-names: Beverley Kent. Victor Daring.
Union Jack (2nd) (anon). Popular (1st) (anon).

Ganpat *(r.n. M. L. G. Gompertz)*
Thriller.

Garbutt, John L. *(r.n.)*
A prolific writer of all types of stories for the Amalgamated Press in the 30's. Lived for a time at Leigh-on-Sea, Essex, but at the outbreak of World War II is known to have gone to Australia.
Pen-names: Peter Q. Forsey. John Templar. John Allen. Clifford Cameron. John Brearley.
Pilot (anon). Popular (2nd). Cricket Article.

Gardner, Earl Stanley *(r.n.)*
Born Malden, Mass, U.S.A., 17th July 1889. Lawyer and writer. Author of the famous Perry Mason series now known to millions on TV. Uses the pen-name of A. A. Fair for adult novels, although, strictly speaking, all his writings are for the adult field.
Detective Weekly.

Garnett, Peter
Champion Library. Triumph. Triumph Annual.

Garratt, J. Hilary *(r.n.)*
Chums.

Garrick, John
Champion Annual.

Garrish, Harold J. *(r.n.)*
Probably one of the most distinguished writers, editors and directors that Amalgamated Press ever had. Held many editorial posts from the beginning – Union Jack, Marvel, Chips, Comic Cuts and Pluck. In his early days was a most prolific writer as well, writing all the serials in the comic papers, in conjunction with E. Newton Bungey and Herbert J. Allingham. Probably his most famous was the 'Cookie Scrubbs' series which ran in Pluck and was later reprinted in The Wonder and Boys Friend. In time he became a director and controlled all the comic papers.
He died 'in harness' in 1956, after over 60 years of service.
Pen-names: John Edmund Fordwych. Grant Foster. George Gerrish. Harry Belbin. Jack Fordwych. Wallace Morrell. Walter Everard.
Fun and Fiction. Pluck (2nd). Boys Friend Weekly (1st).

Garstin, A. *(r.n.)*
One of the Sexton Blake writers under the 'Desmond Reid' pen-name.
S.B.L. (3rd).

Gascoigne, Eric *(r.n. W. J. Mowbray)*
Chums.

Gates, Clifford *(r.n.)*
Was on the staff of Amalgamated Press for a short period before the last war. Served under Hedley O'Mant on Ranger and Pilot. During the Second World War he was in the Royal Navy and was killed in action. Wrote one Sexton Blake story, No 735 (2nd series).
Pilot (anon). S.B.L. (2nd).

Gaunt, Hardy
Aldine Mystery Novels.

Gaunt, Jeffrey *(r.n. George Ernest Rochester)*
Detective Weekly.

148

Gaunt, M. B.
Scout.
'Gaunt Wolf'
Comic Life, Boys Weekly.
Gavin, Wilfred
Chums.
Geary, Stanley
Chums.
Gee, Osman   *(r.n. C. M. Hincks)*
Boys Realm (1st). Boys Friend Weekly (2nd).
Geldart, Peter
Young Britain (1st).
George, Ernest
Chums.
George, Fairfax
True Blue (2nd).
Gerard, Francis   *(r.n.)*
Thriller.
Gerard, John   *(r.n.)*
Pen-name: 'The Cherub'.
Modern Boy.
Gerrard, Peter
Diamond Library (1st).
Gerrard, Robert
Modern Boy.
Gerrish, George   *(r.n. Harold J. Garrish)*
Union Jack (1st). Pluck (1st). Marvel (1st). Boys Friend Weekly
(1st).
Gibb, Spencer J.
Captain.
Gibbon, F. P.
Captain.
Gibbons, Harry Hornaby Clifford   *(r.n.)*
Born at Ealing 17th August 1888. Eldest child of Dr Clifford
Gibbons, a West End dentist. Educated at home until 8 years
old, then went to Durston House Preparatory School, Ealing.
At 14 entered St Paul's School. Was very keen on sports and on
leaving school became a draughtsman designer, later working
up to position of Managing Director of Atlanta Light Car Co.
He wrote the score for a Dick Whittington pantomime, and

there met Andrew Murray. He started 'ghosting' for him in his boys' stories, but later established himself as a first-class author in his own right. He was an extremely clever man and could do expertly practically any trade. He incorporated this knowledge into his stories – dentistry, astrology and music. At one time conducted an orchestra and was very distantly related to Carrol Gibbons.

He died at Brighton on 14th November 1958.

Pen-names: Gilbert Chester. Bert Kempster.

S.B.L. (1st and 2nd). Union Jack (2nd) (anon). Many Thomson boys' papers (all anon).

Gibbons, William *(r.n.)*

Born in Manningham, Bradford, Yorks, 1900. Was the son of William Gibbons, a singer and comedian, whom it is believed later changed his name and became a renowned comedian. Was a prize-winner in the well-known Greyfriars competition in 1915. On the strength of this joined the Amalgamated Press and was on the Boys Friend Library under Willie Back. Contributed bits and pieces for the Companion papers – Greyfriars Herald, etc. Also wrote a Magnet story, published in this paper, to which the war-time editor wrote a sequel the following week.

Later, Will Gibbons joined R. T. Eves's department and wrote a good deal of fiction for his papers, including girls' stories under the 'Helen Gibbons' pen-name. In the 20's, however, he went free-lance and dropped completely out of the writing world just before the last war.

Queries concerning his mysterious disappearance have appeared in the newspapers, but it remains another 'case' which perhaps even Sexton Blake would have been hard-taxed to solve.

Pen-names: Dennis Cross. Frank Richards (Magnet).

Triumph. Champion.

Gibney, Somerville *(r.n.)*

Wrote several books, but mainly contributed to various adult magazines.

B.O.P.

Gielgud, Val Henry *(r.n.)*

Born London, 28th April 1900. Educated at Rugby and Trinity College, Oxford. Dramatic Director of BBC.

Thriller Library.

Gifford, Tom
Scout.
Gift, Theo
Boys Life.
Giggah, K. *(r.n.)*
Pen-name: Stan Kenny.
Gilbert, H. *(r.n.)*
Pen-name: Henry Conner.
Gilchrist, S. D. *(r.n.)*
Editor on the Thomson Adventure, 1929–31.
Gilforde, Robert
Diamond Library (1st).
Gill, – *(r.n.)*
Pen-name: Wilton Mordaunt.
Note: Christian name unknown, but according to Walter
Webb, a great expert on Victorian authors, this may have been
a nom-de-plume to cover the identity of a titled lady; but this
has yet to be confirmed.
Gill, Lawrence
Comet.
Gillander, H.
Boys Champion Story Paper.
Gillanders, W. R.
Henderson's Pocket Budget.
Gillespie, M.
Sport and Adventure.
Gilson, Charles James Louis *(r.n.)*
Born in Dedham, Essex, 1878, and educated at Dulwich
College. At 20 he entered the Army and saw service in the Boer
War in South Africa. It was during a period in hospital, after
being wounded, that he first began to write. Later he was
invalided out of the Army with the rank of Captain. He then
began to write for boys and his first full-length serial appeared
in The Captain in 1907–8, entitled 'The Lost Island', followed
quickly by many others from his pen. In the First World War
he joined the Naval Division and served in Antwerp, being
mentioned in Despatches. On his return he poured out further
contributions to boys' papers, including the B.O.P. Much of his
work was done in bed, as he was more or less an invalid through
ill-health and war experiences.

Chums. Boys Journal. Pluck (3rd). Modern Boy. B.F.L. (2nd). Scout. Chums Annual. B.O.P. Captain.

Gladwin, Peter
Crusoe Magazine.

Glanville, H. L.
Diamond Library (1st).

Glen, Rowan
Chums.

Glieg, Charles *(r.n.)*
Captain. Boys Life.

Glossop, Captain Reginald *(r.n.)*
Came from a big brewery family in Hull. Educated at Repton. Travelled all round the world. Was official war artist at Port Arthur in the Russo-Japanese war with famous writer Jack London. Lived for a time in China and Japan and was a mine of information about the customs of these countries. Collaborated with E. Burton Childs on many stories. Died in Spain and was buried at Gibraltar.
Young Britain (2nd). Chums.

Gloucester, Vernon
True Blue (1st).

Glover, Bruce
Wonder. Merry & Bright (2nd).

Glover, G. Clabon *(r.n.)*
Believed died in 1934.
Pen-name: Mark Glover.
Diamond Lib. (1st). Robin Hood (Aldine 1st and 3rd). True Blue (2nd). Buffalo Bill Lib. (1st and 2nd). Chums. Pluck (2nd). Marvel (2nd). Boys Herald. Boys Wonder Lib. Boys Realm (1st). Boys Friend Weekly (2nd).

Glover, Mark *(r.n. G. Clabon Glover)*
Gem (1st).

Glyn, Anthony *(r.n.)*
One of the Sexton Blake writers under the pen-name of Desmond Reid in the S.B.L. (3rd).

Glyn, Harrison *(r.n. Arthur Steffens)*
Ranger (2nd). Magnet. B.F.L. (2nd).

Goad, W. Arthur
Pluck (3rd).

Goddard, Ernest Hope *(r.n.)*

Born in East Dulwich, 1879. Son of Arthur Goddard, the dramatic critic and editor. Was at one time editor of the Union Jack when he was only 17. He remained on the Harmsworth papers for about 4 years, then moved over to the editorial staff of The Illustrated News and Sketch. Later he became editor of both these papers. In the First World War Goddard joined the Army and did a lot of work for the Ministry of Information, being awarded the C.B.E. in 1919. Afterwards he continued in editorial work up to his death in January, 1939, when he was 59 years of age.

Pen-name: Ernest Hamilton.

Goddard, Norman Molyneux *(r.n.)*

Younger brother of Ernest Hope Goddard, and born in 1881. Much more famous, as far as boys' writing was concerned, than his brother. Was on the regular staff of the Amalgamated Press and wrote under the pseudonym of 'Mark Darran' some really first-class Sexton Blake stories. His first was in 1899, when he was only 18. For a long period, when all the tales were anonymous, he and William Murray Graydon almost shared the stories between them. He also created a very popular character named Inspector Spearing, of Scotland Yard, who worked with Blake. Also wrote stories featuring Spearing as a young man, then much smarter than the rather obtuse person he was later to become. With Michael Storm ceasing to write the Plummer stories in the Blake field, Goddard took over, and also wrote other detective series such as John Smith of 'Doring and Co.'. During the First World War he served as a 2nd Lieutenant, and was killed in France in July 1917.

Pen-names: Captain Fergus Haviland. Henry K. Rich. J. R. Cannon. Peter Pergarth. Claude Custer. Mark Darran. Nat Barr.

Popular (1st) (anon). Marvel (1st) (anon) and (2nd). Pluck (1st) (anon). S.B.L. (1st) (anon). Union Jack (1st and 2nd) (anon). Nelson Lee Lib. (old) (anon). Boys Realm Football & Sports Lib. (anon).

Godwin, Frank *(r.n. Richard Starr)*

Young Britain (1st).

Goff, Charles

Modern Boy.

Going, V. L.
Captain. B.O.P.
Golsworthy, Arnold
Captain.
Gompertz, M. L. G.   *(r.n.)*
Pen-name: Ganpat.
Thriller.
Gooch, Stanley J.   *(r.n.)*
Born in 1894. Joined the Harmsworth Bros. Company when a
boy of 14. Was first office boy on Home Chat, where he re-
mained for 4 years. Then he promoted himself to story editor
of the coloured comic, Puck. After war service in World War I,
he was appointed editor of Funny Wonder and Jester. Later he
took over Merry & Bright and was responsible for 'Crackers'.
1934 saw him originate Tip-Top and Jingles, and when Radio
Fun was born in 1939 he controlled 7 weekly comics and 6
annuals.
He died on 29th June 1958, being then editor of Radio Fun and
TV Fun.
Goodenough, Nat
B.O.P.
Goodwin, Charles
Popular (2nd).
Goodwin, David   *(r.n. Sydney Gowing)*
Boys Herald. Boys Realm (1st). Gem (2nd). Rocket. Boys
Realm. Football & Sports Lib. Popular (2nd). Boys Journal.
B.F.L. (1st and 2nd). Young Britain (1st and 2nd). Union Jack
(2nd). Schoolboys Own Lib. Nelson Lee Lib. (old, 1st and 2nd
new series). Thriller Lib. Dreadnought. Pluck (2nd). Marvel
(2nd). Boys Friend Weekly (2nd). Magnet.
Goodyear, Robert Arthur Hanson   *(r.n.)*
Born in Barnsley, Yorks, 1877. Educated at Archbishop
Holgate's Grammar School, Barnsley. When he was only 17
he wrote a serial called 'The Football Rivals' and sent it to
Hamilton Edwards, who had just launched the Boys Friend.
The editor liked the story so much that he published it immediately (No 47. 1895). Goodyear then wrote further stories
and also for Henderson's Nugget. He also contributed to adult
magazines on sporting themes, especially football.
After some years of this he decided to turn his attention to the

hard-cover books and wrote many popular school stories. 'Blake of the Modern Fifth' was one which had a great success. Goodyear also showed a tremendous interest in producing plays and in collecting Old Boys Books. He wrote many articles on the latter subject and could rightly be termed an expert on Victorian juvenile literature. He died 25th November 1948 at his home in Wheatcroft, Scarborough, Yorks.

British Boy. Nugget. Pluck (1st). Boys Friend Weekly (1st). Best for Boys. Ching Ching's Own. Nugget Library. Lloyds School Yarns. Lloyds Boys Adventure Series. Lot-O'-Fun.

Gookin, M. B.
Scout.

Gordon, Geoffrey *(r.n. J. G. Jones)*
Football & Sports Lib. B.F.L. (1st). Marvel (2nd). Boys Realm (1st). Sports Fun.

Gordon, Richard *(r.n. Adrian Murray)*
B.F.L. (2nd). Pilot (anon). Magnet. Boys Favourite. Sports Budget (2nd). Picture Fun. Football and Sports Lib.

Gordon, S. S. *(r.n. S. Gordon Shaw)*
   Stanley
Union Jack (2nd). Boys Friend Weekly (2nd). Scout. Lloyds Boys Adventure Series. Chums. Pluck (2nd). Dreadnought. Marvel (2nd). Nelson Lee Lib. (old). Young Britain (1st). Rocket. B.F.L. (1st). Champion. Boys Herald. British Boy. Boys Realm (1st and 2nd).

Gordon, Tom
Boys Friend Weekly (1st).

Gordon, W. J.
B.O.P.

Gordon, W. Murray *(r.n. William Murray Graydon)*
Young Britain (2nd).

Gorman, Major T. J.
Chums. B.O.P. Boys Torch Adventure Lib.

Gosfield, H. Heddingham *(r.n. Edwy Searles Brooks)*
Nelson Lee Lib. (2nd new series).

Gould, Harrison
True Blue (2nd).

Gould, Nathaniel *(r.n.)*
Born Manchester, 21st December 1857. Educated at Strath-

more House, Southport. Author of many novels about horse racing, and very popular with the mass public.

Boys Realm (2nd). All Sports.

Gower, Craven *(sometimes Lieutenant) (r.n. Ernest Charles Heath Hosken)*

B.F.L. (1st). Boys Friend Weekly (1st and 2nd).

Gowing, Sydney *(r.n.)*

Born in 1878. His first serial was for the Boys Friend in 1903, followed by many more. Probably was remarkable in that he wrote stories about a war with Germany years before it happened – 'Britain Invaded' (1906), in Boys Friend, to give but one example. Wrote also for adult magazines such as Answers and Penny Pictorial. Some of these serials were later published in book form. One book – 'A Daughter in Revolt' – was made into a silent film. He was very fond of the sea and lived aboard his own yacht, where he wrote his stories, cruising on the Thames and in the North Sea.

Dropped out of writing in the early 30's when he was reported to have gone to live in Kenya, but there has never been any confirmation of his death. He was a very close friend of T. C. Bridges.

Pen-names: David Goodwin. John Tregellis.

Boys Realm (1st).

Goyne, Richard *(r.n.)*

Born at Edmonton, London, 1902, the son of a schoolteacher, who later became a vicar. Goyne, in his early days, had some ambitions to become a missionary (probably due to his father's influence) and his first published work was a hymn accepted by the editor of a missionary magazine. On leaving school he studied at the Royal College of Music and won many awards for his organ- and piano-playing. Goyne later worked as a journalist on the Hornsey Journal in London, and later on the Grocer's Journal, then he turned to free-lance journalism and poured out hundreds of stories for D. C. Thomson papers.

The Red Letter was probably his favourite paper; as he lost count of the amount of stories he wrote for its pages. He also claimed to have written more stories for The Dixon Hawke Library than any other author. Probably his first contribution to the Amalgamated Press group was in the form of articles to the Union Jack supplement, and afterwards he wrote a few

Sexton Blake stories for the same paper, and for the S.B.L. But easily his biggest contribution for this firm was in the Girls Friend Library and Girls Friend, as well as for the Champion and Triumph group of papers. Later he wrote many mystery novels, but probably his greatest claim to fame was the fact that he was 'Paul Renin' of 'lurid' book repute (or disrepute), perhaps the forerunner of today's more sensational sex books.

During the 1939 war he served in the Commandos, despite a lameness which had afflicted him since birth. He wrote two books about his experiences – 'Destination Unknown' and 'International Commando'. After the war he continued writing books under the 'John Courage' and 'David Blair' pen-names, and had over 70 to his credit when he died suddenly in 1957 of heart-failure. He also wrote his autobiography, but this was never published.

Pen-name: Richard Standish.

S.B.L. (2nd). Champion. Union Jack (2nd) (anon). Boxing Novels (1st). Dixon Hawke Lib. (anon). Adventure (anon) and probably all other Thomson papers (anon).

Gracie, L. C.
Hotspur Book for Boys.

Graeme, Bruce *(r.n. Graeme Montague Jeffries)*
Thriller.

Graham, Alexis *(r.n. G. W. Brown)*
Union Jack (1st).

Graham, Armitage *(r.n. John Nix Pentelow)*
    Armytage
Boys Realm (1st). Boys Friend Weekly (2nd). Boys Herald.

Graham, Harold
Football Stories. Boxing Novels (1st and 2nd). Racing Novels (1st).

Graham, William
Boys Friend Weekly (2nd).

Grahame, Arnold
Union Jack (1st). Pluck (1st). Marvel (1st).

Grainger, F. E. *(r.n.)*
Pen-name: Headon Hill.

Granby, Phil
Pluck (2nd). Marvel (2nd).

Grant, Anson
Chums.
Grant, A. R.
Hotspur Book for Boys.
Grant, Denby
Marvel (1st).
Grant, Douglas *(r.n. Oliver Merland)*
Pluck (2nd). Union Jack (2nd). Boys Herald. Boys Realm (1st).
Grant, E. Gordon *(r.n. Robert Hamilton Edwards)*
Marvel (2nd). Pluck (1st).
Grant, Harry
Marvel (2nd).
Grant, Howard *(r.n. W. G. Wright)*
At times this name was used in collaboration with 'Vincent Armitage'.
Sport & Adventure. Football Weekly. Sports Budget (2nd). B. F. Weekly (2nd). Boys Realm (2nd). Rocket. B.F.L. (2nd). Pluck (3rd). Boys Cinema. Champion.
Grant, James
Lads & Lassies Library. Captain Library.
Grant, Leslie
Boys Leader.
Grant, Leslie *(no connection with above name)*
Hotspur Book for Boys. Skipper Book for Boys.
Grant, Maxwell *(r.n. Gladwell Richardson)*
Thriller.
Gratton, Herbert J.
B.O.P.
Graveny, Cecil *(r.n.)*
Joined Amalgamated Press in 1922, first working under editor F. Addington Symonds, then on to the Boys Realm, editor W. G. Wright, who had then taken over from John Nix Pentelow. Later he worked on the Nelson Lee Library under Alfred Edgar; afterwards on The Ranger and Pilot. Since the last war he has worked mainly on the girls' papers as well as writing for them. His wife, Doris, is also a writer of girls' stories and has written many popular series.
Graves, Mortimer
Hotspur Book for Boys.

Gray, Andrew *(r.n. A. C. Murray)*
Sometimes with Ambrose Earle (J. G. Jones).
Sometimes with C. Geoffrey Murray (C. G. Murray).
Sometimes with Geoffrey Gray (C. G. Murray).
Empire Lib. (2nd). B.F.L. (1st). Dreadnought. Boys Friend
Weekly (2nd). Boys Realm (1st and 2nd). Boys Realm Football
& Sports Lib. Boys Herald. Cheer, Boys, Cheer. Greyfriars
Herald (2nd). Gem (2nd). Union Jack (2nd).

Gray, Berkeley *(r.n. Edwy Searles Brooks)*
Thriller. Detective Weekly. S.B.L. (2nd).

Gray, Cecil
Union Jack (1st).

Gray, Dane
Boys Friend Weekly (2nd).

Gray, Don *(r.n. Robert Murray Graydon)*
Football & Sports Favourite. Boys Favourite. Football Weekly.
Football and Sports Lib. Boys Realm (2nd).

Gray, Geoffrey *(r.n. C. G. Murray)*
Sometimes with Andrew Gray (A. C. Murray).
Boys Realm (1st). Boys Herald.

Gray, Gilbert *(r.n. J. S. Margerison)*
B.F.L. (1st). Champion. Boys Leader. Boys Friend Weekly
(2nd).

Gray, Henry
Union Jack (1st).

Gray, J. A. *(r.n.)*
Surprise (anon). Startler (anon).

Gray, Kay
Football Novels (2nd).

Gray, Malcolm
Diamond Library (1st).

Gray, Murray
Sports Budget (2nd).

Grey, Professor
Union Jack (1st). Marvel (1st).

Grey, R. E. *(r.n.)*
Pen-name: Ronald Grayling.

Grey, Roland
True Blue (2nd).

Grey, Walter
Captain.

Graydon, H. Murray
Boys Friend Weekly (2nd).

Graydon, Mark *(r.n. Robert Murray Graydon)*
B.F.L. (1st). Boys Realm (1st).

Graydon, Robert Murray
Born at Harrisburg, Penn, U.S.A. and was the son of William Murray Graydon. As a boy he came to England with his father and young sister and it was logical that he too should in time become a writer. Wrote his first story in an exercise book while at school and had it accepted. A later story traced was 'A Surprise for Uncle Samuel' which appeared in Chums in January 1907. His first Sexton Blake story appeared in the Union Jack in 1916 and some of his creations are exceptionally good – The Criminals Confederation, Dr Satira, Paul Cynos, Mr Reece and Detective Inspector Coutts of Scotland Yard. He also created the popular Captain Justice stories, which ran for years in the Modern Boy. Very fond of football, he also wrote a good many sporting stories under various names. Unfortunately, Robert died at the Sussex County Hospital in 1937, when he was still quite young, leaving a wife and four children. Graydon was, incidentally, editor of the Union Jack for a short time during the war period.
Pen-names: Mark Graydon. Jimmy O'Flynn. Don Gray. Robert Murray. Murray Roberts. Murray Hamilton (with G. H. Teed).
Nelson Lee Lib. (old) (anon). Boys Realm (1st). Boys Friend Weekly (2nd). Startler (anon). S.B.L. (1st and 2nd) (anon). Union Jack (2nd) (anon).

Graydon, William Murray *(r.n.)*
Born at Harrisburg, Penn, U.S.A., 11th February 1864. Was the son of a prominent attorney in that city. Indeed, William Murray Graydon – who in later years was to write so much on history – could trace his own family back to the days of the Roundheads, and his great-grandfather went to America in 1730. On leaving school William first worked in a bank, but after five years decided to turn his talents to full-time writing. After writing prolifically for many American papers he came to

160

England with his wife, Pearl, and two children. He liked England so much that he made it his permanent home.

Graydon poured out thousands of stories for all types of papers, and also some high-class historical novels. In the Blake field he created Mrs Bardell and Pedro, and his own Yard man, Inspector Widgeon. In 1928 he completed the 'double' by having written 100 Blake stories in the Union Jack and 100 in the S.B.L. Other detectives he created in other stories were Carfax Baines, Gordon Fox, Abel Link and Derek Clyde, who also featured in some Scottish newspapers. In the early 1930's Graydon retired from writing and settled for a while in Paris; later, at the outbreak of war, he returned to England and lived in Cornwall.

The death of his wife came as a tremendous shock. Afterwards he fell ill and his daughter took a deep interest in her father's works and career, and spent the last few years with him. He eventually died on the 5th April 1946.

Pen-names: Tom Olliver (at times). Alfred Armitage. William Murray Gordon. G. Murray Graydon (at times probable misprints). William Murray.

Greyfriars Herald (2nd). B.F.L. (1st and 2nd). Pluck (1st, 2nd and 3rd). Nugget Lib. S.B.L. (1st) (anon). S.B.L. (2nd). Boys Journal. Cheer, Boys, Cheer. Detective Lib. Champion. Boys Herald. Boys Friend Weekly (1st and 2nd). Boys Realm (1st). Nelson Lee Lib (old). Union Jack (2nd). Popular (1st) (anon). Football and Sports Lib. (anon). True Blue (2nd). Nuggets.

Grayson, Hubert
All Sports.

Greaves, Captain H. B.
Modern Boy.

Greaves, Norman   *(r.n. Edwy Searles Brooks)*
Cheer, Boys, Cheer. Boys Herald.

Green, Chaile
Boys Torch Adventure Library.

Green, Gerald B.   *(r.n.)*
   Pen-name: Gerald Fitzgerald.
Pluck (1st). Marvel (1st).

Green, Oliver
Captain.

Greene, L. Patrick *(r.n.)*
Modern Boy.
Greene, W. T.
B.O.T.
Greening, Hamilton *(r.n. Charles Hamilton)*
Funny Cuts.
Greenlaw, John
Boys Torch Adventure Library.
Greenwood, James
Young Men of Great Britain. Young Gentlemen of Great
Britain. Boys World. Our Boys Paper. New Boys Paper. Boys
Pocket Lib.
Greenwood, Robin
Scout. Chums.
Gregor, Elmer Russell
Scout.
Gregory, Dave *(r.n. W. T. Taylor)*
Ranger (2nd). B.F.L. (2nd).
Gregory, Duncan
Merry & Bright (2nd).
Gregory, Harry
Picture Fun.
Gregory, Hylton *(r.n. H. Egbert Hill)*
This name was used at times by Jack Lewis and Alfred Edgar
in the S.B.L.
S.B.L. (2nd and 3rd).
Greig, Gustav
B.O.P.
Grenfell, John *(r.n. Gilbert Floyd)*
Boys Journal. B.F.L. (1st). Pluck (2nd). Boys Friend Weekly
(2nd). Playtime. Wonderland Tales.
Gresham, Ivor *(r.n. Miss Ian Grosvenor)*
Chums.
Grey, Carlton *(r.n. C. H. Bullivant)*
According to C. H. Bullivant, he wrote boys' stories under this
name, but so far they have not been traced.
Grey, Gordon *(r.n. E. Flaxman)*
Magnet.
Grey, Ivor
Chums.

Grey, John
Boys Wonder Library.
Grey, Zane *(r.n.)*
Born Zanesville, Ohio. Educated University of Pennsylvania.
World-famous writer of Western stories.
Marvel (2nd). Boys Cinema. Golden Mag.
Gribble, Leonard Reginald *(r.n.)*
Born in London. Educated at the Technical Institute, and
Polytechnic. Joined George Harrap and Co., 1924. Literary
Adviser to a group of London Publishers.
Thriller. Wild West Weekly (anon).
Grierson, Francis Durham *(r.n.)*
Educated St Dunstan's College and privately. Editor of Lloyds
4d. Libraries.
Thriller.
Grieve, Alison
B.O.P.
Griffin, George
Young England.
Griffin, Sercombe
B.O.P.
Griffith, Percy *(r.n.)*
Editor at Amalgamated Press, the man who conceived the idea
of the The Magnet and Gem, and later The Empire Library.
Frank Richards writes at length about him in his autobio-
graphy; Griffith wrote (unknown to Charles Hamilton) some
of the early substitute stories and rewrote a number of B.F.L.s.
He was also the V.C. whom Frank Richards refers to in his
autobiography. Left the Magnet and Gem suddenly and went
to live abroad in 1911. Unfortunately, no further details are
known, as nothing more has been heard of him since just before
the First World War. Was succeeded on the Companion papers
by H. A. Hinton.
Pen-name: Martin Clifford.
Gem. Popular (1st).
Griffiths, Major Arthur
Grip.
Griffiths, Maurice *(r.n. C. D. Lowe)*
Gem (2nd).

Griffiths, Col. R. Boscowen
Boys Journal.
Grimley, Vivian Edmund *(r.n.)*
Was sub-editor on Boys Cinema, 1934. Compiler of Picture
Show's Who's Who on the Screen.
Grimmond, David *(r.n.)*
Editor at one period on The Adventure.
Grimshaw, Mark *(stock name of several authors)*
Special Note: It has been established that many authors wrote
about the famous detective, Colwyn Dane, in the Champion.
E. L. McKeag wrote about 33 stories, with H. W. Belfield
writing them from 1939 until the end; and other authors
filling in odd gaps. It is believed that E. R. Home-Gall started
the series.
Champion. Champion Library. Champion Annual.
Groom, Arthur *(r.n.)*
Born Hove, Sussex. Educated at Whitgift School, Croydon.
Journalist and lecturer. Has written over 100 books and is also
a broadcaster. Took over from Enid Blyton and wrote Sunny
Stories for 2 years. Was a Captain in the R.A.P.C. in the last
war.
Chums. B.O.P.
Groom, Captain Coleman
Marvel (1st). Funny Cuts. Worlds Comic.
Groser, Horace George *(r.n.)*
Editor of Young England in the 1920's.
Grosse, Charles
Knockout Fun Book.
Grosvenor, Ian (Mrs) *(r.n.)*
Pen-names: Reginald King. Ivor Gresham.
Chums.
Groves, William E. *(r.n.)*
Pen-name: Ernest Scott.
Football & Sports Favourite. Football & Sports Lib. Grey-
friars Herald (2nd). B.F.L. (1st). Union Jack (2nd).
Gull, Cyril Ranger *(r.n.)*
Born 1875.
Aldine Mystery Novels.
Gumley, F. W.
B.O.P.

Gunn, Geoffrey
  Champion. Champion Library. Champion Annual.
Gunn, Victor   *(r.n. Edwy Searles Brooks)*
  Thriller.
Gurdon, John Everard   *(r.n.)*
  Born London 1898. Educated Tonbridge School and Royal
  Military College, Sandhurst. Invalided out of the Regular
  Army as a Captain in 1929. Began writing during long spells
  in hospital.
  Ranger (anon). Modern Boy. Thriller. B.F.L. (2nd). Gem
  (2nd). Modern Boy Annual.
Gurr, Thomas Stuart   *(r.n.)*
  Captain.
Gutherie, Thomas Anstey   *(r.n.)*
  Born in London 1856, the son of a tailor and educated at
  Cambridge University. Studied law and in 1881 was called to
  the Bar. Turned to full-time writing following the success of
  his novel 'Vice Versa'. This story is considered to be one of the
  most entertaining school stories ever written.
  Pen-name: F. Anstey.
Guthrie, Archibald   *(r.n. Frank H. Shaw)*
  Chums.
Gwyne, Reginald
  Diamond Library (1st and 2nd). Racing Novels (1st).
Gwynne, Arthur   *(r.n. Gwynfil Arthur Evans)*
  (sometimes with Henry Valentine)
  Rocket. Monster Comic.
Hadath, John Edward Gunby   *(r.n.)*
  Born in Owersby, Lincs, and educated at St Edmund's School,
  Canterbury, where he was the school captain. Later he
  attended Peterhouse College, Cambridge. A schoolmaster and
  also an author he became famous for his authentic and true-to-
  life school stories. His first 'Foozle's Brilliant Idea' appeared in
  the Captain in 1909, and he wrote many others, plus serials,
  until the end of the paper in 1924. Probably his most popular
  character was 'Sparrow' and this appeared also in book form.
  Many of his books were translated into French, and even into
  Braille. A first-class sportsman, he won all his colours at school
  for rugby, soccer and cricket. In World War I he saw active
  service, and on his return became a member of the Inner

Temple; also played cricket for the Gentlemen of Surrey. Despite all his qualifications, his handwriting was said to be almost unreadable, except by his wife, and it was she who typed all his manuscripts before they went to the publishers. Hadath lived at Cricklewood, North West London, and died in January 1954. His books – of which more than 60 were published – are considered to be classics of public-school life.

Pen-names: James Duncan. Shepperd Pearson. John Mowbray. Felix O'Grady.

Modern Boy. Chums. Captain. B.O.P. Chums Annual.

Hadfield, Robert L. *(r.n.)*
Detective Weekly. Union Jack (2nd).

Haggard, Sir Henry Rider *(r.n.)*
Born in Bradenham, Norfolk, 1856. The son of a barrister, he was educated at Ipswich Grammar School. In 1875 was Secretary to the Governor of Natal, and from 1877–79 was Registrar of Transvaal High Court. In 1880 he returned to England and studied law, being called to the Bar in 1884. His novel 'King Solomon's Mines', which was written in 1885, was such a success that he quickly gave up the law and continued to write further novels. 'Allan Quatermain', a sequel to 'King Solomon's Mines', followed, then came 'She', 'Nada the Lily', 'Ayesha', 'Montezuma's Daughter', and 'She and Allan'. He was knighted in 1919 and his books sold (and are still selling) in millions.

Many of his novels have been filmed, in some cases more than once.

Rider Haggard died in 1925.

Marvel (2nd).

Haggeston, Scrope *(r.n. — Richardson)*
Union Jack (1st).

Haines, E.
Chatterbox.

Hale, Clement *(r.n. Arthur Steffens)*
Note: Sometimes Clement Hale and A. S. Hardy.
Boys Realm Football & Sports Library. Pluck (2nd). Dreadnought. Marvel (2nd). Boys Realm (1st and 2nd). Nelson Lee Lib. (old). Boys Herald. B.F.L. (1st and 2nd).

Hale, Geoffrey
Young Britain (1st).

Hale

Hale, Innis   *(r.n. Samuel Clarke Hook)*
Gem (2nd). B.F.L. (2nd).

Hale, Martin   *(r.n. George E. Rochester)*
George Rochester claimed to have written stories under this name, but so far they have not been traced.

Hales, A. G.   *(r.n.)*
Born 1870, and editor of Cassell's 'New Boys World' 1906–7. Also author of several serials in this magazine. Hales, who was known to his acquaintances as 'Smiler' and as 'Hale and Hearty', had certainly led a most colourful life. He was war correspondent, soldier, big-game hunter, gold prospector and globe-trotter, and undoubtedly possessed the knowledge and experience to write interesting stories.
Later in life he wrote a series about a character called 'Mc-Glusky' and these became best-sellers. He wrote an autobiography in 1918 entitled 'My Life and Adventures'. His books are still selling today, and they are mainly published by Wright and Brown.
New Boys World.

Hales, Andrew
Pluck (2nd).

Hales, C. L.
Chatterbox.

Halifax, Dick
Boys Broadcast.

Hall, Anson
Champion Annual.

Hall, Herman
Marvel (1st).

Hall, James Norman   *(r.n.)*
Born 22nd April 1887. Died 5th July 1951.
Thriller.

Hall, Melville
Scout.

Hall, Percy
Chums.

Hall, Richard   *(r.n. Walter H. Holton)*
Boys Friend Weekly (2nd).

Hall, Rupert   *(r.n. Edward R. Home-Gall)*
Champion. Champion Lib. Rocket. Triumph. B.F.L. (2nd).
Boys Friend Weekly (2nd). Champion Annual. Triumph
Annual.

Hall, Saville
Chums.

Hallard, Peter J.   *(r.n. Arthur Catherall)*
Scout. Sun. Ranger (1st).

Halse, Harold
Champion Annual.

Halstead, E. Sinclair   *(r.n. Edwy Searles Brooks)*
Nelson Lee Lib. (2nd New Series).

Halstead S. B. *(r.n. Edwy Searles Brooks)*
Nelson Lee Lib. (2nd New Series).

Hamer, Sam Hield   *(r.n.)*
Born 1869. Was on the editorial staff of Cassells 1886–1907.
Editor of Little Folks 1895–1907. Was Secretary of National
Trust for Places of Historic Interest and National Beauty.

Hamilton, Cecily   *(r.n.)*
Registered at birth as Cecily Mary Hammill in London, 1872,
but adopted the name of Cecily Hamilton. Educated at private
schools in England and Germany. Was well-known as an
actress and playwright, and also as a first-class journalist. She
was a Director of Time & Tide, and wrote a series of travel
books; but it was under her several masculine pen-names that
most people – especially boys – knew her. As 'Max Hamilton'
she wrote many serials of all types for Boys Realm, Boys
Herald, and indeed was the first woman to write Sexton Blake
stories for the early Union Jack. She was a very firm supporter
of Women's Suffrage.
She also penned many stories in The Girls Friend, when
Hamilton Edwards was editor. She lived in Glebe Place,
Chelsea, for some years and wrote her autobiography in 1935,
entitled 'Life Errant'.
Pen-names: Scott Rae. Max Hamilton.
Union Jack (2nd) (anon). Popular (1st) (anon).

Hamilton, Charles Harold St John   *(r.n.)*
Born at Oak Street, Ealing, Middx on August 8th 1876, being
the sixth in a family of five brothers and three sisters. His father,
John Hamilton, was a master carpenter and formerly a

stationer. His grandfather was a landscape gardener, whilst the family can be traced back to 1771, when a great-grandfather owned houses and The Black Horse Inn in Berkshire. Charles, who was a keen reader from an early age, was educated privately and also attended a Private School for Young Gentlemen – Thorne House School, Ealing.

He wrote his first story in 1885. His early work is to be found mainly in the Trapps Holmes boys' papers and comics, and his output was prodigious, as he was writing at least six stories and serials every week under about 20 different pen-names. Apart from school stories he wrote adventure, romance, travel, crime, humour and serious yarns.

In the autumn of 1906 he wrote his first stories of St Jim's in Pluck, followed by the appearance in the new Gem in 1907 of Tom Merry and Co.

In 1908 the best-loved and best-known school of all time – Greyfriars – appeared in the Magnet, complete with the immortal Billy Bunter and Harry Wharton & Co. In 1910 he once again created a new school in the Empire Library (Gordon Gay & Co.) whilst in 1915 the Rookwood stories of Jimmy Silver & Co. commenced in the Boys Friend. 1919 saw him create yet another school which was to delight millions of girl readers – Cliff House, for the Schoolfriend; although to be factually accurate, he had introduced Cliff House in his Greyfriars stories many years previously. Whilst school stories were his favourite theme, he also created the Rio Kid – Outlaw stories for the Popular, Ken King of the Islands in Modern Boy and, for the same paper, Len Lex the schoolboy detective, as well as an unusual series called The School for Slackers. All this in addition to his original contributions for the yearly Holiday Annuals.

His work is still being traced and there seems to be no limit to his output. With the closing down of nearly all the juvenile papers in World War II, Charles Hamilton seemed fated to disappear into obscurity, but with the publication of the Bunter Books by Charles Skilton (later Cassells took them over), the Tom Merry Annuals, and the B.B.C. series of Billy Bunter, the fame which was so rightly due to him came his way.

His autobiography, published in 1952 (republished in 1962), was eagerly bought by countless thousands of his admirers, and although it was in the main disappointing, it did reveal many interesting facts about the characters he created.

It has been an almost impossible task to record all his work, but to date the compilers of this biography have discovered over 100 schools he created, with a total of about 5,000 stories. So well-written were they that more than 3,111 were reprinted into various other publications. Almost 75% of the famous Schoolboys Own Library was comprised of reprints of his stories, and probably he penned about a hundred million words in his lifetime.

Towards the end of his life Charles Hamilton suffered not only from ill-health but from the worst handicap which can befall a writer – failing eye-sight; but despite this he never failed to answer the letters which continued to arrive from old and new readers from all over the world. Indeed, shortly before his death, Charles Hamilton personally autographed a Billy Bunter Annual for the son of the publisher of this biography, and gave him advice on how to succeed at his new school.

On Christmas Eve, 1961, the radio and TV gave the news of Charles Hamilton's death, which must have spoilt the festivities for a large number of admirers. Probably he received more news coverage than any other writer of boys' fiction, and many mourned the loss of 'Frank Richards', 'Martin Clifford' and 'Owen Conquest'. Mrs Una Harrison, Charles's sister, died suddenly a few years ago, but Mrs Una Hamilton-Wright, her daughter, and the niece of Charles Hamilton, is engaged on the writing of a biography of her uncle.

Pen-names: Ridley Redway. Eric Stanhope. T. Harcourt Llewelyn. Harry Clifton. Clifford Owen. Prosper Howard. Owen Conquest. Ralph Redway. Martin Clifford. Frank Richards. Harry Dorian. Sir Alan Cobham. Robert Stanley. Gordon Conway. Gillingham Jones. Frank Drake. Robert Rogers. Robert Jennings. Talbot Wynyard. Cecil Herbert. Nigel Wallace. Raleigh Robbins. Hamilton Greening. Clifford Clive. Freeman Fox. Hilda Richards (girls' stories).

Pluck (1st, 2nd and 3rd series). Empire Lib. (1st and 2nd). Popular (2nd). Boys Realm Football & Sports Lib. Union Jack (1st and 2nd). B.F.L. (1st and 2nd). Dreadnought. Boys Journal. Schoolboys Own Lib. Nugget Lib. Marvel (2nd). Pilot (anon). Modern Boy. Boys Herald. Boys Realm (1st).

Boys Friend Weekly (2nd). Greyfriars Holiday Annual. Modern Boy Annual. Vanguard Library. (Trapps Holmes) Best Budget. Coloured Comic. Funny Cuts. Picture Fun. Smiles. Larks (Trapps Holmes) World Comic.

Hamilton, Ernest *(r.n. E. H. Goddard)*
Union Jack (1st).

Hamilton, George *(r.n. George Heber Teed)*
Detective Weekly.

Hamilton, Max *(r.n. Cecily Hamilton)*
Marvel (2nd). Union Jack (2nd). Boys Realm (1st). Gem (2nd). Boys Herald. Boys Friend Weekly (2nd). B.F.L. (1st). Pluck (1st & 2nd).

Hamilton, Murray *(r.n. G. H. Teed and R. M. Graydon)*
This story was written by both authors in collaboration. In all probability it was started by R.M.G. and finished by G.H.T. Only one story was published.
Thriller.

Hammerton, Grenville *(r.n. Frank H. Shaw)*
Chums.

Hammett, Samuel Dashiell *(r.n.)*
Thriller.

Hammond, Ralph
B.O.P.

Hammond, Walter *(r.n. of famous cricketer)*
Wally
Story was probably 'ghosted' by F. T. Bolton.
Modern Boy.

Hankinson, C. J. *(r.n.)*
Born 1866, lived at Ealing, Middx. Author of many books.
Pen-name: Clive Holland.

Hanson, V. J. *(r.n.)*
One of the modern school of Sexton Blake writers, who wrote his first story in the S.B.L. 1962. Born in the Midlands his work has appeared in many publications under many nom-de-plumes. Once ran a bookshop, a jazz club, even worked on a fairground. Writes mainly for the adult market. Was one of the writers of Sexton Blake stories under the Desmond Reid pen-name.
S.B.L. (3rd).

Hansor, Joyce
Chatterbox.

Harcourt, George
Marvel (1st).
Hardie, W. Auchterlonie
Union Jack (1st).
Harding, Robert *(r.n.)*
Born in Watford, Herts, 1897, and educated at Dorchester Boys School and Weymouth Secondary School, Dorset. During World War I served in the Dorset Territorials, 1914–19. Later he travelled all over the world, especially in India and Arabia. He used his overseas experiences to write hundreds of stories and articles, etc. He was editor of the B.O.P. 1935–6, and the paper celebrated its Diamond Jubilee under his editorship in 1939. He published many boys' books and was a recognised expert on both military and police matters as during World War II he served with the Military Police from 1942 to 1945. Chums. B.O.P. Modern Boy. Boys Wonder Library.
Harding, S. Graham
Scout.
Hardinge, Rex *(r.n. Charles Wrexe Hardinge)*
Born in Poona, India, 1904. Adopted the name of Rex in early boyhood and was known to everyone by that name, legally and otherwise. His father was in the Indian Army, and he travelled all over India and Burma when his father's unit moved from place to place. Returning to England shortly before the First World War, he lived in Exmoor in a farmhouse, and is one of the few Blake authors who read about the great detective when a boy, and can recall many nostalgic memories. Was also 'brought up' on the Magnet and Gem and delighted to act the parts of the boys with his brothers.
Later he joined the Army but was invalided out in the early 1920's. Whilst working on an orange plantation in South Africa he decided to write a Blake story entitled 'The Black Cloud' and sent it to H. W. Twyman, the editor in 1928. 'Twy' liked it so much that Hardinge soon wrote a sequel. He then travelled to India, where he worked on two of Kipling's old papers, 'The Pioneer' and 'The Civil and Military Gazette'. He also wrote more stories for the Union Jack and on his return to England in 1929 wrote stories full-time for S.B.L., Chums and many other papers.
His own particular character was Slim Corrigan, but he

revived successfully the Lobangu and Losely characters. Easily his best stories were those set in India and Africa, and his readable and interesting style made him very much in demand by editors. In World War II he served as an officer in Military Intelligence and was in fact parachuted into China. Probably this gave him the idea for the S.B.L. story 'The Man from Chungking'.

In recent years he wrote one or two S.B.L.s for the modern Blake, and was in the National Press when he captured an escaped convict in his cottage on Dartmoor. He was last known to be living in South London.

Pen-names: Charles Wrexe. Rex Quintin.

Chums. Comet. Union Jack (2nd). Modern Boys Book of True Adventure. Ranger (2nd). Thriller. Detective Weekly. B.F.L. (2nd). S.B.L. (2nd and 3rd).

Hardy, Arthur S. *(r.n. Arthur Steffens)*
Hardy, Arthur Steffens
Hardy, A. S.
Union Jack (1st and 2nd). Pluck (1st, 2nd and 3rd). Marvel (1st and 2nd). Champion. Detective Weekly. Boys Herald. Boys Friend Weekly (1st and 2nd). Jester. Wonder. Popular Book of Boys Stories. Football and Sports Lib. B.F.L. (1st and 2nd). Empire Library (2nd). Boys Journal. Popular (1st and 2nd). Sports for Boys. Boys Realm Football and Sports Lib. Ranger (1st and 2nd). Pioneer. Boys Favourite. Boys Realm of Sport and Adventure. Football Weekly. Dreadnought. Nugget Lib. S.B.L. (1st) (anon) and (2nd). Chums. Boys Realm (1st and 2nd). Football and Sports. Favourite. Gem (2nd). All Sports. Sports Budget (1st). Startler (anon). Sports Fun. Nelson Lee Library (old, 1st and 2nd new series).

Hardy, E. S. *(r.n. Arthur Steffens)*
Marvel (1st).

Hardy, Philip *(r.n. C. D. Lowe)*
Schoolboys Pocket Library (Swan). Gem (2nd).

Harfield, Edmund
Nugget Library.

Hargrave, Sidney
B.F.L. (2nd). Modern Boy.

Harker, John
Chums.

Harmsworth, Alfred C. *(r.n.) later* **Lord Northcliffe**
From the start of his first venture 'Answers to Correspondents' in 1888 he eventually became Head of one of the biggest publishers of juvenile periodicals in the world – the Amalgamated Press, turning our many of the finest and most famous papers ever published – Magnet, Gem, Union Jack, Thriller, Sexton Blake Library, Nelson Lee Library, Boys Friend, Marvel, Champion, Triumph, etc. Their comics sold in millions – Chips, Comic Cuts, Rainbow, Puck, Playbox, Jester, Funny Wonder, Bubbles, Tiny Tots, Chicks Own, Film Fun, and practically all the comics known and loved by generations of children. Nor must one forget the hundreds of Annuals published by the Amalgamated Press, especially the Holiday Annual, which was issued every Christmas. He became Lord Northcliffe in 1905 and died in 1922. Many books have been written about his life, i.e. 'Northcliffe', 'My Northcliffe Diary', etc. Perhaps a fact not generally known is that he once wrote in Young Folks Tales.

Harper, Gillis *(r.n. H. Crichton Miln)*
Chums.

Harper, Harry *(r.n.)*
Well-known as a war correspondent, and later in the First World War was famous as an air correspondent. Was mentioned (though not by name) in Frank Richards' Autobiography as writing a substitute St Jim's story (though it has been proved since that this was not the first). Later wrote many books on flying, and countless articles and stories on the subject. Was still writing in the late 30's, but since that date nothing has been heard of him.
Pen-name: Martin Clifford (in Gem).
Startler (anon). All Sports (anon). Chums (with Claude Graham White).

Harris, Ernest S. *(r.n.) Sometimes Ernest E. Harris*
On the staff of Amalgamated Press for many years; in fact, he had completed 50 years' service when he retired in 1960. His first editorial post was on Answers Library.
Boys Journal. Boys Realm Football & Sports Lib. Rocket. Pluck (3rd). Dreadnought. Marvel (2nd). Boys Realm (2nd). Young Britain (1st). Playtime.

Harris, G. W.
Scout.

Harris, John B.
Aldine Mystery Novels.

Harrison, Edwin *(r.n. Eric Alan Ballard)*
S.B.L. (3rd).

Harrison, F. Bayford
Young England.

Harrison, H.
B.O.P.

Harrison, J. P. *(r.n.)*
Early editor of Comic Cuts in the 1904–5 period.

Harrop, John
Pluck (1st).

Hart, James *(r.n. James Hart Higgins)*
Knockout Fun Book. Western Lib.

Hart, Leonard *(r.n. Alfred Barnard)*
Boys Herald.

Hart, Sackville
Chums. Chums Annual.

Hart, William S. *(r.n.)*
Name of famous Western star of films. Story almost certainly 'ghosted'.
Boys Cinema.

Harte, Oliver *(r.n. J. R. Stagg)*
Boys Journal.

Hartwell, J. M.
Chatterbox.

Harvey, Alick
C.I.D. Library (1st).

Harvey, C. H. Fox
Scout.

Harvey, H.
Scout.

Harvey, Captain Jack
Boys Friend Weekly (1st). Boys Home Journal.

Harvey, Ross *(r.n. H. Clarke Hook)*
Chums. Scout. Champion. Boys Friend Weekly (2nd). Boys Realm (1st).

Haslar, John
Knockout. Sun.
Hastings, Michael
B.O.P.
Hatherley, Captain
True Blue (1st).
Hatherway, Cyril *(r.n. A. S. Burrage)*
Known to have used this name in juvenile publications, but so
far none have been traced.
Havant, H. *(r.n.)*
Was on the editorial staff of juvenile papers at Amalgamated
Press, probably the comics group in the early days c. 1910.
Haviland, Captain Fergus *(r.n. Norman Goddard)*
Union Jack.
Havilton, Jeffrey
Writer of first-class school stories published by Blackie and Son.
As no stories have been traced in boys' magazines, possibly
this may be the nom-de-plume of a well-known author. Wrote
most of his novels between 1920–45, and they had a very good
market. All efforts to trace him, however, have proved fruitless.
Hawk, Sparrow
Chums.
Hawke, G.
Captain.
Hawke, Captain Robert *(r.n. G. M. Bowman)*
(This name was used at times by Hedley O'Mant, but it is now
established that the originator of the pen-name was G. M.
Bowman.)
Greyfriars Holiday Annual. Ranger (1st and 2nd). B.F.L.
(2nd).
Hawkins, John *(r.n. W. L. Catchpole)*
Ranger (2nd). B.F.L. (2nd).
Hawkins, K. J.
Boys Torch Adventure Library.
Hawkins, Michael
Rocket.
Hawley, George
Captain. B.O.P.
Hawley, Herbert
Scout.

Hawton, Hector *(r.n.)*

Born Plymouth 1901, educated Plymouth College. Reporter on Western Morning News 1917–20. National Press Agency 1920–22. Sub-editor Empire News, 1922–24. Before the Second World War he wrote many romantic serials for Daily Mirror, Star and Daily Herald. Is now Managing Director of Rationalist Press Assoc., and C. A. Watts.
Pen-name: John Sylvester.
Thriller. Thriller Library.

Hay, Montague

Football and Sports Lib.

Haycox, Ernest *(r.n.)*

Born Portland, Oregon, 1st October 1899. Author of many best-selling Western novels. Died 13th October 1950.
Western Library.

Haydon, Arthur Lincoln *(r.n.)*

Born London 1872 and educated at Woodhouse Grove, Yorks. Editor of the B.O.P. 1913–24 and editor of Rovering and Empire Annual for Boys. Later edited 'Lady's World' and 'Our Home' magazines. Penned many stories for his own papers and several novels. These included 'The Skipper of the Team' and 'The Book of the V.C.'. Was Assistant Editor of Nuttall's Standard Dictionary and Nuttall's Encyclopaedia, and also Assistant Director of studies at the London School of Journalism.
B.O.P.

Haydon, N. G. *(r.n.)*

Pen-name: Grosvenor Pembury.

Haydon, Percy Montague *(r.n.)*

Born in London 1895, and at an early age he started work at the Amalgamated Press, with his brother Rex. Their father held a position at the printing works. 'Monty', as he was affectionately known, soon rose in position and worked on several boys' sporting papers. After service in the First World War, where her served as an officer with great distinction (winning the M.C.), he was appointed controlling editor in 1922 after the death abroad of Willie Back. His papers included nearly all the successful ones such as Magnet, Gem, Union Jack, Detective Weekly, Nelson Lee Library, Ranger, etc., as well as the Sexton Blake Library and Thriller. Extremely conscientious, he was always ready to give the young and inexperienced writer a chance, and there have been many tributes paid to him by authors and editors.

Charles Hamilton mentions in his Autobiography that 'Monty' once did him a very good turn.

In time he was appointed a Director of Amalgamated Press and eventually retired in July 1961. He now lives in Sussex.

Playtime.

Haydon, Rex *(r.n.)*

Brother of P. M. Haydon, and editor of several papers at Amalgamated Press, including at one stage the Boys Realm. Died some years ago.

Hayens, Herbert *(r.n.)*

Born 1861. Chief editor for Collins. Also very popular writer of boys' school and adventure stories. Wrote several books including a 'Playup' series, which had such titles as 'Play-up, Swifts', 'Play-up, Kings', etc.

Captain. B.O.P.

Hayes, Ivor *(r.n. L. E. Ransome)*

Gem (2nd).

Haynes, Nancy M. *(r.n. Mrs John Freeman)*

Playtime.

Haynes, Pat *(r.n. Ernest L. McKeag)*

Champion Library. Triumph.

Haynes, Robert

Football and Sports Lib.

Haynes, V. A.

Chums.

Hayter, Cecil Goodenough *(r.n.)*

Born on 4th September 1871 in Queensbury Place, South Kensington, London, the son of an export merchant. Went with Alfred Harmsworth (later Lord Northcliffe) on a fishing expedition to Florida in the 1890's, in the role of secretary-companion. Later became a most prolific and popular author for the A.P., writing his first story in the Union Jack in 1903, which featured Frank Ferret – Detective. His first Blake story in 1906 was 'The Slave Market', introducing two very popular characters in the Sexton Blake saga – Lobangu, the Zulu chief of the Etbaia, and Sir Richard Losely, better known to all as 'Spots' and at one time Blake's fag at school and his close friend.

Hayter also wrote series about Sexton Blake at school and later at Oxford, whilst other popular series had Blake in the Sixth. He even wrote about Tinker's schooldays. All these tales were later reprinted in the B.F.L. A great globe-trotter, Hayter brought a great deal of colour into his stories – apart from the Blake field he wrote about Ned Kelly, and another detective who appeared in the Penny Pictorial, Derwent Duff. A great friend of author C. J. Cutcliffe-Hyne, the creator of the famous Captain Kettle series, he often went on cruises with him.

Hayter came from a very well-known and distinguished family, and 'Goodenough' was included in the names of nearly all the male members. He was related to the well-known actor, James Hayter. Cecil Hayter died at his home, Apple Tree Cottage, Thakenham, West Sussex, on the 23rd February 1922.

Pen-names: Howard Steel (in Champion). Lewis Bird.

B.F.L. (1st and 2nd). Pluck (2nd). Marvel (2nd). Boys Friend Weekly (2nd). Boys Herald. Boys Realm (1st and 2nd). Union Jack (2nd). Young Britain (2nd). Cheer, Boys, Cheer. Rocket.

Hayward, Arthur Lawrence *(r.n.)*

Born in Croydon, Surrey, 1885, and educated at Whitgift Grammar School. Editor of Chums from 1924–26 and also wrote many stories for this paper and others. Was a great admirer of Charles Dickens and wrote many books on the subject, and on historical matters. His books included 'The Dickens Encyclopaedia', 'Book of Pirates' and 'Books of Kings and Queens'. Held the position of Chief Editor, Cassell and Co., and also compiled and edited Cassell's English and Italian Dictionaries. Lived at Beaconsfield, Bucks.

Chums.

Hayward, Dagney *(r.n. J. D. Major)*

B.F.L. (1st). Magnet.

Hayward, William Stephens *(r.n.)*

Comrades. Boys Own Magazine (Beetons). Magazine for Boys (Routledge). Young Gentleman of Great Britain. Young Englishman's Journal. Boys of England. Our Boys Paper. Boys World. Boys Journal (Vickers). Boys Friend (Henry Lea, publisher). Sons of Britannia.

Hazard, Buck

Pioneer.

Hazel, Harry *(r.n. J. Jones)*
Wrote very early 'bloods' and juvenile literature.
Hazelwood, Rex *(r.n.)*
Editor of The Scout since 1954. Also editor of the monthly 'Scouting'.
Hearn, Stanley
True Blue, Diamond Library (1st).
Hearne, George Richard Mant *(r.n.)*
Pen-name: Richard Mant.
Hearne, Jack W.
Chums.
Heath, Bernard *(r.n. Bernard Smith)*
Scout.
Heath, Stockton
Lloyds Detective Series.
Heathcote, Claude *(r.n. J. Harwood Panting)*
Boys Leader. Boys Friend Weekly (1st and 2nd). B.F.L. (1st). Marvel (1st). Boys Herald. Boys Home Journal. Union Jack (1st). Pluck (1st). Big Budget.
Heathcote, Claude Jr.
      Claud
Dreadnought. Boys Friend Weekly (2nd).
Heber, Austin *(r.n. Reginald Heber Poole)*
Boys Realm (1st).
Heber, Reginald *(r.n. Reginald Heber Poole)*
Boys Friend Weekly (2nd).
Hedges, Sidney George *(r.n.)*
Born Bicester, 25th March 1897. Educated at elementary schools. Has made many broadcasts and written many articles on games and swimming.
Chums. Scout. Thomson papers.
Hemyng, Bracebridge *(r.n.)*
Born in 1841, and is believed to have become a barrister of the Middle Temple, but this was never confirmed. Creator of stories about Jack Harkaway, the first of which appeared in Boys of England in 1871. Many others followed, such as Jack Harkaway amongst the Pirates, etc. Probably, at a later date, this series could have been as successful as Jack, Sam and Pete, later characters which today seem so outdated.
Jack Harkaway had even greater success in America, while

Hemyng also wrote hundreds of other stories. He died in 1901.
Boys Half-Holiday. British Boys. True-Blue (1st and 2nd).
Boys of England.

Hemyng, Philip B.
Boys World.

Henderson, Bernard William *(r.n.)*
Born 1871. Author of several books on historical facts, including
some on Ancient Rome.
B.O.P.

Henderson, Irving
Young Britain (1st).

Henderson, James *(r.n.)*
Published his first venture, The Weekly Budget, in Manchester
in January 1861, this being one of the first papers where
magazines and newspapers were combined. He then took up
quarters at the famous Red Lion House, Red Lion Court,
Fleet Street. He also started the South London Press in 1856.
Through the years he published such famous papers as Young
Folks Tales, Comic Life and 'Scraps' which appeared in June
1883; was the pioneer of all the modern comic papers.
Around 1920 nearly all of Henderson's juvenile papers were
taken over by the mighty Amalgamated Press, though unfortunately nearly all were soon 'killed off'.

Hendren, 'Patsy' *(r.n. of famous cricketer)*
Stories known to have been 'ghosted' by Alfred Edgar.
Popular (2nd). B.F.L. (2nd). Chums.

Hendryx, James B. *(r.n.)*
Born in Sauk Center, Minnesota, 1880. His father was owner
and editor of the local newspaper and also the postmaster. On
leaving school Hendryx worked in his father's printing office
and post-office, often travelling over thirty miles on horseback
to deliver the mail. Later he spent many years in the Klondike,
was a cowboy and also a trapper in the wild regions of North
West Canada. In 1918 he wrote a serial called 'Sam Morgan's
Boy' for the B.O.P. but in the main his output was for adult
reading.
His adventure stories are still selling today.
B.O.P.

Henley, P. A. *(r.n. Ernest Protheroe)*
Boys Herald.

Henley, Victor
Chips.
Henrich, H. R.
Boys Torch Adventure Library.
Henry, A. L.
Ranger (1st).
Henry, T. S.
Young Britain (1st). Rocket.
Henton, Collett *(r.n. R. A. C. Batchelor)*
Boys Friend Weekly (2nd).
Henty, George Alfred *(r.n.)*
Born in Trumpington, near Cambridge, December 1832 and
educated at Westminster School and Caius College, Cam-
bridge. Originally went to the Crimea in the Purveyor's
Department, and was soon promoted to the post of Purveyor
for the Forces. Tiring of this work he then turned his hand to
mining; later he went into journalism and joined The Standard,
but soon became restless again and went as special correspondent for the Austrio-Italian War. His first novel was for adults,
in 1867, followed in 1868 by his first adventure story for boys,
'Out of the Pampas'. This was succeeded by 'The Young
Frano-Tireurs'.

Soon he was turning out three books a year, and was considered
the best-selling author of boys' books in England. In all, he
wrote about 100 books, many of them selling as well in America
as in England. For years his books sold over 150,000 copies of
each edition, and many of the stories were also serialised in the
high-class boys' papers.

In 1880 Henty succeeded W. H. G. Kingston as editor of
Sampson Low's short-lived boys' magazine, Union Jack. He
had previously been editor of 'Beeton's Boys Own Magazine'.
Even today, first editions of Henty's work, in first-class condition, are eagerly sought after in the U.S.A. His books are
considered to be classics in boys' literature and when he died
in 1902 even the staid London Sketch reported that 'by the
death of George Henty, the boys of England lose one of the best
friends they ever had'. Henty, who died on November 16th,
was a great personal friend of yet another giant in Victorian
literature: George Manville Fenn. A bibliography of all G. A.

Henty's works will one day be compiled in full, including his obscure contributions to hitherto unknown magazines.
Chums. Young England. Boys. B.O.P. Grip.

Hepworth, Carrington
Coloured Comic.

Herbert, Cecil *(Charles Hamilton)*
Vanguard Lib. (Trapps Holmes). Picture Fun.

Herbert, Charles *(r.n.)*
Chatterbox. Young Britain (1st).

Herbert, Frank
Modern Boy.

Herbert, John
Union Jack (1st). Marvel (1st).

Herde, Rossiter
Ranger (1st).

Heritage, John *(r.n. S. Gordon Shaw)*
British Boy. Sport and Adventure. Champion. Boys Friend Weekly (2nd).

Herman, Julius *(r.n.)*
Born in South Africa in 1894, he was a schoolteacher in Tarkastad in that country. Came over to England for a teaching course and entered the famous Greyfriars Story Competition, although he was much older than the other entrants. He won a prize, however, and on the strength of this was able to get some Magnet and Gem stories accepted and published, also bits and pieces for the Greyfriars Herald and Holiday Annuals at a later date. His photograph appeared in the Nelson Lee Library (April 29th 1929) when, according to the late Mrs Frances Brooks, he was in regular correspondence with Edwy Searles Brooks. He also corresponded with Charles Hamilton. He died in South Africa in 1955.
Pen-names: Martin Clifford (Gem). Frank Richards (Magnet).

Herring, Paul *(r.n.)*
Born in Nottingham and lived there all his life. Wrote many serials for Amalgamated Press and Newnes and Pearsons publications. Had the distinction of writing the first story in the Union Jack in 1894, entitled 'The Silver Arrow'. Later penned a few Sexton Blake stories for the same paper. Also wrote many other series on all sorts of subjects including 'Kit

Carson' for Big Budget and a series about cab-drivers entitled 'Pickwick's Club' for Puck. Had published many hard-cover books, mainly thrillers for the adult market; some published under the pseudonym of 'David Raeburn'. He also wrote many articles for the 'Nottinghamshire Weekly Guardian'.

Scout. Union Jack (1st and 2nd). Boys Herald. Boys Realm (1st). Boys Friend Weekly (2nd). Pluck (1st and 2nd). Marvel (1st and 2nd). Puck.

Herrod, Walter *(r.n. Walter H. Light)*
Diamond Library (1st and 2nd). Boys Own Library (1st). Boys Comic Library. Comic Library. Boys Life.

Hervey, Hedley *(r.n.)*
Pen-name: James Strong.
Chums.

Hervey, M. H.
B.O.P. Boys Home Journal.

Heslop, J. W. H.
Boys Life.

Hessell, Henry *(r.n. Henry Hessell Tiltman)*
Champion Annual. Champion. Pluck (3rd).

Heward, May
Chatterbox.

Hewitt, C. Rawleston
B.O.P.

Hewitt, R. C. *(r.n.)*
Joined Amalgamated Press in 1926 and was on the staff of Mr C. M. Down's departments. Was a sub-editor on Boys Realm and also worked on Holiday Annuals, Schoolboys Own Library, Popular Book of Boys Stories, Nelson Lee Library. Later took over the Gem in 1936. Wrote several articles for various papers, but never any stories. Left A.P. in February 1950.

Hickling, W.
Boys Realm (1st).

Higgins, James Hart *(r.n.)*
Born South Norwood 1911 and educated at South Norwood Elementary School and John Rudkin Central School, Croydon. Free-lance fiction writer 1937–40. Editorial writer in Press Dept., R.K.O. Pictures. On the staff of Amalgamated Press for some years and now does mainly picture scripts.

Pen-name: James Hart.
Boys Cinema (anon).
Higgins, Lewis R. *(r.n.)*
Editor of Amalgamated Press in the early days. Was editor of
the comic, 'Chuckles'. A large man with a figure comparable
to Billy Bunter's, it was commonly known at Fleetway House
that he was the editor who 'seemed to overflow his editorial
chair' in Frank Richards' autobiography. It is believed also
that Hamilton based his famous character's circumference on
that of Lewis R. Higgins. He was not a writer, but an artist of
sorts who is believed to be the Frank Nugent artist. He died
suddenly in 1916.
Higgins, Walter *(r.n.)*
All Sports.
Higginson, John A.
B.O.P.
Hild, H. *(r.n.)*
Pen-name: Dudley Brand.
Captain.
Hill, Arnold
Hotspur Book for Boys.
Hill, H. Gregory
  Harry Gregory *(r.n. Harry Egbert Hill)*
  Harry Egbert
A first-class writer of Sexton Blake stories, of whom still very
little is known. Was reported to have been on the early staff of
Answers. Later he went free-lancing and wrote a great deal of
adult fiction. In the Blake field he created Gunga Dass, the
Hindu arch-criminal who came up against Blake so many times.
Hill had an authentic background in all his stories. 'Jackie'
Hunt, editor of Detective Weekly, when a small boy, once met
Hill, who was related to his aunt by marriage. He saw him
working on his typewriter – presumably on a Blake story –
seated in the middle of the aviary in the garden. With dozens
of birds chirping and fluttering around. Hunt marvelled as to
how he managed to concentrate.
H. Gregory Hill, as he was best known, died before the war.
Pen-name: Hylton Gregory.
B.F.L. (1st). Boys Realm (2nd). S.B.L. (1st) (anon). S.B.L.
(anon). Union Jack (2nd) (anon).

Hill, Headon   *(r.n. F. E. Grainger)*
Aldine Mystery Novels.

Hill, John W.
Marvel (1st).

Hilton, James   *(r.n.)*
Born in Leigh, Lancs, in 1900, the son of a schoolmaster, and educated at Leys School and Christ's College, Cambridge. His first novel 'Catherine Herself' appeared when he was still an undergraduate. His world-famous – in fact, immortal – story of public school life, 'Goodbye, Mr Chips' appeared in 1934, and it was set in Brookfield School. It was written in a very short space of time, and first appeared as a serial in The British Weekly. Perhaps it could be classed as one of the most brilliant and emotional studies of a schoolmaster ever penned. Not only was it a best-seller, but it was produced both as a play and a film – the latter starring the late Robert Donat, who won an Oscar for his portrayal of Mr Chips. Today 'Goodbye, Mr Chips' is in the process of being made into a musical film. Hilton wrote a sequel in 1938 entitled 'To You, Mr Chips', but it never had the impact of its predecessor. Other famous novels were 'Lost Horizon' and 'Random Harvest' both of which were made into films starring Ronald Colman. Later Hilton moved to Hollywood, where he wrote for films, and he eventually died there in 1954.

Hincks, Cyril Malcolm   *(r.n.)*
Born in London, 1881. Educated privately. Was sub-editor on Big Budget and on the editorial staff of C. Arthur Pearson for six years from 1903. Wrote his first story for the Union Jack in 1927 and others followed for the Sexton Blake Library and Detective Weekly. But his true medium was in sports stories and he sometimes wrote the whole of a week's issue in the Sports Budget and Football Favourite group of papers under various names. He wrote several books, including 'The Iron Way' in 1920, and was also prolific in adult fiction, writing many serials and romances for the women's market.

He is known to have contributed to D. C. Thomson papers, which are unknown at present. Died October 1954.

Pen-names: Charles Malcolm. John M. Howard. Malcolm Dayle. John Coulsdon. Osman Gee.

Scout. Pioneer. Sports Fun. Modern Boy. Boys Realm (1st and 2nd). Surprise (anon). Boys Favourite. Football Weekly. Boys Realm of Sport and Adventure. Football and Sports Lib. Sports Budget (1st and 2nd). B.F.L. (2nd). S.B.L. (2nd) (anon). Union Jack (2nd). Ranger (anon). Newnes Adventure Lib. Football & Sports Favourite.

Hind, J. R.
Holiday Annual.

Hinkson, H. A.
B.O.P.

Hinton, Herbert Allan *(r.n.)*
Born in 1888 and was educated at a public school. Joined Amalgamated Press in 1905, and it is said that his family were related to Alfred Harmsworth. Was chief sub-editor on Gem and Magnet under Percy Griffith. When Griffith left suddenly in 1911 Hinton was appointed editor of the Companion Papers, a position he held until he went to the war in 1916, where he was an officer in the Guards. His highly colourful editorial letters, supposedly from 'bad' boys, and his moralistic preaching probably made The Boys Friend the most lurid in that period of its history, though he did start publishing the regular stories of Rookwood in 1915.

Later that year he launched the Greyfriars Herald. On his return from war service in 1919 Hinton resumed his editorship of the Companion Papers, but in 1921 he left to bring out a new paper himself. 'School and Sport' was the title, but although Charles Hamilton wrote the main stories, it only lasted for six months, and the firm of 'Popular Publishing Company' almost ceased to exist.

Later, Hinton edited a children's newspaper and just before the Second World War he was on Dalton's Weekly, as editor. In his early days it is worth noting that he wrote a few of the early substitute stories for the Magnet, and also wrote many of the Gordon Gay and Co. stories in the Empire Library, in collaboration with C. M. Down.

Whilst in a train near Weybridge Station on New Year's Day, 1945, during the blackout, Hilton opened the door of the carriage on the wrong side of the platform and fell to his death.
Pen-names: Prosper Howard (Empire Library). Martin Clifford (Gem). Frank Richards (Magnet).

Hoban, John Staveley
Marvel (2nd).
Hobbs, Jack *(r.n. of famous cricketer)*
Story is known to have been 'ghosted' by Sydney Horler.
Chums.
Hobden, Roger
Boys Torch Adventure Library.
Hobson, Carey (Mrs)
B.O.P.
Hobson, Stanley
Marvel (2nd).
Hockley, Lewis *(r.n. Percy W. Longhurst)*
Boys Herald. Pluck (2nd). Marvel (2nd). Magnet.
Hodgetts, James Frederick *(r.n.)*
Famous for his Early Briton/Viking class of stories. Was once in
the Indian Navy and later appointed Professor of Seamanship
at the Royal Prussian Naval Cadet School in Berlin. Later
worked in Moscow and in 1881 decided to write full-time. He
wrote several important books on archaeology, and his first
serial for the B.O.P. in 1883 entitled 'Harold, the Boy Earl' was
about Early Britain. Others followed, and nearly all his serials
were later published in hard-backed form.
B.O.P. Lads and Lassies Lib.
Hodgson, W. E.
Collaborated with Stacey Blake on a story for The Captain.
Captain.
Hoffman, Professor *(r.n. Angelo J. Lewis)*
B.O.P.
Hogan, George
B.O.P.
Hogwood, Mackenzie
Chums. Scout.
Holby, John
Modern Boy.
Holding, Val *(r.n.)*
Born Melbourne, Australia, and came to England just before
the last war. Served in the Royal Marines and Parachute
Regiment as Captain. Joined the Amalgamated Press in 1957
and has held many editorial and, in recent years, managing
editor posts, i.e. Thriller Library, Picture Stories, Radio Fun,

Film Fun, Sun, Comet, Buster, Famous Romances, Hurricane, Lion, Tiger. At Odhams Press for a year on Eagle, Girl, Swift, Robin; and at present Fabulous and Valentine.

Holland, Clive   *(r.n. C. J. Hankinson)*
B.O.P.

Holland, John
Boys Wonder Library.

Holland, Rodney
Boys Wonder Library. Chums.

Hilland, Stephen Bainsbridge
Chums.

Holloway, John   *(r.n.)*
Boys Own Journal. Union Jack (1st). Pluck (1st). Boys World. Our Boys Paper. Bad Boys Paper.

Holloway, Trevor
Scout. Comet.

Holman, E. S.   *(r.n.)*
Wrote the only substitute St Frank's Story in Nelson Lee Library.
Nelson Lee Lib. (2nd New Series) No 41.

Holmscliff, Captain
Nugget Library. Comic Life.

Holme, Gordon   *(r.n. Henry St John Cooper)*
Boys Friend Weekly (2nd).

Holmes, Andrew
Pluck (1st).

Holmes, Angus
Chums.

Holmes, Con
Chums.

Holmes, Edward   *(r.n. George Edward Holmes)*
Detective Weekly.

Holmes, George Edward   *(r.n.)*
Wrote a serial for Detective Weekly in 1939 based on the radio play 'A Case for Sexton Blake'. Was the last editor of Everybody's. On the staff of many Amalgamated Press boys' papers, and is an expert on armour and other historical matters. Left Fleetway Publications a few years ago and lives in Harrow.
Pen-name: Edward Holmes.
Wild West Weekly (anon). B.F.L. (2nd).

Holmes, Leonard
Champion Annual.
Holmes, Martin
Pluck (1st).
Holmes, Radcliffe *(r.n.)*
Boys Friend Weekly (2nd).
Holt, Geoffrey B. A.
Boys Journal.
Holt, Henry *(r.n.)*
Broadsheet Novels. Thriller. Thriller Library.
Holt, Jack
Modern Boy. B.F.L. (2nd).
Holt, Richard *(r.n. Walter H. Holton)*
Greyfriars Holiday Annual. Boys Friend Weekly (2nd).
Holt, Walter J.
Comic Life.
Holton, Walter H. *(r.n.)*
Pen-names: Richard Holt. Richard Hall.
Boys Broadcast.
Home, Andrew *(r.n.)*
Born in Leeds, Yorks, 1864. Wrote his first story in Chums in
the first number in 1892, and became one of its most prolific
contributors. Liked to set his stories in a school, with an element
of mystery about the plot. Nearly all his serials were later
turned into book form and these include 'Well Played' and 'The
Boys of Badminister'.
Chums. B.O.P.
Home, Athol
Chums.
Home, Edwin *(r.n. W. B. Home-Gall)*
Empire Library (2nd).
Home-Gall, Edward Reginald *(r.n.)*
Born in South London, 1899, and is the son of William Benja-
min Home-Gall, also a writer. Edward joined the Amalgamated
Press in 1914 as an office-boy. His first story appeared in The
Sunday Circle and his second in the Boys Realm. Although
under age, he managed to enlist in the Army in World War I
and saw active service in Turkey. Later he was commissioned
and won the M.C. for gallantry on the field. At the age of 21
he returned to the Amalgamated Press with the rank of Captain.

Like many of the other staff he thought of an idea for a sports paper for boys, to be called 'Football Favourite'; this was accepted, and ran for over 8 years. He also wrote many stories for this paper, probably the best being The Terrible Twins series, in which a rich and a poor football fan changed places. When this series finished he left Fleetway House to go free-lance, and wrote hundreds of stories for the Thomson papers. At this time he also wrote some stories featuring Harry Lovell & Co. for Hinton's School & Sport, to continue where Charles Hamilton had left off.

Later Home-Gall had the distinction of writing the first story to feature speedway racing in this country, and could indeed claim to have made the famous Bluey Wilkinson a world star. At about 1923 he switched his writing to R. T. Eves and for his papers, the Champion and Triumph, he turned out at least three complete stories and serials every week. He also started off the famous Colwyn Dane stories.

Probably, next to Charles Hamilton, Home-Gall could claim to be the most prolific writer of boys' stories. Just after the Second World War he began to produce his own stories in a series of libraries, but eventually the Amalgamated Press took them over. In recent years he moved to the South of France, where a modern character of his – 'Judy the Air Hostess' – is very popular and has been published in many books.

Pen-names: Edwin Dale. Rupert Hall. Reginald Home-Gall. Clifford Clive.

Wizard. Rover. Adventure (all anon). Champion Annual. Wild West Weekly. B.F.L. (2nd). Champion. Football Favourite (anon). Boys Favourite Lib. (1st and 2nd).

Home-Gall, Reginald *(r.n. Edward Reginald Home-Gall)*
Young Britain (1st). Boys Realm (2nd).

Home-Gall, William Benjamin *(r.n.)*
Born in Hong Kong in 1861. His father was a sailor who lost his life when his ship 'The Champion' foundered. This seems ironical when one considers that in future years his son was to write several thousand stories for a paper of that name.

W. B. Home-Gall travelled a great deal in his younger days and for a time lived in Texas, where he was a cowboy. At a later date he came to England and got a job as a coachman. His first attempts at writing were unrewarding, but gradually he became an established writer for the early Harmsworth papers. The Boys Friend and Boys Realm saw the bulk of his work, which included 'slapstick' school stories, some of which also appeared in Chums. He did a great deal for the Boy Scout Movement (like his son, Edward) and was the District Commissioner for the Hampton Court area. He died suddenly in 1936, after a heart attack.

Pen-names: T. Home. Reginald Drew. Reginald Wray.

Union Jack (2nd) (anon). Popular (1st) (anon). Boys Realm (1st). Chums. Butterfly (anon). Favourite Comic (anon). Merry & Bright (anon). Fun & Fiction (anon). S.B.L. (1st) (anon). Magnet. Sports Fun (anon).

Home-Gall, William Bolinbroke *(r.n.)*

Son of William Benjamin Home-Gall and elder brother of Edward Reginald Home-Gall. Born at Charlton, 1894 and educated at Hampton Grammar School. Joined the Amalgamated Press in 1912 and was on the staff of many boys' papers. Probably his most important post was on the Sexton Blake Library when it appeared in 1915. For a short time afterwards he edited the Boys Friend. He served in both World Wars, in The Royal Fusiliers 1914–18, and with the R.A.F. 1940–45; he was also the last editor of Chums Annual.

Wrote very little compared to his father and brother, and after editing the R.A.F.A. magazine 'Air-Mail' for a period from 1947 went into engineering. He retired in 1967 and now lives in Surrey.

Pen-names: Will Young. William Bolinbroke.

Boys Realm (2nd).

'Home Goal'

Football Novels.

Home, T. *(r.n. William Benjamin Home-Gall)*

Chums.

Hood, Robert

Champion Annual.

Hood, Stephen *(r.n. Jack Lewis)*

Chips. Jester & Wonder. S.B.L. (2nd). Champion.

Hook, Clarke *(r.n., not established whether father or son)*

Pluck (2nd).

Hook, H. Clarke *(r.n.)*

Son of S. Clarke Hook. First came to notice for his early substi-

tute St Jim's stories for The Gem, and when he contributed a
story of Greyfriars. His own creations were a series about
'Specs and Co.' of Lyncroft School for Pluck. His pseudonym was
'Ross Harvey' and under this name he wrote many high-class
stories for Chums. It is believed he also wrote a great deal of
girls' and adult fiction.

In all, H. Clarke Hook was something of a 'mystery' writer, as
he wrote in many papers, then dropped out for some years;
suddenly appearing on the scene again. Like his father, the
more famous S. Clarke Hook, his death has never been established, nor indeed has he ever been traced.

Pen-names: Ross Harvey. Martin Clifford (Gem and
Popular). Frank Richards (Magnet). Hammond Paine.
Boys Herald. Boys Realm (1st). Boys Friend Weekly (2nd).
Boys Realm Football & Sports Lib. (anon). Pluck (2nd).

Hook, Samuel Clarke *(r.n.)*

Born in Highgate, London, he was a nephew of Theodore
Hook, the 18th-century dramatist and novelist. Educated at
Ewell College. Travelled around the world in his early days
and became an expert in the Spanish language. He later
utilised this knowledge when he became the chief translator at
the head offices of a glass-works in St Helens, Lancs (where,
incidentally, Walter Tyrer also worked). Later he turned to
boys' writing and his creations of Jack, Sam and Pete became
world-famous. These ran in the Marvel from No 385, March
1901, until 940, January 1922, as well as many originals appearing in the Boys Friend Library. Indeed, this venture was
originally called The Jack, Sam and Pete Library, and was to
contain all his stories, but a 60,000 word output in the end
proved too much, so other stories were included and the title
was changed. Apart from writing about his famous trio (and
the situations in which they were involved were, to say the
least, slapstick) he wrote school stories. Unfortunately his
characters lost their appeal in time and he dropped out of the
writing world in 1922. No record has been found of his death,
and it is quite possible he may have died abroad.

Pen-names: Innis Hale. Innis Hael. Hampton Dene. Ewen
Monteith. Owen Monteith. Captain Lancaster. Edgar Hope.
Maurice Merriman. Captain Maurice Clarke.
Boys Friend Weekly (2nd). Marvel (1st and 2nd). Popular

(1st). B.F.L. (1st and 2nd). Pluck (1st and 2nd). Comic Cuts. British Boy. Gem (1st and 2nd). Nelson Lee Lib. (old). Union Jack (1st and 2nd). Dreadnought. Lloyds Boys Adventure Series. Lloyds Detective Series. Funny Cuts. Worlds Comic.

Hooper, Albert E.
Young England.

Hooper, Stanley *(r.n.)*
Probably better known as a sports writer. Was quite a promising boxer until an early injury whilst serving in the R.F.C. terminated his career. He then turned to journalism and won a literary contest run by the Daily Express out of over 4,000 entrants. On the strength of this he got a job on Amalgamated Press as a boxing correspondent writing (for adults) under the nom-de-plume of 'Roy Brandon'. Later he branched out into boys' fiction, probably his best-known being The Night Hawk series in Startler (not to be confused with the Nelson Lee series). He also wrote some Sexton Blake stories for the Detective Weekly in 1939 taking over from Ernest Dudley.
He also wrote a few Nelson Lee stories in the late 20's (not St Frank's tales). He was a great friend of Alfred Edgar, and in recent years was known to be working on a local newspaper in the London area. A friend of many boxers, as well as being a first-class boxing correspondent, Stanley Hooper was a popular figure in the world of sport.
Boys Favourite. Football Weekly. Sports Budget (1st and 2nd). Football & Sports Favourite. Chums Annual. Football & Sports Lib. Detective Weekly (anon). Startler (anon). Nelson Lee (2nd new) (anon).

Hopcroft, George E.
Lloyds Detective Series. Lloyds Boys Adventure Series. Boys Life.

Hope, Alan
Chums.

Hope, Ascott R. *(r.n. R. Hope Moncrieff)*
Chums. B.O.P. Young England. Union Jack (1880). Boys. Captain.

Hope, Cathcart
Boys Realm (1st).

Hope, Colin
B.F.L. (2nd).

Hope, Datchett
Chums.
Hope, Douglas
Lloyds Boys Adventure Series. Lloyds School Yarns.
Hope, Edgar   *(r.n. Samuel Clarke Hook)*
Union Jack (1st). Pluck (1st). Marvel (1st).
Hope, Edwin S.
Boys of the Isles. Boys Champion Paper. Young Briton's
Journal. Boys and Girls. Boys Popular Weekly.
Hope, Evelyn
Marvel (1st).
Hope, Captain G. A.   *(r.n.)*
Educated at Marlborough College. Served in India with the
Armed Forces and later wrote many first-class short stories set
mainly in Castleburgh School for The Captain at the turn of
the century. He also wrote many adventure stories and a serial
later reprinted in book form.
B.O.P. Captain. Chums.
Hope, William Edward Stanton   *(r.n.)*
Born in London in 1889, he was the son of a well-to-do man in
the publishing world. Started work at Amalgamated Press in
1904 as office-boy, and a little later was on the Companion
Papers staff. After the death of Lewis Higgins as editor of
Chuckles he took his place, but shortly afterwards, during the
war, served in Gallipoli with C. M. Down, the Magnet editor.
He later wrote a book about his experiences and presented one
to C. M. Down suitably inscribed. After the war, Stanton Hope
went free-lance, and wrote all kinds of stories. Apart from
substitute Magnet yarns, Sherlock Holmes stories, Sexton
Blake stories (where he introduced his own characters, Petty
Officer Harman and Mike O'Flynn), he explored many other
fields.
A great traveller, he went around the world many times and
wrote his autobiography in 1925 entitled 'Rolling Round the
World for Fun'. He also wrote on technical matters pertaining
to the Merchant Navy, and many bound books on these subjects were published. After the last war he started the 'Stanton
Hope College of Journalism' in Sydney, Australia, where he
settled down in the late 50's confessing that at his age he could
not stand the English winters. After meeting many members of

the Golden Hours Old Boys Book Club in Australia, and enjoying talks with them Hope died suddenly in 1961 at the age of 72.

Pen-names: Will Hope. Donald Dean. William Stanton. Bruce Denver. Frank Richards (Magnet).

Boys Realm (2nd). Chums. Magnet. Football & Sports Favourite. Football & Sports Lib. Greyfriars Herald (2nd). Detective Weekly. Chums Annual. Pioneer (anon). Ranger (1st) (anon). Pilot (anon). S.B.L. (2nd and 3rd). Modern Boy. B.F.L. (1st and 2nd). Nelson Lee Lib. (3rd New Series). Boys Realm of Sport & Adventure. Surprise (anon). Wild West Weekly (anon). All Thomson papers.

Hope, Walter *(r.n. Horace Phillips)*
Boys Journal. Cheer, Boys, Cheer. Boys Herald.

Hope, Will *(r.n. William Edward Stanton Hope)*
Boys Realm (1st). Boys Friend Weekly (2nd).

Hopkins, B. *(r.n.)*
Had a Sexton Blake story published under the Richard Williams pen-name.
S.B.L. (5th).

Hopkins, Robert Thurston *(r.n.)*
Born at Bury St Edmunds 1883. Educated at Thetford Grammar School, Norfolk, and in London. Literary editor to London International Press. Founder & Vice President of Society of Sussex Downsmen. War service, 1916–20.
Thriller.

Horler, Sydney *(r.n.)*
Born 18th July 1888 at Leytonstone, and educated at Colston School, Bristol. Joined Hulton Newspapers as special correspondent and later worked on other papers as reporter. During the 1914–18 war he served with the Air Intelligence and wrote many books, as well as hundreds of stories for boys in various papers. Probably his best football story was 'Goal' which appeared as a serial in Football Weekly and was later reprinted in book form. He also wrote for adults, and had more than 100 novels to his credit, some under the nom-de-plumes of 'Peter Cavendish' and 'Martin Heritage'. Horler, who had a somewhat unusual hobby (he collected pipes), died on the 27th October 1952.
Pen-names: Jack Hobbs. J. O. Standish.

Chums. Scout. Football Stories. Football Novels. Boxing
Novels (1st). B.F.L. (2nd). Football Weekly. Boys Friend
Weekly (2nd). Gem (2nd). Thriller. Sports Budget (2nd).
Newnes Adventure Lib.

Horncastle, George *(r.n.)*
Union Jack (1st).

Hornibroke, J. L.
Captain.

Hornung, Ernest William *(r.n.)*
Born in Middlesbrough, 7th June 1866. Educated at Upping-
ham School. From 1884 to 1886 he had to live in Australia for
health reasons, and whilst there he wrote two novels with
Australian backgrounds. Returning to England, he married
Constance Doyle, sister of A. Conan Doyle, in 1893. In 1899
his first story featuring Raffles, the Gentleman Thief ('The
Amateur Cracksman') appeared something of a foil to Conan
Doyle's Sherlock Holmes. Other stories soon followed. During
the 1914-18 war he served with the Y.M.C.A. in France and
Flanders, travelling with a mobile library for the use of the
troops. His book 'Notes of a Camp Follower' in 1919 told of his
experiences. He wrote many other novels and also a first-class
public school story called 'Fathers of Men'. He died on 22nd
March 1921; and later on Barry Perowne (Philip Atkey) with
permission of the estate, carried on the 'Raffles' stories.
Boys Friend Weekly (2nd).

Horton, F.
B.F.L. (2nd).

Horton, Lance
Marvel (1st).

Horsley, Reginald Ernest (Dr) *(r.n.)*
Born 1863, and was a doctor. Retired in 1903 from the medical
profession and wrote several books.
Young England. B.O.P.

Hosken, Clifford *(r.n. Henry St John Cooper)*
Marvel (2nd). Boys Herald. Boys Realm (1st). Boys Friend
Weekly (2nd).

Hosken, Ernest Charles Heath *(r.n.)*
Born 1875, and wrote many novels. Fiction editor of the Daily
Mail and sometimes collaborated with his wife on stories.

Pen-name: Craven Gower.
Chums. Boys Friend Weekly (2nd).
Hotspur, Paul *(r.n. Lester Bidston)*
Champion Annual. Champion. Rocket. B.F.L. (2nd).
Houblon, A. G.
Captain.
Hough, Lewis
Chums.
Howard, Bruce *(r.n. George Day)*
Pluck (1st and 2nd). Marvel (2nd). Boys Realm (1st).
Howard, Frank
Diamond Library (2nd). Boys Herald.
Howard, Herbert
B.O.P.
Howard, John M. *(r.n. Cyril Malcolm Hincks)*
Sports Budget (1st and 2nd). Boys Favourite. Football Weekly.
Popular Book of Boys Stories. Football and Sports Lib. Football and Sports Favourite.
Howard, Keble *(r.n. J. Keble Bell)*
Captain.
Howard, Langley *(r.n.)*
Boys Herald.
Howard, Louis G. Redmond *(r.n. Louis G. Redmond-Howard)*
Chums.
Howard, Prosper *(stock name of three authors – Charles Hamilton, H. A. Hinton, C. M. Down)*
Chuckles. Empire Library (1st and 2nd). B.F.L. (1st – this was a Charles Hamilton complete story). Gem (2nd).
Howard, Rowland *(r.n. W. L. Catchpole)*
  Roland
Greyfriars Holiday Annual. Ranger (1st and 2nd). Detective Weekly. Nelson Lee Lib. (2nd new series).
Howarth, James *(r.n.)*
Born in Bolton, 1866, and educated at Rivington Grammar School.
Scout. Boys Herald. Boys Realm (1st).
Howe, Frank *(r.n.)*
One of the most prolific writers for D. C. Thomson's. Claimed to have written at least 150 Dixon Hawke Libraries and well over 2,000 stories of all types for all sorts of magazines. Wrote

a book 'The King's Messenger' which had previously appeared as a serial in the Daily Mail.

Dixon Hawke Lib. (anon). Thomson papers (anon). Western Library.

Hoys, Dudley *(r.n.)*
Thriller.

Hubert, Frank *(r.n. Frank H. Shaw)*
Chums.

Huddleston, David R. *(r.n.)*
Chums. Young Britain (1st and 2nd). Rocket. Pluck (3rd).

Hudleston, John *(r.n. C. H. Dent)*
Thriller. Modern Boy.

Hudleston, Robert *(r.n. C. H. Dent)*
B.F.L. (2nd). Modern Boy.

Hudson, J.
Captain.

Hughes, Harry *(r.n. H. Havant)*
Chips. Wonder Library.

Hughes, Thomas *(r.n.)*
Born in Uffington, 1822, the son of a Berkshire squire, he was educated at Rugby and Oxford. He was called to the Bar in 1848. In 1856 he wrote probably the greatest public school story of all time – 'Tom Brown's Schooldays' (incidentally the first known) which gave a true picture of life at Rugby during the days of his own schooling. It was a tremendous success and is still being printed and sold today. The sequel – 'Tom Brown at Oxford' – was a failure, as most sequels are.

Apart from writing school stories, he wrote biographies of Alfred the Great and several others. From 1865 to 1874 he was an M.P. and in 1882 was appointed a County Court Judge. He died in 1896.

Lads and Lassies Library.

Hugill, R.
Scout. Young Britain (1st).

Hugo, Victor-Marie *(r.n.)*
Born 1802. French poet and novelist. After the revolution of 1848 he spent the years 1851–70 in exile. This is a further example of a classical author used to boost Alfred Harmsworth's claim of only utilising high-quality literature in his papers.

Marvel (1st).

Hulbert, Lloyd *(r.n. F. W. Pope)*
Ranger (2nd).
Humber, B. A.
Rocket.
Humber, W. B.
Young Britain (1st).
Hume, David *(r.n. John Victor Turner)*
Thriller. Detective Weekly.
Hume, Fergus *(r.n.)*
Born 1859. Author of over 128 books, including The Mystery
of the Hansom Cab. Lived at Rayleigh, Essex.
Aldine Mystery Novels.
Hume, Oscar
Chatterbox.
Hume, Valentine
Young England.
Humphreys, Gordon
B.O.P.
Hunt, Graham
Champion. Triumph.
Hunt, Rev. H. G. Bonavia *(r.n.)*
Born 1847. Editor of Cassell's Magazine 1874–96. Editor and
founder of Little Folks from start to 1876.
Hunt, J. D. S. *(r.n.)*
Known to all as 'Jackie' he is a Group Editor, at Fleetway
House. As a boy he read the Union Jack, when his aunt was a
Director of Amalgamated Press. He started there as an office
boy in 1926, soon rising to junior editor. His first post was on
his favourite paper, Union Jack. When the Thriller started in
1928 he too helped to run it with Len Pratt, who also managed
the Sexton Blake Library. In 1935, when Len Berry, editor of
the Detective Weekly, left suddenly, he took over from the
temporary editor, James Higgins, and held the position till 1939.
He was probably the first member of the staff to be called up, as
he joined the Forces in August 1939. After his war service he was
on many papers including Knockout Comic, Top Spot, Miracle
and Miracle Library. He also evolved the idea of a series in
the 30's in which Raffles pitted his wits against Sexton Blake.
Hunt, Maurice *(r.n. B. Parsons)*
Boys Friend Weekly (2nd).

Hunter, A. C. *(r.n.)*
Editor of The Skipper.

Hunter, Alfred John *(r.n.)*
Born in 1891 and began to have stories accepted by publishers when he was still almost a schoolboy. The first traced under his own name was in Chums, January 1913. Shortly afterwards he dropped the first initial as he thought that plain John Hunter would sound better. After service in the First World War his writings became so popular that they appeared in almost every boys' paper. He also wrote a great deal for adults. His first Sexton Blake story was in 1935, and at a later date he introduced his famous character, Captain Dack, who was skipper of the Mary Ann Trinder. This character was so striking that his personality even overshadowed that of Blake himself. Hunter also wrote many novels, some under the pen-names of 'Anthony Drummond' and 'L. H. Brenning' as well as girls' fiction under the name of 'Jean Hunter', his daughter.

In early 1961 John Hunter became very ill and was moved to Hopedene Nursing Home, Worthing, not very far from where he lived. He died there on the 22nd August 1961, aged 69. He left a married daughter and a son who is a dental surgeon.
Pen-names: John Hunter. Peter Meriton. Francis Brent.
Chums.

Hunter, H.
Pluck (2nd).

Hunter, John *(r.n. Alfred John Hunter)*
Ranger (post-war). Boys Friend Weekly (2nd). Boys Magazine. Chums. Knockout. Sun. Boxing Novels (1st). British Boy. Football and Sports Library. B.F.L. (1st and 2nd). Boys Wonder Lib. S.B.L. (2nd and 3rd). Thriller. Thriller Library. All Sports. Western Library. Detective Weekly. Modern Boy. Boys Realm (2nd). Flag Library.

Hunter, Rowland *(r.n. W. L. Catchpole)*
Magnet.

Huntingdon, A.
Nugget Library (2nd).

Huntingdon, Harry *(r.n. J. N. Pentelow)*
Scout. Cheer, Boys, Cheer. Boys Herald. B.F.L. (1st). Comic Life.

Hurford, Ian
Young Britain (1st).
'Huron'
Pluck (2nd).
Hurrell, Marion Isobel
Chatterbox.
Hurst, Alec
Pluck (1st). Marvel (1st).
Hurworth, Fred R.
B.O.P.
Hustington, Harry *(r.n. J. N. Pentelow)*
Chums.
Hutchinson, J. R.
Chums. B.O.P.
Hutchinson, R. *(r.n.)*
Boys Broadcast (anon).
Hutchinson, George Andrew *(r.n.)*
The first editor of the B.O.P. who held the position until his death in 1913. He became editor when he was about 37, and probably no man worked harder to make the B.O.P. a success. In his early life he had been a printer's apprentice, and shortly before the B.O.P. had started he founded a new church in a London suburb. Deeply religious, although he took pains not to make the B.O.P. a religious paper, he was also connected with the Sunday School World, and the famous magazine run by a charitable organisation, with which his father was connected before his retirement – 'Toilers of the Deep'.
Hutt, Hector *(r.n.)*
A writer who wrote various articles etc. for the Magnet, Gem, and Holiday Annuals, and some of the Greyfriars Heralds as well as some of the St Sam's stories. Also wrote 'Coker's Cake' in one of the Holiday Annuals, and a few Gem substitute stories. Now works for the G.P.O.
Pen-name: Martin Clifford (in Gem).
Hyatt, Stanley Portal *(r.n.)*
Born 1877. Died 30th June 1914.
Pen-name: Captain Stanley Dacre.
B.O.P. Bulldog Breed Library. Boys Friend Weekly (2nd).
Hyde, A. G.
Captain.

Hyde, D. Herbert   *(r.n. Derek Chambers)*
S.B.L. (3rd).
Hyde, Marston
Boys Realm (1st).
Hyne, Charles John Cutcliffe Wright   *(r.n.)*
Born in Hilbury, Glos., 11th May 1866, the son of a clergyman, and educated at Bradford Grammar School and Clare College, Cambridge. At school he was a very keen sportsman, boxer, oarsman and yachtsman, and it was said he was very good at the high jump as he was over 6ft 3ins tall. Before his writing career started in earnest, he travelled all over the world, probably using his experiences in later years in his world-famous Captain Kettle stories. This fiery small sea captain first appeared in a serial in Answers, but much better stories of him later appeared in Pearson's. Later, of course, they were put into novel form. Apart from his famous character, he also wrote about McTurk and McTodd. He died in 1944.
Modern Boy.
Inglesant, John
Chums.
Inglesant, Paul
Chums. Young Britain (1st).
Inglis, Lieut. Ross
British Boy.
Ingraham, Colonel Prentiss   *(r.n.)*
American writer who continued with the original Buffalo Bill Stories after E. Z. C. Judson died.
Lot-O'-Fun. Boys Champion Story Paper. Weekly Budget. Wild West Library. Nuggets (all anon).
Ingram, Percival H.
Union Jack (1st).
Inman, Escott   *(r.n. Rev. Herbert Escott Inman)*
B.F.L. (1st). Dreadnought. Boys Friend Weekly (2nd).
Inman, Rev. Herbert Escott   *(r.n.)*
Wrote Sexton Blake stories featuring Henri Garrock (The Snake) in the Union Jack around 1913–14. Author of over 40 hard-cover children's fairy stories, and also several boys' stories.
Pen-name: Escott Inman.
Union Jack (2nd) (anon).

Innes, F.
Boys Life.

Intert, Captain G. D.
Nugget Library (2nd). Comic Life.

Ireland, Arthur Joseph   *(r.n.)*
Born 1874. Lived at St Albans, Herts. Wrote an unusual series of school stories called 'The Dormitory Night's Entertainments' in Boys Champion in 1902.
Boys Champion Story Paper. Pocket Budget of Short & Serial Stories. Henderson's Pocket Budget.

Ireton, Henry
Chums.

Ironside, Matthew   *(r.n. John William Bobin)*
B.F.L. (1st). Gem (2nd).

Irving, Horace
Captain.

Islington, Frank
Scout.

Isaacs, Levi   *(r.n.)*
Pen-name: Lewis Essex.

Ivor, Roderick
Diamond Library (2nd).

Jackson, A. M.
Lot-O'-Fun. B.O.P.

Jackson, Eric
Pluck (1st).

Jackson, Harry
Chums Annual. Chums.

Jackson, Harvey
Chums.

Jackson, Howard   *(r.n. J. H. McGraw)*
Boys Realm (2nd).

Jackson, Julian   *(r.n. John Park Wilson)*
Wonder. Union Jack (1st). Pluck (1st). Marvel (2nd). Boys of England. Boys Comic Journal. Surprise.

Jackson, Lewis   *(r.n. Jack Lewis)*
Boys Realm (1st). Nelson Lee Lib. (2nd New Series) revised. Boys Friend Weekly (2nd). Comet. Cheer, Boys, Cheer. Detective Weekly. S.B.L. (3rd). Union Jack (2nd).

Jackson, Philander *(r.n. Alfred S. Burrage)*
Burrage had an ironic sense of humour, as he often used to
follow this name with the initials H.U.A. (Hard-up Author).
Boys Half-Holiday.

Jacobs, T. C. H. *(r.n. Jacques Pendower)*
Western Library.

Jacobs, William Wymark *(r.n.)*
Born in Wapping, London, 1863, the son of a wharf-overseer.
From 1883–89 he worked as a clerk in the Savings Department
of the Post Office. It was during this period that he began
writing his delightful and humorous stories of coasting vessels
and their crews. Many of them were made up during walking
tours he took with fellow-clerk Will Owen, who became his
illustrator. His first collection of short stories, 'Many Cargoes',
came out in 1896 to be followed by a dozen more. Many of his
stories first appeared in such magazines as 'The Idler', 'Strand',
etc. It was reported that a great number of boys enjoyed his
stories around the turn of the early 1900's. He wrote one or
two horrific tales including 'The Monkey's Paw' which is
judged by many to be the most terrifying story of its kind ever
to be written. He also wrote plays. He died in 1943.

Jago, Dr William H. *(r.n.)*
Was a ship's doctor who travelled all round the world and
wrote of his experiences in fiction form. Believed to have
written a great deal under nom-de-plumes in adult fiction, not
traced. Wrote at least one Sexton Blake story for the Union
Jack and had others rejected because they were considered 'too
meaty'. Also wrote many articles.
Union Jack (2nd) (anon). Boys Realm (2nd).

James, Bernard R.
Champion Annual.

James, Bruce
Champion Annual.

James, David
Boys Torch Adventure Library. All Sports.

James, Ernest *(r.n. W. E. Pike)*
Boys Cinema. Gem (2nd). Boys Friend Weekly (2nd).

James, G. P. R.
Marvel (1st).

James, Herbert Wentworth *(r.n.)*
Specialised in humorous and school stories, and often combined the two.
Won Pearson's £200 a year situation prize when he was 21.
Pen-name: Herbert Wentworth.
James, S. T. *(r.n.)*
Boys Realm (2nd). B.O.P. Scout. Young Britain (1st). Pluck (3rd).
James, Vernon *(r.n. Victor Bridges)*
Boys Realm (1st).
Jameson, Robert *(r.n.)*
Was possibly the same writer who called himself 'Roland Jameson', connected with Amalgamated Press. Wrote many stories of the Great War for Chums, which presented the stark realities of war without any attempt to glorify them. He himself was an officer in the Royal Fusiliers, served on the Western Front throughout the war and was twice wounded and gassed. He normally favoured the short story as opposed to the longer serial form.
Champion Annual. Chums.
Japp, May P. *(r.n.)*
Author of the 'Betty' stories in Young Folks Tales.
Young Folks Tales (anon).
Jardine, Warwick *(r.n. Francis Warwick)*
Thriller. Detective Weekly. S.B.L. (2nd). (One Story by W. J. Bayfield) and (3rd).
Jefferson, R. L. *(r.n.)*
Boys Friend Weekly (1st). Union Jack (1st).
Jeffery, W. L.
Chums.
Jeffries, Graeme Montagu *(r.n.)*
Born in London 1900, and educated privately. His famous thriller 'Blackshirt' – telling of the adventures of a Gentleman Crook in the 'Raffles' tradition, was published in 1925 and became an instant best-seller. Subsequently wrote several more stories about this character, some of which appeared in The Thriller. In post-war years his son, Roderick Graeme, took over the Blackshirt books while Graeme himself continued to write other thrillers and novels. Proprietor of the G.M. Literary

Agency. He was actually christened Bruce Graeme Jeffries, but changed his name.
Pen-name: Bruce Graeme.
Jenkins, Alan C.
B.O.P.
Jenkins, Ernest
Captain.
Jennings, Robert   *(r.n. Charles Hamilton)*
Picture Fun.
Jermyn, R. Gordon
Chums.
Jerome, Jerome Klapka   *(r.n.)*
Born Walsall, Staffs, the son of a Nonconformist preacher, in 1859. The family later moved to Poplar, London, and Jerome was educated at Marylebone Grammar School. On leaving he became a railway clerk at Euston Station and later worked as as reporter, schoolmaster and actor. In 1889 he achieved world-wide fame with his two books, 'Three Men in a Boat' and (to a lesser degree) 'The Idle Thoughts of an Idle Fellow'. The first sold several million copies and still sells regularly today.
In 1892 he was joint editor of The Idler, which introduced several writers later to become famous, including W. W. Jacobs. In 1893 Jerome started his own 2d weekly 'Today' with Stevenson's 'Ebb-Tide' as the serial, but a costly law-suit brought it to an end. In World War I, Jerome was an ambulance driver. His autobiography appeared in 1926. As a point of interest, proof of the perennial popularity of 'Three Men in a Boat' is shown by the fact that it was not only filmed, but was in recent years serialised in 'Look and Learn' with great success. The story was particularly enjoyed by schoolboys, who were in many cases introduced to it by their masters.
Jessop, Gilbert L.   *(r.n.)*
The famous cricketer. It is quite possible that his work was 'ghosted'. *See F. T. Bolton.*
Boys Friend Weekly (2nd).
Jocelyn, Noel
Boys Life.
Johns, Gilbert   *(r.n. James Stagg)*
S.B.L. (3rd).

Johns, William Earle *(r.n.)*
Born in Hertford, 1893, and educated at Hertford Grammar School. He had early ambitions to join the Army and find adventure abroad, but his parents had other ideas and articled him at the age of 16 to a local Municipal Surveyor, for which he qualified. After a spell in the Yeomanry during the First World War, and serving in the Middle East, he joined the R.F.C. in 1916 and learned to fly.
Served as a Regular officer in the R.F.C. and R.A.F. until 1929. Then he resigned, on reaching the rank of Captain, to become Air Correspondent to a number of British and overseas periodicals. Began writing in 1930 and for boys in Modern Boy 1932. Was the founder editor of 'Popular Flying' and it was in the pages of this magazine that the immortal Biggles stories started to appear, and have since run to over 80 books. He also had a fondness for pirate history and many articles about this were to be found in the 30's. During World War II he was commissioned to create a female counterpart for recruiting purposes, and 'Worrals of the W.A.A.F.' was the result. At this time he also created Gimlet, the Commando. They were gracefully retired in 1945, however, and 'Biggles' was given a new lease of life, when he was seconded to the new powerful force of Interpol as the Air Detective. Also began and edited 'Flying' in 1935.
In the last years of his life he lived in Scotland, where he died in 1968. Biggles was also featured in a TV series.
Modern Boy. Modern Boy Annual. Modern Boy Book of Pirates. Thriller. B.F.L. (2nd). Gem (2nd). Ranger (1st). (anon).

Johnson, Dudley Vaughan *(r.n.)*
Brother of H. T. Johnson and occasionally collaborated on stories with him.
Pen-name: Dudley Vaughan.

Johnson, George M.
Captain.

Johnson, Henry T. *(r.n.)*
Born in Wolverhampton 1858. Originally intended for the Law. Began writing at the age of 14 and had verses published in Lloyds Weekly Newspaper. Later he became one of the most prolific boys' story writers of his time, turning out stories for all

the well-known publishers. Was equally at home in stories of school, stage, Ancient Rome, medieval England, sport, circus or mystery. His best-known story was probably 'Pride of the Ring' which originally appeared in 'Funny Wonder' and ran for about three years. Johnson was famous for his colourful, melodramatic style – his heroes were one-hundred-per-cent 'good', his villains equally black and bad, but his heroines were the essence of purity and sweetness. He also wrote humorous stories and several plays, was very fond of acting and often appeared on the stage, sometimes in his own plays. Was editor of 'Fun' and also last editor of 'Vanguard' (Trapps Holmes). Later he became a prominent Member for Hammersmith, being the Independent Councillor for the River Ward for about 20 years, from 1906.

Was editor of 'Kensington News' for many years from 1910 and was incidentally one of the pioneers for dealing with London's traffic problems. He had a large family of children, and one of his daughters worked as editress at Amalgamated Press, whilst another son named Athol (after one of the characters in his stories) studied Law, which was his father's ambition. He passed successfully and was the legal advisor at Amalgamated Press for many years until his retirement.

Henry T. Johnson, who in his declining years went almost blind, died in 1930.

Pen-name: Neil Thomson.

Boys Herald. Football and Sports Favourite. B.F.L. (1st). Union Jack (1st). Dreadnought. Nugget Lib. Champion. Boys Realm (1st and 2nd). Boys Friend Weekly (1st and 2nd). Boys Realm Football and Sports Lib. Cheer, Boys, Cheer. Football and Sports Library. Comic Cuts. Chips. Funny Wonder. Boys Own Library (1st). Diamond Lib. (1st and 2nd). Big Budget. Boys Life. Boys Leader.

Johnston, William *(r.n.)*
Born 1856. Wrote several books, but mainly for the adult market and adult magazines.
B.O.P.

Jolling, Jack *(r.n. Alfred Judd)*
Chums.

Jones, Barry
Football Weekly. Football and Sports Library.

Jones, Gerald Norman
B.O.P.
Jones, Gillingham *(r.n. Charles Hamilton)*
Vanguard Lib. (Trapps Holmes). Funny Cuts. Picture Fun.
Jones, H. Bedford
B.O.P. Captain.
Jones, J. *(r.n.)*
Pen-name: Harry Hazel.
Jones, J. G. *(r.n.)*
Was in 1918 editor of a woman's magazine, probably 'Violet
Magazine', but later he became a free-lance writer and wrote
mainly for girls' papers. Wrote a Sexton Blake story in No 345,
1st series, 'The Secret of the Bucket Shop' in 1924. Unfortun-
ately his eyesight failed and he went completely blind. He con-
tinued writing, however, his daughter typing the stories. He
had a somewhat unique method of writing a story – plotting
out incidents to, say, 100 words for each situation. Was also
regarded as quite a mathematician.
Pen-names: Geoffrey Gordon. Dighton Trew. Ambrose
Earle. Steve Bloomer.
B.F.L. (1st) (anon). Boys Realm Football & Sports Lib. S.B.L.
(1st) (anon). Union Jack (2nd) (anon). Popular (1st) (anon).
Jones, Tom
Pluck (1st). Marvel (1st).
Jones Minor of St Agnes School
Modern Boy.
Jordan, J. A.
Aldine War Stories.
Josling, Harold
Boys Life.
Joughlin, Clueas
Captain.
Joy, Dickson
Boxing Novels.
Joyce, Captain Ernest
Chums.
Joynson, Barry *(r.n. Barry Joynson Cork)*
B.F.L. (2nd). Modern Boy.
Judd, Alfred *(r.n.)*
Began life as a bookseller, but on winning a prize for a story he

wrote for Chums, he decided to write books for a living instead of selling them. Wrote many popular boys' stories, especially school tales, one of the first being 'The Lie Direct' in B.O.P. in 1913. He had many of his stories printed in book form.
Pen-names: Jack Jolling. Nelson Power.
B.O.P. Chums. Scout. Boys Herald. Boys Journal. Cheer, Boys, Cheer. Nugget Library. Little Folks.

Judson, Edward Zane Carroll   *(r.n.)*

Judson goes down in history as the American writer who originally wrote stories of Buffalo Bill. He was a close friend of W. F. Cody, the real-life 'Buffalo Bill' and had almost as adventurous a life as Cody himself, having served with distinction in the Union Army in the U.S. and later working in the West alongside Cody. Judson had already achieved some success under the pen-name of 'Ned Buntline', as a writer of sensational adventure stories and 'Dime Novels' in the 1860's. After many long talks with Cody, Judson decided to try his hand at a series of stories about his friend. He succeeded in selling them to Street and Smith, the publishers, in New York, and his hero appeared in the first story in New York Weekly on December 23rd, 1869. It was called 'Buffalo Bill – King of the Border Men'. It was an immediate success and the series continued over the next twenty years.

When Judson eventually died, the series was continued by Colonel Prentiss Ingraham.

Kahler, Hugh Macnair
Born in the U.S.A. 1883.
Lloyds Detective Series.

Kahm, Harold S.
B.O.P.

Kay, A. K. Clark
B.O.P.

Kay, Bernard
Scout.

Kay, Ray
Boys Friend Weekly (2nd).

Kay, Wallace   *(r.n. Wallace E. Arter)*
Ranger (2nd).

Kaye, Anstey
Pluck (1st). Marvel (1st).

Kaye, Crawford
Hotspur Book for Boys. Skipper Book for Boys.

Kaye-Cook, L.
Comic Life.

Keary, Peter *(r.n.)*
Born 13th December 1865. Died 29th January, 1915.
Young Folks.

Keene, Roy
Lloyds Boys Adventure Series. Big Budget.

Keiler, Ralph
Union Jack (1st).

Keith, Louis
Boys Friend Weekly (2nd).

Kemp, Alec M. *(r.n.)*
On the staff of the Amalgamated Press in the early days, when
he served under F. G. Cordwell. Wrote quite a large number of
stories for the comics, and also several early substitute Magnet
stories. Had a style uncannily similar to Edwy Searles Brooks,
and his yarns could, quite wrongly, have been credited to the
latter author. He died some years ago.
Pen-name: Frank Richards (in Magnet).
Boys Friend Weekly (2nd). Film Fun. Kinema Comic. Fun &
Fiction. Surprise. Butterfly. Favourite Comic. Merry & Bright
(all anon).

Kempster, Bert *(r.n. H. H. Clifford Gibbons)*
Greyfriars Holiday Annual.

Kempster, Jim
Chums.

Kendall, Oswald
B.O.P.

Kendrick, Michael
Schoolboys Pocket Library (Swan).

Kennedy, W. W.
Wrote many stories about the 'Iron Teacher', that popular
mechanical robot schoolmaster in Hotspur, although the name,
of course, was only given in the Hotspur Annual.
Holiday Annual. Hotspur Book for Boys.

Kennedy-Bell, Douglas
B.O.P.

Kenny, Stan *(r.n. K. Giggah)*
Western Library.

Kent, Arthur *(r.n.)*
A newspaper man, for many years on the staff of the Daily
Express. A prolific writer of stories, articles, he also had several
books published. Lived in Aldwych, London.
S.B.L. (3rd and 5th).

Kent, Beverley *(r.n. E. J. Gannon)*
Boys Friend Weekly (2nd). Boys Realm (1st). Gem (2nd).
Magnet. Union Jack (2nd). Pluck (2nd). Dreadnought. Marvel
(2nd). Boys Herald.

Kent, Phillip
B.O.P.

Ker, David *(r.n.)*
A distinguished journalist, he was a War Correspondent for the
Daily Telegraph and other papers, and also a permanent cor-
respondent for the New York Times. He saw service in Central
Asia with the Russian Army and later in European campaigns.
He began writing boys' stories in the 1880's. He was chiefly
associated with B.O.P., when many of his stories appeared in
book form. He wrote every word of his stories in microscopic
handwriting on small sheets of very thin notepaper.
B.O.P. Lads and Lassies Library.

Kerridge, W. T.
Boys Life (with Witton Rix).

Keveren, A. G. *(r.n.)*
Pen-name: Gilbert Veren.

Killingsworth, W.
Chums.

King, Arthur
Captain.

King, Frank L. *(r.n.)*
Born Halifax, 1892. Educated at Rishworth and Bradford
Schools. Also Leeds University. Wrote for many adult maga-
zines, such as Blue Magazine, Chambers Journal. Died 5th
December, 1958.
Thriller.

King, Hilary *(r.n. James Grierson Dickson)*
S.B.L. (3rd).

King, Hyam
True Blue (2nd).
King, Kennedy
Worlds Comic.
King, Reginald *(r.n. Mrs I. Grosvenor)*
Boys Friend Weekly (2nd).
King, Robert (Jnr)
Boys Life.
King, Talbert
Boys World (Storey).
King, Tom
Chums.
King, T. Staneyan
Detective Tales (2nd). Young Britain (1st). Football Novels.
Aldine Mystery Novels. Boxing Novels (1st and 2nd). Lot-O'-
Fun. Sparks.
Kings, Leslie *(r.n.)*
Boys Friend Weekly (2nd).
Kingsford, Guy *(r.n. C. G. Murray)*
Chums.
Kingsland, Peter
B.F.L. (2nd).
Kingsley, Hamilton *(r.n. W. Martin)*
Chums.
Kingsley, Captain Horace
British Boys.
Kingston, Brian *(r.n. Percy William Longhurst)*
Gem (1st and 2nd). Boys Herald. Boys Realm (1st). Cheer,
Boys, Cheer. B.F.L. (1st). Marvel (2nd).
Kingston, Conrad
Wonder.
Kingston, Kit
Rocket.
Kingston, William Henry Giles *(r.n.)*
Born in London 1814, but spent much of his youth abroad in
Oporto, where his father was a merchant. His first book 'The
Circassian Chief' appeared in 1844 and his first story for boys,
'Peter the Whaler', was published in 1851 and had such a
success that he retired from business and devoted himself to
writing. Over the next 30 years he wrote over 130 books and

had the distinction of writing the first serial in the B.O.P. in 1879, 'From Powder Monkey to Admiral'. He was the first editor of Sampson Low's boys' magazine, 'Union Jack', in January, 1880, but died in August of the same year. He was succeeded by G. A. Henty. Kingston also edited other papers including 'The Colonist', the 'Colonist Magazine' and 'East India Review'. He was also interested in emigration problems and various philanthropic schemes. For services in negotiating a commercial treaty with Portugal, he received a Portuguese knighthood, and for his literary labours a Government pension. B.O.P. Union Jack (1880). Boys World. Our Boys Paper.

Kingsway, Bradney
Scout.

Kipling, Rudyard *(r.n.)*
Born in Bombay, India, 1865. He was the son of John Lockwood Kipling, a Methodist minister. Rudyard was named after Rudyard Lake in Staffordshire, where his parents first met. Was sent home to England in 1871 and lived in Southsea, Hants. In 1878 he went to the United Services College at Westward Ho! in Devon. His schooldays there were immortalised in the pages of his classical story 'Stalky and Co.' in 1899, one of the first 'modern' school stories. Kipling died in 1936.

Kirby, Arthur *(r.n. Arthur George Maclean)*
S.B.L. (3rd).

Kirkham, Reginald S. *(r.n.)*
On the staff of the Amalgamated Press for a short time before going free-lance around 1920. Wrote several substitute stories for Magnet, Gem, and then took over the Cliff House stories from Charles Hamilton in the Schoolfriend. Kirkham was a very humorous writer and he usually wrote the amusing stories of Bessie Bunter, whilst Horace Philips penned the serious ones. Later, Kirkham contributed many girls' and boys' stories for various papers. Around 1940 he inherited his father's business and made several world trips. After tiring of travel he set up his own fruit business in Kent. During the First World War he served in the Royal Navy. He died some years ago.
Pen-names: Frank Richards (Magnet). Martin Clifford (Gem). Also in Boys Friend Weekly (Cedar Creek). Frank Vincent.
Boys Journal. Boys Friend Weekly (2nd).

Kirkland, Captain
Pluck (1st).
Knew, George
Chums.
Knight, Arthur Lee
B.O.P.
Knight, Derek
Lion.
Knightley, Miss D. G. *(r.n.)*
Pen-name: Harry Prior.
Knollys, Bodley
Boys Friend Weekly (2nd).
Knowles, G. H.
B.O.P.
Knowles, Mabel Winifred *(r.n.)*
Born Streatham, London, 1875. Wrote many best-selling novels.
Pen-name: May Wynne.
Knowles, Thomas E. *(r.n. R. McClure)*
Captain. Boys Friend Weekly (2nd).
Knox, Thomas Wallace
Young England.
Kuppord, Skelton
B.O.P.
Kuruppu, D. S. C. *(r.n.)*
A Ceylonese newspaper reporter who works on The Times of
Ceylon and who takes a great interest in the history of Sexton
Blake.
Pen-name: Stephen Christie.
Lamb, Harold M. *(r.n.)*
Editor of many papers at Amalgamated Press, chiefly comic
ones. Was also quite a prolific writer in the latter.
Chips. Comic Cuts. Wonder. Larks. Merry & Bright. Butterfly.
Film Fun. Kinema Comic (all anon). Boys Cinema. Wonder
(anon).
Lamb, J. P.
Scout.
Lambe, F. *(r.n.)*
One of the writers of Sexton Blake under the Desmond Reid
pen-name.
S.B.L. (3rd).

Lambe, Robert Justyn

Specialised in rousing historical stories which were published in Bretts and Newnes publications in the 90's. His series for Newnes 'British Boys' included 'The Mystery of the Old Abbey' and 'Shoulder to Shoulder'. Liked to set his stories against a historical background which was authentic, such as the Great Fire of London, and the Plague, etc.

British Boys. Boys Jubilee Journal. Boys Comic Journal. Boys of England.

Lambert, T. H. *(r.n.)*

Pen-name: 'Lumberjack'.

Lamburn, Richmal Crompton *(r.n.)*

Born in Bury, Lancs, in 1890 and educated at Elphins School and Royal Holloway College. Held a B.A. (London) degree and was a classical schoolmistress in the early 20's. When she first began to write she wrote chiefly short stories about children, amongst them a story about William, Ginger, Douglas and Henry, the 'Outlaws'. The editor of the Home Magazine, in which the stories appeared, asked for more and Miss Crompton continued to write them. They proved so popular (also appearing in the 'Happy Magazine') that Newnes brought out the first 'William' book in 1922 entitled 'Just William'.

She gave up her teaching career and wrote full-time over 30 William books. They appeared in films, radio and TV. Originally the character of William was based on her younger brother, then later on her nephew. In addition to the William books, Miss Crompton wrote many adult novels.

She was unmarried and lived at Chislehurst, Kent, where she died suddenly on January 11th 1969.

Pen-name: Richmal Crompton.

Lampen, Herbert Dudley

Captain.

Lancaster, Captain *(r.n. Samuel Clarke Hook)*

Union Jack (1st). Pluck (1st). Marvel (1st).

Lancaster, Jack *(r.n. A. M. Burrage)*

Boys Herald. Empire Library (1st and 2nd). Dreadnought.

Lancaster, Percival

Chums.

Lancaster, William Joseph Cosens *(r.n.)*

Born Weymouth, 23rd May 1851. Died June 1922.

Pen-name: Harry Collingwood.
Lance, John *(r.n. E. Newton Bungay)*
S.B.L. Boys Friend Weekly (2nd). B.F.L. (2nd).
Landon, Herman *(r.n.)*
Born 1882.
Thriller. Union Jack (2nd).
Landor, Owen
Union Jack (1st). True Blue (2nd).
Landsborough, G. H. *(r.n.)*
Pen-names: Stone Cody. Mike M'Cracken.
Lane, Marston
Chums.
Lang, Peter *(r.n. C. Eaton Fearn)*
Champion. Champion Library. Triumph. Champion Annual.
Lang, Stewart *(r.n. Ward Muir)*
Boys Herald. Nugget Library.
Langbridge, Rev. Frederick *(r.n.)*
M.A. Oxon. Rector of St John's, Limerick. Was born 1849.
Wrote several books of poems, novels, and children's books.
B.O.P.
Langley, Colin
Football and Sports Favourite.
Langley, John
Western Library.
Langton, Charles
Marvel (1st).
Laurie, A.
B.O.P.
Lavell, Charles
Captain.
Law, Stephen
Detective Weekly.
Lawn-Newark, J.
Greyfriars Holiday Annual.
Lawrence, Chester *(r.n. S. G. Campbell)*
Ranger (1st).
Lawrence, Christopher George Holman *(r.n.)*
Born 19th February 1866. Died 16th March, 1950. Wrote
prolifically for Aldine's. A great friend of A. C. Murray. First

published story was for a girls' paper in 1897. Served many years as a volunteer in Territorial Army.

Pen-names: Lawrence Abbott. Escott Lynn. Jackspur (adult fiction). Captain W. C. Metcalfe.

Lawrence, Herbert
Boys Journal. Boys Realm (1st).

Lawrence, Michael
Young Britain (1st).

Lawrence, W. E.   *(r.n. W. L. Emmett)*

Laws, Percy
Boys World.

Lawson, C. G.
Boys Champion Story Paper.

Lawson, Warren J.   *(r.n. Donald Bobin)*
Champion Library. Triumph. Triumph Annual.

Lawton, Leslie
British Boys.

Lea, Charlton
Probably the real name of the author, and a member of a boys' publishing firm, but this has never been confirmed with any authenticity. He did more to weave a halo of romance around such dubious characters as Dick Turpin, Jack Sheppard, Claude Duval, etc., than anyone else. Wrote the first 100 issues of the famous Aldine 'Dick Turpin Library' before Stephen Agnew took over. Also the majority of the same firm's 'Claude Duval Library' which ran for 48 numbers, beginning in 1902.
Wrote many other similar stories, including the 'Chronicles of Newgate'. Had a habit of mixing hair-raising adventures with slapstick humour. Dropped completely out of writing 1906–7, and it is presumed he died around this time. (Just before going to press it has been stated that 'Charlton Lea' could have been A. S. Burrage but this needs careful checking.)
Red Rover. Dick Turpin Library. Diamond Library (1st). Claude Duval Library. Springheel Jack Library. Boys Own Lib. (1st).

Lea, John   *(r.n.)*
Born 1871 and educated at Gonville School and Caius College, Cambridge, where he gained his M.A. Later became Registrar at the University of London. His special interests were adult education and art. Wrote many stories and serials for various

boys' papers, chiefly B.O.P. His first serial for this paper, 'Swinton's Open Secret', appeared in 1905. Published several books, including 'The Romance of Bird Life'.
B.O.P.

Leach, D. *(r.n.)*
Boys Broadcast (anon).

Leach, Owen
Pluck (2nd).

Learmouth, Captain D. L. *(r.n.)*
All Sports.

Leatherdale, G. F.
Captain.

LeBlanc, Maurice *(r.n.)*
Born France 1864, died 6th November 1941. His sister was Georgette LeBlanc, the actress. Wrote fiction for some time without noticeable success until 1906, when he wrote a short story on crime which completely changed his life. Creator of the famous Arsine Lupin.
Detective Weekly.

Le Breton, Thomas *(T. Murray Ford)*
Boxing Novels (1st). Racing Novels (1st).

Lee, Albert, Rev. *(r.n.)*
Born 1855. Wrote a number of novels.
B.O.P. Captain.

Lee, Edgar
Pluck (1st). Marvel (1st).

Lee, Raymond *(r.n. E. Le Breton Martin)*
Boys Friend Weekly (2nd). Young Britain (1st). Rocket. Pluck (3rd). Champion.

Lee, Stanhope
Marvel (1st).

Leemans, H.
Boys Standard.

Lees, Captain
Boys Realm (1st).

LeFevre, Captain
Marvel (1st).

LeFevre, Lieutenant Paul *(r.n. Henry St John Cooper)*
Gem (2nd. Boys Friend Weekly (1st and 2nd). Union Jack (1st). Pluck (1st). Marvel (1st).

LeGrand, Jack *(r.n.)*
Joined Amalgamated Press in 1936 and was on the staff of F. Cordwell Group. Film Fun, Bullseye, etc. Used to think up many ideas for the famous Jack Keen detective stories. Became the editor of the Valiant, Buster group.

Leicester, Henry
Marvel (1st).

Leigh, Adrian
B.O.P.

Leigh, Arnold
Young Britain (1st).

Leigh, Captain Arthur *(r.n. Arthur Steffens)*
Union Jack (2nd).

Leigh, Brian
Tiger.

Leigh, Felix
Comic Life.

Leighton, Robert *(r.n.)*
Born 1859, Ayr, Scotland. Married Marie Conner Leighton. Educated Liverpool. Editor of 'Young Folks' 1884–5. Director of Answers Ltd. Wrote many books in collaboration with his wife. His daughter, in a biography of Marie, once said that 'Robert was a meek little man dominated by his wife'. Whilst he was editor of Young Folks, Stevenson's famous 'Treasure Island' was accepted for serialisation in that paper.
Cheer, Boys, Cheer. Boys Realm (1st). Boys Herald. Comic Cuts. Chums. Scout.

Leighton, Marie Connor *(r.n.)*
Wife of Robert Leighton, and collaborated with him on many serials. Also wrote the famous serial 'Convict 99' and many of her stories were published in Answers.

Lelland, Frank *(r.n. Alfred McLelland Burrage)*
Detective Weekly.

Lennox, Henry
Pluck (3rd).

Leonard, Henry *(r.n. Hugh W. Fennell)*
Monster Comic.

LePage, Richard
Champion.

Leroux, Gaston *(r.n.)*
Born France 1868 and died 16th April 1927. After becoming well-known as a journalist and author of popular fiction he turned in 1907 to the detective story. Wrote half a dozen adventures featuring Joseph Rouletabille, reporter. Thriller.

LeRoy, Miss
Pen-name: Esme Stuart.

Leslie, Arthur Forbes
B.O.P.

Leslie, Captain *(r.n. J. J. G. Bradley)*
Boys Standard.

L'Estrange, James *(Biographical details under the name of Herbert Strang)*

LeStrange, W. D. L. (Captain)
Boys Own Library (1st). Boys World. Weekly Budget.

Lever, Charles
Pluck (1st). Marvel (1st).

Levi, Riso *(r.n.)*
World-famous billiard champion.
All Sports.

Lewdrock, John
Merry and Bright.

Lewins, C. A. *(r.n.)*
Pen-name: Tex Rivers.

Lewis, Angelo J. *(r.n.)*
Pen-name: Professor Hoffman.

Lewis, Charles *(r.n. John Gabriel Rowe)*
Marvel (1st). Champion Library.

Lewis, Edgar
Marvel (1st).

Lewis, Harold G. *(r.n.)*
All Sports.

Lewis, Jack *(r.n.)*
Began writing when a sub-editor with Harmsworth (later A.P.) in 1911 and also wrote short stories and verse for Answers. Then contributed to many of the A.P. boys' papers. Began writing for the Union Jack in 1915 and introduced one of the most famous and popular characters to the Sexton Blake saga – Leon Kestrel, the Master Mummer. The first story featuring

him was in Union Jack No 620, 'The Case of the Cataleptic'. During the First World War he served with the Royal Navy and on his return he wrote many school stories for Rainbow and other comic papers.

A more-than-average cricketer, it could be said that in his later life he resembled the popular Colin Milburn in size. He lived in his declining years near Newhaven, Sussex, and died there in the late 50's.

Pen-names: Phylis Lewis. Stephen Hood. Lewis Jackson. S.B.L. (1st and 2nd) (anon). Union Jack (2nd) (anon). Boys Friend Weekly (2nd). Boys Journal. Pluck (2nd). Rainbow. Pilot (anon).

Lewis, J. Morton
Fun & Fiction.

Lewis, Leon
Our Boys Paper. Boys World.

Lewis, Matthew Gregory *(r.n.)*
Born 1775. Died 1818.
Wrote 'The Monk', 1796.

Lewis, Phylis *(r.n. Jack Lewis)*
Thriller. Union Jack (2nd).

Leyland, Eric *(r.n.)*
Born 1911, son of a Church of England parson. Educated at Brentwood and University College, London. Trained as a librarian, eventually being appointed Borough Librarian and curator, Walthamstow. Resigned 1949 to devote whole time to writing. Written nearly 150 books for young people as well as short stories, articles, etc. Editor of various works including Commander and Coronet Annuals. Written another 100 books under various pen-names which are strictly private.
B.O.P. Eagle.

Leys, John K. *(r.n.)*
Writer of several novels.
Chums.

Lidstone, F. *(r.n.)*
On the staff of Amalgamated Press and in C. M. Down's group of papers. Sub-editor on Modern Boy and Look and Learn. Editor of the Fleetway House Magazine until he retired in 1968.

Light, Walter H.
Editor of the famous Aldine Publishing Company from the early 1900's, including 'Boys Own Library', 'Football Novels', 'Aldine Home Library', 'Buffalo Bill Novels', 'Diamond Library' and 'Tales for Little People'. Was well-known for his practice of putting different invented names to stories every week, to give the impression that he had plenty of authors on his staff. In fact, the Aldine firm paid very poor rates for stories, in comparison with other publishers, and the offices at Crown Court, London, consisted of two small and dingy rooms occupied by Walter Light, the editor, his assistant, and an office boy – not very impressive headquarters in view of the large number of papers and libraries they produced.
Pen-names: Wingrove Wilson. Walter Herrod.
Bullseye (Aldine) (anon).
Lincoln, Maurice *(r.n.)*
B.F.L. (2nd).
Lincoln, Seymour
Pluck (1st).
Lind, Anton
An author who confined himself almost entirely to writing a series of books set in Altonbury School and published from the 1930's up to the present day, when they were still being re-printed. Titles included 'Riot at Altonbury' and 'Secret Service at Altonbury'. Leading characters include 'The Three Angels' (Sid West, Stan Arnold and Jack Garner), Andrew Locking, Beacon (the fat boy), Dinghy and Pips. The general atmosphere is knockabout, unsubtle and plebian, but the yarns are enjoyable enough in a simple way, with plenty of amusing sequences. The books are published by Sampson Low and their early history is uncertain, as are any details about the author.
Linden, A. R. *(r.n.)*
One of the first authors of the famous Red Circle School stories which appeared in The Hotspur; although he was not the creator, this honour belonging to the editorial staff of D. C. Thomson Ltd, particularly W. Blain. Lived at Portsmouth.
Hotspur (anon).
Lindridge, James
Wrote 'bloods' for George Purkess, including 'The Merry Wives of London' (1850).

Lindsay, Edward
 Scout.
Linley, Julian *(r.n. Alec G. Pearson)*
 Scout.
Linley, Mark *(r.n. G. R. Samways)*
 Magnet. Greyfriars Herald.
'Little Owl'
 Scout.
Llewellyn T. Harcourt *(r.n. Charles Hamilton)*
 Smiles.
Lloyd, Edward *(r.n.)*
 Born at Thornton Heath, Surrey, in 1815. At an early age he
 opened up a shop at Shoreditch, London, where he sold papers
 and magazines. His first venture as a publisher was 'Lloyds
 Stenographer'. He began publishing boys' papers and 'dread-
 fuls' in 1836, and was soon most successful. Perhaps 'boys'
 papers' is an incorrect phrasing, as the majority of them were 1d
 instalments of lurid stories designed for all ages, if not tastes.
 They usually fell into three categories: Gothic Horrors (such
 as 'Varney the Vampire'), historical romances, and domestic
 romances. They had an enormous sale amongst the working-
 class readers of the mid-19th century. It was in Lloyd's publications that the infamous 'Sweeney Todd' made his bow. Lloyd
 also blatantly plagiarised the works of Charles Dickens as they
 came out, and he made a fortune by publishing such tales as
 'Penny Pickwick', 'Oliver Twiss' and 'Nicholas Nickleberry'.
 They were eagerly snapped up and, indeed, often exceeded the
 sales of the originals, being much cheaper. He later published
 many better-class magazines and papers and it is said he be-
 came ashamed at the way he had made his fortune. He was
 the founder of Lloyds Newspaper, Lloyds Shipping List and
 Daily Chronicle, and died a very wealthy man in 1890.
 An excellent reference to his 'bloods' can be seen in 'A Biblio-
 graphy of the Penny Bloods of Edward Lloyd' (Medcraft 1945).
Lloyd, E. M. S.
 Chums.
Lloyd, Tom
 Boxing Novels (1st).
Lomax, W. J. *(r.n.)*
 Famous as the Sexton Blake author who created the detective's

assistant, Tinker. Lomax made his bow in the Union Jack No 53 (New Series) 'Cunning Against Skill' in 1904, under the pen-name of 'Herbert Maxwell'. He was believed to have been a schoolmaster by profession. He went abroad just before the 1914–18 war, and was not heard of again by his colleagues in Fleet Street.

Pen-names: Commissioner Fulke. Herbert Maxwell. Union Jack (1st and 2nd) (anon). Popular (1st) (anon).

London, Jack *(r.n.)*

Born in San Francisco, 1876, and brought up in poverty. Finally managed to study for a year at the University of California, but the open sea and the open road soon called him. In 1897 he took part in the Klondyke Gold Rush. He got no gold, but from his experiences wrote 'Call of the Wild' (1903) which sold a million-and-a-half copies and established him as an author.

In 1905 The Captain published one of his stories, 'The King of Lazy May', a story of the Klondyke Goldfields. It was so complex that a special editorial had to be written explaining the technique of 'claim-jumping'. After an adventurous life ashore and afloat, London took to drink and extravagant living, and finally committed suicide in 1916.

Captain.

Long, Derek *(r.n.)*

Comes from a family where all are in the writing field. As a boy was an avid reader of the Magnet and Gem, also a tremendous admirer of the great Edgar Wallace – who, as a boy, sold newspapers outside the Press Club of which he is a member. On the staff of the Amalgamated Press in the early 30's, he dealt with women's fiction alongside Walter Tyrer. Mainly his work appeared in that field, but he did write two Sexton Blake stories in the 1940's, and some other short boys' stories for Montague Haydon. He is today a prolific writer of women's fiction.

S.B.L. (3rd).

Long, H. W. Shirley *(r.n.)*

Born London 1905 and as a boy used to roam the dockland areas. His experiences stood him in good stead as in later years he was able to write many articles about them and the shipping docks for Chums Annual, as well as many articles on jazz. An expert on music – he has held quite a few managerial positions,

including manager of Rich and Cowen, Publishers. At present is Public Relations Officer at Fleetway Publications.
Chums. Chums Annual.

Longhurst, Percy William *(r.n.)*
Born London 1874. Educated at London University. Official at every Olympic Games 1908–32. Favourite writings were, of course, about sport, especially boxing. Wrote also numerous articles in every field of sport.
Pen-names: Hubert Spence. 'Agent 55'. Brian Kingston. Lewis Hockley.
Pluck (2nd). Marvel (2nd). Boys Realm (2nd). Magnet. Boys Herald. All Sports. Boys Friend Weekly (2nd). Sport & Adventure. B.F.L. (1st). Sports for Boys. B.O.P.

Lounsberry, Lionel
Chums.

Lovel, Vera *(r.n. Mrs N. Murch)*
Young Britain (1st). Chips.

Lover, Samuel
Marvel (1st).

Low, R. D. *(r.n.)*
A Managing Editor of the Thomson Group of boys' papers: Hotspur, Rover, Skipper, Wizard, Adventure, Vanguard and Red Arrow.

Lowe, A. H.
Captain.

Lowe, Claud D. *(r.n.)*
A script writer who, it is believed, wrote a scenario for a Tom Merry film after the 1914–18 war, which was shelved. As recompense he was allowed to write some substitute Gem stories including 'Glyn's Colour Ray' and 'The Mystery of the Mill'. The writer was certainly as good as many, and also wrote stories under two pen-names.
Pen-names: Maurice Griffiths. Phillip Hardy. Martin Clifford (Gem).

Lowe, Major T. A. *(r.n.)*
    Lt. Col.
Army (retired), D.S.O., M.C. Editor of Services Territorial Magazine. Wrote for Adult magazines such as Picture Show, Picturegoer, Men Only, Strand, Titbits.
Boys Realm (2nd).

Lowry, Henry Dawson *(r.n.)*
Born 1869. Wrote several novels.
Captain.
Lowther, Fred
Boys Realm (1st).
Loxley, Raymond   *(r.n. C. G. Murray)*
Chums.
'Lumberjack'   *(r.n. T. H. Lambert)*
Scout.
Luxemberg, Claude
Chums.
Lynch, John Gilbert Bohun   *(r.n.)*
Wrote several books, was boxing correspondent for 'Field and Sport', and 'Dramatic News'. Book reviews on art and antique furniture. Caricature designer of book wrappers and posters.
Pen-name: Jack Bloomer.
Lyndon, Barre   *(r.n. Alfred Edgar)*
Thriller.
Lynk, Warder   *(r.n. G. M. Bowman)*
Ranger (2nd). B.F.L. (2nd).
Lynn, Escott   *(r.n. Christopher George Holman Lawrence)*
Robin Hood Lib. (1st, 2nd and 3rd). Buffalo Bill Lib. (1st and 2nd). Bullseye (Aldine). Tip-Top Detective Tales. True Blue (1st and 2nd). Scout. Lot-O'-Fun. Little Folks. Big Budget.
Lynn, Max   *(r.n. G. J. B. Anderson)*
Chums.
Lyons, Captain John
Wrote 'bloods', including 'Black Rollo the Pirate' (1860).
Lyons, Ronald Samuel   *(r.n.)*
Born London 1904. Publicity Manager, C. A. Pearson. Sub-editor Pearsons Magazine, 1925–29. Assistant comp. editor to Pearsons 1930–33. Assistant editor of the Scout 1924–25. Produced and partly wrote comic papers which Lilley and Skinner issued monthly through their shops. Also produced and wrote comics issued quarterly by C. Arthur Pearson, and wrote adult fiction for Thomsons.
Scout. Comet.
Lytton, Lord Edward George Lytton Bulwer   *(r.n.)*
Born 1803, died 1873. Educated at Trinity College and Trinity Hall, Cambridge. M.P. for St Ives and later Lincoln. Author

of 'Paul Clifford', 'The Last Days of Pompeii', etc. Alfred Harmsworth abridged his stories for publication in the 'classic' period of the following papers:
Union Jack (1st). Marvel (1st).

Maas, William Harold   *(r.n.)*
Served under Lord Northcliffe, C. Arthur Pearson. Worked on Daily Express, editor of 'Black and White Budget', Daily Chronicle (1906), 1st editor of Big Budget. Editor of Pluck, Union Jack, asst. editor of The Winner (1931).

McArdle, Brian   *(r.n.)*
One of the original writers of stories published under the 'Desmond Reid' pen-name.
S.B.L. (3rd).

McClintock, Buck
Modern Boy.

McClintock, Neil
Young Britain (1st).

McCormack, James   *(r.n.)*
Pen-name: Max Patrick.

McCracken, 'Bullet'
Ranger (2nd). B.F.L. (2nd).

McCracken, Mike   *(r.n. G. A. Landsborough)*
Western Library.

McCulley, Johnston   *(r.n.)*
Born Ottawa, 1883. Educated public school and privately.
Pen-names for adult fiction: Grant McAlpin, George Drayne, Kaley Brien.
Pen-name for boys' fiction: Harrington Strong.
Lloyds Detective Series.

McCulloch, Derek   *(r.n.)*
Born 1897 in Plymouth. Educated Croydon High School, Plymouth. Joined the staff of the B.B.C. in 1926. Became Director of Children's Hour in 1938. Wrote several books and had several children's Annuals published. Became known to millions of children as 'Uncle Mac' in the days of radio. Also contributed numerous articles to all the leading papers, as well as doing book reviews. Was awarded the O.B.E.
Pen-name: Uncle Mac.

McCulloch, J. H.   *(r.n.)*
Pen-name: J. R. Rawlings.

McCutcheon, Hugh
B.O.P.
MacDonald, Alastair *(r.n.)*
Son of R. J. MacDonald, the famous Gem artist. Last heard of
when he was working at the Ministry of Education in White-
hall.
Chums.
McDonald, Alex
Popular Book of Boys Stories.
MacDonald, Alexander *(r.n.)*
Born 1878. Wrote many adventure books and contributed to all
leading magazines. Lived in Queensland, Australia.
Captain.
MacDonald, Eric
Chums.
McDonald, F. S.
Scout.
McDonald, William Colt
Western Library.
McElwee, Andrew
Scout.
McEnvoy, C. N. *(r.n.)*
Pen-name: Kemble Strange.
McFarlane, Harold
Captain.
McGraw, J. H. *(r.n.)*
Pen-name: Howard Jackson.
MacGregor, A. (Commodore)
Boys Friend Weekly (1st).
MacGregor, John *(r.n.)*
Captain.
MacIntosh, Sophiel
Captain.
MacIntyre, H.
Marvel (1st).
MacIvor
Boys World.
McKeag, Ernest L. *(r.n.) (sometimes incorrectly spelt 'McKeagh')*
Born in Newcastle-on-Tyne, 1896, where his father was in the
Insurance business. Educated at South Shields Marine School,

Armstrong College and Durham University. Joined the Merchant Navy at 16 and travelled around the world several times. Returned to England in 1916 and joined the Royal Navy as a midshipman, rising to the rank of Lieutenant. On demobilisation in 1919 he became a newspaper reporter. When Lloyds Newspapers Ltd started British Boy in 1921 he had his first boys' story accepted for the paper. Became editor of The Northern Weekly Review in 1922. In 1923 he joined the staff of the Amalgamated Press, working on the girls' papers under R. T. Eves. Wrote his first girls' story for the new paper, 'Ruby'. Later he wrote many stories for the Aldine publications and for many of their Annuals; chiefly these stories dealt with the sea and the Navy, on which subject he was, of course, an expert. Later he wrote many boys' and girls' stories for the Champion-Triumph group. Of the former he wrote over 300 Colwyn Dane detective tales, after E. R. Home-Gall, the creator. In the Magnet he wrote the interesting features in 'Come into the Office, Boys and Girls', which title he created. This ran from No 1092 (1929) to 1446 (1937). He was on the editorial side of many girls' papers and eventually retired as editor of The Schoolgirls Picture Library in 1961.

Pen-names: Mark Grimshaw (one of a syndicate). Pat Haynes. Jack Maxwell.

Chums Annual. Lloyds Boys Adventure Series. Champion Annual. Champion. Chums. Magnet. Nelson Lee Lib. (2nd new series) (anon). B.F.L. (2nd). War Stories. British Boy. Lloyds School Yarns.

MacKenna, S. J.

Union Jack (1880).

McKibbon, J. E. *(r.n.)*

Wrote his first stories for Cheer, Boys, Cheer and Boys Realm around 1912. Wrote complete stories for women in Family Journal, on which he was employed as a junior sub-editor when he was 16. Wrote humorously as 'John Ellis' for London, Premier, Red Magazines. Used the name of John E. Probyn for Family Journal and Home Companion. Also wrote many stories for girls under the 'Elise Probyn' pen-name. In 1927 left the staff of Amalgamated Press to free-lance.

Boys Journal.

Mackie, John *(r.n.)*
Born in Stirling, Scotland, 1862, and educated at Stirling High School. An author who had almost as many adventures as those he wrote about. He once said he never wrote about incidents of which he had not had personal experience in the course of his world-wide travels. He had hand-to-hand fights with cannibals, hunted down notorious cut-throats with the Canadian Royal Mounted Police (with whom he served for a period), existed on crows, snakes and roots in the desert and jungle. Fought in the Boer War (and was awarded the South African War Medal with five clasps) and rode 800 miles on horseback in search of gold. Began writing in the 1890's and contributed articles and short stories to the Daily Mail, Wide World Magazine and Pearsons before writing his first serial for The Captain – 'The Heart of the Prairie' in 1899. Many more serials followed, also hard-cover books of adventure and novels for adults. In his spare time he was a keen amateur flyer.
Captain. Chums. B.O.P. Boys Life. Adventure Library (Newnes).

McKinney, A. J. *(r.n.)*
Football and Sports Favourite. Sports Fun. Football and Sports Library. Boys Realm (2nd).

Mackinrodd, Andrew
Scout.

Mackworth, John *(r.n.)*
Modern Boy.

McLaren, J. A. *(r.n.)*
Pen-name: John Adams.

Maclean, Angus
Rob Roy Library.

MacLean, Arthur George
Born Middlesbrough, Yorks, and was brought up on the Thomson papers, especially Wizard. Was a librarian when he started writing and made his début in the Sexton Blake Library in 1956. Created the aged and rather brittle character of Eustace Craille for the saga and also wrote a modern story of George Marsden Plummer. Is also one of the authors responsible for re-writing the Desmond Reid stories in the S.B.L.
Pen-name: Arthur Kirby.
S.B.L. (3rd and 5th).

McLean, Eric W. *(r.n.)*

A most popular author in the early 20's, who wrote really first-class adventure stories, and whose work was in great demand by editors. After the Second World War, he was last reported to be tramping the roads, picking flowers in Cornwall and helping with the potato crops. A great deal more could be written about this author, but perhaps it is best to remember him as a man who once entertained countless thousands of readers with his writing.

Pen-names: Geoffrey Rayle. Eric W. Townsend.

MacLeod, Alan George

Thriller.

MacLeod, Fiona *(r.n. William Sharp)*

Young Folks.

McLeod, Philip

Pluck (2nd).

MacLeod, Walter A. *(r.n.)*

Thriller. Pilot (anon).

McLoughlin, Maurice *(r.n.)*

Not strictly a boys' writer or editor, but deserves a mention for producing many Billy Bunter plays in the West End of London, and also merits the highest praise for introducing to the stage one of the greatest fictional characters of all time in boys' stories – Billy Bunter. The playwright was born in London in 1918 and works by day as secretary to a fish-curing company in London's fish-market, Billingsgate.

The first play was in 1958, entitled 'Billy Bunter's Mystery Christmas', and the others since that date have been:

Billy Bunter Flies East	1959
Billy Bunter's Swiss Roll	1960
Billy Bunter Shipwrecked	1961
Billy Bunter's Christmas Circus	1962
Billy Bunter Meets Magic	1963

The plays were put on by City Stage Productions Ltd., headed by Michael Anthony and Bernadette Milnes. McLoughlin has written many other plays and began writing and producing them for his local amateur Dramatic Club in Ilford, Essex, where he lives. Other Billy Bunter plays have been produced in Scotland, but by different producers.

Macluire, David *(r.n.)*
Detective Weekly. Union Jack (2nd).

Maclure, K.
Chums. B.O.P.

McLure, R. *(r.n.)*
Pen-name: Thomas E. Knowles.

MacMillan, William
Captain. B.O.P.

McNeill, Archibald
Union Jack (1880).

McNeilly, Wilfred *(r.n.)*
Born in Ulster, Northern Ireland. Was in war-time (1940) an
officer in the British Yeomanry, Indian Cavalry and Royal
Indian Navy. Has written all kinds of fiction for all types of
papers from Punch to juvenile fiction. After writing a few
S.B.L.s under the 'Desmond Reid' pen-name, had several
published under his own. Hobbies are sea-fishing and under-
water swimming, and he is also an international archer. Has
appeared many times on TV and now lives in a fishing port in
Ireland.
S.B.L. (3rd and 5th).

MacPherson, Captain Angus *(r.n. A. J. Colinski)*
Boys Friend Weekly (2nd).

MacPherson, Barclay
Marvel (1st).

McPherson, Jock
Football and Sports Lib. Football and Sports Favourite.

McPherson, Paul
Big Budget.

McRae, George
Football and Sports Library.

MacRae, Herbert *(r.n. C. Eaton Fearn)*
Rocket. Boys Friend Weekly (2nd). Champion. Champion Lib.
Triumph.

MacRae, Roy *(r.n. Bernard Buley)*
Football and Sports Lib.

Mac, 'Uncle', of B.B.C. *(r.n. Derek McCulloch)*

Magnus, Gerald *(r.n. Gerald M. Bowman)*
Modern Boy. B.F.L. (2nd).

234

Mais, Stuart Peter Brodie *(r.n.)*
Born 1885 and educated at Christ Church, Oxon. Wrote for many leading daily papers and School World. Also author of many adult fiction books. Lived at Hove, Sussex.
Modern Boy.

Maitland, H. A.
Boys World.

Maitland, J. A.
Young Folks.

Maitland, T. G. Dowling *(r.n.)*
Author in the early days of Harmsworth papers and who, it is reported, acted as agent for other writers. His initials were given sometimes as J. G. or S.
Pen-names: Herbert Chandos. H. Winter Gale. Tristam K. Monck.
Boys Realm (1st). Union Jack (1st and 2nd). Pluck (1st). Marvel (2nd). True Blue (2nd). Red Rover. Diamond Library (1st). Aldine Half-Holiday.

Major, Dagney *(r.n. J. D. Major)*
Gem (2nd).

Major, J. D. *(r.n.)*
Pen-names: Dagney Major. Dagney Hayward.

Makin, William James *(r.n.)*
Born Manchester, 1894. Sub-editor of Manchester Guardian 1916–18. Travelled extensively in India, Malaya, China, Japan, United States and Africa.
Thriller.

Malan, A. N. *(r.n.)*
The Rev. Dr Malan was one of the most prolific and popular of the regular B.O.P. writers, and wrote between 20 and 30 serials, though they were often shorter than those, say, by Gordon Stables. Malan's stories were usually of school life, a subject about which he obviously knew a great deal, being for some years the Headmaster of Eagle House School, Wimbledon. He wrote for the B.O.P. chiefly in the 1880's and 1890's, when apart from serials he also contributed numerous stories and seemed to confine his output mainly to this paper.
He later held Chaplaincies in Switzerland and France.
Union Jack (1880). B.O.P. Captain.

Malcolm, Charles　*(r.n. Cyril Malcolm Hincks)*
Boys Favourite. Sports Budget (2nd). Football and Sports Lib.

Malling, Acton
Marvel (1st).

Mallinson, R. Russell　*(r.n. Russell Stannard)*
Boys Friend Weekly (2nd). B.F.L. (2nd).

Manfield, Herbert
Marvel (2nd).

Mannering, Melville
Marvel (1st).

Manning-Foster, Alfred Edge　*(r.n.)*
Born in London. Educated at U.C.S. and U.C.L. Editor and proprietor of 'Bridge Magazine', 'The Country Gentleman' and 'Land and Water'.
Boys Friend Weekly (1st).

Manningham, Maurice
Marvel (1st).

Mansfield, Charles E.
Pluck (1st).

Mansfield, George　*(r.n.)*
Champion.

Mansfield, Harold　*(r.n.)*
Merry & Bright (anon). Fun and Fiction (anon). Butterfly (anon). Favourite Comic (anon).

Mansfield, H. T. E.
Editor on the comic papers in the early days at Amalgamated Press. Worked in Fred Cordwell's group. Possibly he may be the same writer as above, who was on the same comics, but this has never been confirmed.

Mansfield, John
Pluck (2nd). Marvel (1st).

Mansford, Charles J.
A schoolmaster by profession and a B.A. Wrote many stories about Westbourne School for The Boys Realm. Also wrote several hard-cover school stories.
Boys Friend Weekly (1st and 2nd). Boys Realm (1st). B.F.L. (1st). Chums.

Manson, Lieutenant A.　*(r.n. – Pope)*
Union Jack (1st).

Mant, Richard *(r.n. George Richard Mant Hearne)*
True Blue (2nd). Boys Comic Lib. Robin Hood (1st and 3rd).
Diamond Library (1st).

Manville, George *(r.n. George Manville Fenn)*
Boys Leader.

March, Dicky *(r.n. of footballer)*
Queens Park Rangers half-back in the 30's and 40's. Story
certainly 'ghosted' editorially. March is the uncle of Derek
Adley, the joint compiler of this biography.
Football Weekly.

March, John
Boys Broadcast.

Marchant, L. S.
Boys Life.

Margerison, John S. *(r.n.)*
Prolific writer of stories, usually with a sea background, in the
20's.
Pen-names: Gilbert Grey. James S. Mellalieu.
Boys Friend Weekly (2nd). Boys Realm (2nd). Sports Fun.
B.F.L. (1st). Football and Sports Favourite. Dreadnought.
Football and Sports Library. Marvel (2nd). British Boy. Lloyds
School Yarns. Chums. Scout.

Marland, Bart
Captain Lib.

Marlow, Stephen
Diamond Lib. (1st and 2nd). Chums.

Marlowe, Felix
Captain Library.

Marlowe, Francis *(r.n.)*
Captain. Captain Library. Chums. Aldine Mystery Novels.
B.O.P. Boys Life.

Marmur, Jacland *(r.n.)*
Born in Poland, 1901.
Chums.

Marne, Silas
Ranger (2nd). Pioneer. B.F.L. (2nd).

Marquis, M. *(r.n.)*
One of the writers of the modern Sexton Blake Library. Had a
story published under the name of 'Richard Williams'.
S.B.L. (5th).

Marr, James
Chums.
Marr, Ray
Lion.
Marriott, Buck *(r.n. Miss M. Meagher)*
Champion.
Marryatt, Frederick *(r.n.)*
Born in London 1792, the son of a West Indian merchant, and educated at Ponders End. In 1806 he entered the Royal Navy as a midshipman under Lord Cochrane, and saw much service in the Mediterranean, at Walcheron, and in the Burmese War of 1824. Returned 1830 as a Captain and C.B. He also invented a code of signals, still widely used in the Navy today. His experiences at sea were to form the basis for a series of popular novels, the first of which was 'Frank Mildmay', published in 1829. It was followed by 30 others, including 'Midshipman Easy' and 'The Pirate'. He also edited 'The Metropolitan'. In his time he inherited and spent three fortunes, was an equerry to Royalty, and a man of fashion. He ended his days as a farmer in Norfolk and died in 1848.
Union Jack (1st). Pluck (1st). Marvel (1st).
Marryat, Hugh
Scout.
Marsh, John
B.O.P.
Marshall, Archibald *(r.n.)*
Born 1866. Educated at Highgate School and Trinity College, Cambridge. Author of many books.
Chatterbox.
Marshall, Arthur C. *(r.n.)*
Was probably better known as 'Arthur Brooke', the editor of Pearsons 'Big Budget' throughout most of its run, 1897–1909. He was only 18 when he first took up the post. Was an ideal editor who took a keen interest in his young readers and their letters. Also edited 'Boys Leader' and 'Boys Friend Weekly' for a time. Was an expert horticulturist and his home, on the outskirts of Hounslow, was said to be a paradise of flowers. He died on the 4th March 1945. His editorship on the Big Budget so impressed a young reader – F. Addington Symonds – that in later years he not only moulded his creation 'The Champion'

on the old paper, but employed his old editor on the staff. **Pen-names:** Arthur Brooke. Berkeley Crane. Carras Yorke and Howard Steele (one of a syndicate of writers).
Chums. Scout. Champion Annual.

Marshall, D.
Scout.

Marshall, H. P. *(r.n.)*
Pen-name: Jonathan Stark.

Marshall, James *(r.n. Claude Rister)*
Western Library.

Marshall, John *(r.n. Frank S. Pepper)*
Tiger. Champion. Champion Library. Champion Annual. Triumph Annual.

Marshall, S. P.
Chums.

Mart, Donovan *(r.n. E. Le Breton Martin)*
Champion Annual. Young Britain (1st). Pluck (3rd). Champion. Boys Leader. Big Budget.

Martin, A. L. *(r.n.)*
One of the writers in the Modern Sexton Blake Library. Had a story published under the 'Desmond Reid' pen-name.
S.B.L. (3rd).

Martin, Ernest . *(r.n.)*
Born 1862. Author of several dramas and plays. Wrote for many leading magazines and newspapers.
B.O.P.

Martin, E. Le Breton *(r.n.)*
Born in 1874. Prolific writer of boys' stories during the 1900–20 period. His most famous serial was in The Scout entitled 'Boys of the Otter Patrol' which was later reprinted in book form. He was killed in a road accident in Kensington, London, in 1944.
Pen-names: Martin Shaw. Raymond Lee. Donovan Mart.
Newnes Adventure Library. Bulldog Breed Lib. Chums. Scout,

Martin, Harold
Merry & Bright (2nd).

Martin, Harry W.
Scout.

Martin, James
Sports Budget (2nd). Football and Sports Lib.

Martin, John
Champion. Modern Boy. Triumph Annual.
Martin, John S.
Captain.
Martin, P.
Schoolboys Pocket Library (Swan).
Martin, Radcliffe
Chums.
Martin, R. D'O.
B.O.P.
Martin, Stuart *(r.n.)*
Sometimes spelt 'Stewart' as Christian name.
Modern Boy. Boys Realm (2nd). B.F.L. (1st and 2nd). Scout.
Popular (2nd). Magnet. Boys Friend Weekly (2nd).
Martin, Thomas *(r.n.)*
An expert on the Sexton Blake saga, and has written quite a few stories for the modern S.B.L. Has also written numerous stories and articles for other magazines and papers, often with a supernatural theme. Lives at Bristol.
Pen-name: Martin Thomas.
Martin, W. *(r.n.)*
Pen-name: Hamilton Kingsley.
Martineau, Harriet *(r.n.)*
Born in Norwich 1802. Author of what was probably the first school story (The Crofton Boys) published in 1841 – 16 years before 'Tom Brown's Schooldays'. It had some well-told episodes and even touches of humour, but its characters were merely puppets and the story overloaded with morals. It was popular for many years and several eminent authors praised it, including George Eliot and Maurice Baring. She also wrote several other children's books, and works on political economy and history. She died in 1876.
Martyn, Fred.
Chums.
Martyn, Ivor *(r.n. Bernard Smith)*
Young Britain (1st). Rocket. Pluck (3rd). Champion.
Martyn, Tom
Boys Friend Weekly (1st).
Marvel, Holt *(r.n. Eric Maschwitz)*
Thriller Library.

Marviss, Charles
Football Novels.
Marwick, J. D.
Chatterbox.
Marx, William James
B.O.P.
Maschwitz, Eric *(r.n.)*
Born 1901, Birmingham. Educated at Repton School, Gonville and Caius College, Cambridge. Wrote for Sovereign Magazine, Women's Pictorial, Blue Magazine. With the BBC 1926-27. Wrote plays, films, songs, was a Lt. Col. in Intelligence Corps.
Pen-name: Holt Marvel.
Masefield, John *(r.n.)*
Born at Ledbury 1878 and educated at Kings School, Warwick. Was Poet Laureate from 1930 until his death in 1967, when apart from his fine verse, he wrote many novels and several books for young people.
Chatterbox.
Mason, Bower
Modern Wonder.
Mason, E.
Chums.
Masterman, Rex
Champion.
Masters, Bat *(r.n. Bernard Buley)*
Boxing Novels (1st). Football & Sports Lib. Racing Novels (1st and 2nd).
Masters, Paul *(r.n. G. R. Samways)*
Gem (2nd). B.F.L. (1st).
Masterson, Val *(r.n. H. T. Wright)*
Western Library.
Mathams, W. J.
B.O.P.
Matheson, Duncan
Lion.
Matthews, Leonard James *(r.n.)*
Born Islington, London, 10th October 1914. As a small boy, his father provided him weekly with every comic and boys' paper then published. At school his essays were regularly printed in

the school magazine, and he looked forward to a journalistic career. At an early age, however, his family (who were in the hotel business) moved to Liverpool, and Fleet Street seemed very far away. After a succession of jobs, which included working as an apprentice for a firm of Liverpool architects, and in the hotel business, he eventually settled down in London.

For a time he worked for the Bayswater store of William Whitely, where he not only edited the house magazine but – being a talented musician – he conducted both the Whitely Light Orchestra and the Golden Rhythm Boys. For a short time before the war he contributed to D. C. Thomson's comics, but he eventually joined the Amalgamated Press in May 1939. Serving in the R.A.F. in the last war, he did very valuable work in writing technical scripts for the Air Ministry.

Afterwards he returned to the Amalgamated Press on the staff of 'Knockout', which around this period was featuring both Billy Bunter and Sexton Blake. He soon rose to the position of Managing Editor, and with the retirement of P. Montague Haydon in July 1961 as Director of Juvenile Publications, it was natural that he should take his place. Already a writer of children's books, serials, and a cartoonist regularly contributing picture strips, he has to date produced around twenty new magazines, nearly all with great success. Probably the greatest was 'Look and Learn', followed closely by 'Treasure'.

Historically minded, Mr Matthews is an expert on history, especially on Napoleon. Also, he has a deep interest in Old Boys' papers, and especially artists; and his knowledge of them is probably as good as many of the other experts in this field. One must also remember Comet (1949–51) which had original Greyfriars stories by Frank Richards, 'Sun' (1952–3) Tom Merry Tales, Film Fun (1961) stories of St Frank's, 'Knockout' (1960–61) stories of Rookwood, 'Look and Learn' (1963) stories of Greyfriars.

Founder of Magazine Editors Club to which important speakers are invited.

Maurelly, A. R.
B.O.P.

Maxwell, Allan *(r.n. William J. Bayfield)*
S.B.L. (2nd).

242

Maxwell, Gordon *(r.n. Walter Shute)*
Boys Realm (2nd). Boys Realm of Sport & Adventure. B.F.L. (2nd).
Maxwell, Herbert *(r.n. W. J. Lomax)*
Marvel (1st). Boys Friend Weekly (2nd). Chums. Scout. Union Jack (1st and 2nd). B.F.L. (1st). Boys Herald. Pluck (1st). Big Budget.
Maxwell, Jack *(r.n. Ernest L. McKeag)*
Modern Boy. Triumph Annual. Champion. Champion Lib. Triumph. Boys Wonder Lib.
Maxwell, Thomas D.
B.O.P.
May, A. H. S. *(r.n.)*
Probably Harold May, who was educated at Dulwich College, and who became editor of The Nelson Lee Library until 1926 – according to experts, the best period of all its run. May, who was a newspaper man, was a very clever individual and when he left the Amalgamated Press in 1926, it has been said that the Nelson Lee Library gradually declined in readership until it finished in 1933. May, who lived at Richmond, was last seen in 1940 at Hammersmith, London, but all attempts to trace him for important data on his period of office have proved fruitless.
Young Britain (1st). Rocket.
May, W. J.
Boys Torch Adventure Library.
Maycock, Sidney Arthur *(r.n.)*
Scout.
Mayland, W. W.
Captain.
Mayne, Arthur *(r.n. R. A. C. Batchelor)*
Marvel (2nd). Boys Herald. Boys Friend Weekly (2nd). Chums.
Mayne, Maurice
B.F.L. (1st). Boys Realm (1st).
Mayne, Talbot
Diamond Library (1st). Detective Tales (2nd).
Mayo, Douglas
Vanguard Library (Trapps Holmes).
Mead, Charles
Triumph.

Mead, Matt *(r.n. Ross Richards)*
S.B.L. (5th).
Mead, Philip
Boys Realm (2nd).
Meade, Ronald
Comet.
Meadows, Wilson
Marvel (1st).
Meagher, Miss M. *(r.n.)*
Pen-name: Buck Marriott.
Mecair, F. C.
B.O.P.
Mee, Shirley
Union Jack (1st). Pluck (1st). Marvel (1st).
Melbourne, Ivor *(r.n. L. E Ransome)*
Champion Annual.
Mellalieu, James S. *(r.n. John S. Margerison)*
B.F.L. (1st). Boys Friend Weekly (2nd).
Meredith, David
B.O.P.
Meredith, Geoffrey
Champion Library. Triumph. Chums Annual.
Meredith, Hal *(r.n. Harry Blyth)*
Union Jack (1st). Marvel (1st).
Meredith, Captain Tom
Pluck (1st).
Meriton, Peter *(r.n. Alfred John Hunter)*
S.B.L. (3rd).
Merivale, J.
Scout. Boys Torch Adventure Library.
Merland, Oliver *(r.n.)*
Wrote stories of Sexton Blake for the Union Jack and S.B.L.
introducing the character, Topper, who was an extra assistant
to Blake. Merland himself was said to be an aristocratic-looking
man who wore a monocle – an older version of Arthur
Augustus D'Arcy. A photo-drawing of him appeared in an early
Union Jack.
Pen-names: Colin Collins. Singleton Pound. Douglas Grant.
Union Jack (1st). S.B.L. (1st). (anon).

Merrick, Jim *(r.n. C. Eaton Fearn)*
Triumph.
Merriman, Maurice *(r.n. S. Clarke Hook)*
Marvel (2nd). Young Britain (1st). B.F.L. (1st). Pluck (2nd).
Gem (1st).
Merrion, Nick
Comic Library.
Merry, Malcolm James *(r.n.)*
One of publisher Edward Lloyd's most prolific and lurid
'Penny Dreadful' writers. He was reputed to have had as many
as ten serials running at the same time. Amongst his titles were
'Ada the Betrayed' and 'The Unspeakable'. His works ran in
various papers including Lloyds Miscellany, but mainly
appeared in penny parts.
Pen-names: James Malcolm Rymer. Malcolm J. Errym.
Merton, Alma
Young Britain (1st).
Metcalfe, Eric *(r.n.)*
Boys Realm (1st). Union Jack (1st). Pluck (1st). Marvel (1st).
Metcalfe, W. C. *(r.n. C. Lawrence)*
Bullseye (Aldine).
Metford, Major Lionel Seymour *(r.n.)*
Born in Kent. Lived in British Columbia. Commissioned in the
Infantry and transferred to the R.F.C. in 1915. Was a pioneer
of the parachute. Started writing in 1921, when his air stories
were very popular in the U.S.A.
Chums. Chums Annual.
Methley, A. A.
Chatterbox.
Methley, Noel T. *(r.n.)* **F.R.G.S.**
Boys Herald. Chums.
Methley, Violet M. *(r.n.)*
Wrote several plays and books, also wrote for all leading
magazines such as Strand, Pearsons, etc.
Chatterbox. B.O.P.
Methuen, John *(r.n. John Keble Bell)*
Bell in his lifetime claimed to have written boys' stories under
this pen-name, but so far they have not been traced.
Miall, Derwent *(r.n.)*
Wrote mainly for Henderson's publications, for which he did

many fine serials, including 'Schoolboys Three' which featured a boy named Bunter, the date being 1905, some three years before the Magnet came out.
Boys Champion Story Paper. Nuggets. Lot-O'-Fun. Marvel (1st). Young Britain (1st). Pluck (1st). Pocket Budget. Nugget Library. (1st and 2nd). Comic Life. Chums.

Michael, John *(r.n. Ernest Sempill)*
Boys Journal.

Michael, Paul *(r.n. Ernest Sempill)*
Boys Journal.

Middleton, Desmond
Chums.

Mighels. P. V.
Boys Friend Weekly (1st).

Miles, M. E.
Thriller.

Miles, Stanley
Ranger (2nd).

Millar, Ashton
Football Weekly.

Miller, C. N.
Pioneer.

Miller, G. M.
Chums Annual.

Miller, J. *(r.n.)*
Surprise (A.P.) (anon).

Miller, Lawrence *(r.n. E. W. Alais)*
Empire Library (1st). B.F.L. (1st).

Milligan, W. H.
B.O.P.

Millington, Ernest
Diamond Library (1st).

Millington, T. S.
B.O.P.

Mills, Clifford
Captain.

Mills, George *(r.n.)*
A schoolmaster in a Sussex preparatory school who has also written three highly enjoyable prep. school stories – 'Meredith & Co.', 'King Willow' and 'Minor and Major'. All were

published in 1939 and have been reprinted in more recent years.

Mills, Morris
Chums.

Mills, T. Flower
Young England.

Miln, H. Crichton   *(r.n.)*
Educated at Eton and was the son of a well-known authoress. Turned out a vast amount of stories of all types for the Amalgamated Press in the 1920–30 period, but wrote far more in the girls' fiction field than in the boys'. Was believed to be at one time on the staff of the Girls Friend Library, where as often as not he was writing all the stories. Died in Bulowai, South Africa in 1957, where he was working on a newspaper.
Pen-names: Jack Crichton. Gillis Harper.
All Sports. S.B.L. (1st) (anon). Boys Friend Weekly (2nd). Startler (anon).

Milton, Mark   *(r.n. S. Rossiter Shepherd)*
Pluck (3rd).

Mitchell, Allan *(r.n.)* **Captain**
Son of artist Hutton Mitchell, who contributed many short stories for boys' papers in the 1920's. Was last heard of in charge of an art gallery in Canada. His father, who was the first Greyfriars artist, is reputed to have based one of his famous illustrated characters on his son, Allan.
Boys Realm (2nd). Gem (2nd) Scout.

Mitchell, Hutton   *(r.n.)*
Strictly an artist, and whose claim to fame is probably because he was the very first artist to illustrate Greyfriars in the Magnet in 1908, although there is evidence that he was a far better artist in other fields. Probably wrote for adult papers, but this is the only story traced in boys' fiction.
Cheer, Boys, Cheer.

Mitchell, Ogilvy
Aldine Half-Holiday Lib. Robin Hood (1st and 3rd). True Blue (1st and 2nd).

Mitchell, Randolph
Hotspur Book for Boys.

Mitford, Bertram   *(r.n.)*
Captain.

Mix, Tom *(r.n.) Famous film star*
Story obviously 'ghosted'.
Boys Cinema.

Mizzen
Chums.

Moberley, Lucy Gertrude *(r.n.)*
Born 1860. Wrote serials for all leading magazines. Windsor,
Cassells, etc., and also women's magazines.
Captain.

Mole, M. *(r.n.)* **Miss**
Chums.

Molohan, Brew
Captain.

Monck, Tristam K. *(r.n. T. G. Dowling Maitland)*
Pluck (1st). Marvel (1st and 2nd). Union Jack (1st and 2nd).
Boys Herald. Boys Realm (1st).

Moncrieff, R. Hope *(r.n.)*
A schoolmaster who was educated at Edinburgh University.
He retired in 1868 to devote himself full-time to writing. The
first volume of B.O.P. saw his serial 'At the Masthead' and he
later had many more published. Moncrieff travelled widely
in Europe and the Far East, and was an expert on American
History. He had many hard cover books published and 'My
Schoolboy Friend' was regarded as a classic by many people.
Pen-name: Ascott R. Hope.

Monk, Richard
Boxing Novels (1st).

Monteith, Ewen *(r.n. S. Clarke Hook)*
Union Jack (1st). Marvel (1st).

Monteith, Owen *(r.n. S. Clarke Hook)*
Union Jack (1st). Pluck (1st).

Moon, George P. *(r.n.)*
Pen-name: Montague Pembury.
Boys' Journal.

Moor, J. Marston
True Blue (2nd).

Moorcock, Michael *(r.n.)*
After producing several amateur magazines he became editor
of Tarzan Comics. Later sub-editor on the Sexton Blake
Library. Always retaining a deep interest in science fiction he

248

later became editor of a science fiction magazine and has written a considerable number of stories, also had books published, with excellent reviews. Wrote only one Blake story, published under the 'Desmond Reid' pen-name. S.B.L. (3rd).

Moore, Amos
Western Library.

Moore, Hilda F.
B.O.P.

Moore, L. P.
Captain.

Moore, Tony *(r.n.)*
Pen-name: Tony Morris.
Champion.

Moray, Dugald *(r.n. Dugald Matheson Cumming-Skinner)*
Champion. Champion Library.

Mordaunt, Wilton *(r.n. — Gill)*
Union Jack (1st). Marvel (1st).

Morgan, F. L.
Young England. Captain.

Morgan, Geoffrey
B.O.P.

Morion, John
Comet, Sun, Knockout.

Morland, Bart *(r.n. E. Harcourt Burrage)*
New Boys Paper.

Morland, Nigel *(r.n.)*
Writer of well-known thrillers featuring his character, Miss Pym. Was a great friend of Edgar Wallace. Editor of Edgar Wallace Mystery Magazine and now editor of The Criminologist. Thriller.

Morley, C.
Chatterbox.

Mornington, John
Young Britain (1st).

Morrell, Dennis
Chums.

Morrell Wallace *(r.n. Harold G. Garrish)*
Morel
Marvel (1st).

Morris, David
Sun.
Morris, Henry
Ranger (1st). Chums. Chums Annual.
Morris, Patrick   *(r.n. Viscount Mountmorres)*
Boys Friend Weekly (2nd). Chips.
Morris, Stanley
Wrote at least two excellent public school stories in novel form, published by Thomas Nelson in the 1930's. Both were later reprinted. Titles were: 'The Senior Prefect' and 'The Penalty Area'.
Morris, Tony   *(r.n. Tony Moore)*
Modern Boy.
Morris, William H.   *(r.n.)*
Favourite Comic. Chips. Puck. Rainbow. Wonder, Butterfly. Chicks Own (all anon). Chums. Little Folks, Captain. Scout. Boys Magazine. Young England. B.O.P. Adventure (anon). Gem (2nd). Startler (anon). Greyfriars Holiday Annual.
Morton, N. Douglas   *(r.n.)*
Gem (2nd).
Morton, Paul
Thriller.
Moss, R. A.
Chums.
Mountmorres, Viscount   *(r.n.)*
Born 23rd September 1872. His full title was William Geoffrey Bouchard de Montmerency, Sixth Viscount Mountmorres. Was an Irishman from County Galway. Contributed to Answers in his early days as a free-lance journalist. Also wrote serials, probably his most famous being one featuring Sexton Blake in Chips. In 1935 he was Rector of Wokingham, and he died on the 2nd December 1936.
Pen-name: Patrick Morris.
Chums.
Mowbray, John   *(r.n. Gunby Hadath)*
Scout.
Mowbray, Martin
Football Novels.
Mowbray, W. J.   *(r.n.)*
Pen-name: Eric Gascoigne.

Moxon, Stanley
    Buffalo Bill Lib. (1st and 2nd). True Blue (2nd).
Muddock, Joyce Emerson Preston *(r.n.)*
    Lived at Harrow and wrote many novels, as well as contributing to all leading magazines.
    Pen-name: Dick Donovan.
Mugford, J. Trounsell *(r.n.)*
    Boys Friend Weekly (1st). Union Jack (1st).
Muir, Augustus *(r.n.)*
    Born in Ontario, Canada, 1892 and educated at George Heriot's School, Edinburgh, and also at the same city's University. Entered journalism and became assistant editor, and later editor of 'The World' Magazine. Wrote several humorous stories about a character called 'Penny Farthing' for the Captain, when he was still in his twenties. Later wrote many detective novels, including some featuring a detective named Dr Louis Raphael. Also contributed to The Strand and other leading magazines. Was an authority on Scotland and published several Scottish travel books.
    Captain.
Muir, Wardrop Openshaw *(r.n.)*
    Born in 1878, the son of a clergyman and educated at Merchant Taylors School and Brighton College. Author of several novels and essays. Died in June 1927.
    Pen-name: Stewart Lang.
Mulford, Clarence Edward *(r.n.)*
    Born 3rd February 1883. Author of many Western novels, including the world-famous cowboy character 'Hopalong Cassidy' in 1907.
    Western Library.
Mulholland, Clara
    Young England.
Mundy, Talbot *(r.n.)*
    Born in London, April 23rd, 1879. Educated at Rugby and served nearly ten years as Government official in Africa and India, which gave him the authentic background for many of his stories. Travelled over India on horseback, even going into dangerous Tibet. Visited the U.S.A. in 1911 and decided to stay there and become a citizen. Joined the U.S.A. Theosophical Society in the twenties and those of his books written after

this date show the influence of occultism. His most famous story – 'King of the Khyber Rifles' – was made into a film and all his books are much sought-after today, particularly in the U.S.A. where first editions fetch very good prices. Died August 5th, 1940.
Boys Journal. Thriller.

Munro, A. G. (B.A.)
Boys Friend Weekly (1st). Chums.

Munro, J.
B.O.P.

Murch, Mrs N.
Born 24th May 1868. Sister of Richard Starr. Continued with Starr's stories when he was in the R.F.C. in the First World War and wrote stories for boys for about twenty years. At one time she and her brother were practically writing the whole of Young Britain between them.
Pen-name: Vera Lovel.

Murdoch, Temple
Ranger (2nd). B.F.L. (2nd).

Murphy, J. M.
Union Jack (1880).

Murray, A. C. *(r.n.)*
A prolific writer of stories in the 1906–15 period, mainly those with a military flavour, when according to an ex-officer editor, Murray was 'in the ranks'. Very little is known about him except that a photograph once appeared of him in a boys' paper showing him as a rather tough-looking individual with a crew-cut. Had a brother named C. G. Murray, as revealed in an editorial chat. A. C. Murray had the distinction of writing the very first story in the Nelson Lee Library – 'The Mystery of Limehouse Reach'. Was reported to be a personal friend of Christopher Lawrence.
Pen-names: Hubert Feveril. Andrew Gray.
Popular (1st) (anon). Union Jack (2nd) (anon). Nelson Lee Lib. (old) (anon). Boys Realm. Football & Sports Lib. (anon).

Murray, Adrian *(r.n.)*
Pen-name: Richard Gordon.

Murray, Andrew Nicholas *(r.n.)*
Born in 1880 and wrote his first Sexton Blake story for the Union Jack in March 1911, entitled 'Sexton Blake, Boxing

Trainer'. Served as an officer in the Army and so was able to write a great deal on military themes. He created several famous characters for the saga, including Count Ivor Carlac (U.J. 468), Professor Kew (U.J. 511), The Honourable John Lawless, Trouble Nantucket and Adrian Steele. He later paired Carlac and Kew together in several stories for the S.B.L. Altogether he wrote approx. 173 Blake stories, not counting those he probably wrote in Answers and Penny Pictorial. Later he owned his own publishing business and was a good friend of G. R. Sims. Wrote several books under the pen-name of 'Nicholas Islay' but in the mid-twenties he suffered a severe mental illness. Died at Epsom, Surrey, in 1929. As stated in the entry of H. H. Clifford Gibbons, this writer 'ghosted' for Murray when he first started.

Pen-names: Malcolm Arnold. Capt. Malcolm Arnold. Vesey Deane.

Pluck (3rd). Nugget Lib. (2nd). S.B.L. (1st) (anon). S.B.L. (2nd). Football & Sports Favourite. Nelson Lee Lib. (2nd New Series revised). Detective Weekly (rewrite). Champion. Union Jack (2nd) (anon). Startler (anon) (rewrite). Boys Realm Football & Sports Lib. (anon).

Murray, C. Geoffrey *(r.n.)*

Brother of A. C. Murray and likewise nothing is known about him at all. An editor revealed in his editorial that A.C. and C.G. were brothers. Both surprisingly dropped completely out of writing just after the First World War.

Pen-names: Raymond Loxley. Guy Kingsford. Geoffrey Gray.

Dreadnought. Boys Journal. Cheer, Boys, Cheer. B.F.L. (1st).

Murray, Edgar Joyce *(r.n.)*

Born 1878. Most prolific writer of stories in the 1895–1925 period. Probably his most famous creation was Ferrers Lord, the multi-millionaire genius, and his arch enemy Prince Michael Scaroff, who appeared in the Boys Friend. Another character was Graydon Garth, who appeared in rival publications published by Pearson's. He also wrote stories of a school called Calcroft. In the Boys Realm he wrote an account of 'Charlie Chaplin's Schooldays' which was later republished in the B.F.L. In the Sexton Blake field he introduced Ferrers Lord, as well as another character named Gun Waga. Murray was a countryman who used to write all his stories in microscopic handwriting, so small that an editor friend who remembers him and his work had to get his wife to read them to him. Really very little is known about this author, as another editor can recall him only by the large pair of squeaky boots he wore!

Pen-names: Sidney Drew. Max Rover.

S.B.L. (1st and 2nd) (anon). Union Jack (2nd) (anon). Boys Realm Football and Sports Lib. (anon).

Murray, Marr *(r.n.)*
Chums. Dreadnought.

Murray, Robert *(r.n. Robert Murray Graydon)*
Union Jack (2nd). Boys Herald. Pluck (2nd). Boys Friend Weekly (2nd). Gem (2nd). Boys Realm (1st and 2nd). Boys Realm of Sport and Adventure. Football and Sports Lib. B.F.L. (1st and 2nd). Boys Journal. Thriller. Cheer, Boys, Cheer. Detective Weekly.

Murray, Sidney
True Blue (2nd).

Murray, William *(r.n. William Murray Graydon)*
Nelson Lee Library (old).

Mylne, W. C. R.
Union Jack (1880).

Neilson, Vernon *(r.n. Percy A. Clarke)*
Ranger (2nd). B.F.L. (2nd).

Neish, Duncan *(r.n. A. Carney Allan)*
Chums Annual. Chums.

Neish, R.
Captain.

Nelson, Barry *(r.n. R. G. Thomas)*
Champion.

Nelson, George
Champion Annual.

Nelson, Stanley H. *(r.n.)*
One of the editors of Boys Magazine.
Football & Sports Lib. Chums Annual. Pioneer. Sports Budget (2nd). Boys Broadcast.

Nelson, Steve *(r.n. John William Bobin)*
Sports Fun. Football & Sports Lib. Football & Sports Favourite.

Nelson, T. *(r.n.)*
Pen-name: Duncan Brown.
Nelson, Victor *(r.n. John William Bobin)*
Champion Lib. Football & Sports Lib. Magnet. Pluck (3rd).
Triumph. Champion. Boys Friend Weekly (2nd). B.F.L. (1st
and 2nd).
Nendick, Victor R. *(r.n.)*
Boys Herald. Boys Friend Weekly (2nd). B.O.P. Scout. Boys
Journal. Cheer, Boys, Cheer. Chums.
Neolan, Ned
Pluck (1st). Marvel (1st in coll. with Ben Brightly).
Newcome, Colin *(r.n. F. W. Young)*
Chums.
Newman, Kenneth E. *(r.n.)*
Editor and author of the short-lived 'School Yarn Magazine'
which appeared in 1947. The stories were about Rippingham
School and were based on a B.B.C. radio series written by
Newman in 1936. Newman also wrote a number of substitute
St Jim's, Rookwood and Greyfriars stories. Now a Civil
Servant, Newman still writes for the B.B.C. at times.
Pen-names: Martin Clifford (Gem). Owen Conquest (Gem)
(short Rookwood stories). Frank Richards (Magnet). School-
yarn Magazine.
Newman, L. J.
Schoolboys Pocket Library (Gerald Swan).
Newton, Wilfred Douglas *(r.n.)*
Born in London 1884 and educated at St Aloysius College,
Highgate and St Edmund's College, Ware. Special Correspon-
dent Hants Advertiser 1913. Acting editor T.P.'s Journal 1914.
Leader and feature writer Lloyds Weekly News and Daily
Chronicle. Book critic for The Sketch and Illustrated London
News. Special Correspondent Daily Chronicle and New York
Times and was with M.O.I. 1940–45. Wrote several books,
when for stories he dropped his first Christian name.
Thriller. Detective Weekly.
Nicholls, Anthony *(r.n. Anthony Parsons)*
Modern Boy. B.F.L. (2nd).
Nimmo, John A.
Chums.

Nixon, F. J.
Boys Torch Adventure Library.
Nolan, John Vincent *(r.n.)*
Western Library.
Nordhoff, Charles Bernard *(r.n.)*
Born 1st Feb. 1877 and died 11th April 1947 at Santa Barbara, California.
Thriller.
Norman, Marshall
Captain.
Norman, Philip *(r.n. George Norman Philips)*
Detective Weekly.
Norman, Victor *(r.n. L. E. Ransome)*
Champion Annual. Lion.
Norris, Arthur
Scout.
North, Colonel *(r.n. Cecil Bullivant)*
Boys Life.
North, Captain George *(r.n. Robert Louis Stevenson)*
Young Folks Tales.
North, Jack *(r.n. John Nix Pentelow)*
Dreadnought. Marvel (2nd). Champion. Boys Herald. Sport and Adventure. B.F.L. (1st and 2nd). Pluck (2nd). Boys Realm (1st). Boys Friend Weekly (2nd).
North, James
Champion Annual.
North, Pearson *(r.n. T. E. Pearson)*
Boys Realm (2nd).
Northcroft, George J. H. *(r.n.)*
Born 1868 at Liverpool. Was general editor of the Religious Tract Society for some years, and editor of the B.O.P. from 1933–35. He wrote several books, including 'The Story of London' and 'How to Write Verse'. His wife, Dorothea Northcroft, was also a journalist and editress of 'Housecraft' Magazine for some years.
Norton, Victor *(r.n. G. L. Dalton)*
Ranger (1st and 2nd). B.F.L. (2nd).
Nutbrown, Maurice *(r.n.)*
Sub-editor on several Amalgamated Press boys' papers in the 1916–25 period. The comic Chuckles was one, and Boys Realm

another. Wrote short pieces and stories, probably his best being substitute St Frank's stories for the latter paper. Unfortunately Nutbrown became seriously ill and later a permanent invalid. His wife, Hetty Nutbrown, was once on the Red Magazine and also acted as a literary agent.
Pen-name: Maurice Denbigh.
Boys Realm (2nd St Frank's sub. stories) (anon).

Nye, Whitworth
True Blue (2nd).

O'Brien, Captain
Boys Friend Weekly (2nd).

O'Brine, Paddy Manning *(r.n.)*
Wrote a screen play for the Sexton Blake film 'Murder at Site Three' (based on W. Howard Baker's S.B.L. 'Crime is my Business') which was released in 1960, with Geoffrey Toone appearing as Blake. Also published several hard-cover mystery novels featuring a Secret Service agent hero named Mike O'Kelly.

O'Dare, Kerry *(r.n. Richard Starr)*
Young Britain (2nd).

O'Donnell, Peter *(r.n.)*
Pen-name: John Barnes.

O'Flynn, Jimmy *(r.n. Robert Murray Graydon)*
Football & Sports Library. Football & Sports Favourite

Ogalvay, George
Aldine Half-Holiday.

O'Grady, Felix *(r.n. John Edward Gunby Hadath)*
Bulldog Breed Library.

Ogrady, Standish *(r.n.)*
Born 1846.
Chums.

Old Boy, An *(r.n. Talbot Baines Reed)*
B.O.P.

Old Cap
Football Novels

'Old Fag' *(r.n. R. S. Warren Bell)*
Captain.

Oldham, Hugh R. *(r.n. Joan Whitford)*
Western Library.

Oliver, Gertrude Kent *(r.n.)*
  Pen-name: Kent Carr.
Oliver *(r.n.)*
Olliver, Tom
  Name was also at times used by William Murray Graydon.
  Pluck (1st). Boys Herald. Boys Realm (1st). Boys Friend
  Weekly (2nd). Marvel (2nd).
O'Mant, Hedley Percival Angelo *(r.n.)*
  Was Irish on his father's side and Italian on his mother's side.
  Born 2nd September 1899. Attended King Edward VI School
  at Whitley with G. R. Samways and H. W. Twyman, and
  where yet another writer, Ernest Brindle, attended some years
  before. After leaving school he went to work for Walter Light
  I/C of Aldine Publications at Crown Court, but found the offices
  depressing and joined his former school friends at Amalgamated
  Press in the Magnet and Gem offices. Later he became Chief
  Sub-Editor on the Magnet. During the First World War he
  joined the Army, but was later transferred to the R.F.C., ending
  up as a pilot. On returning to Fleetway he edited many boys'
  papers: Nelson Lee Library for a very short time, Ranger, and
  Pilot. Was also a prolific writer and, apart from writing, quite
  probably the most popular editor of all time at Amalgamated
  Press. Wrote quite a few substitute stories of Greyfriars, St
  Jim's and Rookwood. His best stories were those of flying,
  written under the name of 'Hedley Scott', and sometimes
  'Captain Robert Hawke' (also used by G. M. Bowman). He
  also continued the Ferrers Locke stories after Charles Hamilton
  had left off. His last editorial post was probably on 'Wild West
  Weekly' as during the Second World War he served in the
  R.A.F. as a Squadron Leader (non-op.). His last contributions
  appeared in comics such as Radio Fun, etc. He became ill
  in the 1950's and eventually died on the 30th December 1955
  of bronchial pneumonia.
  Pen-names: Hedley Owen. Hedley Scott. Captain Robert
  Hawke. Hamilton Scott. Martin Clifford (Gem). Frank
  Richards (Magnet). Owen Conquest (Boys Friend Weekly).
  Pilot (anon). Thomson Papers. Wild West Weekly (anon).
O'Neill, Lucas
  Vanguard Library (Trapps Holmes).

Openshaw, G. H. *(r.n.)*
Pen-names: Duncan Sterne. Justin Shaw. John Gale. Dick Shaw.
Surprise (anon).

Oppenheim, Edward Phillips *(r.n.)*
Born in London 1866 and educated at Wyggeston Grammar School, Leicester. Followed in his father's footsteps and became a leather merchant in Leicester. He held this job until he was 40, writing books only in his spare time. Then he left the leather business to devote himself to full-time authorship. His first novel 'Expiation' appeared in 1887 when he was 21. Later came over 100 novels and 40 books of short stories. Used the name of 'Anthony Partridge' for some of his novels. Although not strictly a writer of boys' fiction his stories nevertheless did appear in The Thriller.
Thriller.

Orme, K. *(r.n.)*
A writer of a few substitute Gem stories, and probable contributor of short pieces for the Companion papers and Holiday Annuals.
Pen-name: Martin Clifford (Gem).
Holiday Annual.

Orton, Hugh
B.F.L. (2nd).

Osborne, Adrian T.
Diamond Lib. (1st). True Blue (2nd). Pocket Budget of Short and Serial Stories. Boys Leader.

Osborne, Mark *(r.n. John William Bobin)*
Detective Weekly. S.B.L. (2nd) (one story by W. J. Bayfield).

Outhwaite, Ernest
Scout.

Overton, Robert
Made his début in boys' papers in the first numbers of Sampson Low's 'Boys' in 1892 with the serial 'Lights Out'. Usually specialised in school stories with a background of mystery and adventure. Also published several boys' books.
Chums. Boys.

Owen, Clifford *(r.n. Charles Hamilton)*
Diamond Library (1st).

259

Owen, Miss D. E. *(r.n.)*
Pen-name: Don English.

Owen, Hedley *(r.n. Hedley O'Mant)*
Modern Boy.

Owen, Norman *(r.n. J. Walters)*
B.F.L. (1st).

Owen, Vincent *(r.n. Fred Gordon Cook)*
Gem (2nd).

Oxley, J. MacDonald
Captain. B.O.P.

O-X-O
Scout.

Ozanne, C. H.
Chums.

Packard, Frank Lucius *(r.n.)*
Born Montreal, Canada, 2nd Feb. 1877. Died 17th Feb. 1942.
Wrote quite a few novels and stories, usually in adult magazines.
Union Jack (2nd).

Padgett, Henry J.
Football and Sports Lib.

Page, Richard
Triumph. Champion.

Page, Walter
Newnes Adventure Library.

Pain, Allison
Chums. B.O.P.

Pain, Barry Eric Odell *(r.n.)*
Born Cambridge 1864, the son of a draper. He was educated at
Sedburgh, where he edited the school magazine. Likewise at
Cambridge University, where he edited 'Granta'. Became a
journalist and succeeded Jerome K. Jerome as editor of
'Today'. As a writer he excelled in humorous stories of working-
class life. His best-known books are those about 'Eliza', the
first appearing in 1900. He had the honour of writing the first
serial in Chums in 1893, entitled 'Two'. He died in 1928.
Chums.

Pain, G. O.
Chums.

Paine, Hammond   *(r.n. H. Clarke Hook)*
Chums.
Painton, Herbert
Dreadnought.
Palk, Arthur J.
Was the last 'new' author to write a Sexton Blake story in the Union Jack in 1933, before it became Detective Weekly. The 'write-up' about the author says that he was an Australian who came from Melbourne, and the story is set in that city; obviously written by someone with local knowledge. H. W. Twyman, the editor, thinks however that it may possibly be an old story by Arthur J. Patterson (same initials) re-written. It has at least been established that there was an author of that name, in Australia, who wrote a book.
Union Jack (2nd).
Palmer, E. Vance   *(r.n.)*
Pen-name: Vance Palmer.
Palmer, John Leslie   *(r.n.)*
Born 1895. Permanent secretariat to League of Nations, 1920.
Pen-name: Francis Beeding (with H. A. St G. Saunders).
Palmer, Vance   *(r.n. E. Vance Palmer)*
Chums. Boys Friend Weekly (2nd).
Panting, Arnold Clement   *(r.n.)*
Was editor of Boys Friend Weekly for a time and also wrote a few boys' stories himself. He was killed in World War I, whilst serving as a 2nd Lieutenant, as the result of a tragic flying accident on 23rd January 1917.
Pen-name: Clement Arnold.
Panting, James Harwood   *(r.n.)*
Prolific writer of boys' stories around the turn of the century. Was editor of Young Folks for a time. Wrote many hard-cover books for boys, which dealt mainly with school and circus life. Was believed to be the father of Clement and Phylis Panting.
Pen-name: Claude Heathcote
                    Claud
Panting, Phylis   *(r.n.)*
Editress of 'My Favourite' comic and was reported by all to be an extremely attractive woman. Later married Mr Digby Morton.

261

Parbuckle, Lieut (Royal Navy)
Union Jack (1880).
'Pard'
Chums.
Pardepp, R.
Boys Friend Weekly (1st).
Parker, Eric   *(r.n.)*
Born East Barnet, Herts., 1870 and educated at Eton and
Oxford. Was Assistant Editor of 'St James Gazette' 1900–2 and
editor of 'The Country Gentleman' 1902–7. Also wrote regularly
for 'The Spectator' and 'The Field'. Was editor-in-chief of the
latter 1930–37. Edited the famous Lonsdale Library of Sport,
with the Earl of Lonsdale. In 1922 wrote the classic story of
life at Eton College, 'Playing Fields', which has since gone into
many editions and is one of the most famous school stories ever
published. Wrote and edited many other books, but is no
relation to the famous Sexton Blake illustrator of the same name.
Parker, Martin
Scout.
Parry, David Harold   *(r.n.)*
Born in 1868 and came from a long line of distinguished
painters. His father and uncle were well-known artists of the
Manchester School. Parry himself studied art in London under
Calderon and Julian, and later in Paris. Painting throughout
his life was always his great love. In his early literary career in
the late 1880's he wrote for Cassell's Saturday Journal, Answers
and New York Herald. But it was through his friend, Max
Pemberton, that his work was guided into boys' fiction.
Pemberton was starting a new paper for Cassells called Chums,
and invited Parry to write the first serial for it. Parry accepted
and the serial – 'For Glory and Renown' began in the first
number of Chums in 1892. He began a long association with
this paper and was still writing for it in 1935.
In his time he wrote an enormous amount of fiction and factual
articles and in one seven-year period he wrote more than two
million words about Robin Hood.
He was also regarded as one of the greatest experts on the
Napoleonic Wars, as well as being an authority on all historical
and military matters, when his details in stories were correct
to the last minutiae.

He wrote his first serial for the Captain in 1899, entitled 'The King's Red Coat'. Parry lived and wrote in Norfolk all his life, in a little secluded cottage known as 'Ben Gunn's Cottage' near Barton Broad. A bad fall left him lame, but he was still a very enthusiastic shot and fisherman. He died there in January 1950, at the age of 82.

Pen-names: Morton Pike. Captain Wilton Blake.

Union Jack (2nd) (anon). Chums. Chums Annual. Lloyds Boys Adventure series. Captain. Cheer, Boys, Cheer. B.F.L. (1st and 2nd). Popular (1st) (anon). British Boy.

Parry, Peter

Sports Budget (2nd). Football & Sports Library. B.F.L. (2nd).

Parry, Reginald R.

Boys Life.

Parry, Richmond

Scout.

Parsons, Anthony *(r.n.)*

Born at Nuneaton, Warwickshire, June 21st 1893. Educated at Nuneaton Grammar School. He enlisted in the First World War and was given a commission and drafted to India. Whilst there was drafted into the R.F.C. becoming a pilot. He spent most of his time flying over the North West Frontier and later went on to Egypt.

In 1920 and out of the services he left England again for Africa, shooting elephants for a living, but later came home and started to write for a living. His first contributions were to the adult magazines such as Strand, Royal, Wide World and Blackwoods, etc. and it was not until 1937 that he wrote his first Blake story, and continued over the next 20 years, doing much to keep the S.B.L. going over the difficult war years. He took over the character of Gunga Dass, but he is chiefly re-membered for his conception of that brilliant Yard man, Superintendent Venner, and his Indian backgrounds. In all he wrote exactly 100 Blake stories; 99 in the S.B.L. and one in a Sexton Blake Annual. Six feet three inches tall, he was a very handsome man, even in his middle sixties. He died at Brighton on June 8th, 1963, at the age of 69. His favourite writer – not surprisingly – was H. Rider Haggard.

Pen-name: Anthony Nicholls.

Sexton Blake Annual. Thriller. S.B.L. (2nd and 3rd).

Parsons, B. *(r.n.)*
Pen-names: Warwick Young, Maurice Hunt.

Parsons, Harcourt
Chums.

Passingham, William John *(r.n.)*
Born in Essex 1897, educated at The Coopers County School.
In the 1930's was an instructor and lecturer in journalism and
short-story writing at the Regent Institute in London. Literary
editor, London General Press, 1933. He also contributed to
papers and magazines all over the world. His main subject was
boxing and his works on this sport have been widely read and
translated into every European language except Russian.
Football and Sports Lib. S.B.L. (3rd.) All Sports. Scout.

Pateman, J. S.
Union Jack (1st)

Paterson, Arthur Henry *(r.n.)*
Born in Bowden, Cheshire, 15th July 1862 and educated at the
University College School, London. Worked as a sheep rancher
in New Mexico, U.S.A., between 1877–79 as a farmer in
Western Kansas, 1879–80 and later as a clerk in a Merchants
Office in Birkenhead on returning to England in 1881, afterwards being promoted to a sub-manager in 1884.
1885–96 saw him District Secretary of the Charity Organisation in London. Between 1896 and 1909 he wrote 11 novels,
biographies, historical dramas and reference works. He later
wrote half-a-dozen books, and after being connected with many
other charitable organisations wrote his autobiography. His
first Sexton Blake story was written at the age of 64, easily the
oldest writer ever to do so, and he died 18 months later on the
16th January 1928. He left behind him a further 8 Blake stories,
which were all published. For the last two years of his life he
lived in Hampstead, London.
B.F.L. (2nd). Union Jack (2nd). Boys Realm (2nd). Gem (2nd).

Patrick, John
True Blue (2nd). Captain.

Patrick, Max *(r.n. James McCormack)*
Western Library.

Patterson, Ewen K.
Scout.

Patterson, George Andrew
B.O.P. Chums.

Paul, Policeman *(r.n. Harry Blyth)*
The son of Harry Blyth stated that his father had written boys'
stories under this name, but so far they have not been traced.

Paull, Harry Major *(r.n.)*
Born Monmouth, 1854, educated privately. Was a Civil
Servant, and lived at Hampstead. One of the B.O.P.'s earliest
and most popular authors. His first story 'The New Boy', a
serial, appeared in 1881, as did another 'A Week on the
Thames', followed by many more, as well as short stories.
Pen-name: Paul Blake.

Paxton, Alfred
B.O.P.

Payne-Crutchley *(r.n. F. H. Evans)*
Chums.

Pearce, Charles Edward *(r.n.)*
Editor of South London Press, 1878–82. Editor of Funny Folks
1882–86. Wrote several stories for Answers 1896–97. About 50
novelettes for Aldine 1895–1910. Many novels and about 70
serials, also over 500 short stories for various publications.
Lloyds School Yarns. Lloyds Detective Series. Young Folks.
Boys Leader. True Blue (1st). Aldine Mystery Novels. Comic
Cuts. Union Jack (2nd). Boys Friend Weekly (1st). Football &
Sports Favourite. Sports for Boys. Pluck (1st). Marvel (1st).
Lot-O'-Fun. Lloyds Boys Adventure Series.

Pearce, Charles Louis St John *(r.n.)*
Son of C. E. Pearce; their respective writings are still confused.
Before First World War used to play soccer in London's senior
games. Served throughout the war and originally intended to
become an artist. A skilled amateur actor and producer. Died
some time before Second World War.
Pen-names: Nat Fairbanks. St John Pearce.
Vanguard Lib. (Trapps Holmes). Boys Herald. Young
Britain (1st).

Pearce, C. S.
Pluck (1st).

Pearce, St John *(r.n. Charles Louis St John Pearce)*
Champion Annual. Chums Annual. Champion. Chums.

Pears, John
Chums.

Pearson, Alec George *(r.n.)*
A most prolific writer of boys' stories at the start of the century, especially for Aldine's and Amalgamated Press. Wrote several early Sexton Blake stories in the ½d Union Jack, also in the 2nd series. Created a number of detectives including Stanley Dare, the Boy Detective, Royston Gower, Herbert Trackett, Frank Ferrett, Dr Nevada and Dr Messina. Lived at Southsea, Portsmouth, during the latter part of his life, when he was reputed to be an ex-Naval man. It is presumed he died there just before the First World War.

Pen-names: Julian Linley. George Pearson. Capt. Russell Scott.
Boys Friend Weekly (1st and 2nd). Chums. Scout. Aldine Half-Holiday. True Blue (2nd). Wonder. Merry & Bright (2nd). Boys Leader. Lloyds Boys Adventure Series. Lloyds Detective Series. Cheer, Boys, Cheer. Detective Lib. Union Jack (1st and 2nd). Boys Realm (1st and 2nd). Sport and Adventure. Boys Journal. B.F.L. (1st). Pluck (1st and 2nd). Gem (2nd). Dreadnought. Magnet. Marvel (1st and 2nd). Popular (1st) (anon). Boys Herald. Boys Own Library (1st).

Pearson, E. V.
Chatterbox.

Pearson, George *(r.n. Alec G. Pearson)*
Diamond Library (1st).

Pearson, Shepperd *(r.n. Gunby Hadath)*
Cheer, Boys, Cheer.

Pearson, T. E. *(r.n.)*
Pen-name: Pearson North.

Peattie, Donald Culcross *(r.n.)*
Born 1898, Chicago. Educated at the Universities of Chicago and Harvard. Wrote several books, his special subjects being botany and natural history. Married to Louise Redfield Peattie, and collaborated with her on many stories.
Chums.

Peattie, Louise Redfield *(r.n.)*
Born 1900 in Illinois. Educated privately. Wife of Donald

266

Culcross Peattie. Wrote several books in collaboration with her husband, also stories.

Chums.

Peck, Franklin M.

Chums.

Peele, Ernest H.

Scout.

Pemberton, Sir Max *(r.n.)*

Born in Birmingham 1863 and educated at Merchant Taylors' School and Caius College, Cambridge. Was the first editor of Chums 1892-93 and wrote a first-class adventure serial for the first volume ('The Iron Pirate'). It was a great success and was later published in book form several times. Gave up the editorial position after a year to concentrate on writing novels, etc. Returned to become editor of Cassell's Magazine, 1896-1906, in which he had many stories published. Founded the London School of Journalism in 1920. Later became a Director of Northcliffe Newspapers and was also knighted. Wrote the biography of Lord Northcliffe and also his own autobiography 'Sixty Years Ago – and After'. Wrote several stage reviews and plays, as well as contributing many stories for magazines, including Strand. Was a Master of Arts and a Justice of the Peace, also a very keen sportsman in his day. Died on 2nd February 1950 at the age of 86.

Chums.

Pembroke, Richard

Boys Realm (2nd).

Pembroke, Ronald

Champion Annual.

Pembury, Grosvenor *(r.n. N. G. Haydon)*

Boys Realm (1st).

Pembury, Montague *(r.n. G. P. Moon)*

Boys Realm (1st).

Pendexter, Hugh

Scout.

Pendower, Jacques *(r.n.)*

One of the D. C. Thomson Group's leading Dixon Hawke writers and also wrote for all their main juvenile papers. Wrote a Sexton Blake story, revised and published as by 'James Stagg'.

Wizard. Rover. Dixon Hawke Casebook. Dixon Hawke Lib.
Adventure (all anon). Knockout. Sun.

Pentelow, John Nix *(r.n.)*
Born at St Ives, Huntingdonshire on the 26th March 1872, and
the son of Ebeneezer Pentelow, the local shopkeeper. His unusual middle name was his mother's maiden name. Educated
locally and was for a very short time employed as a schoolmaster at his old school. Began writing at a very early age
(about 15), his first work appearing in several Victorian boys'
papers, including some by Guy Rayner. He soon became one
of the most versatile and prolific boys' writers of his time,
turning out hundreds of school, sports and adventure stories, of
which Haygarth and Wycliffe are the best known.

He was a very keen and expert cricket writer and was author
of several books on the game, as well as contributing to Wisden,
the Bible of the cricket world. Was at one time co-editor of
'Cricket' with A. C. MacLaren, though it is no secret that he
wrote nearly all the material and did all the work, the famous
cricketer's name being used to boost sales. Was the war-time
editor of Magnet and Gem (1916–19) and wrote a large number of substitute stories, as well as compiling Greyfriars and St
Jim's Galleries.

Afterwards edited Boys Realm and then Sport & Adventure.
Also editor of Boys Realm Football and Sports Library and
Robin Hood and Prairie Libraries. Retired from Amalgamated
Press in 1924 and died at Carshalton, Surrey, at the age of 59
on the 5th July 1931.

Pentelow probably had the distinction of being the only boys'
writer to have a review of one of his stories in The Times by
Sir John Squire, the famous reviewer. This was one of Pentelow's cricketing stories. He was also a member of Middlesex,
Sussex and Surrey Cricket Clubs.

Pen-names: Harry Hustington. Richard Randolph. John
West. Randolph Ryle. Harry Huntingdon. Jack North. Frank
Richards (Magnet). Martin Clifford (Gem and Popular (2nd).
Boys Jubilee Journal. Boys Popular Weekly. Gem (2nd).
S.B.L. (1st and 2nd) (anon). Union Jack (2nd) (anon). Cheer,
Boys, Cheer.

Pepper, Frank S. *(r.n.)*
Prolific contributor to many boys' papers, from the 1930's.
Today lives in Essex and is a contributor to the picture strips.
Pen-names: John Marshall. Hal Wilton.
Tiger.

Peppercorn, E. L.
Schoolboys Pocket Library (Swan).

Pergarth, Peter *(r.n. Norman Goddard)*
Union Jack (2nd).

Perowne, Barry *(r.n. Philip Atkey)*
Thriller. Detective Weekly. S.B.L. (2nd).

Perry, George B.
B.O.P.

Perry, Vincent
Captain.

Pete, 'Lariat'
Boys Cinema. Champion.

Philips, George Norman *(r.n.)*
Born c. 1888. Was a full-time surveyor in H.M. Office of
Works and wrote only in his spare time. Was an avid reader of
Pluck, Union Jack and Marvel when a boy and wrote his first
story in the former in 1916. His first Blake story was in Union
Jack No 837 in 1918 entitled 'A Duel to Death', and introduced his famous character, Zenith the Albino, who was soon
to become one of the most popular characters ever to pit his
wits against Blake. He wrote, in all, about 125 Blake stories in
various papers and apart from this wrote numerous articles for
the London Evening News.

His first hard-cover mystery novel, 'Five Dead Men', was published in the mid-thirties, and he later wrote other books. His
character, Zenith, appeared in 'Monsieur Zenith' but without
Sexton Blake.

George Norman Philips is not the same writer who has penned
the radio and TV plays, although it is a coincidence that he
has used at times an 'Anthony Juan Skene' pen-name. He is
now living in the Isle of Wight in retirement.
Pen-names: Anthony Skene. Philip Norman. Victor Fremlin.
S.B.L. (1st and 2nd) (anon). Union Jack (2nd) (anon). Dixon
Hawke Case Book (anon).

Phillips, Alfred R. *(r.n.)*
A better-than-average writer, who penned a large amount of stories at the turn of the century.
Comic Life. Boys Champion Story Paper. Boys World. Young Folks.

Phillips, Derek *(r.n.)*
Son of Horace Phillips, who once worked on the staff of girls' papers at Fleetway House, and contributed a few girls' stories and others. Was a few years ago working with the I.C.I. Group.
Champion Annual.

Phillips, Forbes A. *(r.n.)*
Pen-name: Athol Forbes.

Phillips, Horace *(r.n.)*
Born around 1880 and in his early days wrote many boys' stories for various publications under his own name. Was the second editor of Scout for about a year in 1910, then went over to the Amalgamated Press and became editor of Cheer, Boys, Cheer (1912–13), Boys Journal (1913–15) and Pluck (1915). In July 1919 he took over the stories of Cliff House in the Schoolfriend from Charles Hamilton and continued them in conjunction with Reginald Kirkham until 1921. Phillips got tired of writing about someone else's creations and so introduced probably one of the best schools in girls' fiction for Schoolgirls Own Weekly in 1921. These featured stories about Betty Barton & Co., and the Morcove School had a successful run of nearly 16 years – a total of 798 issues. It is believed that Phillips wrote them all under the famous nom-de-plume of 'Marjorie Stanton'.
As a boy Phillips was a keen reader of the B.O.P. and the writer last heard from him a few years ago, when he was living on a farm in the West Country.
Pen-names: Walter Hope. Derek Duke.
Dreadnought. Boys Journal. Boys Herald. Scout. Boys Realm Football and Sports Library. Champion Annual. Chums Annual. Lot-O'-Fun. Boys Friend Weekly (2nd). Boys Realm (1st). B.F.L. (1st). Cheer, Boys, Cheer.

Phillpots, Eden *(r.n.)*
Born in Mount Aboo, India, 1862, and educated at Plymouth. Was a clerk in an insurance office between 1880–90, before he

went to London to study for the stage, having always been something of a frustrated actor. Gave it up when he found that his talents in that direction were not as promising as he had imagined. He then turned to writing. His first book 'Lying Prophet' was an immediate success and he subsequently wrote other books and plays. He contributed to 'The Idler' in the 1890's and penned warmly written and beautifully characterised stories about 'The Human Boy', set in a small private school. Many experiences in these stories were supposed to have been based on the author's own school life. These later appeared in an omnibus collection entitled 'The Complete Human Boy'. He was a shy, retiring man and confessed that he had never seen one of his plays performed.

Died in 1961 at the age of 98, and was probably the oldest writer of school stories of all time.

Phipps, Sidney Arnold
Captain.

Pickering, Edgar *(r.n.)*
Prolific writer of stories around the turn of the century. Wrote 9 Sexton Blake stories for the Union Jack (1905-9).
Pluck (2nd). Marvel (2nd). Union Jack (2nd). Popular (1st) (anon).

Pickford, Charles
Boys Favourite. Football and Sports Library.

Pierce, Frank Richardson
Captain.

Pike, Morton *(r.n. D. H. Parry)*
Lloyds Detective Series. Chums. Champion Annual. Greyfriars Holiday Annual. Boys Herald. Popular (2nd). Pluck (2nd). Champion. Magnet. Cheer, Boys, Cheer. Prairie Library. Robin Hood Lib. (A.P.). B.F.L. (1st and 2nd). Young Britain (1st). Boys Journal. Boys Friend Weekly (2nd).

Pike, William Ernest *(r.n.)*
As a boy was very interested in running amateur magazines, and ran the West Norwood League, details of which were shown in Magnet, No. 370, 13th March 1915. Also ran a magazine called 'The Red Crusader' (1914–18). Joined the Amalgamated Press 1st February 1915 as sub-editor on the Magnet. Joined the Army 14th March 1917 and returned October 1919. Wrote

one substitute story for the Magnet and one of Rookwood for the Boys Friend, of which he was the last editor.

Worked on the editorial staff of the following papers: Boys Friend Weekly, Boys Cinema, Fun & Fiction, Chuckles, Chicks Own, Crackers, My Favourite, Chips, Funny Wonder, Merry & Bright, Merry Mag, Comic Cuts, Sunbeam, Tiny Tots, Thriller Picture Library, War Picture Library.

Retired from A.P. in 1963 and now lives at Coulsdon, Surrey.
Pen-names: Ernest James. Owen Conquest (Boys Friend Weekly). Frank Richards (Magnet).
Pluck (3rd). Fun & Fiction (anon). Champion. Boys Friend Weekly (2nd).

Pile, D. W. *(r.n.)*
Pen-name: Stawford Webber.

Pilot, John
Scout.

Pirbright, Robert
Chums.

Pitcairn, John
Football Weekly. Football & Sports Library.

Pitt, David
True Blue (2nd).

Platt, Edward
Captain.

Player, Eddie *(r.n.)*
Wrote a Sexton Blake story under the name of 'Desmond Reid'. S.B.L. (3rd).

Plummer, T. Arthur *(r.n.)*
Started his working life as an actor, but soon turned to writing, when it proved more profitable. Had over 57 books published by Stanley Paul and John Long.
Thriller. Detective Weekly. Sports Fun. Football & Sports Lib.

Pocklington, Geoffrey Richard *(r.n.)*
Born in Chelsworth 1879 and educated at The United Services College, Rossall School, and Balliol College, Oxford. Worked for some years as a newspaper reporter, features writer and publicist, after gaining his B.A. degree. In 1914 became editor of 'Newsboy', a trade paper, and held this post until 1931. Was editor of the B.O.P. from 1924 until 1933, successfully steering it through the difficult days of the General Strike. Wrote for

several boys' papers including Scout, as scouting was a particular interest of his. He also wrote several books, including 'The Story of W. H. Smith & Son'. Became a West Suffolk Councillor in 1937 and Chairman of the Education Committee 1942.
Scout.

Pocock, Doris Alice *(r.n.)*
Born Highgate, educated privately. Wrote many books and contributed to many Annuals, Blackies, etc.
B.O.P. Boys Torch Adventure Library. Chums. Little Folks.

Pocock, Guy Noel *(r.n.)*
Born Hampstead 1880. Educated Highgate School and St John's College, Cambridge. Wrote many novels and books of poetry.
Captain.

Pocock, H. E. D.
Chums.

Pocock, Roger *(r.n.)*
Born 1865 at Tenby. Educated at Ludlow Grammar School. Special Correspondent, Lloyds Weekly 1897–1901. Author of several novels. Wrote his first Autobiography 'A Frontiersman' and a follow-up, 'Chorus to Adventures'.
Boys Realm (1st).

Podmore, Charles T.
Young Briton's Journal. Boys Popular Weekly.

Poe, Edgar Allan *(r.n.)*
Born at Boston, Mass, 1808, of actor parents, he became an orphan in early childhood. Poe was brought to England and sent to school at Stoke Newington. Later he studied at the University of Virginia for a year and enlisted in the U.S. Army in 1828. Began to write poems but met with no success and so turned to journalism. Later he wrote many tales of horror, which are regarded as classics, including 'The Fall of the House of Usher' and 'The Pit and the Pendulum'. Poe also goes down in posterity as being the writer of the first detective story. He died 7th October 1849.
The Union Jack published one story by him in their 'classic' period.
Union Jack (1st).

Pollard, Eliza F. *(r.n.)*
Young England.

Pollock, William
B.O.P.
Polo, Eddie *(r.n. of film-star)*
Story probably 'ghosted'.
Boys Cinema.
Pond, S. T. R. *(r.n.)*
Pen-name: Trevace Reay.
Ponting, Clarence
Chums.
Poole, Michael *(r.n. Reginald Heber Poole)*
B.O.P. Modern Boy. Chums. Gem (2nd). Scout. Boys Friend
Weekly (2nd). Champion Annual. Chums Annual. Greyfriars
Holiday Annual. Schoolboys Own Lib. B.F.L. (2nd). S.B.L.
(2nd). Champion. Boys Mag.
Poole, Reginald Heber *(r.n.)*
Born in Northwich, 1885, and educated at Manchester Gram-
mar School. His first short story was in The Captain in March
1907, entitled 'Washington Minor', whilst his first serial was in
B.O.P. 1908-9 called 'Dr Silver'. He joined the staff of Amalgamated Press in 1910 and was editor of Answers 1912–14.
Later became Fiction Editor for United Newspapers Ltd., a
post which he held from 1921-23. Editor of British Boy in
1921. He also contributed many humorous stories to such
magazines as Happy, Strand, etc. Wrote what was probably
the finest series ever to appear in Boys Magazine – 'The Blott of
Berisford', which later was reprinted in the S.O.L. and in book
form. Wrote a number of hard-cover school stories. After the
Second World War he was engaged on editorial work for
Pictorial Knowledge, the 10-volume Newnes publication. Lived
for many years in Horsell, Woking, Surrey.
Pen-names: Austin Heber. Reginald Heber. Michael Poole.
Anthony Thomas. Henry Valentine.
There is evidence that the last name was also used by Geoffrey
Prout.
S.B.L. (1st and 2nd) (anon). Aldine Mystery Novels. Union
Jack (2nd) (anon).
Pope *(r.n.)*
Pen-name: Lieutenant A. Manson.
Pope, E. Legh
Chums.

Pope, F. W.   *(r.n.)*
Pen-name: Lloyd Hulbert.
Porter, Frederick   *(r.n.)*
Born Jedburgh, Scotland, 1871 and educated at The Nest
Academy, Edinburgh and Edinburgh University. Was a prac-
tising doctor and contributed many articles to medical journals, etc., also wrote three plays and many short stories for
various publications. Contributed his first serial to The Captain
in 1912, this being entitled 'White Man's Gold'. The following
year he wrote a very popular serial called 'Muckle John' for the
same paper. In 1917–18 came a school serial called 'Waking up
Warrenders', also in Captain. Was also a first-class painter and
exhibited in the Royal Scottish Academy and for the Society
of Scottish Artists.
Pen-name: Frederick Watson.
Pothecary, Raymond   *(r.n.)*
Pen-name: Quinton Ford.
Potten, Phil
Union Jack (1880).
Poultney, S. Vic
Chums. B.O.P.
Pound, Singleton   *(r.n. Oliver Merland)*
Buffalo Bill Lib. (1st and 2nd). Robin Hood Lib. (1st and 3rd).
Diamond Lib. (1st). True Blue (2nd). Boys Leader. Union
Jack (1st and 2nd). Boys Herald. Boys Realm (1st). Boys Friend
Weekly (2nd). Rocket. Pluck (1st and 2nd). Marvel (2nd).
Powell, Barclay
True Blue (2nd).
Powell, Frank
Wrote a famous adventure serial 'The Wolf Man' for Boys
World in 1905. It was the subject of a detailed article by
Margaret Lane in Punch in 1962, in which she admitted that
the story had haunted her all her life. This was later reprinted
in book form. In 1906 came the sequel, 'The Vengeance of the
Wolf Man' in the same paper.
Boys World (Cassells).
Power, Anthony   *(r.n.)*
Young writer who penned 'Tinker's Challenge' in Valiant
Sexton Blake Annual.

Power, Nelson *(r.n. Alfred Judd)*
Boys Journal. Cheer, Boys, Cheer. B.F.L. (1st).

Pratt, Leonard E. *(r.n.)*
Joined the Amalgamated Press in 1903 and was on the early papers such as Marvel, Pluck, etc. During the First World War he served in the Rifle Brigade. After war service he controlled The Robin Hood and Prairie Libraries. In 1921 he took over the Sexton Blake Library and held that position until 1955. During his career he was also editor of The Thriller and he originated the famous women's paper, The Oracle. Retired to his home at Westcliff, Essex and died there a few years ago.
Pen-name: Fenton Smith.

Prescott, G.
B.O.P. Scout.

Prest, Thomas Peckett *(r.n.)*
Born around 1810 and was a relative of an Archdeacon of Durham, and prepared many of his sermons for the printer. Was publisher Edward Lloyd's most prolific writer and turned out numerous 'bloods' during the mid-19th century. Wrote well over 100 full-length stories, including Gothic Horror tales, historical adventures, and domestic romances. But easily his most famous story was 'The String of Pearls' which introduced the immortal Sweeney Todd, Demon Barber of Fleet Street. This set the pattern for all subsequent stories about this character. Publisher Edward Lloyd first issued 4 penny parts in 1840 and later republished it in his 'People's Pictorial'. It had an immense success. Prest also worked as a crime reporter and was famous for his graphic descriptions of murders and trials of murderers. Amongst his book titles were 'The Female Fiend', 'The Maniac Father' and 'The Victim of Seduction'. Some authorities, including the famous expert Montague Summers, attributed the rarest 'blood' of all – 'Varney the Vampire' – to him, but many others, including the British Museum, credit it to his fellow-scribe at Lloyds, M. J. Merry. Prest was editor of 'The Calendar of Horrors' and also a fine musician and writer of songs.
He died in 1879.

Preston, Walford *(r.n. Houghton Townley)*
Rocket. Pluck (3rd).

Preston, Whyatt
Boys Friend Weekly (2nd).
Price, Evadne *(r.n. Helen Zenna Smith)*
Thriller.
Price, N. Penton
True Blue (2nd).
Pride, Merlin
Ranger (1st).
Prior, Harry *(r.n. Miss D. G. Knightley)*
Pluck (3rd).
Prior, Vivian
Newnes Adventure Library.
Proctor, H. G.
Boys Torch Adventure Library.
Proctor, Paul *(r.n. G. R. Samways)*
Merry & Bright (2nd). B.F.L. (2nd). Popular (2nd).
Protheroe, Charles
Captain.
Protheroe, Ernest *(r.n.)*
Pen-name: P. A. Henley.
Boys Realm Football & Sports Lib. (anon). Chums. School-
boys Own Lib. B.F.L. (1st). Boys Realm (1st). Boys Friend
Weekly (2nd).
Proudfoot, John
Scout.
Prout, Geoffrey *(r.n.)*
Born in Saxilby in 1894 and educated at Devonport High
School. Was a prolific contributor to the Scout, in which he
wrote stories, serials and articles on boating, etc. Was an expert
on boats and sailing and ran his own boat business at Canvey
Island, Essex. Wrote many hard-cover boys' stories and also
technical manuals on boating and yachting. Collaborated at
times with his great friend, Francis Warwick, on stories.
Served in both World Wars. Died some years ago.
Pen-names: Roland Spencer. Henry Valentine.
There is evidence that the second pen-name was also used
by Michael Poole.
B.O.P. Wizard (anon). Scout. Lloyds Detective Series. Lloyds
Sports Library. Young England. Boys Magazine. Chums.
Detective Tales (2nd). Boys Journal. Gem (2nd).

Pugh, Roger *(r.n.)*
Pen-name: Ben Rogers.

Pumphrey, F. M.
Captain.

'Puncher'
Young Britain (2nd).

Punshon, Ernest Robinson *(r.n.)*
Born London 1872. Author of many novels and contributed to all leading magazines. Strand, Pearsons, etc.
Aldine Mystery Novels.

Purcell, J. S. *(r.n.)*
Pen-name: Maurice Stapleton.
True Blue (2nd).

Purchase, Walter H. *(r.n.)*
On the editorial staff of Fred Cordwell and a contributor to many of the serials and stories that appeared in them. Probably his most famous was 'The Woman with the Black Heart' in Fun & Fiction about 1912, which was later taken over by other authors. Was very much at home with the melodramatic type of story which was so popular in those days. Was later sub-editor of Chips, Comic Cuts, Joker and later editor of Puck.
Fun and Fiction (anon). Firefly (anon).

Purley, John *(r.n. Reginald George Thomas)*
S.B.L. (3rd).

Purves, E. Eric
Scout.

Pye, Clifford H.
B.O.P.

Pym, J. H.
Editor of the Union Jack (succeeded W. Maas) and Pluck.

Quiller-Couch, Sir Arthur T. *(r.n.)*
Born Cornwall 21st November 1863. Educated at Newton Abbot College, Clifton College, Trinity College, Oxford. Professor of English Literature at the University of Cambridge from October 1912. Wrote mainly books and poems. Died in 1944.
Union Jack (2nd).

Quiller-Couch, Lilian
Larks (Trapps Holmes).

Quilter, Eddie *(r.n. Thomas E. Woodman)*
Ranger (2nd). B.F.L. (2nd).

Quintin, Peter
Football & Sports Lib. Pioneer. Football Weekly. Football & Sports Favourite.

Quintin, Rex *(r.n. Rex Hardinge)*
Western Library.

Quintin, Paul *(r.n. W. G. Wright)*
B.F.L. (1st and 2nd). Pluck (3rd).

Quirroule, Pierre *(r.n. W. W. Sayer)*
Nelson Lee Lib. (2nd New Series revised). Thriller. Detective Weekly. S.B.L. (2nd and 5th). Thriller Lib.

Quittenton, Bertram *(r.n.)*
Son of R. M. H. Quittenton, wrote a few brief stories for Henderson's publications around 1909–10.
Pen-name: Roland Quiz (jnr.).

Quittenton, Richard Martin Howard *(r.n.)*
Born in 1833. Best known for his popular fantasy stories of giants, fairies, magicians, etc., which ran as serials in Henderson's 'Young Folks' in the 1870's and later. Most famous are 'Tom Pippin' and 'Giantland' which were later republished in Nuggets and also in book form. He died in 1914.
Pen-name: Roland Quiz.

Quiz, Roland *(r.n. Richard Martin Howard Quittenton)*
Young Folks Tales. Nuggets.

Quiz, Roland (jnr.) *(r.n. Bertram Quittenton)*
Young Folks.

Radcliffe, Arthur
Hotspur Book for Boys. Skipper Book for Boys.

Rae, Scott *(r.n. Cecily Hamilton)*
Boys Herald.

Rae, William Shaw *(r.n.)*
One of the earliest Sexton Blake writers. Created We-Wee, one of Blake's assistants before Tinker came on the scene.
Boys Friend Weekly (1st). Union Jack (1st). Pluck (1st). Marvel (1st). Popular (1st) (anon).

Raife, Raymond
B.O.P.

Raine, William Macleod   *(r.n.)*
Born 22nd June 1871 in London and educated at Oberlin College. Author of over 70 books, many of them Westerns. Died at Denver Hospital 25th July 1954.
Western Library. Boys Herald.

Randali, W. C. B.
Scout.

Randolph, Richard   *(r.n. John Nix Pentelow)*
Boys Herald. Boys Realm (1st and 2nd). B.F.L. (2nd). Pluck (3rd). Nugget Lib. Marvel (2nd). Sport & Adventure. Sports for Boys. Football & Sports Lib. Champion. Boys Friend Weekly (2nd). Gem (2nd). Magnet. Champion Annual. Comic Life.

Ransome, Charles A.   *(r.n. John G. Rowe)*
Adventure Lib. (Newnes).

Ransome, L. E.
Born in London. As a boy he was an avid reader of the Magnet and Gem. He entered the Greyfriars Story Competition in 1915 and won a prize, a book of poems by Longfellow, which he still has. He entered the Companion Papers in 1916 as there was a severe shortage of staff; nearly all had been called up or were away on war occupations. During part of the war years he worked with John Nix Pentelow, the war-time editor. About 1918 he switched to The Boys Friend office with R. T. Eves, mainly checking proofs and reading the Rookwood scripts. He also helped to prepare the first dummies, etc., of the new girls' paper The Schoolfriend.
In 1921 or thereabouts he decided to go free-lance and since that date had written thousands of stories for both boys' and girls' papers. His early work consisted of a St Jim's story published in the Gem when he was only 18, apart from other contributions to the Greyfriars Herald, etc. In 1924 he took over the Cliff House stories of Bessie Bunter in the Schoolfriend from Reginald Kirkham and wrote them until the final issue in July 1929.
He also carried on with the stories in The Schoolgirl.
Later he contributed further substitute stories for the Magnet and Gem. In all, he probably contributed far more for the girls' market than for the boys'. Has also written for adult fiction in John Bull, Modern Woman, etc.

Pen-names: Ivor Hayes. Ivor Melbourne. Victor Norman. Tom Stirling. Martin Clifford (Gem). Frank Richards (Magnet).

Ratcliffe, Frederic
Nugget Lib. Comic Life.

Raven, G.

Ravenglass, Hal *(r.n. Samuel Andrew Wood)*
Chums.

Rawlings, Clyde
Pioneer.

Rawlings, James R. *(r.n. J. H. McCulloch)*
Modern Boy.

Rawson, T. W.
Lot-O'-Fun.

Ray, Saxon
Boys Herald.

Ray, Stacey
Football Novels.

Rayle, Geoffrey *(r.n. Eric W. McLean)*
Champion.

Raymond, N. G. *(r.n.)*
Startler (anon).

Rayne, Clifford
Champion.

Rayner, Guy *(r.n. S. Dacre Clarke)*
Bad Boys Paper.

Raynes, Robert
Champion.

Read, Alfred
Scout.

Read, C. A.
Young Folks.

Reade, Sidney
Captain Library.

Reay, Trevace *(r.n. S. T. R. Pond)*
Boys Realm (1st).

Reck, Franklin M. *(r.n.)*
Born in Chacago, 1896.
Chums.

Redknapp, E. E.
Flag Library.

Redmond-Howard, Louis G. *(r.n.)*
Born 1884. Authority on Irish Politics and History. Writer of detective stories, serials, verse, plays and many books.
Pen-name: L. G. Redmond Howard (no hyphen).

Redway, Ralph *(r.n. Charles Hamilton)*
Modern Boy. Ranger (1st). Popular (2nd). B.F.L. (2nd).

Redway, Ridley *(r.n. Charles Hamilton)*
Vanguard Lib. (Trapps Holmes). Funny Cuts. Picture Fun. Smiles.

Reed, Lucas
Nugget Library. Comic Life.

Reed, Talbot Baines *(r.n.)*
Born in Hackney, London, 1852, the son of Sir Charles Reed, M.P., who was Chairman of the London School Board. Is best known as the 'king' of the B.O.P. school-story writers. His first real school story appeared in August 1879, a two-chapter story called 'The Troubles of a Dawdler'. Then he wrote his first serial for the B.O.P., 'The Adventures of a Three-Guinea Watch'. It was an immediate success and he subsequently wrote another 10 serials for the paper. All were later reprinted in book form and ran into many editions.

Although he himself attended a day school, Reed's fine descriptions of public school life were generally agreed to be extremely accurate. He was an expert in matters pertaining to printing and typography (a trade in which he worked in earlier days), and he wrote a book on the subject.

He died at Highgate, London, in 1893 at the early age of 42. At the time of his death he was still working on a story about the Rebellion of 1798 and called 'Kilgoran'.
B.O.P. Lads and Lassies Lib.

Rees, David *(r.n. Trevor C. Wignall)*
B.F.L. (1st). Marvel (2nd). Boys Realm (2nd).

Rees, Edward
Scout.

Rees, George *(r.n.)*
Was serving in the Royal Navy about 1920 when he met the famous Blake author, Gwyn Evans, and they became great friends. Was not strictly a writer of juvenile fiction, but often

used to write chapters of a Blake story when Gwyn was unable to do so. It could be said that Rees at times 'ghosted' for him. Rees's main output was for Government propaganda, including articles for foreign newspapers explaining the British way of life.

Was also a naturalist and published several books for children. During the Second World War he was employed on the B.B.C.'s Monitoring Service, being an expert linguist. In 1953-4 Rees wrote two Sexton Blake stories, which were so good that when they were published many readers believed they were old unpublished stories of Gwyn Evans's, so uncannily like his stories were they.

S.B.L. (3rd).

Rees, J. Roger
B.O.P.

Rees, Walter
Boys Best Story Paper.

Reeves, Percy
Boys Life.

Reginald, F.
Vanguard Library (Trapps Holmes).

Reid, Desmond *(editorial name)*

The above name was used when submitted stories had to be rewritten for various reasons, or when old stories were revised. These were rewritten usually by W. Howard Baker, Philip Chambers, Arthur MacLean and W. McNeilly. The following authors had stories under the Desmond Reid pen-name:

S. J. Bounds. Noel Browne. J. F. Burke. Cahill. John Newton. Chance. Anthony Douse. A. Garstin. R. C. Elliott. Anthony Glyn. Stephen Frances. V. J. Hanson. Frank Lambe. Brian McArdle. Wilfred McNeilly. A. L. Martin. Michael Moorcock. Eddie Player. Ross Richards. Lee Roberts. Colin Robertson. Gordon Sowman. James Stagg. G. H. Teed. Ross Story. Rex Dolphin.

S.B.L. (3rd and 5th).

Reid, J. Dougall
Boys Life.

Reid, Mayne *(r.n.)*

Born in Ballyroney, County Down, Ireland, in 1818. The son of a Presbyterian minister. His parents set him up as a tutor when he left college, but Reid wanted to see something of the world. In 1839 he sailed for New Orleans and was soon working as a store clerk in the lawless town of Natchez, Missouri. Later he became tutor to a judge's family in Nashville, Tennessee, before setting up as a schoolmaster in a school built mainly by his own efforts. Soon tired of teaching he became a trader, making several journeys up the Plate, Missouri and Red Rivers, where he had dealings with the Red Indians, getting to know them and their customs very well. Later he became a Lieutenant in the U.S. Army and fought in the Mexican War in 1847. He had been writing regularly for the New York Herald and 'The Spirit of the Times' and continued sending back despatches from the Front. During a dashing and brave war career he was severely injured and retired with the rank of Captain.

During his convalescence he began writing fiction. His first adventure book – 'The Rifle Rangers' – was turned down by the American publishers but accepted by a British one. Reid then came to London, where his work appeared in two volumes in 1850. It was followed by over 50 more books. In 1867 Reid started and edited a new London paper, 'The Little Times'; much of its contents, aimed at evening readers, was written by himself. It only lasted a month, however. A year or so later Reid and his wife settled in Rhode Island, U.S.A., and he became an American citizen.

He then started an original boys' paper called 'Onwards' but this only ran for 14 monthly numbers, leaving Reid almost penniless. He suffered from failing health in his later years and at the end walked with the aid of crutches. He died in October 1883, leaving behind books which are regarded as classics of adventure literature.

Boys Journal (Brett). Boys Friend (Houlston & Wright). Boys of England. Marvel (1st). Captain Library.

Reid, Sybil
    Captain.

Reilly, William K. *(r.n. John Creasey)*
    Western Library.

Remington, Rex *(r.n.)*
    Champion.

Revel, Harry *(r.n. Gilbert Floyd)*
B.F.L. (1st). Sparks.

Reynolds, Basil C. Hope *(r.n.)*
Born London, son of Basil Reynolds, artist, and nephew of the famous Gem illustrator, Warwick Reynolds. On the staff of Mickey Mouse Weekly and later moved to Amalgamated Press, where he was last editor of Tiny Tots. An artist himself, he now free-lances for the present-day comic papers. He lives at Botley, Chesham, Bucks.

Reynolds, E. Cockburn
Captain.

Reynolds, George William McCarther *(r.n.)*
Born in Sandwich, Kent, 1814 and educated at a local Council School in Ashford. His father was Sir George Reynolds, a distinguished captain in the Royal Navy. His parents died when he was in his early teens and left him a considerable fortune. He went on a grand tour of the Continent, and in 1835 was to be found in Paris, running a bookshop and publishing business and issuing daily papers in English.
Back in England two years later he translated French novels, edited obscure magazines and became political correspondent for a leading journal. He had by now spent most of his inheritance and in 1835 he published an immature first novel called 'The Youthful Imposter', while in 1839 came a study of French modern literature. Then he published his popular 'follow-up' to Dickens – 'Pickwick Abroad' which had a tremendously successful run and became almost as popular as the original 'Pickwick Papers'. Around 1846, he became editor of the London Journal, in which he began his lengthy 'Mysteries of London', which was to run in various guises for over 12 years. The same year came his magazine 'Reynolds' Miscellany' which lasted 23 years.
Later still came many sensational novels in illustrated weekly numbers, which were so popular that they were bought up before the ink was barely dry. He was also the leader of the Chartist Movement and travelled England addressing numerous meetings. In 1850 he published the first number of 'Reynolds Weekly Newspaper' which soon became the mouthpiece of advance working-class opinion. This later became Reynolds News which was published until 1962.

Many sensational novels came from his pen and he became the leading best-seller of his day. He died in Woburn Square, London, in 1879, aged 65.

Reynolds, Warwick *(r.n.)*
According to official records, he wrote a single Sexton Blake Library story in 1924. (No 316, 1st series, 'Mawpeth Millions'.) It is still a puzzle how this famous illustrator came to write this story, although it is strongly suspected that it may have been submitted by him on behalf of a friend who thought that Warwick's name would get it accepted. Certainly this is his only known literary work, although his father, Warwick senior, was a writer as well as an artist.

Warwick Reynolds died in 1946, acclaimed by nearly all fellow-artists as the most talented and best of all Amalgamated Press artists.

S.B.L. (anon).

Rhoades, Walter C.
Author who wrote mainly school stories and serials in various papers for many years beginning in the 1880's. Wrote also several hard-cover school stories.

Young Folks. Boys Champion Story Paper. Nugget Library.

Rhodes, Oakmead *(r.n. Thomas Burke)*
Boys Realm (1st).

Rich, Henry K. *(r.n. Norman Goddard)*
Boys Herald. Pluck (2nd).

Richards, Frank *(r.n. Charles Hamilton)*
Probably the most famous name in boys' fiction history. The Christian name came from Scott's Frank Osbaldistone. Richards came from the name of Richard (the younger brother of Hamilton) pluralised into a surname. At times, however, other writers penned stories of Greyfriars under this name, usually only when stories from Charles Hamilton were not available. Whilst this list seems lengthy it is only fair to point out that out of 1,683 numbers, Charles Hamilton wrote approximately 1,380 of them.

Substitute writers in the Magnet:
S. E. Austin. Alfred Barnard. S. Barrie. Edwy Searles Brooks. W. L. Catchpole. F. G. Cook. A. W. Davis. C. M. Down. M. Duffy. Will Gibbons. Julius Herman. H. A. Hinton. W. E. S. Hope. H. C. Hook. A. M. Kemp. R. S. Kirkham. K. E.

Newman. Hedley O'Mant. J. N. Pentelow. W. E. Pike. L. E. Ransome. G. R. Samways. S. R. Shepherd. H. W. Twyman. Noel Wood-Smith.
The following had stories reprinted in the Popular (2nd).
S. E. Austin. E. Searles Brooks. C. M. Down. G. R. Samways. S. R. Shepherd. Noel Wood-Smith.
C. M. Down also wrote a few odd Greyfriars stories in Chuckles. Popular (1st and 2nd). Dreadnought. Ranger (1st and 2nd). Gem (2nd). Magnet. Boys Friend Weekly (2nd). B.F.L. (1st). Schoolboys Own Library. Chuckles. Greyfriars Holiday Annual. Knockout Fun Book. Tom Merry's Own. Billy Bunter's Own. Mascot Schoolboy Series. Sparshott Series. Wonder Book of Comics, and other post-war publications.

Richards, Gordon
Pluck (1st). Marvel (2nd).

Richards, Ross *(r.n.)*
Pen-name: Matt Mead, and some stories as Desmond Reid.
S.B.L. (5th).

Richards, Walter
Boys Friend Weekly (1st).

Richardson – *(r.n.)*
Pen-name: Scrope Haggerston.

Richardson, Flavia   *(r.n. Christine Campbell Thomson)*
Thriller.

Richardson, Gladwell   *(r.n.)*
Wrote many novels under the following names for adult fiction: George Blacksnake. Orman Clarkson. John Haines. Calico Jones. Pete Kent. Maurice Kildare. Warren O'Riley. Frank Warner. John Winslowe.
The following name was used only in the Thriller:
Pen-name: Maxwell Grant.

Richardson, Robert
Chums.

Richmond, Court
Boys Realm (1st).

Richmond, George   *(r.n. George Richmond Samways)*
Boys Friend Weekly (2nd).

Richmond, H. B.   *(r.n. E. Newton Bungay)*
Wonder Library. Chips

Rickwood, E.
Boys Own Library (2nd). Boys Pocket Lib.
Rideout, Harold
Wild West Weekly.
Ridge, W. Pett
One of the best-selling light novelists of the late 1890's and early 1900's. His work was mainly of the light romantic and humorous variety. He also wrote many stories for juvenile publications in the early part of the century.
Puck.
Rigby, Arthur
Chums.
Rigby, Hugh
Boys Life.
Rigot, Sebastian
True Blue (2nd). Bullseye (Aldine).
Rishton, William *(r.n. W. G. Wright)*
Boys Friend Weekly (2nd).
Rister, Claude *(r.n.)*
Western Library.
Ritchie, Balfour *(r.n.)*
Was on the staff of the Amalgamated Press for some years, and various boys' papers. At one time he was editor of the Boys Friend Library and wrote stories himself in several papers. Later he inherited the family business at Richmond, Surrey, and retired completely from writing and editing. Believed to have died some years ago.
Pen-name: Basil Baldwin.
Rittenberg, Max
Born in Sydney, Australia, in 1880 and educated at Tonbridge College, Kent, and Cambridge University, where he gained his B.A. Became a leading practitioner in advertising and wrote many books with such titles as 'Mail Order Made Easy', etc. Was probably the country's leading expert on Mail Order salesmanship. Also turned out numerous articles and short stories for many different magazines. In 1912 he wrote a fine public school serial called 'The Cockatoo' for The Captain, but never repeated this success, despite many letters of appreciation from readers.
Captain.

288

Rivers, Tex *(r.n. C. A. Lewins)*
Ranger (2nd). Pioneer. Western Library. B.F.L. (2nd).
Rix, Witton
Boys Life (with W. T. Kerridge).
Robbins, L. H.
Union Jack (2nd).
Robbins, Raleigh *(r.n. Charles Hamilton)*
Funny Cuts.
Roberts, D. H.
Young Britain (1st).
Roberts, Franklin
B.F.L. (2nd).
Roberts, Holt *(r.n. Ben Draper)*
Ranger (2nd).
Roberts, John Llewellyn *(r.n.)*
One of the finest writers of school stories the B.O.P. ever had. Always wrote of Greystone School and usually in short-story form, although some of the stories were long enough to be shortish novels. One exception to this was his only serial for the B.O.P. – 'The Glory of Greystone' in 1926, which was earlier printed in book form.
His Greystone stories were usually high-spirited with plenty of first-class character-drawing in them. Not much is known about Roberts, although it is believed he was killed in the Second World War.
B.O.P.
Roberts, Lee *(r.n.)*
Author of a Sexton Blake story published under the Desmond Reid pen-name.
Roberts, Louis
Marvel (1st).
Roberts, Murray *(r.n. Robert Murray Graydon)*
It has been established that at least one other author (John L. Garbutt) wrote a few stories of Captain Justice in the latter part of its run.
B.F.L. (2nd). Modern Boy.
Roberts, Ralph
Scout.
Roberts, Theodore *(r.n.)*
Chums.

Robertson, Colin *(r.n.)*
Born 1906. Wrote only one story for D. C. Thomson, in the
Wizard in 1933. Wrote about 40 books and 3 stage plays, also
plays for broadcasting. During the last war was Senior Press
Censor for Scotland. Founder member of Crime Writers
Association and served on its Committees since it commence-
ment in 1953. Wrote one Blake story published under the
Desmond Reid pen-name, in S.B.L. (3rd).
B.O.P. Wizard (anon). Modern Boy.

Robertson, Frank Chester *(r.n.)*
Born 1890.
Western Library.

Robertson, Henry
Larks (Trapps Holmes).

Robertson, James
Dreadnought. B.F.L. (2nd).

Robertson, J. B.
Union Jack (1880).

Robertson, J. G.
Skipper Book for Boys. Hotspur Book for Boys.

Robins, Fenton *(r.n. D. J. Gammon)*
Thriller.

Robinson, Ben C.
Scout.

Robinson, Ernest Herbert *(r.n.)*
Born in London 1880 and educated at Alleyns School, Dulwich.
Joined staff of George Newnes at the age of 15 in 1895 and then
became sub-editor on a magazine called 'The Free-Lance' in
1897. Was appointed Assistant Editor of the Education Department of George Newnes in 1898 where he remained until
1905. He then became assistant editor of Home Chat and The
World and His Wife. Became editor of Chums in 1907 and held
the post until he was called up in the R.F.C. in 1915. During
his career on this paper he contributed many serials, short
stories and articles. An expert rifle-shot (he won the King's
Prize at Bisley in 1923) he introduced the famous Chums Sharp-
shooters League, which had a membership of thousands of
schoolboys. He also wrote for several Amalgamated Press
papers as well as for The Times, Observer, Wireless World, etc.
During his war service he was attached to the Royal Arsenal,

Woolwich, where he was an expert and authority on firearms, wireless, and later television. He had many books published on these subjects. Lived for some years in Pirbright, Woking, Surrey and died in 1947.
British Boy. Lloyds Detective Series. Lloyds School Yarns. Detective Tales (2nd). Boys Own Lib. (2nd). Boys Pocket Lib. Chums.

Robinson, Gunner
Boys Herald.

Robinson, Hubert J.
Popular Book of Boys Stories.

Robson, Ralph
Football & Sports Library.

Roche, Arthur Summers *(r.n.)*
Born 1883. Wrote several novels of suspense and mystery. Lived in the U.S.A.
Thriller. Broadsheet Novels.

Roche, Eric *(r.n. George E. Rochester)*
Modern Boy. Schoolboys Own Lib.

Rochefort, Julian *(r.n.)*
Pen-name: Christopher Stevens.
Pluck (1st) (anon). Union Jack (1st).

Rochester, George Ernest *(r.n.)*
Born in Northumberland in the mid-1890's. During World War I served as a Flight-Lieutenant in the R.F.C., mainly with the 97th Squadron. Was shot down whilst flying bombers over the Germans' lines and made a P.O.W. After his war service he was working as a golf caddy when he wrote his first story for the B.O.P. in 1926 entitled 'Funk'. He then started to write a serial for that paper, and this was 'The Flying Beetle', a story of aerial adventure, in 1927. It was so successful that it launched him on a long writing career, and from then onwards he wrote serials and stories for all the popular boys' papers. He also wrote over 70 books, some of which were hard-cover editions of his serials.
In the 1950's he concentrated chiefly on writing for the women's market, especially 'The Miracle', under such names as Elizabeth Kent, Martin Hale, Mary West, Hester Roche and Allison Frazer. The loss of his wife seemed to break him up completely and he suffered a stroke in 1962, which left him

partly paralysed and unable to continue with his writings. He went to live with a daughter in the U.S.A. but returned to England, suffered a relapse, and died at an R.A.F. hospital a few years ago.

Pen-names: Jeffrey Gaunt. Frank Chatham. Barton Furze. John Beresford. Eric Roche. Hamilton Smith. Wizard. Rover. Adventure. Vanguard. Beano. Dandy (all anon). Popular (2nd). Boys Wonder Lib. S.B.L. (3rd). Magnet. Thriller. Schoolboys Own Library. Western Lib. B.F.L. (2nd). Detective Weekly. Nelson Lee Lib. (1st new series). Ranger (1st and 2nd). Thriller Library. Modern Boy. Chums. Gem (2nd). Comet. Knockout. Greyfriars Holiday Annual. Knockout Fun Book. Modern Boys Annual. B.O.P.

Rochester, W. F.
Captain.

Rodway, Roland *(r.n. Charles Hamilton)*
Vanguard Lib. (Trapps Holmes)

Roe, E. P.
Lads and Lassies Lib.

Rogers, Ben *(r.n. Roger Pugh)*
Detective Weekly.

Rogers, G. M.
B.O.P.

Rogers, Robert *(r.n. Charles Hamilton)*
Funny Cuts. Picture Fun.

Rogers, Steve *(r.n. Percy A. Clarke)*
B.F.L. (2nd).

Rogers, Tom *(r.n. Alfred Edgar)*
Modern Boy.

Rohmer, Sax *(r.n. Arthur Sarsfield Ward)*
Thriller.

Roizel, Albert
Aldine War Stories.

Rollem, John W. *(r.n.)*
Boys Friend Weekly (2nd).

Rollington, Ralph *(r.n. James W. Allingham)*
New Boys Paper. Boys Pocket Lib. Boys World. Our Boys Paper. Boys Holiday.

Rome, Stewart
Boys Cinema.

Ronald, Grayling *(r.n. R. E. Gray)*
Boys Friend Weekly (2nd).
Ronald, Guy
Chips.
Ronald, James *(r.n.)*
Thriller. Wild West Weekly. B.F.L. (2nd).
Roper, Archibald G.
Chums. Boys Realm (1st). Boys Friend Weekly (2nd). B.O.P.
Roper, Mary E.
B.O.P.
Rose, Charles E.
Boxing Novels (1st).
Ross, Alan *(r.n. Alan Ross Warwick)*
Scout.
Ross, C. H. *(r.n.)*
Wrote for Reynolds 'Miscellany' and Bow Bells adult papers, and was also an artist.
Boys of England. Boys Herald (1877). Young Men of Gt Britain.
Ross, Edgar
Union Jack (1st).
Ross, Phillip
Chums.
Rothery, Guy Cadogan *(r.n.)*
Born in France, educated privately. Author of many books of a technical nature. Lived at Ivor, Bucks.
Captain.
Rousselet, Louis
B.O.P.
Routledge, Edmund *(r.n.)*
Editor of Boys Journal (1863)
Rover, Max *(r.n. Edgar Joyce Murray)*
Boys Friend Weekly (2nd).
Rowan, Jack
Sports Budget (2nd).
Rowe, H. M.
Union Jack (1st).
Rowe, John Gabriel *(r.n.)*
Born in Liverpool 1873 and educated at Everton Valley Convent, St James School, Bootle, and St Francis Xaviers

College, Liverpool. On leaving school he became a junior reporter on his local 'Bootle Times'. While there, and at the age of 16, he placed his first story, 'Cupid's Dart'. It was the first of a great number of stories he wrote for Pearsons, Newnes, Aldine's, Henderson's and Harmsworth's (later Amalgamated Press). He wrote many of the popular 'Tufty and Co.' school stories for Nugget, although he did not actually create the characters. He remained on the staff of Bootle Times until 1903. Edited the Catholic Home Journal 1906–7 and later edited 'Boys School and Adventure Annual', and its companion volume for girls. Subsequently he became Scenario reader for the Alliance Film Corporation and also wrote over 70 screenplays himself. He wrote 'A Popular History of the Great War' (1918) and biographies of such people as Queen Alexandria and Lord Baden Powell, etc. For adult works he used the name of T. B. Walters and for girls Alice E. Rowe.

Lived in the East End of London in his later years, when it has been said he wore a beard in order to disguise a scar he had acquired during a bad accident in childhood. Although he used the pen-name of 'John Gabriel' it seems that there was another author who wrote sports stories in the Boys Realm in the 20's, who also used this name, this being his real name.

Pen-names: Charles Lewis. Mortimer Austin. Arthur Ferris. Gregory Dunstan. Charles A. Ransome. James Bright. John Gabriel.

The stories by 'Arthur Ferris' have so far not been traced, though the author in correspondence with an editor admitted using that name in boys' fiction.

Diamond Lib. (1st and 2nd). Adventure Lib. (Newnes). Briton's Own Lib. Boys Own Lib. (1st and 2nd). Boys Pocket Lib. Boys Champion Story Paper. Comic Life. Vanguard Lib. (Trapps Holmes). Nuggets. Marvel (1st and 2nd). Boys Friend Weekly (1st). Union Jack (1st). Pluck (1st). Nugget Library. Pocket Budget. Lot-O'-Fun. Lloyds Boys Adventure Library. Boys Life.

Rowe, W. *(r.n.)*
Pen-name: Major Arthur Bingham.
Rowe, W. I.
Union Jack (1st).

Royal, Rex
True Blue (2nd).

Rudolf, R. de M.
Chums. B.O.P.

Rush. Stanley
Champion.

Russ, Richard P.
Chums.

Russan, Ashmore
Popular B.O.P. author, who made his début in 1889, with a school serial 'The New House Mystery' followed immediately with 'A Strange Epidemic'. In 1891 he co-operated with Frederick Boyle to write the famous 'The Orchid Seekers'.
Boys Friend Weekly (1st). B.O.P. Union Jack (1880). Young England.

Russell, C. *(r.n.)*
Was at one time Chief Literary Cashier at Amalgamated Press, and in his early days on the staff wrote a few stories. Died a few years ago.
Pen-names: Geoffrey Wood. Martin Clifford (Popular) (2nd).

Russell, George Hansby *(r.n.)*
Born 1895. Wrote several books and stories for magazines, pertaining mostly to South African matters. Lived at Lyme Regis, Dorset.
B.O.P.

Russell, Herbert
Worlds Comic.

Russell, Philip
Union Jack (1st). Marvel (1st).

Russell, Sinclair
Greyfriars Herald (2nd).

Russell, Spike
Pioneer.

Russell, William Clark *(r.n.)*
Born in 1844 and went to sea with the Merchant Navy at the age of 13. Spent several years in the Service. Wrote his first novel 'John Holdsworth, Chief Mate' in 1874. Subsequently became a leading sea-story writer of his generation. Lived in Bath for many years and in later life became an invalid, losing

the use of his legs. He was the uncle of Henry St John Cooper.
Died 8th November 1911.
Nuggets. Lads and Lassies Lib. B.O.P.

Ruthven, Jack
Football & Sports Lib. Flag Library.

Rutledge, Archibald *(r.n.)*
Born 1883. Captain.

Ryder, Steve *(r.n. Alfred Edgar)*
Champion.

Ryle, Randolph *(r.n. John Nix Pentelow)*
Marvel (1st). B.F.L. (1st).

Rymer, James Malcolm *(r.n. Malcolm James Merry)*
This was one of the pen-names used by Merry when he was
writing the 'Penny Bloods' over 100 years ago. Many of them
are quite valuable today and are most sought-after collectors'
pieces.

Sabatini, Raphael *(r.n.)*
Born 1875 in Jesi, Italy. Educated Ecole Cantonale, Switzerland. Author of many classical books and magazine stories,
including 'Captain Blood', 'Scaramouche' and 'The Sea Hawk'.
Union Jack (2nd).

Sadler, S. Whitechurch *(r.n.)*
Paymaster-in-Chief to the Royal Navy for some years around
the 1870's and 1880's. His naval experiences served him in good
stead when he turned to writing. He wrote three rattling sea
serials for the B.O.P., the first in 1880 entitled 'The Adventurous Voyage of the Polly'. The others were 'Adventures on the
Southern Main' (1882) and later the same year 'Mutineers of
the Good Intent'.
B.O.P.

Sagon, Amyot
True Blue (2nd).

St Clair, A.
B.O.P.

St John, Arthur
Vanguard Lib. (Trapps Holmes).

St John, Henry *(r.n. Henry St John Cooper)*
Fun & Fiction. B.F.L. (1st). Pluck (1st and 2nd). Marvel (1st
and 2nd). Cheer, Boys, Cheer. Champion. Union Jack (1st
and 2nd). Popular (2nd). Young Britain (2nd). Boys Realm

Football and Sports Lib. Boys Herald. Boys Friend Weekly (1st and 2nd). Boys Realm (1st and 2nd).

St John, Percy Bolingbroke *(r.n.)*

Born 1821 and popular boys' writer for the early Victorian papers. His most famous serial, later reprinted many times in book form, was 'The Blue Dwarf'. He also wrote the popular series about different types of castaway Crusoes, including 'Sailor Crusoe', 'Arctic Crusoe', and 'Cannibal Crusoe'. Was the brother of Vane St John. Died in 1889.

Boys Friend (1864). Our Boys Paper. New Boys Paper. Boys Pocket Library. Young Men of Great Britain. Boys of England. Boys World. Boys Journal. Young Gentlemen of Great Britain.

St John, Vane *(r.n.)*

Prolific writer of boys' stories in the very early Victorian days. Was editor of 'Young Men of Great Britain' for a time. Wrote 'The Night Guard' for the first volume of the latter paper and later serials. Was at his best on stories of Irish life, which included 'That Larry of Ours' and 'Pat o' the Hills'. One of his best-remembered stories is 'The Link Boy of Old London' which introduced Sweeney Todd as a secondary character. Like so many of the Victorian boys' authors, he lived carelessly and died penniless. Was the brother of Percy St John.

Boys World. Our Boys Paper. Young Men of Great Britain. New Boys Paper. Boys Pocket Library. Young Gentlemen of Great Britain. Boys Standard (2nd). Boys of England.

St Johnston, Alfred

Chums.

St Lawrence, J.

Boys Leader.

St Mars, F. (Frank) *(r.n.)*

Wrote many stories for boys' papers, including a famous 'War with Germany' serial in Pluck before the 1914–18 war had even started. But his main output was nature stories and articles, for many magazines and yearly Annuals. Died in the 1920's, according to a magazine to which he contributed, but there is no trace in this country of his death. For years it was presumed that the 'F' of his name stood for 'Florence' and that this writer was a woman. He was a friend of C. M. Down, the Magnet and Gem editor, and contributed much work for his papers. A photograph of him can be seen in the collection of F. Vernon Lay, who is greatly interested in his work and background. Boys Realm (1st). Boys Friend Weekly (2nd). Empire Library (1st and 2nd). Popular (2nd). Pluck (2nd). Gem (2nd). Boys Herald.

St Mervyn, Guy
Chums.

Sala, George Augustus *(r.n.)*
Born 24th November 1928. Began his literary career as editor of 'Chat' in 1848. After writing regularly for 'Household Words' 1851–56, he joined the staff of the Daily Telegraph in 1857. Was special correspondent for that paper in the American Civil War. Wrote 'Charley Wag' in 1861 and other similar 'Bloods'. Died 8th December 1895.

Salmon, Edward G. *(r.n.)*
Born 1885 and author of several biographies, also contributed to leading magazines.
B.O.P. Worlds Comic (with W. W. Fenn).

Salzmann, Alice
Young England.

Samways, George Richmond *(r.n.)*
Born 1895 at Kingsclere, Hants, and educated at King Edward VI School, Witley, Surrey. Was a reader of Magnet and Gem at school and after leaving started work in a stockbroker's office as a junior clerk at Southsea. He earned 15s. a week and supplemented this income by supplying the Magnet with verses under the titles of 'Greyfriars' Lyrics' and for the Gem 'St Jim's Jingles'. They were so successful that he was offered a job in the Magnet office in London.

Soon afterwards he was asked by H. A. Hinton, the editor of the Companion Papers, to write a full-length Magnet story. This he did, and it appeared under the title of 'Reign of Terror' in No 353 in 1914. Later came 'The Sunday Crusaders', in Magnet No 400 which had a religious background. Copies were sent to hundreds of clergymen and headmasters throughout the country to prove that the Magnet was suitable reading matter for young people. In all Samways wrote about 90 substitute stories for the Magnet and approximately 50 for the Gem.

Some were written in collaboration with John Nix Pentelow,

the war-time editor, which has made the exact authorship of the substitute tales somewhat difficult to define. At the outbreak of war, in August 1914, he took over the job of sub-editor of the Companion Papers from C. M. Down, who had joined up. Around this time he was asked by H. A. Hinton to write a full-length story for the B.F.L. with sport the main theme. 'School and Sport' eventually came out, and despite criticism today of its lack of plot, there is no question but that it was tremendously popular with boys at the time, and it is regarded as a rare collectors' item today.

After serving under John Nix Pentelow, the war-time editor, for a time, he eventually joined up himself, serving in the R.F.C. and returning to his old job in 1919. He originated the popular Greyfriars Herald and St Jim's Gazette, and created the humorous stories of Dr Birchemal of St Sam's (taken from the first half of Samway's name) which ran for many years. He also wrote thousands of verses and rhymes for the Companion Papers, as well as short stories.

He created the characters of Archie and Phyllis Howell in the Magnet, and also Dennis Carr of the Remove. A long original series about this character appeared in the Popular. He also created Claremont School, and Teddy Baxter and Co. for Chuckles. In 1921 he resigned from the firm to become free-lance, and went to live in the Isle of Wight. Between 1921–28 he continued to pour out stories, poems and jingles, and also wrote for such papers as Flying, Answers, Passing Show and Punch. He also had several books published, including a book of poems entitled 'War Lyrics'.

In 1929 he decided to concentrate on full-time competition work and become a professional solutionist. This he did, winning many big prizes for himself and clients.

During the last war he served in the R.A.F. in Iceland 1942–45 and today is still busy with his competition work at his home in Dursley, Glos.

Pen-names: Paul Proctor. Paul Masters. Mark Linley. George Richmond. Martin Clifford (Gem and Popular). Frank Richards (Magnet and Popular). Owen Conquest (Boys Friend Weekly – 2nd).

Scout. Boys Realm (2nd). Football and Sports Favourite. B.F.L. (1st) (anon). Greyfriars Herald (1st) (anon).

Sandell, Courtney
Boys Realm (2nd).

Sapt, Arkus *(r.n.)*
Union Jack (2nd) (anon). Boys Friend Weekly (2nd) (anon).

Sapte, W. *(r.n. Robert Hamilton Edwards)*
Union Jack (2nd).

Sargent, Maud E.
Chatterbox.

Saunders, Charles Wesley
Lloyds Detective Series.

Saunders, D. M.
Modern Boy.

Saunders, Hilary Aidan St George *(r.n.)*
Librarian at the House of Commons. Wrote several novels, some in collaboration with John Palmer.
Pen-name: Francis Beeding.

Saville, Malcolm *(r.n.)*
Born Hastings, Sussex, 1901. Educated at Richmond Hill School, Richmond. Publicity and Sales Promotion, Amalgamated Press 1922–36. Sales Promotion George Newnes 1936–41. Assc. editor of 'My Garden' 1946. Editor of general books for Newnes and Pearson in 1950's. Has written over 40 books for boys and girls and lives in Lewes, Sussex.

Saville, Ray
Boys Own Library (2nd). Boys Pocket Library. Detective Tales (2nd).

Saxby, Argyll *(r.n.)*
Son of Jessie Saxby, a well-known Scottish writer. After an early career in which he roamed Canada, he became a schoolmaster and the initials which sometimes appeared after his name are rightly his – M.A. and F.R.G.S. His schoolmaster duties took him all over the Middle East, teaching in Cyprus, Syria, etc. He also taught in India before serving in the First World War. He wrote several adventure serials set in many different parts of the world for the B.O.P., the first being 'The Fiery Totem' in 1912. Other titles included 'The Black Lizard', 'Living it Down' and 'Kookaburra Jack', the latter appearing in 1924 and consisting of escapades at an Australian school.
B.O.P. Young England.

Saxby, Jessie Margaret Edmondston *(r.n.)*
Born 1842, and wrote about 30 books, and volumes of poetry.
Mother of Argyll Saxby.
B.O.P.

Saxon, Peter *(r.n. William Howard Baker)*
S.B.L. (3rd and 5th).

Sayer, Wal *(r.n. W. W. Sayer)*
Rocket. Pluck (3rd) Champion Annual.

Sayer, Walter William *(r.n.)*
Born at Forest Hill, London, S.E., March 1892. Educated at
the grey-coat Roan School at Greenwich Village. Good at
mathematics and writing, he edited the school magazine.
Probably he inherited this ability from his grandfather, who
was a school manager and master of the famous Kingsland
Birkbeck School. On leaving school he worked at the Midland
Bank in Fleet Street. It was probably those Amalgamated Press
writers who paid in big cheques that decided him to become a
writer, and his first stories were for the old Pluck, featuring
Detective Inspector Will Spearing. He also wrote for the Tubby
Haig Library, and Titbits.
The First World War saw him on war service in France, and on
his return he set up a small office in Fleet Street as a free-lance
writer. In 1919 he wrote his first Sexton Blake story for the
S.B.L. and it was published in No 110, 1st Series – 'The Case of
the King's Spy'. It featured Granite Grant, a character of his
own invention. His second story introduced Mademoiselle
Julie, a French Secret Service agent, and from then on she and
Grant were to feature as a pair of secret agents in probably the
best-written of all the Blake stories. Such was their popularity
that most of them were later reprinted.
Apart from his Blake stories, he wrote for many of the D. C.
Thomson papers. A Blake yarn of his once appeared in the
London Evening Standard (23rd November 1936) in a feature
edited by Miss Dorothy Sayers. In 1930, Sayer left his juvenile
writings behind him and joined the London General Press, a
feature agency. Later he formed the International Press, but
resigned and joined the British Lion Company. He then became licensee of a public house at Winkfield near Windsor,
Berks. Eventually he moved next door to help his wife run a
garden ornament business titled 'Rustic Crafts'.

Writer of many novels, he once had a compliment paid to him by an editor who said that his writing was 'too good' for the juvenile market.

His unusual pen-name of 'Pierre Quiroule' means 'the Rolling Stone' in French. He is married, his wife being French. His writings were exceptionally good, and his prose far above the majority of other Sexton Blake writers.

Pen-names: Wal Sayer. Pierre Quiroule.

S.B.L. (1st and 2nd). Union Jack. Dixon Hawke Lib. Pluck. Tubby Haig Lib. Wizard. Rover. Adventure (all anon).

Sayers, Edgar *(r.n. Alfred Edgar)*
Champion. Boys Friend Weekly (2nd). Gem (2nd).

Sayers, James Denson *(r.n.)*
Pen-name: Denver Bardwell.

Scarth, Paul
Champion.

Schisgall, Oscar *(r.n.)*
Born U.S.A. 1901.
Thriller. Detective Weekly. B.F.L. (2nd).

Schooling, Geoffrey Holt
Pluck (2nd).

Scotland, Kennedy
Thriller.

Scott, Captain Angus *(r.n. A. J. Colinski)*
Boys Friend Weekly (2nd).

Scott, Captain Digby
Boys Herald.

Scott, Ernest *(r.n. W. E. Groves)*
Champion. Boys Friend Weekly (2nd). B.F.L. (1st).

Scott, G. Firth
Captain. Chums.

Scott, George
Pluck (2nd).

Scott, Hamilton *(r.n. Hedley O'Mant)*
Boys Realm (2nd).

Scott, Hedley *(r.n. Hedley O'Mant)*
A serial 'The Phantom Bat' in the Magnet was written by F. W. Young. But this is the only time that another writer used the 'Hedley Scott' pen-name.

Pluck (3rd). S.B.L. (2nd). Gem (2nd). Magnet. Boys Realm

(2nd). Nelson Lee Lib. (1st New Series). Ranger (1st and 2nd). B.F.L. (2nd). Boys Own Lib. (2nd).

Scott, Kingsbury
Scout.

Scott, Maxwell *(r.n. Dr John William Staniforth)*
Boys Realm Football and Sports Lib. Cheer, Boys, Cheer. Detective Lib. B.F.L. (1st). Pluck (1st and 2nd). Marvel (1st and 2nd). Nelson Lee Lib. (Old Series and 2nd New Series revised). Union Jack (1st and 2nd). Boys Friend Weekly (1st and 2nd). Boys Herald. Boys Realm (1st). Gem (2nd). Comic Home Journal. Wonder. Chums. Boys Leader. Big Budget. Jester.

Scott, Michael
Pluck (1st).

Scott, Nigel
Captain.

Scott, Reginald Thomas Maitland *(r.n.)*
Born Ontario 1882, and educated at Royal Military College, Canada.
B.F.L. (2nd).

Scott, Captain Russell *(r.n. Alec G. Pearson)*
Boys Leader.

Scott, Sir Walter *(r.n.)*
Born 1771 in Edinburgh and educated at Edinburgh High School and University. Was apprenticed to his father; called to the Bar in 1792. He devoted much of his leisure time to exploration of the Border Country. Went on to write many novels that were to become classics, such as 'Waverley', 'Guy Mannering', etc. His stories were published in the following papers during Alfred Harmsworth's 'classical' period:
Union Jack (1st). Pluck (1st). Marvel (1st).

Scratton, Howel
Racing Novels (1st).

Scribe, The
Scout.

Seabrook, William Buehler *(r.n.)*
Born U.S.A. 22nd Feb. 1886. Died 20th Sept. 1945.
Thriller.

'Seamark' *(r.n. Austin J. Small)*
Thriller.
Seamer, H. St John
Captain.
'Seawrack'
B.O.P.
Seed, H. A.
Rocket.
Segar, James
Modern Boy.
Sellick, G. Godfrey
B.O.P.
Seltzer, Charles Alden *(r.n.)*
Born 15th Aug. 1875 and well-known author of many Westerns.
Died 9th April 1942 at Lakeside Hospital, Cleveland, Ohio.
Western Library.
Selwyn, Jack
Boys of the Isles. Bad Boys Paper.
Sempill, Ernest *(r.n.)*
Probably the most mysterious writer of boys' fiction of all time.
Known to all at old Amalgamated Press about 1906 as 'Michael
Storm' and creator of George Marston Plummer, the ex-
detective Yard man turned crook. His first story about him
was 'The Man from Scotland Yard' in Union Jack No 222 in
January 1908. Several other stories followed, until his presumed
death abroad in 1909. Apart from his Sexton Blake stories, he
wrote fine school stories featuring Abbotscrag and Ravenscar
for Pluck and Marvel, as well as about Nigel Dorn, Private
Investigator. Sempill, or Storm as he was known, was a man of
about 50 in 1908 and spent nearly all his time between Bognor
and Boulogne in France. It is suspected that he may have been
connected with the famous Sempill family. G. H. Teed met the
widow of 'Michael Storm' when she was returning to England
from Australia and it was due to her influence that Teed started
writing for A.P. Mrs 'Storm' disappeared in 1912 and many
researchers have spent years still trying to accumulate authentic facts about her husband.
Pen-names: Rupert Storm. Michael Storm. Alan Gale.
Detective Inspector Coles. John Michael. Paul Michael.

Popular (1st) (anon). Union Jack (2nd) (anon). Detective
Weekly (anon) re-write.

Senarens, Louis P.   *(r.n.)*

Born in New York, 24th April 1865. Took over from Harry
Enton, the original creator of Frank Reade and Frank Reade
Jnr., the father and son inventors, whose popular adventures
with their incredible 'Steam Man', 'Steam Horse', etc., appeared
in the Aldine Invention, Travel and Adventure Library in the
1890's. The stories originally appeared in the Frank Reade
Library in the U.S.A. Senarens began writing when he was
14, and by the age of 16 he was earning 200 dollars a week. For
many years he wrote about 50,000 words a week, and all
written in longhand. Other writers in time took over the Frank
Reade stories, and Senarens died in 1940.

Invention, Travel and Adventure Lib. (anon).

Senior, Charles

Marvel (1st).

Senior, Walter, Rev.   *(r.n.)*

B.O.P.

Sennett, Tertia

Chatterbox.

Serjeant, Escort

Marvel (1st).

Sewell, William G.

Boys Torch Adventure Library.

Seymour, W. J.

Scout.

Shackleford, Martin

Boys Pictorial (new series).

Shadwell, Detective Inspector

Marvel (1st).

Shah Ali Ikbal   *(r.n.)*

Pen-name: Sheikh Ahmed Abdullah.

Shallard, E. F.

B.O.P.

Shanan, C. H.

Scout.

Shand, Captain   *(r.n. Gilbert Floyd)*

Boys Realm (1st).

Shannon, A. Donnelly   *(r.n. A. Donnelly Aitken)*
Dreadnought.
Sharp, William   *(r.n.)*
Pen-name: *Fiona Macleod.*
Shaw, Dick   *(r.n. H. Openshaw)*
Champion Annual. Modern Boy. Champion. Champion Lib.
Triumph.
Shaw, Frank H.   *(r.n.)*
Born 24th October 1878. Joined the Royal Navy as an ap-
prentice on a windjammer and soon rose up in rank to become
a Captain. Also served his country in the air when he piloted
Naval sea-planes in 1916. Wrote his first story in the form of a
serial in Chums in 1908, a story about a great war with Russia,
set in the future. A sequel appeared later. Throughout the years
he contributed many other stories and serials, and all were first-
class in every way as well as being authentic regarding locality,
etc. He also wrote for adults in such high-class magazines as
Strand, Cassell's, Red Magazine, etc. Published his auto-
biography in 1958 – 'Seas of Memory' – when he was 80, and at
the time of writing is living in South London.
His brother was S. Gordon Shaw.
Pen-names: Archibald Guthrie. Frank Hubert. Grenville
Hammerton. Frank Cleveland.
Thriller. Modern Boy. Chums. Boys Life.
Shaw, Gordon   *(r.n. Stanley Gordon Shaw)*
Champion. Boys Herald. Chums. Young Britain (1st). B.F.L.
(2nd). Pluck (3rd). Chums Annual.
Shaw, Herbert
Thriller.
Shaw, Justin   *(r.n. H. Openshaw)*
Ranger (2nd).
Shaw, Martin   *(r.n. E. Le Breton Martin)*
Boys Realm (1st). Boys Friend Weekly (2nd). Boys Herald.
Young Britain (1st). Champion. B.F.L. (1st and 2nd).
Shaw, Reeves   *(r.n.)*
Born in Brighton 1886, and educated at Brighton Grammar
School. Was Editor-in-Chief of George Newnes Ltd., and ran
such famous papers as The Captain, Tubby Haig Lib. and the
comic Merry Moments. Held the post of editor of the former
paper for a time in 1910 and later became editor of The Grand

Magazine in 1920. After other editorial posts he became editor of Strand Magazine, a post he held for some years. He wrote mainly for adult magazines, and was still working for George Newnes in post-war years. Died some years ago.

Shaw, Stanley Gordon *(r.n.)*

Born 1884, and had an adventurous early life, emigrating to Canada, tramping the countryside, living with Red Indians, working as a lumberjack, trapper and farm hand. He used all his experience to good advantage when he took up writing on his return to England in 1908. He wrote for most of the Amalgamated Press papers and served throughout the First World War with the 49th Division, getting several mentions in Despatches. He wrote many Sexton Blake stories – one of them called 'Sexton Blake, Lumberjack', based on his own experiences. His own character was Janssen the Moonslayer, and his last story was in the late 30's. Gordon Shaw, who was the brother of Frank H. Shaw, died about 1938.

Pen-names: John Heritage. Captain Dare. Harry Strange. S. S. Gordon. Gordon Shaw. Gordon Wallace. Stanley Gordon. Union Jack (2nd) (anon). Detective Lib. (anon). Pluck (3rd). S.B.L. (2nd). (anon). Boys Realm. Football & Sports Lib. Chums.

Shea, Victor

Chums.

Sheldrake, S.

B.O.P.

Shepherd, S. Rossiter *(r.n.)*

The famous Sunday People theatre and holiday expert, now on the staff of News of the World. Wrote several substitute stories for the Magnet in 1921–25 period. The first was 'Sleepers of the Remove', No 697. Later worked on the Union Jack Supplement and wrote several articles. Has held other important editorial posts, including editor of 'Picturegoer'. Also crime reporter on the Daily Express and Features editor and film critic of The People. He is a well-known and popular figure in the world of entertainment.

Pen-names: Mark Milton. Frank Richards (Magnet).

Boys Realm (2nd). Detective Tales (2nd).

Sherlock, A. B.

Captain. B.O.P.

Sherliker, James
Boys Journal.
Sheriff, Katherine E.
Chatterbox.
Sherrington, Alf *(r.n. A. S. Burrage)*
Champion Journal.
Sherwood, Captain
Ranger (2nd).
Sherwood, L.
B.F.L. (2nd).
Shiel, Matthew Phipps *(r.n.)*
Born 21st July 1865 in the West Indies. Was the son of a
Methodist preacher. A whole chapter about this author can be
seen in 'Explorers of the Infinite' by Sam Moskowitz. Shiel
died in 1947.
Boys Friend Weekly (1st).
Shirley, Mostyn
Chums.
Shirvell, Michael
Chums.
Shultz, James Willard
Boys Cinema.
Shute, Walter *(r.n.)*
A most prolific writer of boys' stories for Amalgamated Press of
whom very little is known. Was editor of the Union Jack before
H. W. Twyman in 1921, then went free-lance. Was reported to
be driving a taxi-cab in the West country shortly before his
death, which is believed to have been around 1940.
Pen-names: Walter Edwards. Johnson Edwards. Gordon
Maxwell. Charles Wentworth.
Pilot (anon). S.B.L. (2nd) (anon). Union Jack (2nd) (anon).
Surprise (anon).
Sidney, Frank *(r.n. Alan Ross Warwick*
Sydney *Francis Warwick, Sidney Warwick)*
This pen-name was used at times by all the three authors:
father and two sons. B.F.L. (2nd). Pluck (3rd). Champion.
Silas, Ellis
Chums.
Simmonds, Ralph *(r.n.)*
Wrote hard-cover books for Cassells.

Nugget Lib. Boys Herald. Boys Journal. Cheer, Boys, Cheer.
B.F.L. (1st). Chums.

Simpson, Horace J.
Pluck (2nd).

Sims, George Robert   *(r.n.)*
Born 1847 and wrote many books. Was a great friend of
Andrew Murray. Died 4th September 1922.
Fun & Fiction. Boys Friend Weekly (2nd). Dreadnought. Grip.

Sinbad   *(r.n. A. E. Dingle)*
Thriller. Detective Weekly. Modern Boy.

Sinclair, Captain   *(r.n. Harry Blyth)*
According to the son of Harry Blyth, his father wrote boys'
fiction under this name, but so far it has not been traced.

Sinclair, Harry
Marvel (1st).

Sinclaire, Gavin
Hotspur Book for Boys.

Sizer, Kate T.
Young England.

Skene, Anthony   *(r.n. George Norman Philips)*
Union Jack (2nd). B.F.L. (2nd) Thriller. Thriller Lib. Detective Weekly. S.B.L. (2nd and 3rd).

Sketchley, Sidney
B.O.P.

Skilton, Charles   *(r.n.)*
Not an author or editor, but certainly deserves a place in this
biography for the idea of publishing the Billy Bunter books.
The first one in 1947 was entitled 'Billy Bunter of Greyfriars
School' and he produced 9 others until 1951, when he sold out
to Cassells, who published their first book in 1952. These continued up to and after Charles Hamilton's death in 1961. Many
are still being reprinted today as paperbacks.
Charles Skilton also republished 'Frank Richards' Autobiography' but it was unsuccessful without the promised
revisions (because of his death) by Charles Hamilton.

Skinner, James T.   *(r.n.)*
Boys Friend Weekly (2nd).

Slade, Gurney   *(r.n.)*
Wrote many hard-cover books for boys including 'The Black

Pyramid' and 'Ships that Pass in the Night'. Lived at Sidcup, Kent, and died in 1956.

Sleigh, Stanton
Diamond Lib. (1st and 2nd). True Blue (2nd).

Small, Austin J. *(r.n.)*
Pen-name: 'Seamark'.

Smart, Hegan
Boys Cinema.

Smeaton, Fred *(r.n. Fred Gordon Cook)*
F. G. Cook has stated that he once wrote boys' stories under this pen-name, but so far they have not been traced.

Smiles, Sam
Marvel (1st).

Smith, Bernard *(r.n.)*
Was assistant editor of Scout to F. Haydon Dimmock, just after World War I, and stayed with him until November 1922. He then joined the Amalgamated Press and was editor of the Champion after F. Addington Symonds. Later he used to convert the old serials into long complete tales for The Champion Library. Worked also for a time on Pearson's Weekly. In later years he was editor of Lion and Air Ace Picture Library, and has devoted much of his life to the Boy Scout Movement.
He retired from Fleetway Publications in 1966.
Pen-names: Jack Smith. Fred J. Williams. Ivor Martyn. Harry Campbell. Bernard Heath.
Scout.

Smith, D. M. Percy
Chatterbox.

Smith, Fenton *(r.n. L. E. Pratt)*
Boys Journal. Boys Realm (2nd).

Smith, Fowler
Boys Life.

Smith, George
Chums.

Smith, Hamilton *(r.n. George E. Rochester)*
George E. Rochester recalled writing boys' stories under this pen-name, but so far they have not been traced.

Smith, Helen Zenna *(r.n.)*
Dramatist, journalist and author. Wrote film scenarios, stage and radio plays. Special features writer for the Sunday People

1930–34. Was War Correspondent for the same paper 1944–46. Wrote many books and contributed to many leading magazines.

Pen-name: Evadne Price.

Smith, Jack   *(r.n. Bernard Smith)*
Champion.

Smith, Joe
Football Weekly.

Smith, Stewart
Chums.

Smith, W. V.
Chums.

Snell, Edmund   *(r.n.)*
Born London 1889. Educated Ashford Grammar School. Author of many books. Wrote for many leading magazines such as Chambers' Journal, Windsor Magazine, Pearsons, Premier, Hutchinsons, Sovereign, Grand, Red, Yellow, Green, Blue Magazines. Served in the First World War. Was cinema and travel bureau proprietor after the war.
Thriller. Thriller Library. Detective Weekly.

Snell, E. L.   *(r.n.)*
Pen-names: Ellis Ellsen. Ellis Ellison.
Boys Life.

Snell, Roy Judson   *(r.n.)*
Born 1878 at Laddonia, Missouri. Educated at Wheaton Academy and Chicago University. Wrote a number of novels.
Captain.

Snow, Edward C.
Lived at Windsor, Berks, and joined the Amalgamated Press in 1919 when a lad of 15. Worked as a junior sub-editor in the Companion Papers office. Although like many others on the staff he did not write any St Jim's or Greyfriars tales, he did however contribute a great many articles for the Popular and Holiday Annuals. He also created the St Jim's News in the Gem, and drew maps for the Holiday Annuals.
He left Amalgamated Press in 1922 to go free-lance and sailed to a new life in Australia in 1924.
He is now a successful journalist, and regularly writes for travel magazines, covering with authority such subjects as Pacific

travel and luxury passenger ships. According to C. M. Down, the Companion Papers editor, he was an expert on the Magnet and Gem, and left with him a book filled with data and drawings of all the Hamilton characters.

Snow, Phil
Boys Realm (1st). Football and Sports Favourite.

Soloman, David R.
Detective Weekly.

Somers, Boston
True Blue (2nd).

Sorrell, Lucian
Young England.

Soutar, Andrew   *(r.n.)*
Born 1879. Wrote many serials and stories for Chums 1912–15 mainly with sporting backgrounds. Later he turned to adult fiction, when he became an established writer of thrillers and detective stories. Was Special Correspondent for the London Times in North Russia, 1919. At least 16 of his books have been filmed, and he took a six-month visit to the U.S.A. in 1920 to supervise the filming of four of his novels.
Chums. B.F.L. (1st).

Southwick, David (Captain)
British Boys Paper.

Sowerby, Temple
Boys Journal.

Sowman, Gordon   *(r.n.)*
Wrote an S.B.L. under the Desmond Reid pen-name in S.B.L. (3rd).
Western Library.

'Sparrowhawk'
Chums.

Speed, H. Fiennes (Rev.)
B.O.P.

Spence, Hubert   *(r.n. Percy Longhurst)*
Boys Herald.

Spencer, Captain   *(r.n. Hugh Tuite)*
Union Jack (1st). Pluck (1st). Comic Cuts.

Spencer, John   *(r.n. Roy C. Vickers)*
Gem (2nd).

Spencer, Roland *(r.n. Geoffrey Prout)*
At times the name was used by Geoffrey Prout and Francis
Warwick.
Scout. B.F.L. (2nd). Football Novels. Aldine War Stories. Gem
(2nd).

Spicer, Howard Handley (Sir) *(r.n.)*
Born 1872, editor of Sandow's Magazine 1899–1901. Resigned
to edit 'Boys of our Empire' 1901. Co-founder of 'Boys Empire
League'. Author of several books.

Spiers, C. L.
Hotspur Book for Boys.

Spiller, Leonard
Scout.

Sprigg, William Stanhope *(r.n.)*
Born 18th August 1867 in Dublin and educated at Kings School,
Worcester. Spent several years editing provincial newspapers at
Nottingham and Sheffield, also in Southampton. Was advisory
editor to C. A. Pearson and later became an editor of the
Amalgamated Press. Sprigg claimed to have first introduced
Dr Staniforth to the firm, who later created the famous detec-
tive, Nelson Lee. Sprigg also wrote a large number of stories,
including a Sexton Blake story for the Union Jack. He died
15th May 1932.
Boys Herald. Union Jack (1st) and anon in (2nd). Pluck (1st).
Comic Cuts. Chips.

Sprigg, T. Stanhope *(r.n.)*
Editor of magazine 'Fantasy'.
Rocket (anon).

Squire, Peter
Knockout.

Stables, Dr William Gordon *(r.n.)*
Born in Banffshire, Scotland, 21st May 1840 and educated at
Aberdeen University, where he studied medicine and qualified
as a doctor. Whilst still a student he served on a small whaling
brig as a surgeon. He was able to use his experiences in later
years when he wrote about the Frozen North. For 9 years he
served as a surgeon in the Royal Navy, at home, in India and
the Middle East. Eventually he was invalided out with half-
pay.

The first of his many serials for the B.O.P. was in 1880, entitled 'The Cruise of the Snowbird', and over the next 28 years he contributed a further 18 full-length serials for the same paper. Many of his serials were reprinted into book form, and he once also contributed a serial for the Captain in 1901.

An expert on Natural History, dogs, and taxidermy, he lived largely in a caravan and toured the countryside writing as he went. His home was in Berkshire, where he died on the 10th May 1910.

Captain. B.O.P. Boys Own Novels.

Stacpoole, H. de Vere *(r.n.)*

Born in Kingstown, Ireland, and educated at Malvern College. Wrote an exciting and first-class adventure serial for Chatterbox in 1913, which concerned hidden treasure. Called 'Bird Cay', this was so popular that it was not only reprinted in book form many times but the B.B.C. used it as a serial. Probably his most famous book was 'The Blue Lagoon', the story of two children who were shipwrecked on a desert island and who grew up there. It was later filmed, with Jean Simmons and Donald Houston in the leading roles.

Also contributed to Strand, Pearsons, Argosy, etc. His hobbies were travelling and deep-sea fishing. He was a J.P. and lived at Chelmsford, Essex. Collaborated with William A. Bryce a few times on stories in B.O.P.

Chatterbox. B.O.P.

Stafford, Arthur

Chips.

Stagg, J. Cecil

Boys of England

Stagg, J. R. *(r.n.)*

Pen-names: John Barnet. Oliver Harte.

Stagg, James *(r.n.)*

Has been a Fleet Street journalist for many years, and has contributed many stories to newspapers. Later joined the Amalgamated Press and became sub-editor on the Sexton Blake Library under W. Howard Baker. Wrote his first Blake yarn in 1956 and apart from writing others, re-wrote quite a few more. In 1962 he was awarded the £500 E. Nesbit Children's Book Award for his book 'A Castle for the Kopchecks' (pub-

314

lished by Benn, 1963). Later he left Fleetway to go free-lance, and was last known to be living on the edge of Dartmoor.
Pen-name: Gilbert Johns. Was one of the Desmond Reid writers in S.B.L. (3rd).
S.B.L. (3rd).

Stainforth, Frank
Boys World.

Stamper, Joseph *(r.n.)*
Born at St Helens, Lancs, 1886 and educated locally. Originally worked in an iron foundry but later, after much hardship and unemployment, went on the road as a tramp, travelling all over England. In the 1920's he tried his hand at writing and was fairly successful. His articles appeared in many papers and he worked for Amalgamated Press, D. C. Thomson and Pearson's. Probably his greatest work was his autobiography entitled 'Less than the Dust, or the Memoirs of a Tramp'. In 1940 he wrote one S.B.L. (No 51, 3rd series) 'The Shipyard Menace'. A few years ago he was living at Brentford, Middlesex and seemingly retired from writing.
S.B.L. (3rd).

Standish, J. O. *(r.n. Sidney Horler)*
Boys Friend Weekly (2nd). Boys Realm (1st and 2nd). Dreadnought. B.F.L. (1st).

Standish, Richard *(r.n. Richard Goyne)*
S.B.L. (3rd) Triumph. Champion.

Standring, Robert
Rocket.

Stanford, E. E.
Scout.

Stanhope, Eric *(r.n. Charles Hamilton)*
Vanguard Lib. (Trapps Holmes). Picture Fun.

Staniforth, Dr John William *(r.n.)*
Born in Sheffield, Yorks, 14th November 1863. Won his M.R.C.S. and L.R.C.P. diplomas in 1887. His first job was that of a temporary medical officer in charge of a fever hospital, this being the time of the great smallpox epidemic in Sheffield. He was almost completely isolated from the rest of the world during this period and took up writing to pass the days. His first story, 'Told at Totley', appeared in the March 10th issue of Sheffield Weekly Telegraph in 1887. When the epidemic

ended he was appointed Senior Assistant House Surgeon at the Sheffield Royal Hospital. Later, after marrying a nurse, he moved out to the moors and settled down to a steady practice; then once more took up writing to supplement his income. His first story for boys, entitled 'Nelson Lee, Detective', appeared in the Marvel, dated 31st October 1894, and further stories of Nelson Lee appeared later that year in the Union Jack. Apart from Nelson Lee, he created many other detectives such as Kenyon Ford, Vernon Read, Martin Dale, etc., but none lasted or had the same popularity as his first-named. In the Boys Herald he introduced Nipper, who became Lee's assistant; this story was entitled 'Nelson Lee's Pupil'. Apart from his detective stories Scott also wrote a considerable number of other stories, school, sport and mystery, as well as several early Sexton Blake stories in the Union Jack. So methodical was he that he was known to work with a copy of the Bradshaw Railway Guide and Lloyds Shipping List by him, to make sure that the details in his stories which involved journeys were 100% authentic. Later in life he became a J.P. and gradually ceased writing. He died at Bamford, Sheffield, on 3rd November 1927, and was buried at Hinderwell.

Pen-name: Maxwell Scott.
Nelson Lee Lib. (old series) (anon).

Stanley, Robert *(r.n. Charles Hamilton)*
Vanguard Lib. (Trapps Holmes). Best Budget. Funny Cuts. Larks (Trapps Holmes).

Stanley, Robert
This is presumed to be another author as distinct from Charles Hamilton.
Chums.

Stannard, Russell *(r.n.)*
Pen-name: Russell Mallinson.
Boys Friend Weekly (2nd). All Sports.

Stanovitch, Boris
Boys Friend Weekly (2nd).

Stanton, James
Boys Realm (1st).

Stanton, John *(r.n. G. C. Wallis)*
Boys Herald. Union Jack (1st and 2nd). Boys Friend Weekly (2nd).

Stanton, William *(r.n. William Edward Stanton Hope)*
B.F.L. (2nd).

Stapleton, Maurice *(r.n. J. S. Purcell)*
Union Jack (1st).

Star, Martin
B.O.P.

Stark, Jonathan *(r.n. H. P. Marshall)*
All Sports.

Starr, Frank (Captain)
Boxing Novels (1st and 2nd).

Starr, John
Junior Pyramid Books.

Starr, Richard *(r.n.)*
Started writing about 1910 and was in the R.F.C. 1915–18 during the First World War. Wrote mainly for the comic papers at first, but soon concentrated on boys' fiction. His favourite characters were Irishmen, including Kerry & Co., for Young Britain. Wrote also for Picture Show and Girls Cinema. Was a great friend of H. J. Allingham and they used to collaborate at times on stories. Starr wrote over 50 novels and his sister, Mrs N. Murch, was also a boys' writer. He retired to Sussex in late 1968 and died there, aged over 90. He had no connection with Lewis Essex.
Pen-names: Captain Essex. Kerry O'Dare. Richard Essex. Frank Godwin.

Stebbing, G.
Union Jack (1880).

Steele, Frank
Boys Cinema. Boys Friend Weekly (2nd).

Steele, Howard
An editorial pen-name to cover the identities of many writers who were penning stories featuring 'Panther Grayle' in the Champion. These tales appeared in the early 1920's, when the character was originally created by Alfred Edgar.
Writers were: F. Addington Symonds. Alfred Edgar. A. C. Marshall. L. H. Brooks and Cecil Hayter.
Stories also appeared in Young Britain and B.F.L. (2nd).

Steele, S.
In collaboration with Andrew Fletcher.
Marvel (1st).

Steen, Colin
Boys Own Library (1st).
Steevens, G. W.
Boys Friend Weekly (1st).
Steffens, Arthur *(r.n. Arthur Joseph Steffens)*
Born in London, on the 28th Sept. 1873, the son of a Polish
tailor. Spent his early life as an actor-manager touring all over
England. Later he turned to writing and seemingly adopted the
name of Arthur S. Hardy, by which he was known at Amalgamated Press. Wrote many of his early stories whilst in his
dressing-room waiting for his call. A great sportsman, his
stories of football, racing and Olympic events were first-class
and accurate in every way.

His early famous stories were about Tom Sayers, the boxer-
actor in The Marvel. Later he created the Blue Crusaders
Football team, which ran in the Boys Realm. He held several
editorial posts, being editor of All Sports, Football Favourite
and Sports for Boys. He also contributed to adult papers.
Hardy was a great sportsman himself and knocked up a several-
hundred break in billiards. Steffens dropped out of writing in
the early 30's and although he supposedly died before the last
war, there has never been any trace of his death, either under
his own name or that of Arthur S. Hardy.

Pen-names: Freemont Cooper. W. G. Walters. E. S. Hardy.
A. S. Hardy. Capt. Arthur Leigh. Dare Dee. Clement Hale.
Charles Wentworth (B.F.L. 2nd, No 358). Harrison Glyn.

B.F.L. (2nd). Boys Realm (2nd). Football and Sports Favour-
ite. All Sports. Ranger (1st). Football and Sports Lib. Magnet.
Stein, J. H. *(r.n.)*
One of the writers of the Red Circle School stories in the
Hotspur.

Pen-name: Don Dixon.

Hotspur (anon).
Stembridge, Frank
Lloyds Boys Adventure Series. Lloyds School Yarns.
Stenner, Thomas Robert *(r.n.)*
Born in Minehead, Somerset, 1886. Wrote for various Amalga-
mated Press and D. C. Thomson papers, his speciality being
horse-racing, speedway racing and ice-hockey. Was responsible
for the National Speedway Trophy Competition and was also

the originator of the first speedway test match in 1930. He also more or less 'invented' ice-hockey in this country. Became Publicity Controller of the Greyhound Racing Association and Harringay Arena, and ran his own yearly and weekly Speedway Annual and magazine. He wrote two Sexton Blake stories for the Union Jack, 1927, being the first to have a horse-racing background.

Boys Friend Weekly (2nd). Wizard (anon). Popular (2nd). Union Jack (2nd) (anon). Adventure (anon). B.O.P.

Step, Edward *(r.n.)*

Born in 1855 and was editor of the very short-lived Sampson Low paper 'Boys' which ran from 1892–94. Later he became Natural History editor of the Captain for a few years, on which he was a recognised expert.

Stephen, Handley

Hotspur Book for Boys.

Stephen, Roy

Dreadnought. Football Novels.

Stephens, Arthur *(r.n. S. H. Agnew)*

Chums.

Stephens, Donald Ryder *(r.n.)*

Worked as a free-lance writing stories for the Amalgamated Press. Served in Second World War in Malta for 4 years. Afterwards was staff writer on Children's Newspaper. Wrote adult novels under name of Donald Sinderby.

Stephens, Jack

Football and Sports Lib.

Stephens, Kenneth *(r.n. S. H. Agnew)*

Chums.

Sterne, Duncan *(r.n. H. Openshaw)*

Champion. Champion Lib. Triumph.

Stevens, Arthur

All Sports.

Stevens, Charles

The first editor of Edwin J. Brett's famous paper, Boys of England, which began in 1866, and also wrote the first serial. Stevens was probably one of the best writers for boys of his period, but he made the mistake of thinking he was also a good editor and publisher – his own 'Boys Book of Romance' was a failure. Apart from his own writings, perhaps the best thing

Stevens did was to discover and encourage the later-to-become-famous Edwin Harcourt Burrage, in his early days.
Boys Own Journal. Boys Popular Weekly.

Stevens, Christopher   *(r.n. Julian Rochfort)*
Union Jack (1st).

Stevens, C. L. McLuer   *(r.n.)*
Boys Journal. Scout. British Boys.

Stevens, Lieutenant   *(r.n.)*
B.O.P.

Stevenson, Robert Louis   *(r.n.)*
Born in Edinburgh, 13th November 1850. Was expected to follow his father and grandfather in the engineering profession, but was too delicate in health, so studied Law instead, and was called to the Bar in 1875, but never practised. Always interested in writing, he first wrote for several obscure magazines. His first book appeared in 1878 entitled 'An Inland Voyage'. In Henderson's Young Folks, October 1881–January 1882, he wrote an adventure serial entitled 'The Sea Cook' under the pen-name of Captain George North, without creating much interest, yet later on when this was reprinted in book form and re-titled 'Treasure Island' it was a best-seller and became a classic of its kind. It has been filmed many times, and performed on the stage. It was also serialised in many later boys' papers. Later he wrote many other famous books and eventually settled in Samoa, in the South Sea Islands, in 1890, where he died in 1894.
Pen-name: Captain George North.
Cheer, Boys, Cheer. Union Jack (2nd). Chums. Young Folks. Nuggets.

Steward, Colin
Modern Boy.

Stewart, Hubert
Boys Life.

Stewart, Paul
Scout.

Stewart, Ronald
Cheer, Boys, Cheer.

Stewart, Stuart
Young Folks Tales. Comic Life.

Stirling, Bruce
Chums.
Stirling, Jack
Champion. Champion Lib. Triumph. Champion Annual.
Stirling, Captain John
Boys Realm (2nd).
Stirling, Tom   *(r.n. L. E. Ransome)*
Triumph. Champion. Lion. Champion Annual. Triumph Annual.
Stock, Ralph   *(r.n.)*
Born London 1881. Author, playwright and scenario writer. Captain.
Stockton, Wallace
Chums.
Stone, Martin
Marvel (1st).
Stoneham, Charles Thurley   *(r.n.)*
Born London 1895. Educated at Brighton College. Published several novels and wrote for all leading newspapers and magazines.
Modern Boy.
Storey, Basil   *(r.n.)*
Actually christened William Basil Storey at Low Fell, Newcastle-on-Tyne, 1909. Was speedway correspondent and ice-hockey reporter for the Daily Express. Launched several speedway magazines and a post-war (1950's) boys' paper entitled The School Cap, which did not, however, have a long run.
Tom Merry's Annual. School Cap.
Storm, Duncan   *(r.n. Gilbert Floyd)*
Greyfriars Holiday Annual. B.F.L. (1st and 2nd). Dreadnought. Boys Friend Weekly (2nd). Gem (2nd).
Storm, Harold
Pluck (3rd).
Storm, Ivan   *(r.n. R. G. Thomas)*
Ranger (2nd). B.F.L. (2nd).
Storm, Leslie
Modern Boy.
Storm, Michael   *(r.n. Ernest Sempill)*
B.F.L. (1st). Pluck (2nd). Marvel (2nd). Boys Friend Weekly (2nd).

Storm, Rupert *(r.n. Ernest Sempill)*
Cheer, Boys, Cheer.
Stormalong, Rex *(r.n.)*
B.F.L. (2nd). Champion.
Storrie, J. A. *(r.n.)*
Western Library.
Story, Alfred Thomas *(r.n.)*
Captain.
Story, Jack Trevor *(r.n.)*
Born at Cambridge, 1918. His father was killed in the First
World War, when Jack was only 18 months old. Worked in
Pye Radio factory, then in electronic engineering at Marconi's,
St Albans. Sold a number of short stories to Evening News,
Argosy and John Bull, then wrote his first novel, 'The Trouble
With Harry'. This was later filmed by Alfred Hitchcock, and
more successful novels followed, including 'Mix Me a Person',
'Live Now, Pay Later', 'Something for Nothing,' The Urban
District Lover', and 'One Last Mad Embrace'. Many of his
books have been filmed and his last novel – 'I Sit in Hanger
Lane' – is also being made into a film.
Writes many film and TV scripts for popular series and has also
written many modern Sexton Blake stories, nearly all with a
humorous slant.
Lives in Hampstead in a house overlooking the Heath.
S.B.L. (3rd and 5th).
Story, Rosamond Mary *(r.n.)*
Born at Watford, Herts., the daughter of an accountant. As a
girl she read all the boys' papers, including Magnet, Gem, and
Nelson Lee, but the Nelson Lee remained her favourite. She
was always 'scribbling' and had her first story published, at the
age of 7, in her school magazine. Later continued to write for
her own amusement and she was persuaded to send an 80,000
word Western novel to an agent, who immediately placed it
with Herbert Jenkins. Continued to write for them, mainly
Westerns, and has since written under the names of Ross Woods,
Catherine Tracy, Charles H. Lee, Josephine Lindsay and
Richard Jeskins, covering Westerns, the Deep South, family
romance and a novel of 150,000 words set in a boys' public
school. Also wrote boys' Westerns for Collins.

322

Apart from an almost complete set of Nelson Lee Libraries probably one of her most treasured possessions is a letter from Edwy Searles Brooks, shortly before he died, complimenting her on a St Frank's story she had written.

Also wrote a Sexton Blake story (published under the Desmond Reid pen-name): only the second woman to have done so. Lives with her son and daughter at Wimbledon.

S.B.L. (3rd).

Stovell, Dennis H.
Scout.

Stow, Fred G. *(r.n.)*
Boys Cinema. Football & Sports Lib. Football Novels.

Stradling, Arthur (Dr)
B.O.P.

Strand, Sidney
Scout.

Strang, Herbert
A famous name in boys' fiction history and probably the most unusual, as this name actually hid the identity of two writers, George Herbert Ely (who died in 1958) and James L'Estrange (who died in 1947). The name was coined from both their names. They wrote around 50 books and neither ever wrote one on his own. The plots were usually worked out together, L'Estrange doing the research and Ely the actual writing. The partnership began in Glasgow in 1903 and, after later joining the Oxford University Press, they worked together for over 30 years. Six serials of theirs appeared in The Captain, and some stories in Scout, but mainly their work appeared in the yearly 'Herbert Strang's Annual' which began in 1908 and was continued as 'The Oxford Annual for Boys' until the late 30's. Their stories were very readable and extremely popular in their day, and the Annuals are sought after by many collectors.

Captain. Scout. Herbert Strang's Annual. Oxford Book for Boys.

Strange, Harry *(r.n. S. Gordon Shaw)*
Champion. B.F.L. (2nd).

Strange, Kemble *(r.n. C. N. McEnvoy)*
Marvel (2nd).

Strange, Oliver
Chums.

Street, F.
Lloyds School Yarns.
Stringer, Arthur *(r.n.)*
Born 1874 at Chatham, Ontario. Educated at London Collegiate, Inst./Universities of Toronto and Oxford. On staff of Montreal Herald and wrote many novels at the turn of the century.
Thriller.
Strong, Harrington *(r.n. Johnson McCulley)*
Lloyds Detective Series.
Strong, Jack
Young Britain (1st).
Strong, James *(r.n. H. Hervey)*
Boys Friend Weekly (2nd).
Strong, Philip
Boys Realm (1st).
Strong, Stephen
Chums.
Stroud, Len *(r.n.)*
Was editor at times on some of the coloured 2d comics.
Young Britain (1st). Bullseye (anon).
Struan, Lesley
Chatterbox.
Stuart, Donald *(r.n.)*
Is so well-known also as 'Gerald Verner' that many people think this is his real name. Wrote his first story in 1927. Was highly successful and he soon established himself as a first-class writer. Has written many stage plays including one of Sexton Blake, and also adapted many Peter Cheyney novels for the stage. Stuart has also written the radio scripts for the Sexton Blake series.
Pen-names: Gerald Verner. Ronald Stuart.
Thriller. Detective Weekly. S.B.L. (2nd). Union Jack (2nd).
Stuart, Esme *(r.n. Miss Leroy)*
Union Jack (1880).
Stuart, Michael *(r.n. R. G. Thomas)*
Modern Boy.
Stuart, Oliver
Boys Best Story Paper. Bulldog Breed Library.

Stuart, Ronald   *(r.n. Donald Stuart)*
B.F.L. (2nd).
Stuart, W. E.   *(r.n. W. E. Pike)*
Pluck (3rd).
Studd, Burton F. J.
Scout.
Sturmer, Dudley
Ranger (1st).
Sullivan, Edward D.
Thriller.
Sullivan, Jake
Pioneer. Sports Budget (2nd).
Summers, Colin   *(r.n. S. H. Agnew)*
Chums.
Summers, Somers John   *(r.n.)*
Born 1876, and was one of Alfred Harmsworth's youngest
editors, being only 18 years of age when he controlled Union
Jack, Pluck and Marvel. Was earlier a sub-editor on Answers,
alongside another popular boys' writer, T. C. Bridges. Later
Summers was promoted to the editorship of Answers, which
was the senior Harmsworth publication, and became a close
friend of Alfred Harmsworth. Summers was, however, a very
sick man and died aged only 29, his death cutting short a
brilliant career.
Summers, W. Lloyd
B.O.P. Captain.
Surrey, G.
Boys Torch Adventure Library.
Suter, Harry
Scout.
Sutherland, William Colin
B.O.P.
Swainson, Fred
A writer who wrote some splendid school stories for the Captain
in the early 1900's. Also wrote in the Scout.
Captain. Scout.
Swainson, Leslie R.   *(r.n.)*
Champion Annual.
Sweet, John W.
Chums.

Swinnerton, Phillipe Charles   *(r.n.)*
Born 10th August 1879 in London. Was the brother of the famous Frank Swinnerton, novelist. An artist, for a time he drew Weary Willie and Tired Tim, became editor of Chicks Own and Wonderland Weekly later on, when he also drew comic characters. Died a few years ago.

Sydney, Frank   *(see Frank Sidney)*
Young Britain (1st). Champion.

Sydney, George   *(editorial name: S. J. Bounds)*
S.B.L. (3rd).

Sylvester, John   *(r.n. Hector Hawton)*
Thriller. Chums. Gem (2nd). Magnet. Football & Sports Lib. B.F.L. (2nd). S.B.L. (3rd). Boys Wonder Library.

Symonds, Francis Addington   *(r.n.)*
Born in Southampton, 1893 and educated in Cape Town, South Africa and Rhodesia. As a schoolboy he read 'The Big Budget' and had a great admiration for its editor, Arthur Brooke. He began a correspondence with him and declared that one day he would edit a paper on the same lines. But his first job on leaving school was as auctioneer's clerk in Salisbury, then he worked on a small newspaper, and did a little acting as well. Returning to England, he obtained a post at Amalgamated Press as a manuscript reader in the editorial department. Soon the Directors were impressed with his drive and determination, and gave him the job of starting a new boys' paper. This he did with great success and it was called 'The Champion', the first issue appearing in January 1922.

Later he edited Rocket, Pluck and Young Britain. Probably the greatest satisfaction he experienced was in employing his own boyhood hero, editor Arthur Brooke (real name A. C. Marshall), to write stories for his ventures. Apart from editing, Symonds was also a writer of merit, and wrote many Sexton Blake stories, his creations being Claire Delisle, The Raven, Dr Queed and Vedax the Dwarf. He resigned from the firm in 1924 and went free-lance. Since then he has written for the Dixon Hawke Library and many hard-cover books, as well as hundreds of short stories for the newspapers.

Was the editor of Gregg Publishing Co. Ltd., the shorthand firm, and is also connected with many South African magazines and newspapers. Now lives near Hendon, London, and has written the whole history of his boys' editorships in several collecting magazines.

Pen-names: Howard Steele. Earle Danesford.

S.B.L. (1st and 2nd) (anon). Union Jack (2nd) (anon). Dixon Hawke Lib. (anon).

Taffrail *(r.n. Captain Henry Taprell Dorling)*
Scout.

Tait, W. *(r.n.)*
First editor of Wizard.

Talbot, E.
B.O.P. Chums.

Tarkington, Newton Booth *(r.n.)*
Born 29th July 1869. Educated Indianapolis public schools. Phillips and Exeter Academy and Purdue & Princeton Universities. Author of many books.
Sport and Adventure.

Taylor, Allan M.
B.O.P.

Taylor, Eric
Thriller.

Taylor, F. W.
B.O.P.

Taylor, James
Scout.

Taylor, Norman *(r.n. Noel Wood-Smith)*
Boys Friend Weekly (2nd). Young Britain (1st). B.F.L. (1st and 2nd). Pluck (3rd). Triumph. Sport for Boys. Champion. Champion Lib. Boys Realm (2nd). Union Jack (2nd). Sport and Adventure.

Taylor, Reginald S. *(r.n.)*
Started as an office boy on Magnet, Gem and Nelson Lee Library. Became a sub-editor 1933–36. Had to count the words of Charles Hamilton's manuscripts and proof-read them.

Taylor, W. T. *(r.n.)*
Pen-names: Dave Gregory. John Bredon. Arch Whitehouse. Wild West Weekly (anon). Many obscure boys' Annuals.

Teed, George Heber *(r.n.)*
Hamilton
Born at St Johns, New Brunswick, Canada, 13th April 1878. His father was the wealthy owner of saw-mills and a fleet of

fishing and trading boats. At school he was considered quite a brilliant pupil and later he attended McGill University. In his teens he travelled around the world and eventually settled down in Australia as a sheep farmer. A drought caused the financial ruin of this venture and Teed, on his way to England, met Mrs Storm – the widow of Michael Storm. The outcome of this meeting was that after a time of 'ghosting' he established himself as a first-class author in his own right.

In the First World War, Teed served in the Forces, and on his return got tired of writing and went out to Indo-China as manager of a large export firm. Later, when the branch closed down, he returned to England and continued writing where he had left off.

His creations and writings are considered the best in Blake history before the Second World War: Yvonne Cartier, Nirvana, Huxton Rymer, Roxane Harfield, Marie Galante, and Prince Wu Ling. He set his stories in all parts of the world and could bring colour and authenticity to them, as well as drama. Teed was a well-known figure in Fleet Street, and his sudden death in the London Hospital, Whitechapel, on Christmas Eve 1939 was a shock not only to his many friends, but to all his readers.

Pen-names: Louis Brittainy. George Hamilton. Murray Hamilton (with R. M. Graydon).

Had a story published under the Desmond Reid pen-name in S.B.L. (3rd).

Detective Weekly. Union Jack (2nd). N.L. Lib. (old) (anon). Boys Realm (1st). Sexton Blake Annual. Boys Journal. Ranger (1st and 2nd). B.F.L. (1st and 2nd). Pluck (2nd). Dreadnought. S.B.L. (1st) (anon). S.B.L. (2nd). Thriller. Thriller Lib. Boys Friend Weekly (2nd).

Temperley, W. H.
B.O.P.

Tempest, Alan
Comic Life. Scout. Sparks.

Tempest, E. Dudley
Wonder (anon). Wonder Library.

Tempest, Jack
Dick Turpin Library (Aldine).

Templar, John   *(r.n. John L. Garbutt)*
Modern Boy.
Temple, William
Rocket (N.O.W.)
Tench, C. V.   *(r.n.)*
Thriller. Boys Broadcast (anon).
Terrill, G. Appleby
B.O.P.
Terry, Noel   *(r.n. Noel Wood-Smith)*
Chums.
Thoborn-Clark, L. B.
Young England. B.O.P.
Thomas, Annie   *(r.n. Mrs Pender Cudlip)*
Worlds Comic.
Thomas, Anthony   *(r.n. Reginald Heber Poole)*
British Boy. Gem (2nd). Magnet. Chums. B.F.L. (1st and 2nd).
Boys Wonder Lib. Dixon Brett Lib. Adventure Lib. Thrillers
(Aldine). Champion. Lloyds School Yarns. Lloyds Sports Lib.
Thomas, Colin F.   *(r.n.)*
On the staff of Amalgamated Press and on many comic papers.
Was on the last editorial of Comic Cuts, and is now on the
managing side of Fleetway juvenile papers.
Western Library.
Thomas, D.   *(r.n.)*
Union Jack Library (anon).
Thomas, Evan
Sports Budget (2nd).
Thomas, Ivan
B.F.L. (2nd).
Thomas, Lowell
Modern Boy.
Thomas, Martin   *(r.n. Thomas Martin)*
S.B.L. (3rd and 5th).
Thomas, P. R.
Scout.
Thomas, Reginald George   *(r.n.)*
Born in Worcester 1899 and educated at Merthyr Tydfil
Secondary School and the University College of Wales,
Aberystwyth. Considered to be one of the most prolific of
D. C. Thomson's group of anonymous authors, when his out-

put was said to be enormous. Wrote many romantic stories for such papers as Red Star Weekly, Woman's Way, as well as thousands for the boys' papers. Was also a prominent author of the Red Circle School stories in the first seven or eight years. As well as all this, he was still able to write stories under at least five different names for Amalgamated Press, including one Sexton Blake story. Thomas died some years ago and had a son working on one of the Fleetway papers, who also lived at Wanstead Park for some years.

Pen-names: Reg. Wilson. Ivan Storm. John Purley. Barry Nelson. Michael Stuart.

Hotspur. Adventure. Wizard. Skipper. Dixon Hawke Lib. Scoops (all anon). Chums Annual. Champion. Lion. Tiger. Chums. Scout. Boys Ace Library.

Thompson, E. W.
B.O.P. Young England.

Thompson, J. H. *(r.n.)*
Wrote a Sexton Blake story in Union Jack (1st series) No 44, called '10,000 Pounds Reward'. In it Blake appeared with an American Detective named Jefferson Hart.
Union Jack (1st) (anon).

Thompson, Reginald George
Boys Journal.

Thompson, Stephen *(r.n. Draycot Montagu Dell)*
Triumph Annual (mis-spelt Thomson). Triumph. Champion Lib.

Thompson, W. Harold *(r.n.)*
Novelist and lecturer. Was for five years in the fiction department of Amalgamated Press Ltd.
Chums Annual. Chums. Young Britain (1st).

Thomson, Christine Campbell *(r.n.)*
Born London. Educated at Queens College, London. Was a literary agent and wrote her autobiography 'I am a Literary Agent' in 1961. Editor of the famous macabre series of books 'Not at Night', etc., published in the 20's.
Pen-name: Flavia Richardson.

Thomson, Neil *(r.n. Henry T. Johnson)*
Union Jack (1st).

Thorne, Rushden
B.O.P. Scout. Chums.

Thornhill, C.
Boys World.
Thornhill, Major J.
Scout.
Thornicroft, J.
B.O.P.
Thornton, Dorothy K.
Young England.
Thornton, Edward *(r.n. Edwy Searles Brooks)*
Schoolboys Pocket Library (Gerald Swan).
Thornton, Norman
Scout.
Thorpe, P. J.
Captain.
Tiddeman, Lizzie Ellen *(r.n.)*
Author of many books for young people.
Young England.
Tiltman, Hugh Hessell *(r.n.)*
Born 2nd February 1897.
Pen-names: Henry Hessell. Tex Davenport.
Timmis, Norman L. S. *(r.n.)*
Boys Broadcast.
Todd, James
Boys Life.
Tolmie, James
Hotspur Book for Boys.
Tomlinson, Everett
Young England.
Townley, Houghton *(r.n.)*
On the staff of Amalgamated Press for many years, especi
on the comic papers. Also wrote a great deal for them. D
many years ago.
Pen-name: Walford Preston.
S.B.L. (2nd) (anon). Dreadnought (anon). Merry & Brig
Butterfly. Comic Cuts. Favourite Comic (all anon).
Townley, Langton *(r.n.)*
Editor at one time of Chips, Comic Cuts, Chicks Own and T
Tots.
Townsend, Eric W. *(r.n. Eric W. McLean)*
Boys Friend Weekly (2nd). Sport & Adventure. B.F.L. (1st a

2nd). Chums Annual. Chums. Champion. Boys Realm (2nd). Boys Wonder Lib. Scout.

Townsend, W. T.
Wrote a great deal for Brett's Journals.

Townshend, Richard Baxter   *(r.n.)*
Lot-O'-Fun.

Tracy, Horace Ernest Humphrey   *(r.n.)*
Born 1883 at Bury St Edmunds. Educated Haileybury and Guys Hospital. Squadron Leader, R.A.F. Medical Branch 1923–24. Civil Health Service Iraq 1920–22. During the First World War served in the R.A.M.C.
Detective Weekly.

Travanion, Tracy
True Blue (2nd).

Trease, Geoffrey   *(r.n.)*
Born in Nottingham, August 1909 and educated at Nottingham High School and Queens College, Oxford. Has written many contemporary books for children, also adult novels. Also an excellent study of children's books entitled 'Tales out of School'. As a boy he was very fond of reading Chums, and an interesting book about him was published in 1960 called 'Geoffrey Trease' by Margaret Meek. Trease lived in Malvern, Worcestershire.
B.O.P. Boys Torch Adventure Library.

Tree, Travers
Football Stories. Football Novels.

Treeton, Ernest A.   *(r.n.)*
Lloyds School Yarns. Lloyds Boys Adventure Series. Lloyds Detective Series. Boys Friend Weekly (2nd). Boys Herald. Boys Friend Football and Sports Library. Boys Realm (1st). Union Jack (2nd) (anon).

Treaves, Norman
Writer who penned Red Circle School stories in the Hotspur Book for Boys. Almost certainly a nom-de-plume.
Hotspur Book for Boys. Skipper Book for Boys.

Tregellis, John   *(r.n. Sidney Gowing)*
Boys Friend Weekly (2nd). Gem (2nd). Boys Herald. Boys Realm (1st). B.F.L. (1st). Pluck (2nd and 3rd). Dreadnought. Marvel (2nd).

Trelawney, Hubert   *(r.n. Hugh Tuite)*
Chips.

Trelease, Harold
Young England.
Tremaine, Roger
Modern Boy.
Tremayne, Hartley *(r.n. R. Coutts Armour)*
Rocket. Champion.
Tremelin, Wilfred *(r.n.)*
Modern Boy. Chums. Union Jack (2nd).
Trent, James
Young Britain (1st).
Trent, Jeffrey
Comet.
Trevor, Edward C.
Champion Annual. Boys Friend Weekly (2nd).
Trevor, Elleston
B.O.P.
Trevor, Gordon
Boys Herald.
Trevor, Sid
Champion.
Trew, Dighton *(r.n. J. G. Jones)*
Boys Friend Weekly (2nd).
Trowbridge, G. T.
Lads and Lassies Lib.
Truss, Leslie Seldon *(r.n.)*
Born in 1892. Wrote for Picture Show, Strand, Answers and other adult papers. Also several novels. Served in the Army in the 1914–18 war.
B.F.L. (2nd).
Tubb, E. C. *(r.n.)*
Mainly a writer of science-fiction.
S.B.L. (3rd). Under the name of Arthur Maclean.
Tuck, A. L.
B.O.P.
Tucknor, R. I.
World Comic.
Tuite, Hugh *(r.n.)*
Author of many romantic novels published by Herbert Jenkins. Editor of the women's romantic paper in the early days, 'Forget-Me-Not'.

Pen-names: Hubert Trelawney. Captain Spencer.

Turley, Charles *(r.n.)*

Born 1871. Educated at Cheltenham College. In 1902 he published a now famous school story called 'Geoffrey Marten, Schoolboy' which was based on his own schooldays at Cheltenham. This was, however, thinly disguised under the name of Cliborough College in the book. He later wrote further school stories.

Captain. Herbert Strang's Annual.

Turnbull, Patrick

B.O.P.

Turner, Ernest Sackville *(r.n.)*

Born in Liverpool in 1909 and educated at Priory School, Shrewsbury and Orme School, Newcastle-under-Lyme. Held various editorial posts on such papers as the Glasgow Evening Times and other Scottish papers between 1930–41. After war service became editor of the War Office publication 'Soldier' and held the post 1946–57. In 1948 he published his first book, 'Boys will be Boys', a brilliant, readable and entertaining survey of boys' papers over the years, dealing with characters from Sweeney Todd to Dick Barton. Also since then has written books on surveys of other popular topics, but none have had the impact of the first. Was also a regular contributor to Punch and lives at Orpington, Kent.

Turner, John Victor *(r.n.)*

Pen-name: David Hume.

Turville, Henry *(r.n. Cecil Henry Bullivant)*

Boys Friend Weekly (2nd). Pluck (2nd). Boys Herald. Boys Realm (1st).

Twiner, J. V.

B.F.L. (2nd).

Twist, John C. *(r.n.)*

True Blue (1st). British Boys. Boys Friend Weekly (1st).

Twyman, Harold William *(r.n.)*

Born in London 1898 and educated at King Edward's School, Witley, Surrey, where G. R. Samways, Ernest Brindle and Hedley O'Mant were also educated. Started at the Amalgamated Press in 1914 as a proof reader on the Magnet/Gem group, but soon after was appointed chief-sub editor on the comic, Chuckles. He later joined up, serving with the A.S.C.

(later the R.A.S.C.). After war service, he returned to the firm and was made editor of a new paper entitled 'Detective Library' in 1919, followed by Nugget Weekly. Most of the stories were reprints, but Twyman himself wrote several original yarns for it. In 1921, with the editor of the Union Jack – Walter Shute – going free-lance, he took over the editorship. He held this post right up until 1931, when he temporarily left the paper to prepare the dummy of a new project. With the Union Jack ceasing in 1933, and then continuing with the new Detective Weekly, he remained as chief editor until about No 47, when he left the firm.

During his career at Fleetway House he contributed many articles and ideas, which were usually used, as well as a few stories. During his early days he drew a Greyfriars Map for the Magnet, and much later created a Billy Bunter game as well as writing two substitute stories in 1926. These were No 941 'Billy Bunter's Legacy' and No 949 'The Temptation of Peter Hazeldene'. After leaving the Amalgamated Press, he joined the staff of the Sunday Pictorial and later worked for the Ministry of Information Overseas Features Dept., joining them in 1941 during the war. Later still he was on the editorial staff of 'Man of the World' in 1945 and 'Commonwealth Review' in 1946. In later years he went free-lance and wrote for the American True Crime Magazines, and also produced several novels. He has unfortunately suffered ill health in recent years and is now almost in retirement.

Pen-names: A. Cartwright. John Forge. One story in Union Jack (2nd) as Robert Murray. Frank Richards (Magnet). Detective Library. B.F.L. (2nd). Union Jack (2nd). Chums.

Tylee, E. S.
B.O.P.

Tyler, Charles Wesley *(r.n.)*
Lloyds Detective Series.

Tyrer, Walter *(r.n.)*
Born at St Helens, Lancs, 1900. Originally worked as a clerk in a local glassworks and served in the R.N.A.S. in the latter part of World War I. His first story was sold to the A.P.'s Detective Magazine in 1921 for £5. But in 1924 he started a long association with D. C. Thomson's, writing mainly for their girls' papers, although he also contributed to their boys' papers.

In 1935, however, he went over to Amalgamated Press, where he started the famous 'Miracle' and also wrote extensively for it. He had no equal in the 'She Sent Her Mother to the Scaffold' type of story which were read by the masses in the 1930's. His first Sexton Blake story was in 1943 for the S.B.L. No 53 'The Mystery of Squadron X' and he continued writing Blakes from then onwards until the 'new look' in 1957.

In an article in Lilliput magazine in 1947, Tyrer admitted to writing at least 20,000,000 words of juvenile fiction. He also published several hard-cover mystery novels, including 'The Hangman's Daughter' and 'Jane the Ripper'.

In his early days Tyrer was also something of an artist. He now lives in retirement at Hove, Sussex.

Rover (anon). Wizard (anon). Champion. Thriller. Broadsheet Novels. Western Library. B.F.L. (2nd). S.B.L. (3rd).

Tyson, Wallace
Champion.

Ullerton, Herbert
Chums.

Underwood, F.
Boys Cinema.

Unpunga
B.O.P.

Urquhart, Paul *(r.n. Ladbroke Lionel Day Black)*
Sports Budget (1st). Sports Fun. Football & Sports Favourite. Thriller Library. Football & Sports Library. Detective Weekly. B.F.L. (2nd). S.B.L. (2nd).

Vachell, Horace Annesley *(r.n.)*
Born in Sydenham, Kent (now London) 1861, a great-grandson of the first Lord Lyttleton. Educated at Harrow, about which he wrote his famous school story 'The Hill' in 1905.

Between 1883 and 1889 he lived on a ranch in California, where he began writing. Subsequently wrote numerous successful novels and plays, once having three plays running simultaneously in the West End.

Two of his more famous books are 'Quinneys' and 'John Verney' but to most people his name is most associated with his public school classic, 'The Hill'. He had over 100 books published and died in 1955 at the age of 93.

Valentine, Henry *(r.n. Reginald Heber Poole)*
B.F.W. (2nd). Gem (2nd). Monster Comic (in collaboration with Arthur Gwynne).

Vallence, Peter
Chums.

Van Druten, John *(r.n.)*
Born London 1901. Educated at University College School. Became a lawyer and his posts included Solicitor of the Supreme Court of Judicature and lecturer in English law at University College, Aberystwyth, Wales. Later he took up writing and his first big success was his story of public school life, 'Young Woodley' 1929, which became a best-selling novel and a hit stage-play. It was also filmed, with Frank Lawton in the lead. Other well-known plays included 'After All' and 'London Wall'. 'Young Woodley' was highly controversial when it first appeared, as the story concerned the love affair between a senior schoolboy and his housemaster's attractive wife. It has since been produced on radio and TV several times. John Van Druten resided in the U.S.A. from the 1930's.

Vane, Derek
Triumph. Champion.

Vaughan, Dudley *(r.n. D. V. Johnson)*
Cheer, Boys, Cheer. Boys Realm (1st) (also wrote tales of the latter in collaboration with his father, Henry T. Johnson).

Veren, Gilbert *(r.n. A. G. Keveren)*
Boys Realm (2nd).

Verne, Jules *(r.n.)*
Born in Nantes, France, 8th February 1828, the son of a successful lawyer. His father wanted him to follow in his footsteps and at the age of 16 he began to study law in his father's office. When in Paris in 1848 to take an examination he met Alexandre Dumas the younger, and the two men became friends, the latter producing a play which Verne had written as a relaxation from his law studies.

Encouraged to carry on with his writing, Verne went to live in Paris and at first gave lessons to young law students in order to earn money. Then in 1863 came the publication of his first book, 'Five Weeks in a Balloon', which was an immediate success and made him famous.

Later came a large number of books, chiefly adventure and

337

science-fiction (although some of his 'fiction' later turned out to be fact and Verne prophesied such inventions as the incandescent bulb, the submarine, the electric clock and many more). His most famous books include 'Twenty Thousand Leagues under the Sea', 'Around the World in 80 Days', 'From the Earth to the Moon and a Trip Around It', 'A Journey to the Centre of the Earth', 'The Mysterious Island' and 'Michael Strogoff'. The B.O.P. serialised no fewer than 16 of his stories, the first being 'The Boy Captain' (later published as 'Dick Sands') in Vol 2 in 1879. He was one of the most popular contributors the B.O.P. ever had. His story 'Adrift in the Pacific' was also serialised in the first issues of the Boys Leader in 1903 and also appeared in the B.F.L.

In recent years many of his books have been made into films, including 'Twenty Thousand Leagues Under the Sea', 'A Journey to the Centre of the Earth' and 'Around the World in 80 Days'. Jules Verne was honoured by the French Academy and received the Legion of Honour Medal. He died on 24th March, 1905.

B.F.L. (1st). B.O.P. Boys Leader. Lads and Lassies Lib.

Verner, Gerald *(r.n. Donald Stuart)*
Thriller. Thriller Lib. Detective Weekly. B.F.L. (2nd). **S.B.L.** (2nd).

Vickers, Roy C. *(r.n.)*
Educated at Charterhouse, Brasenose College, Oxford. Wrote a great many stories for D. C. Thomson papers.
Pen-name: John Spencer.
Thriller.

Vickery, William Paul *(r.n.)*
Thriller. S.B.L. (2nd).

Victor, J. *(r.n. J. A. V. Edwards)*
Boys Journal.

Viles, Edward *(r.n.)*
Author of the long-running 'Black Bess' published by E. Harrison.

Viles, Walter *(r.n.)*
Pen-name: Brenchley Beaumont.
Boys World.

Villiers, Walter
Young Folks Tales.

Vincent, Frank *(r.n. Reginald S. Kirkham)*
Champion Annual. Scout.

Vise, Toye
Comic Life (in collaboration with Brian M. Bellasis).

Vivian, Evelyn Charles *(r.n.)*
Thriller Library. B.O.P.

Waddy, Stacy (Rev.)
B.O.P.

Wade, George Alfred *(r.n.)*
Born 1863. Was a B.A. Wrote for Pearsons, Windsor, Sphere, Answers, Titbits, Weekly Telegraph, Daily Mail, Daily News. Lived at Twickenham, Middx.
B.O.P. Boys Realm (1st).

Wade, John Reed *(r.n.)*
Born Highgate, editor of Pearson's Magazine and Royal Pictorial. Joined staff of Strand Magazine 1898. Assistant-editor Boys Leader and Pearson's Weekly. Editor of Pearson's Magazine, 1919.

Walker, A. B.
B.O.P.

Walker, Martin
Chums. Scout. Gem (2nd).

Walker, N. Bradbury
B.O.P.

Walker, Rowland *(r.n.)*
Author of many boys' adventure and school-story books, which include 'Pepper's Crack Eleven' and 'The Lost Expedition'. Contributed many articles to both juvenile and adult publications, especially about flying and aircraft. When writing about these subjects he often used the pen-name of 'Hugh Kenworthy' for adult books. He also wrote several books for the cinema in the U.S.A. and saw service in both the R.F.C. and R.A.F. Lived in Barnet, Herts.
Pen-name: Anthony Blair.
War Stories. Boys Realm (2nd). Chums.

Walker, W. H. *(r.n.)*
A footballer who played for Aston Villa, when the story was probably 'ghosted'.
Chums.

Walkey, Samuel *(r.n.)*

Born in Cornwall 1871–72 period, and at the age of 16 entered a bank as a clerk. Being good at his job promotions came quickly and regularly. By the turn of the century Walkey had become a bank inspector and later a staff controller. These jobs necessitated being away from home a great deal, so he took up writing boys' stories to while away the evenings. A Cornish acquaintance, the distinguished author Sir Arthur Quiller-Couch, saw Walkey's work, liked it a lot, and introduced him to Max Pemberton in 1895.

The latter had recently relinquished the editorship of Chums, but still held an important post with Cassells, the paper publishers. It was largely through him that Walkey's first serial 'In Quest of Sheba's Treasure' appeared in 1895–96 volumes of Chums. It was illustrated by George Hutchinson and was well received. But with his next serial the following year, Walkey really 'hit the bullseye'. It was a stirring, swashbuckling pirate yarn called 'Rogues of the Fiery Cross' and was illustrated by the man who subsequently illustrated all his work: the artist Paul Hardy.

From then on Walkey wrote many adventure serials for Chums, mainly dealing with pirates, sailors, adventurers and French Revolution heroes. Many of his stories were later reprinted in book form.

He always signed himself 'S. Walkey' and never used his actual Christian name. He wrote only in his spare time, and retained his bank position for many years.

Eventually he retired to his native Cornwall and died there in the 1950's.

Aldine Adventure Library. Chums Annual. Chums. B.F.L. (2nd).

Wallace, Alfred

Left school early 1939 determined to become a journalist and joined Amalgamated Press. Worked on such papers as Funny Wonder, Tip-Top and Radio Fun until war service with the Royal Navy. After the war was a sub-editor on a number of boys' papers and then became editor of Sun, Comet and Cowboy Picture Library. The highly successful range of Fleetway War Libraries (War Picture Library, Air Ace Library, Battle Picture Library, War-at-Sea Library) were launched under his editorship. These successes earned him promotion to a Managing Editorship in 1960. He was Managing Editor of Look and Learn when it was launched and also responsible in this capacity for Lion, Tiger and many of the Fleetway monthly libraries. After the Daily Mirror Group takeover of Odhams Press, Wallace moved from Fleetway to become Managing Editor of the ex-Hulton group of papers which included Eagle.

Wallace, Bryan Edgar *(r.n.)*
Son of the famous Edgar Wallace, he followed in his father's footsteps by writing mystery novels, but he never achieved a modicum of his father's fame. Titles of his novels include 'Death Packs a Suitcase', 'The Device' and 'The Man Who Would Not Swim'. In the 1930's he wrote a 1½-page Sexton Blake playlet for The Detective Weekly. Lives in Switzerland.
Thriller.

Wallace, Carlton
Thriller.

Wallace, Dillon
B.O.P.

Wallace, Edgar *(r.n.)*
Born in Greenwich, London, December 1875. His first two Christian names were actually Richard Horatio, but he never used them as a writer. His first jobs included printer's boy, newspaper seller, ship's cook, milk roundsman, soldier reporter in South Africa during the Boer War, and Fleet Street reporter on the Daily Mail and Standard. He was also racing editor on the Evening Times. In 1905 came his first novel, 'The Four Just Men' and it was the beginning of an incredible and prolific career as a best-selling author. He subsequently wrote several hundred novels, stories, plays and film scenarios, including such famous titles as 'The Squeaker', 'Sanders of the River' and 'The Case of the Frightened Lady'.

Wallace was a very swift worker and often produced three or four full-length novels and several short stories a month. (It was once said that he wrote a full-length novel while held up in a traffic jam!) He also directed stage plays and silent films based on his books.

His income often exceeded £50,000 a year, but his generosity and reckless expenditure – mainly horse-racing – often left him short of money.

He died in Hollywood on the 10th February 1932, and his body was brought back to this country and buried in Buckinghamshire. A plaque was erected to his memory and can be seen on the corner of Ludgate Circus, only a stone's throw from where he once sold newspapers as a boy, and where he was Chairman of the Press Club.

Chums. All Sports. Wild West Weekly (anon). Thriller. Boys Favourite. Detective Weekly. Union Jack (2nd).

Wallace, Gordon   *(r.n. Gordon Shaw)*
Gem (2nd). Boys Journal. Cheer, Boys, Cheer. B.F.L. (1st). Boys Friend Weekly (2nd). Greyfriars Holiday Annual. Chums. Nugget Library. Boys Herald.

Wallace, Nigel   *(r.n. Charles Hamilton)*
Vanguard Lib. (Trapps Holmes).

Wallace, William
British Boy. Lloyds Boys Adventure Series. Lloyds Sports Lib. Lloyds School Yarns.

Walley, Clive Phillips
Captain.

Wallis, George C.   *(r.n.)*
Pen-name: John Stanton.
Lot-O'-Fun. Boys Herald. Cheer, Boys, Cheer.

Walpole, Sir Hugh   *(r.n.)*
Born in Auckland, New Zealand, 1884, the son of a clergyman who later became Bishop of Edinburgh. Came to England and was educated at Kings School, Canterbury and Cambridge. Was a schoolmaster for a year after leaving Cambridge, an experience on which he drew when he wrote his third novel 'Mr Perrin and Mr Traill' in 1911, which was set at school. Between 1919–27 he wrote a trilogy of autobiographical stories of boyhood – 'Jeremy', 'Jeremy and Hamlet' and 'Jeremy at Crale', the latter being a fine public-school story. It was loosely based on Walpole's own days at Kings School, Canterbury.
He wrote many other fine novels and was knighted in 1937. Unmarried, he died in 1941.

Walsh, George Ethelbert
B.O.P.

Walshe, Douglas   *(r.n.)*
A prolific author just after the turn of the century, but mainly for adult fiction. Wrote several novels and also a play.

Pen-name: Adams Carr.

Cheer, Boys, Cheer. Union Jack (2nd) (anon). Boys Friend Weekly (2nd).

Walters, J.   *(r.n.)*

Pen-name: Norman Owen.

Walters, Leonard

Arrow Schoolboy Series.

Walters, W. G.   *(r.n. Arthur Steffens)*

Boys Friend Weekly (2nd).

Walton, L. L.

Chums.

Walton, Robin

Detective Weekly.

Wangle, Captain

Scout.

Ward, Arthur Sarsfield   *(r.n.)*

Born 1883 in Birmingham, the son of Irish parents. Educated at Kings College and studied art with the intention of becoming a black-and-white artist, but soon lost interest when his literary work was accepted. Creator and author of the famous 'Dr Fu Manchu', which novels have been made into many films. Wrote for all the leading magazines such as Pearsons, London, Novel, Premier, Red Magazine, Chambers, Graphic, Story Teller, Cassells Magazine of Fiction, New Magazine, Colliers, Munseys, McClures, Blue Book, etc. Most certainly never wrote a Sexton Blake story, as claimed by one writer. Died 3rd June 1959.

Pen-name: Sax Rohmer.

Ward, G. Whiteley

Chums.

Ward, Herbert (F.R.G.S.)

Chums.

Ward, Leighton

Marvel (1st).

Warren, John Russell   *(r.n.)*

Born 1886 at Reading, educated privately. Was a sub-editor at Amalgamated Press from 1905. Wrote several novels.

Chums.

Warri, K.

Chums.

343

Warwick, Alan Ross *(r.n.)*

Son of Sidney Warwick and brother of Francis. Has held several Fleet Street staff appointments, including that of Picture Editor of John Bull Magazine in the late 1940's. Wrote many stories about Markhurst School for the Scout, together with many serials. Wrote most of the book – 'Fifty-Two Stories for Boys' – himself.

Pen-names: Frank Sidney. Frank Sydney. Allan Ross. Young Britain (1st). Champion. Scoops. Scout. Champion Annual.

Warwick, Francis Alister *(r.n.)*

Son of Sidney Warwick and brother of Alan. As a boy he was an enthusiastic reader of The Magnet each week. Had his first story, 'The Hatchester Centre Forward', published in The Scout when he was only 16, and soon afterwards his first story for the Amalgamated Press appeared in the Boys Friend Weekly, this being a historical serial. Many of his early stories were written in collaboration with his father, and appeared mostly in the F. Addington Symonds group of boys' papers in the early 1920's. Those in the Champion usually appeared under the name of 'Frank Sydney' although other pen-names were used as well, for at one time the two Warwicks were writing all the serials which were running in the same paper.

Francis Warwick wrote at least two serials for the Gem in the early 1920's in collaboration with Geoffrey Prout, the titles being 'Chums of the Iron Way' and 'Tom of the Ajax', and they appeared under the name of Roland Spencer.

Late in 1928 C. M. Down, the Magnet and Gem editor, invited Warwick to write substitute stories for The Gem, and he wrote in all 56, including all those stories featuring such characters as Lady Pegg, Bully Burkett, Cyrus P. Handcock and those featuring Spalding Hall.

When his work on the Gem finished because of the policy of reprinting the old stories, Warwick began writing Sexton Blake stories. His first was No 325 (2nd series) for the S.B.L. – 'The Great Dumping Mystery', although he had previously penned a single Union Jack Blake story in 1930. His Blake stories always appeared under the name of 'Warwick Jardine' and he wrote in all 32 of them. Some featured the character Dearth Tallon and Sandra Sylvester, both his own creations.

344

In 1933 he took over those two famous characters of W. W. Sayer 'Granite Grant' and 'Mlle Julie' for two S.B.L.s, but his style simply did not fit in and they flopped. Apart from the Blake field he wrote several serials about a popular schoolboy called 'Fisher of the Fishshop' for the Scout.

During World War II he served in the Military Intelligence and some of his post-war stories in the S.B.L., when he featured Cliff Gordon of M.I.5, were based on personal experiences. He also contributed to women's magazines.

Pen-names: Warwick Jardine. Frank Sidney. Frank Sydney. Martin Clifford (Gem).

Magnet. Pluck (3rd). Boys Friend Weekly (2nd). Popular (2nd). Champion. Scout. Chums. Union Jack (2nd). B.F.L. (1st and 2nd).

Warwick, Sidney *(r.n.)*

Born 1870 and educated at St Peters, York, and Oxford University, where he gained a B.A. degree. Was the father of Alan and Francis Warwick. In his early days he contributed many popular serials to such papers as Daily Mail, Daily Mirror, Evening News, Sunday Chronicle and Answers.

Soon he had produced many novels, including 'House of Lies', 'Dreams to Sell' and 'Night of Secrets'. In the 1920's Sidney Warwick, with his son Francis, wrote several serials for the Champion, Pluck, Magnet and B.F.L. The results of this partnership often appeared under the name of 'Frank Sydney'. He died in Torquay in December 1953, at the age of 83.

Pen-names: A. W. Drayson. Frank Sidney. Frank Sydney. Boys Realm (1st). Union Jack (1st). B.F.L. (1st and 2nd). Pluck (3rd). Champion.

Waters, Eddie *(r.n. A. Fryars)*

Boys Realm (2nd).

Watson, Frederick *(r.n. Frederick Porter)*

Captain. Newnes Adventure Library.

Watson, Matt

Racing Novels (1st).

Watson, Philip

Hotspur Book for Boys.

Watson, St John *(r.n. Percy A. Clarke)*

B.F.L. (2nd).

Watson, Spencer
Thriller.
Watson, T. C.
Hotspur Book for Boys.
Watt, J. E.
Modern Boy.
Watts-Phillips, E.
Aldine Life & Adventure Library.
Waugh, Alexander Ratan *(r.n.)*
Born in London, 1898, and better known as 'Alec'. The brother of Evelyn Waugh the novelist, and son of Arthur Waugh the publisher. Educated at Sherbourne, where he edited the school magazine. His first novel was written immediately he left school and published in 1917. Entitled 'The Loom of Youth', it was based on his own schooldays at Sherbourne. It was highly controversial and Waugh's name was removed from the School Roll. He subsequently went to Sandhurst and served in both World Wars in the Dorset Regiment. Has written many other novels and travel books and also two autobiographies.
Way, H. J.
B.O.P. Scout.
Wayne, Richard
Flag Library. Boys Cinema.
Webb, Harry
Boys Journal.
Webb, T. C. P. *(r.n.)*
Wrote a Sexton Blake story for the S.B.L. (3rd) which was re-written and published under Arthur MacLean's name.
Webb, W. S. K.
Author of a paperback publication called 'The Truth About Wilson' – Wilson being the famous character who appeared in the Wizard. (See article in appreciation of D. C. Thomson papers.) As mentioned in this article, several authors had a hand in different series about him, and this name is almost certainly a nom-de-plume.
Red Lion Library.
Webber, Stawford *(r.n. D. W. Pile)*
Detective Weekly. Union Jack (2nd).
Webster, Captain Frederick Annesley Michael *(r.n.)*
Born 1886 at St Albans, and educated at St Albans. Author of

many books and wrote for all the leading magazines, Windsor Magazine, etc. Was special correspondent for News of the World, Daily Chronicle and York Post. Was a F.Z.S. and F.R.G.S.

Chums. Modern Boy.

Webster, Ronald

Boys Herald.

Wedgewood, Eric

Chips. Wonder.

Weekes-Wylde, Rev. Oliver

Boys Friend Weekly (1st).

Weldon, Pat

Boxing Novels (1st).

Wells, Harford

Boys Favourite. Boys Realm of Sport & Adventure.

Wells, Herbert George   *(r.n.)*

Born in Bromley, Kent, 1866, the son of a professional cricketer, and educated at Midhurst Grammar School. Was apprenticed first to a draper, then to a chemist, then won a scholarship to the Royal College of Science, where he studied under Huxley and edited the college magazine, finally gaining a B.Sc. degree at the University Correspondence College, Cambridge. He became a science instructor and began writing when his academic work was interrupted by ill-health.

His first real success was 'The Time Machine' in 1895, and this was followed by such now-famous science fiction stories as 'The 'Invisible Man', 'The War of the Worlds' and 'The First Men in the Moon', plus many short stories.

Other famous novels include 'Kipps' and 'The History of Mr Polly'. The most popular of all his books, however, was 'Outline of History' which sold over 3,000,000 copies.

In the final period of his life Wells became mainly a political (Socialist) and sociological writer. His best-known later work was 'The Shape of Things to Come', which was made into a film in the 1930's, like many of his other writings. Together with his French counterpart, Jules Verne, Wells provided the originals on which so many later scientific stories were based. He died in 1946.

Look and Learn.

Wells, William
Scout.
Wentworth, Charles *(r.n. A. W. Bradley)*
Marvel (1st).
Wentworth, Charles *(editorial name)*
Name used when old stories were rewritten and brought up-to-date for republication. Authors or editorial staff who have done this and used the name were Percy A. Clarke and Walter Shute. It has been established that Arthur Steffens's stories were mainly used in this way.
Boys Realm of Sport and Adventure. B.F.L. (2nd). Gem (2nd).
Wentworth, Herbert *(r.n. Herbert Wentworth-James)*
Boys Leader. Big Budget. Boys Life. Marvel (2nd).
West, Avonmore
Boys Broadcast.
West, Edgar *(r.n. Gordon Carr)*
Pluck (2nd). Boys Herald. Boys Friend Weekly (2nd).
West, John *(r.n. John Nix Pentelow)*
Marvel (2nd).
West, Montague
Lot-O'-Fun.
West, Peter
Boys World (Storey).
Westell, William
Nuggets.
Wescombe, Charles *(r.n. Gordon Carr)*
Boys Realm (1st). Boys Friend Weekly (2nd).
Westerman, J. F. C. *(r.n.)*
Prolific and popular boys' adventure-story writer of the 1920's and 1930's. He wrote many hard-cover books including a series dealing with the exploits of such characters as 'John Wentley' and 'Jaggers'. In 1928 Oxford United Press published the J. F. C. Westerman omnibus.
B.O.P. Chums.
Westerman, Percy Francis *(r.n.)*
Born in Portsmouth, 1876, and educated at Portsmouth Grammar School. A prolific writer of boys' adventures he specialised in tales of the sea. Published numerous adventure books for boys including such titles as 'The White Arab', 'Under the White Ensign' and 'The Pirate Submarine' and many

others, amounting to nearly 200 books. Also wrote for such papers as 'Motor Boat' and 'Yachting World', and was an expert in anything to do with sea and ships.

Was at one time Commodore of Redclyffe Yacht Club, and lived for many years on a large converted barge at Wareham, Dorset. His most popular books were translated into Danish, Dutch, Norwegian, Swedish, Polish and Hungarian. During the 1930's he was voted the most popular boys' author at many Public Libraries up and down Britain, during a nation-wide contest. He died in 1958 at Wareham (see article in Book Collecting and Library Monthly, October, 1968).

Captain. Scout. Chums. B.O.P. Modern Boy.

Western, Barry *(r.n. Gwynfil Arthur Evans)*
B.F.L. (2nd).

Weston, Cedric
Chums Annual. Chums.

Weston, G. A.
Boys Best Story Paper.

Wetherby, Captain John
B.F.L. (2nd).

Weyman, Louis
Pluck (1st). Marvel (1st).

Whadcoat, Gordon Cuming *(r.n.)*
Born 1873, author of several novels.
Boys Friend Weekly (2nd).

Whalley, George H.
Captain.

Wheeler, Edmund L.
Aldine Life and Adventure Library.

Wheway, John W. *(r.n.)*
Joined the staff of Amalgamated Press in 1922 from the printing works and was one of the original staff on The Champion under F. Addington Symonds. He also combined the sub-editorship of Pluck with this job; and wrote numerous serials, short stories and articles on every kind of sport for these two papers, and for many other periodicals as well. He had an unusual working system in which he turned out his stories on long strips of paper fed into his typewriter from a roll in front of him, and cutting off pages as he went along. He is probably best known for his stories of Cliff House School, which

he wrote under the name of 'Hilda Richards', after Charles
Hamilton and other substitute writers. These were in the
revived Schoolgirl in 1931, when, apart from a few stories by
L. E. Ransome, he wrote them all in this paper until the end
in May 1940. A single Sexton Blake story also came from his
pen in the Union Jack, 1924. In 1958 he was still writing half
a million words a year for girls' papers. He retired some years
ago when editor of Pets Annual, and lives in London.
Pen-name: Vincent Armitage.
Union Jack (2nd) (anon). Boys Friend Weekly (2nd). Gem
(2nd). Sport and Adventure. B.F.L. (1st and 2nd). Pluck (3rd).
Boys Realm (2nd). Chums. Champion Annual. Boys Wonder
Lib. Marvel (2nd). Triumph. Champion.

Whishaw, Fred *(r.n.)*
A popular novelist of the later 19th–early 20th century, also
wrote several serials and books for boys. Amongst his adult
novels were 'The Emperor's Englishmen', 'A Race for Life' and
'The Diamond of Evil'. Lived at Paignton, South Devon.
Captain. Boys of Our Empire. Boys Herald. Chums.

Whistler, John
Football Novels.

White, Claude Graham
Chums (in collaboration with Harry Harper).

White, Fred M.
Racing Novels (1st). Aldine Mystery Novels. Comic Cuts.
Chips.

White, Jean
Aldine Cinema Novels.

White, Joan
All Sports.

White, J. Harrington
Aldine Cinema Novels.

Whitechurch, Rev. Victor L. *(r.n.)*
Author of several books. Wrote for many adult magazines such
as Pearsons, Strand, Royal, etc. Lived at Aylesbury, Bucks.
B.O.P. Boys Realm (1st).

Whitehouse, Arch *(r.n. W. T. Taylor)*
Thriller. Modern Boy.

Whitehouse, F. Cowley
B.O.P.

Whitelaw, David *(r.n.)*
Born in London. Editor of Premier and London Magazines.
Also author of many books. Collector of all Warwick Reynolds'
art work.
Thriller.
Whiteman, L.
Captain.
Whitefield, Raoul
Wild West Weekly.
Whitford, Joan *(r.n.)*
Born about 1922. Lived for 12 years in the heart of cowboy
country in the U.S.A. Has written many articles, stories and
books about the Wild West.
Lives in North Harrow, Middlesex.
Pen-names: Barry Ford. Hugh R. Oldham.
Whitley, Reid *(r.n. Coutts Armour)*
Chums. B.F.L. (1st and 2nd). Pluck (3rd). Champion. Boys
Realm (2nd). Gem (2nd). Aldine Adventure Lib. War Stories.
Boxing Novels (1st). Nelson Lee Lib. (old). Union Jack (2nd).
Sport and Adventure. Young Britain (1st). Rocket. Detective
Weekly.
Whitlock, Charles
Boys Life.
Whyte, H.
Boys Comic Journal.
Whyte, Melton *(r.n. G. J. B. Anderson)*
Buffalo Bill Novels. Marvel (1st). Boys Realm (1st). Boys
Friend Weekly (2nd). Tip-Top Tales. True Blue (2nd).
Buffalo Bill Library (1st and 2nd). Diamond Lib. (1st and 2nd).
Boys Journal. Union Jack (1st). Pluck (1st and 2nd).
Whyte-Melville, G. J.
Lads and Lassies Library.
Wightman, Warren
Boys Ace Library. Scout.
Wignall, Trevor *(r.n.)*
Born in Swansea, 1883, and educated there. First job on leaving
school was a junior reporter on the 'Cambria Daily Leader' in
Swansea. Later worked on other Welsh papers and then came
to London. He worked mainly as a sporting journalist on The
Standard, Evening Times, Sporting Life, Daily Mail and sub-

sequently the Daily Express, in which his famous 'Daily Spotlight' column ran for many years.

In all he spent 10 years on the latter newspaper. He also wrote many sporting stories for boys' papers, including two Sexton Blake stories for the S.B.L. in 1920, receiving for these, as he revealed in his autobiography, £60 each. He also had many books published, including several on sport. Lived for many years, towards the latter part of his life, in Ferrers, South Devon. Died 22nd March 1958 at Hove, Sussex.

Pen-names: Alan Dene. David Rees.

S.B.L. (1st) (anon). Boys Realm (1st). Chums. B.F.L. (1st). Young Britain (1st). Boys Realm Football & Sports Library.

Wilcox, W. M.
Captain.

Wilkes, W. *(r.n.)*
Pen-name: A. W. Evelyn.

Wilkinson, T. W.
B.O.P.

Williams, Fred J. *(r.n. Bernard Smith)*
Champion.

Williams, Graeme *(r.n.)*
Pen-name: Denis Dent.
Cheer, Boys, Cheer.

Williams, Herbert Darkin *(r.n.)*
Editor of 'Quiver' from 1909. Editor of Little Folks from 1915. Was also for some time editor of Girls Realm, British Girls Annual and Cassells children's Annuals.

Williams, H. J.
Chums.

Williams, Leslie *(r.n.)*
Boys Friend Weekly (2nd). Boys Realm (2nd).

Williams, Richard *(editorial name)*
Name used on Sexton Blake stories when most of the original story has had to be revised. The following authors have had stories published under this name: W. Howard Baker. Stephen Francis. S. O. Franes. Rex Dolphin. M. Marquis. B. Hopkins and at times Peter Chambers has done the revision.
S.B.L. (3rd and 5th).

Williams, Valentine *(r.n.)*
Born in London, 20th January 1883. Educated at Downside

School, sub-editor Reuters, 1902. Reuters Correspondent, Berlin, 1904. Daily Mail Paris Correspondent 1909–13. Travelled extensively as Daily Mail War and Special Correspondent (Russia, Ireland, Spain, Portugal and Balkans, 1910–14). Wrote several books and did war service (1915–19), being twice wounded and receiving the Belgian Order of the Crown. Died 20th November 1946.
Detective Weekly.

Williams, W. H.
B.O.P.

Williamson, C. H.
Boys Friend Weekly (1st).

Williamson, Jack
Chums.

Williamson, Kay
Chums

Williamson, Thomas
Boxing Novels (1st).

Williamson, William Alan *(r.n.)*
Born in West Hartlepool in 1893, wrote and sold his first story in 1907 when he was 14. It appeared a year later in Pearson's Novel Magazine, June 1908, entitled 'How Wilmer Fought the Fourth'. Because of this success he at once left school and embarked on a journalistic career. After working as a free-lance journalist and advertising copywriter, he joined the staff of C. Arthur Pearson in 1910.
After several assistant posts he was later transferred to Pearson's Weekly. At the age of 18 he wrote the first of two Sexton Blake stories, which appeared in the Union Jack in 1912. After war service, 1915–19, he became publishing manager and Film Editor of the M.D. Sales Agency Ltd. in 1920 he joined the editorial of Odham's Press, becoming the first editor of 'Picturegoer' in 1921.
The following year he edited 'Pan', then 'Twenty Story Magazine'; in 1925 he became editor of 'Passing Show', a post he held for many years. He contributed to many adult papers and magazines.
Union Jack (2nd) (anon). Fun & Fiction. Pluck (2nd). Boys Cinema. Various D. C. Thomson juvenile papers.

Willis, Captain Anthony Armstrong *(r.n.)*
Born 1897.
Pen-name: Anthony Armstrong.
Willis, Thomas John *(r.n.)*
Scout. Chums.
Wilson, Andy
Chums.
Wilson, J. and P.
B.O.P.
Wilson, John Park *(r.n.)*
Born Glassford, Lanarkshire, 15th October 1867. Spent all his
life in the remote Perthshire village of Deanston. He added the
name of 'Park' to his own (which was his mother's maiden
name) to avoid confusion in his mail, as there was another John
Wilson living nearby. He also taught himself French, German
and shorthand. He first started writing in the 1890's, when for
two years he was ill with a back disablement. Died 10th March
1932.
Pen-name: Julian Jackson.
Wilson, Matt
Racing Novels (1st and 2nd).
Wilson, Reg. *(r.n. R. G. Thomas)*
Champion. Champion Library.
Wilson, Rex
Scout.
Wilson, Robert
Chums.
Wilson, Wingrove *(r.n. Walter H. Light)*
Diamond Lib. (2nd). Chums. B.F.L. (2nd). Boys Wonder
Library.
Wilton, Hal *(r.n. Frank S. Pepper)*
Champion Annual. Triumph Annual. Champion. Champion
Lib. Triumph. Tiger.
Wimbury, Harold *(r.n.)*
Thriller. Chums.
Winchester, Clarence *(r.n.)*
Was for many years chief editor and Managing Director of
Winchester Publications Ltd. Before then he had held several
important appointments in Fleet Street, including those of
Assistant Chief Editor of Cassells, Chief Editor of a group of

Amalgamated Press Publications, Literary Editor and Assistant Editor of The Daily Sketch, Chief Editor of Argosy and Storyteller, editor of Film Pictorial, World Film Encyclopaedia, etc. Contributed to many American newspapers and magazines. Wrote many books including 'An Innocent in Hollywood' and 'The Devil Rides High'. Was editor of 'Ideas' 1920 and editor of Chums from 1920–24. Used pen-name of Ornis for adult work.
Chums. Boys Magazine.

Winchester, Mark
Chums. Pluck. Scout.

Windham, Basil *(r.n. P. G. Wodehouse)*
Chums (in collaboration with W. Townend).

Windsor, Frank *(r.n. Derek A. W. Birnage)*
Chums.

Witzen, A. E.
B.F.L. (2nd).

Wodehouse, Pelham Grenville *(r.n.)*
Born in 1881 and educated at Dulwich College. His first job was as a clerk in the Hong Kong and Shanghai Bank in the City of London, where he remained for two years. He then joined the staff of the Globe, then a London evening paper, and wrote a column entitled 'By the Way' for eight years, with the exception of a period of one year, which he spent in America. He sold two short stories in New York for 300 dollars apiece and decided to stay there. Eventually he sold a serial to the Saturday Evening Post and for the next 25 years almost all his books appeared first in this paper.
He also wrote lyrics to music by Jerome Kern and other composers and a few years later formed a partnership with Guy Bolton, which resulted in a number of musical shows and plays. Also wrote screenplays in Hollywood. Today, famous as the creator of the immortal Jeeves, Mulliner, Psmith, Lord Emsworth, etc., he is the author of over 70 books.
Was a regular contributor to Punch, for whom he reported on the current American scene. Wodehouse's earliest writings appeared in such papers as Titbits, Fun, Sandows Magazine, Weekly Telegraph, The Universal and Ludgate Magazine, Answers, The Globe, Today, and The Public School Magazine,

which had the honour of serialising 'The Pothunters', his first full-length story.

Today, at 88, he lives in New York and still turns out a book a year. He is President of The Northern Old Boys Book Club, with its headquarters in Leeds, England.

Pen-name: Basil Windham.

Captain. Boys Friend Weekly (2nd). Greyfriars Holiday Annual.

Wolfe, Cedric *(r.n. E. W. Alais)*

Boys Herald. Pluck (2nd). Marvel (1st and 2nd). Boys Friend Weekly (2nd). B.F.L. (1st).

Wood, Andrew *(r.n. Samuel Andrew Wood)*

Thriller. Captain. Chums. Scout. Merry Moments. Joe Pickford Lib.

Wood, Edward

Boys Cinema.

Wood, Elizabeth

Young England.

Wood, Eric *(r.n. F. Knowles Camplin)*

Boys Friend Weekly (2nd). B.O.P. Chums. Scout. B.F.L. (2nd). Popular (2nd). Gem (2nd).

Wood, Geoffrey *(r.n. C. Russell)*

Boys Realm (2nd). Football and Sports Favourite.

Wood, George

Scout.

Wood, Innis

Boys Realm (1st).

Wood, J. Claverdon *(r.n.)*

Wrote several popular adventure serials for the B.O.P. based on his personal knowledge of the countries he described so well, having travelled widely all over the world. His first serial appeared in 1910 and was 'Sinclair of the Scouts'. His main recreation was sailing and yachting and he held the silver cup for 'open-boat sailing' in Britain.

B.O.P.

Wood, J. G. *(r.n.)*

The first Natural History editor of the B.O.P. under the title, 'Out with a Jack-knife' he wrote on animals, birds, insects, fish, etc., for some years. He was previously editor of a predecessor to the B.O.P. – 'The Boys Own Magazine'.

B.O.P.

356

Wood, Rodney
   Scout.
Wood, Samuel Andrew *(r.n.)*
   Born 1890 Ashton-under-Lyne, educated privately, and at
   Manchester Grammar School. Was a talented musician and
   was organist at Bridge of Terth Church for 26 years. Wrote
   hundreds of stories for Chums and Captain up to the 1920's.
   Also wrote some of the Tubby Haig stories.
   Pen-names: Andrew Wood. Hal Ravenglass. Thomson Cross.
   Scout.
Wood, Walter *(r.n.)*
   Born 1886 at Bradford. Author of many books and wrote many
   serials for leading magazines.
   B.O.P. Scout. Boys Realm (2nd).
Woodhouse, Lawrence
   B.O.P. Sports for Boys.
Woodman, George D. *(r.n.)*
   Went to Australia when he was 16. Wrote his first short piece
   for 'Melbourne Age'. Back once again in England he wrote his
   first boys' story for The Rover. Worked at several jobs and in
   between had several novels published. When he was a young-
   ster he modelled for an artist doing a sketch of Sherlock
   Holmes's head for the dust-cover of 'The Omnibus Volume of
   Holmes's Stories'. Wrote two Sexton Blake stories for Detective
   Weekly in 1934 and one for the Sexton Blake Annual. The
   original drawing of him as 'Sherlock Holmes' was exhibited in
   the 1951 Sherlock Holmes Exhibition in London. Brother of
   Thomas E. Woodman.
   Rover. Skipper. Buzzer (all anon). Sexton Blake Annual.
   Detective Weekly.
Woodman, Thomas *(r.n.)*
   Brother of George D. Woodman, and wrote for D. C. Thomson's
   Red Letter as well as for many juvenile papers.
   Pen-name: Eddie Quilter.
   Rover. Adventure. Wizard. Skipper (all anon). Scout. Buzzer
   (anon). Scoops (anon). Boys Ace Lib. (anon).
Woodruff, Peter
   Boxing Novels (1st and 2nd). Football Stories. Football Novels.
Woods, James
   Comic Cuts.

Woods, L. H.
Lot-O'-Fun (in collaboration with C. R. L. Farley).
Woods, W. O.
Chums.
Wood-Smith, Noel *(r.n.)*
On the staff of the Companion Papers and served with the R.N.A.S. during the First World War. Was chief sub-editor and deputy to C. M. Down on the Magnet during the 1920's when he also wrote some substitute Greyfriars stories. As well, he wrote some Sexton Blake stories for the Union Jack. He was a very clever inventor and had many inventions accepted by leading business firms. Died about 1955.
Pen-names: Norman Taylor. Noel Terry. Frank Richards (Magnet). Owen Conquest (Boys Friend Weekly). Martin Clifford (Gem). Union Jack (2nd) (anon). Boys Realm (1st). Boys Friend Weekly (2nd). Dreadnought.
Woodward, Edward
Racing Novels (1st).
Woolley, Horace A. *(r.n.)*
Cheer, Boys, Cheer. Boys Herald. Boys Journal. B.O.P. Chums. Scout.
Wooton, Edwin *(r.n.)*
Flag Lib. Rocket. Magnet. Union Jack (1st). Pluck (1st and 3rd). Champion.
Worsleigh, David
Aldine Mystery Novels. Union Jack (1st).
Worth, Richard
Racing Novels (1st). Boxing Novels (1st and 2nd). Lloyds Detective Series.
Worthing, Jack
        John
Chums.
Wortley, Beatrice
Chatterbox.
Wray, Reginald *(r.n. William Benjamin Home-Gall)*
Union Jack (1st and 2nd). Boys Friend Weekly (1st and 2nd). Boys Herald. Gem (2nd). Boys Leader. Chums. B.F.L. (1st). Pluck (1st and 2nd). Nugget Lib. Boys Realm (1st and 2nd). Boys Journal. Cheer, Boys, Cheer. Dreadnought. Marvel (1st and 2nd).

Wren, Percival Christopher   *(r.n.)*
Born Devonshire, 1885, educated at Oxford. Served in the
French and Indian armies and was a member of the French
Foreign Legion. He used his experience to good advantage in
several best-sellers, including 'Beau Geste' and 'Beau Sabreur'.
Died 23rd November 1941.
Thriller.

Wrexe, Charles   *(r.n. Rex Hardinge)*
Western Library.

Wright, Franklin   *(r.n. Henry Farmer)*
Union Jack (1st). Marvel (1st). Pluck (1st).

Wright, H. Philpott
Probably one of the most interesting authors in the early days
of the century and certainly the most mysterious. Wrote a long
and popular school series for Vanguard (Trapps Holmes) between 1907–10 called 'Taffy Llewellyn's Schooldays', the
school being Blackminster, and one of the boys in the school
was named Billy Bunter. This was at least a year before the
famous Owl of Greyfriars appeared in The Magnet.
Philpott Wright is certainly a nom-de-plume and was, without
question, nothing to do with Charles Hamilton, as in his lifetime Hamilton denied any connection with him. The style of
the two authors is also very different.
It is believed that Wright was the nom-de-plume of a writer
named J. Weedon Birch, as a story with a photograph of this
author in the Aldine Diamond Library is exactly the same as
one shown in True Blue, the author's name in this case being
H. Philpott Wright. But this is not conclusive.
Birch was an officer and transport rider to the Chartered
Companies of Rhodesia and disappeared from the writing scene
before the First World War.
H. Philpott Wright will most certainly go down in history of
Old Boys story papers as being the most intriguing writer of
them all.
True Blue (2nd). Robin Hood Lib. (1st, 2nd and 3rd). Dia-
mond Library (3rd). Buffalo Bill Lib. (1st and 2nd). Vanguard
Lib. (Trapps Holmes).

Wright, Philip Mercer
B.O.P.

Wright, Walter B.
Chums.
Wright, Warwick
Boys Life.
Wright, W. George *(r.n.)*
Editor of Boys Realm around 1922–24 period, and after John
Nix Pentelow.
Pen-Names. William Rishton, Howard Grant, Paul
Quinton, Bruce Bryant, William Bouchard, Val Masterson.
Wroxham, Cecil *(r.n. H. Wedgwood Belfield)*
Boys Realm (2nd). Boys Friend Weekly (2nd).
Wyatt, Ben *(r.n. F. W. Young)*
Chums.
Wylde, Anson
Chums.
Wylde, Jack
Detective Tales (2nd). Jack's Paper.
Wylie, — *(r.n.)*
Merry & Bright. Butterfly. Favourite Comic (all anon).
Wyllie, Crichton *(r.n.)*
This may possibly be the same person as 'Wylie' but given from
a different source and with different spelling.
Boys Friend Weekly (2nd).
Wyndham-Gittens, Herbert *(r.n.)*
Chums.
Wynne, May *(r.n. Mabel Winifred Knowles)*
Lloyds Boys Adventure Series. Chums. Scout. Boys Herald.
Boys Weekly.
Wynnton, Patrick *(r.n.)*
Born 1899. Educated at Marlborough College and Manchester
University. Wrote several novels.
Thriller.
Wynyard, Talbot *(r.n. Charles Hamilton)*
Picture Fun.
Y. Viscount *(r.n. G. J. B. Anderson)*
Union Jack (1st).
'Yangtzepoo'
Chums.
Yare, Edmund
Football Stories. Football Novels.

Yates, H. S. *(r.n.)*
Boys Realm (1st). B.F.W. (2nd).
York, Harrison
Thriller.
Yorke, Carras *(r.n. Arthur C. Marshall)*
Rocket. Champion. Chums. Champion Annual.
Yorke, Edward G. *(r.n.)*
Cheer, Boys, Cheer.
Yorke, Sidney
Newnes Adventure Library.
Young, Charles
B.O.P. Scout.
Young, Dick
Boys Realm (2nd).
Young, Frank W.
Fred W. *(r.n.)*
Pen-names: Frank Arnold. Hedley Scott (serial 'Phantom Bat' in Magnet). Colin Newcome. Ben Wyatt.
All Sports. U.J. (2nd) (anon). Boys Realm (1st). B.F.W. (2nd). Chums. Scout. Diamond Library (1st and 2nd). Adventure Lib. Britons Own Lib. Comic Life. Chums Annual.
Young, Stewart *(r.n. A. M. Burrage)*
Cheer, Boys, Cheer. Boys Herald.
Young, Warwick *(r.n. B. Parsons)*
Boys Realm (1st).
Young, Will *(r.n. W. B. Home-Gall Jnr.)*
Boys Realm (2nd). Playtime.